DEBATING THE AMERICAN DREAM

Debating the American Dream

HOW EXPLANATIONS FOR INEQUALITY POLARIZE POLITICS

Elizabeth Suhay

Russell Sage Foundation NEW YORK

ROR: https://ror.org/02yh9se80
DOI: https://doi.org/10.7758/trap6910

Library of Congress Cataloging-in-Publication Data

Names: Suhay, Elizabeth, author.
Title: Debating the American dream : how explanations for inequality polarize politics / Elizabeth Suhay.
Description: New York : Russell Sage Foundation, [2025] | Includes bibliographical references and index. | Summary: "The American Dream—the idea that economic success is available to all who work hard—is one of Americans' most cherished ideals. Does the U.S. public believe the nation lives up to this important ideal? For decades, scholars argued that most Americans indeed believed the economy to be meritocratic, meaning affluent people earned their riches fair and square and lower-income people were primarily responsible for their economic difficulties. In the twenty-first century, however, faith in the American Dream no longer dominates. Recent surveys indicate economic pessimism has overtaken optimism. Why the change? One straightforward explanation is that the economy worsened for most Americans. Yet, while there is little question that the state of the economy contributes to beliefs about the American Dream, Suhay argues that we tend to overlook an important second contributing factor: politics. Drawing on representative public opinion surveys from over four decades, the author demonstrates that people on the political left—Democrats and liberals—are, on average, more skeptical of the "reality" of the American Dream than those on the political right—Republicans and conservatives. Disagreements over the nature of opportunity in the U.S. can be found across many social divides, including educational and religious ones, but none is greater than that between the political left and right. The book provides an explanation for why these partisan disagreements exist—and persist"— Provided by publisher.
Identifiers: LCCN 2025001144 (print) | LCCN 2025001145 (ebook) | ISBN 9780871548627 (paperback ; alk. paper) | ISBN 9781610449380 (ebook)
Subjects: LCSH: Income distribution—United States—History—21st century. | Equality—United States—History—21st century. | American Dream—History—21st century. | Success—United States—History—21st century. | Polarization (Social sciences)—United States—History—21st century. | Right and left (Political science)—United States—History—21st century.
Classification: LCC HC110.I5 S88 2025 (print) | LCC HC110.I5 (ebook) | DDC 339.2/20973—dc23/eng/20250512
LC record available at https://lccn.loc.gov/2025001144
LC ebook record available at https://lccn.loc.gov/2025001145

The paper used in this publication meets the minimum requirements of American National Standard for Information Sciences--Permanence of Paper for Printed Library Materials. ANSI Z39.48-1992.

Text design by Linda Secondari. Front matter DOI: https://doi.org/10.7758/trap6910.8065

RUSSELL SAGE FOUNDATION
112 East 64th Street, New York, New York 10065
10 9 8 7 6 5 4 3 2 1

This book is dedicated, with much love, to my parents,
Barbara Harner Suhay and Jim Suhay

CONTENTS

LIST OF ILLUSTRATIONS *ix*

ABOUT THE AUTHOR *xv*

ACKNOWLEDGMENTS *xvii*

Introduction *1*

Chapter 1. Debating the American Dream *11*

Chapter 2. The Politics of the American Dream in
Historical Perspective *32*

Chapter 3. Americans' Beliefs About Inequality and Opportunity over
Four Decades *68*
  With Mark Tenenbaum and Qingya Xu

Chapter 4. How Americans Explain Socioeconomic Inequalities *99*

Chapter 5. Demographic Divides over Explanations for
Socioeconomic Inequality *136*

Chapter 6. Partisan Divides over Explanations for Socioeconomic
Inequality *157*

Chapter 7. Political Preferences and Explanations for Inequality *186*

Chapter 8. The American Dream: Belief, Rhetoric, and Reality *215*

APPENDIX *243*

NOTES *265*

REFERENCES *291*

INDEX *325*

ILLUSTRATIONS

Figures

Figure 1.1. Relationship Between Household Income and Partisanship in 2020 *16*

Figure 1.2. Image Accompanying *Wall Street Journal* Essay "The American Dream Is Alive and Well" *21*

Figure 2.1. Rate (per 1,000 Words) of Explanations for Economic and Related Inequalities in Party Platforms (1980–2020) *49*

Figure 2.2. Proportion of Three Types of Explanations for Economic and Related Inequalities by Party and Year (1980–2020) *50*

Figure 2.3. Number of Times Specific Social Groups Were Mentioned in Conjunction with Concerns over Unequal Opportunity in Democratic Party Platforms (1980–2020) *51*

Figure 3.1. Americans Who Agree That Most People Can Get Ahead If They Work Hard *80*

Figure 3.2. Americans Who Agree That Poor People Have It Easy Because of Government Benefits *82*

Figure 3.3. Americans Who Agree That We Don't Give Everyone an Equal Chance *84*

Figure 3.4. Americans Who Agree That African Americans Have Worse Jobs, Income, and Housing Due to Lack of Access to Education *86*

Figure 3.5. Americans Who Agree That African Americans Have Worse Jobs, Income, and Housing Due to Discrimination *87*

Figure 3.6. Americans Who Agree That African Americans Have Worse Jobs, Income, and Housing Due to a Lack of Will *88*

Figure 3.7. Americans Who Agree That African Americans Have Worse Jobs, Income, and Housing Due to a Lesser Ability to Learn *89*

Figure 3.8. Partisans' Beliefs That We Don't Give Everyone an Equal Chance by Level of Political Interest *92*

Figure 3.9. Partisans' Beliefs That Lack of Access to Education and Discrimination Cause Racial Inequality by Level of Political Interest *93*

Figure 3.10. Partisans' Beliefs That Lack of Will and Inborn Ability to Learn Cause Racial Inequality by Level of Political Interest *94*

Figure 4.1. Explanations for Economic Inequalities, 2002 ANES *112*

Figure 4.2. Explanations for Economic Inequalities (2016) *115*

Figure 4.3. Explanations for Economic Inequalities (2018) *117*

Figure 4.4. Correlations Among Explanations for Economic Inequality (2016) *120*

Figure 5.1. Frequency Distributions of the Three Unequal Economic Opportunity Indexes (2016) *147*

Figure 5.2. Coefficient Plot of Unequal Opportunity Indexes Regressed onto Demographic Characteristics (2016) *150*

Figure 5.3. Coefficient Plots of Explanations for Inequality Regressed onto Demographic Characteristics (2018) *152*

Figure 5.4. Coefficient Plots of Additional Explanations for Inequality Regressed onto Demographic Characteristics (2018) *154*

Figure 6.1. Frequency Distributions of the Unequal Economic Opportunity Index for Democrats, Independents, and Republicans (2016) *170*

Figure 6.2. Coefficient Plot of Unequal Opportunity Indexes Regressed onto Partisanship and Demographic Variables (2016) *171*

Figure 6.3. Coefficient Plot of Unequal Opportunity Indexes Regressed onto Partisanship, Ideology, and Prejudice (2016) *172*

Figure 6.4. Associations Between Partisanship and Societal Explanations for Socioeconomic Inequality *174*

Figure 6.5. Associations Between Partisanship and Individual Explanations for Socioeconomic Inequality *176*

Figure 6.6. Explanations for Race and Sex Inequality by Level of Political Attention and Partisanship (2018) *182*

Figure 6.7. Explanations for Rural-Urban and White-Asian American Inequality by Level of Political Attention and Partisanship (2018) *183*

Figure 7.1. Distributions of Items in Government Responsibility for Social Welfare Index (2016) *195*

Figure 7.2. Distributions of Items in Decrease Economic Inequality Index (2016) *196*

Figure 7.3. Distributions of Affirmative Action Items (2018) *197*

Figure 7.4. Relationship Between the Unequal Economic Opportunity Index and Political Attitudes (2016) *200*

Figure 7.5. Associations Between the Unequal Opportunity Index and Political Attitudes Holding Potential Confounders Constant (2016) *202*

Figure 7.6. Association Between the Unequal Opportunity Index and Political Attitudes by Respondent Party Identification (2016) *205*

Figure 7.7. Relationship Between the Unequal Opportunity Index and Political Attitudes by Partisanship (2016) *206*

Figure 7.8. Coefficient Plots of Political Attitudes Regressed onto Three Unequal Opportunity Indexes (2016) *208*

Figure 7.9. Coefficient Plots of Affirmative Action Support Regressed onto Two Unequal Opportunity Indexes (2018) *210*

Figure 7.10. Coefficient Plots of Social Welfare Support Regressed onto Specific Explanations for More and Less Scripted Inequalities (2018) *211*

Figure A.1. Frequency of Specific Types of Explanations for Economic and Related Inequalities in Party Platforms (1980–2020) *243*

Figure A.2. Number of Times Specific Social Groups Mentioned in Conjunction with Concerns over Unequal Opportunity in Republican Party Platforms (1980–2020) *244*

Figure A.3. Predicted Probabilities from Logit Regression with Demographic Controls for "Most Can Make It If They Work Hard" Outcome (Corresponding to Figure 3.1) *244*

Figure A.4. Predicted Probabilities from Logit Regression with Demographic Controls for "Poor People Have It Easy" Outcome (Corresponding to Figure 3.2) *245*

Figure A.5. Predicted Probabilities from Logit Regression with Demographic Controls for "We Don't Give Everyone an Equal Chance" Outcome (Corresponding to Figure 3.3) *245*

Figure A.6. Predicted Probabilities from Logit Regression with Demographic Controls for Education Explanation for Racial Inequality Outcome (Corresponding to Figure 3.4) *246*

Figure A.7. Predicted Probabilities from Logit Regression with Demographic Controls for Discrimination Explanation for Racial Inequality Outcome (Corresponding to Figure 3.5) *246*

Figure A.8. Predicted Probabilities from Logit Regression with Demographic Controls for Lack of Will Explanation for Racial Inequality Outcome (Corresponding to Figure 3.6) *247*

Figure A.9. Predicted Probabilities from Logit Regression with Demographic Controls for Inborn Ability Explanation for Racial Inequality Outcome (Corresponding to Figure 3.7) *247*

Figure A.10. Correlations Among Explanations for Inequality in 2018 Survey *248*

Figure A.11. Coefficient Plot of Unequal Opportunity Difference Measures Regressed onto Demographic Characteristics (2016) *249*

Figure A.12. Associations Between Partisanship and Cultural Explanations for Socioeconomic Inequality *250*

Figure A.13. Distributions of Presidential Candidate Feeling Thermometers (2016) *251*

Figure A.14. Coefficient Plots of Political Attitudes Regressed onto Specific Explanations for Economic Inequality (2016) *252*

Figure A.15. Coefficient Plots of Specific Political Attitudes Regressed onto Unequal Opportunity Index (2016) *253*

Figure A.16. Coefficient Plots of Political Attitudes Regressed onto Three Unequal Opportunity Indexes—Racial Subgroups (2016) *254*

Tables

Table 2.1. Party Platform Coding Scheme *48*

Table 4.1. Typology and Examples of Causal Attributions for Economic Outcomes *103*

Table 4.2. Characteristics of 2016 EIPS Sample *109*

Table 4.3. Characteristics of 2018 EIPS Sample *110*

Table 4.4. Open-Ended Explanations for Four Types of Socioeconomic Inequality (2018) *127*

Table 6.1. Republican Versus Democratic Odds of Mentioning Five Explanations for Four Types of Inequality, Results from Twenty Independent Logit Regressions (2018) *179*

Table A.1. Unequal Opportunity Indexes Regressed onto Demographic Characteristics (2016) *255*

Table A.2. Unequal Opportunity Indexes Regressed onto Partisanship and Demographic Variables (2016) *256*

Table A.3. Unequal Opportunity Indexes Regressed onto Partisanship, Ideology, and Prejudice Variables (2016) *257*

Table A.4. Explanations for Economic Inequality Regressed onto Partisanship and Demographic Variables (2016) *258*

Table A.5. Economic Policy Attitudes Regressed onto Unequal Opportunity Index and Potential Confounders (2016) *259*

Table A.6. Presidential Preferences Regressed onto Unequal Opportunity Index and Potential Confounders (2016) *260*

Table A.7. Political Attitudes Regressed onto Unequal Opportunity Index, Party Identification, and Their Interaction (2016) *261*

Table A.8. Political Attitudes Regressed onto Three Unequal Opportunity Indexes (2016) *262*

Table A.9. Affirmative Action Support Regressed onto Two Unequal Opportunity Indexes (2018) *263*

ABOUT THE AUTHOR

ELIZABETH SUHAY, PHD◉ is associate professor in the Department of Government, School of Public Affairs, American University.

ACKNOWLEDGMENTS

IF YOU ARE LUCKY, as I was, the long process of writing a book can bring you countless rewarding conversations with colleagues, friends, and family. I am very grateful for the earnest and smart feedback I have received from so many people. I want to especially thank Larry Bartels, Don Herzog, and Leon Porter for reading the entire manuscript (in Larry's case, twice!), as well as the people who shared their advice at a wonderfully productive book conference organized by Suzanne Nichols at the Russell Sage Foundation— Scott Allard, Stanley Feldman, Matt Grossmann, Jacob Hacker, Eunji Kim, Leslie McCall, Samuel Myers, Jr., Laura Stoker, Kris-Stella Trump, and Amber Wichowsky. Three anonymous manuscript reviewers provided constructive criticism that helped me improve the manuscript a great deal. I deeply appreciate additional comments, perspectives, and support from Laura Antkowiak, Nick Carnes, Oren Cass, Dalton Conley, Martha Farah, Jake Grumbach, Marc Hetherington, Jennifer Hochschild, Leonie Huddy, John Jost, Cindy Kam, Marko Klašnja, Jon Krosnick, Jan Leighley, Kris Miler, Michael Morrell, Kerem Oktar, Hannah Tesler, Emily West, Sam Zacher, and John Zaller. This book would not exist without the late Toby Jayaratne, who awakened my interest in causal attributions. I wish she were still here to read this.

This work benefited from the input of many other academic colleagues at presentations and workshops hosted by the American Political Science Association, Cooperative Election Study, Georgetown University Department of Government, International Society of Political Psychology, University of Maryland Department of Government and Politics, McGill University Center for the Study of Democratic Citizenship, National Capital Area Political Science Association, New York Area Political Psychology Meeting, Stony Brook University Department of Political Science, University of North Carolina Department of Political Science, Vanderbilt University Center for the Study of Democratic Institutions, and Yale Center for Empirical Research on Stratification and Inequality. I wish also to thank the Russell Sage Foundation for providing a grant (grant number 83-16-17) that funded the original survey research discussed in chapters 4 through 7, and the three anonymous grant reviewers who provided crucial early direction. From this book's conception through to publication, American University's Department of Government and School of Public Affairs have provided me with a lively and supportive intellectual home.

Writing this book took many more years than I expected, and it certainly would have taken much longer but for the assistance of a number of promising young scholars working as research assistants. I would like to especially thank Austin Bartola, Mark Tenenbaum, and Qingya Xu for their conscientiousness and dedication to this project over several years. Early on, Austin cheerfully helped me explore the survey data that forms the backbone of the book. Mark and Qingya provided many, many hours of assistance, including producing the final figures and tables that appear throughout the book. They are also coauthors on chapter 3, going above and beyond to analyze four decades of data from three different survey providers. Kristen Munnelly and Sarah Thorne provided helpful research assistance, and Vaishnavi Menon and Vanessa Sousa coded the many qualitative survey responses.

Finally, I would like to recognize my husband and parents, who provide unconditional love, and support for this project conditioned on me actually finishing it. My husband and life partner, Rich Gallagher, is one of the smartest and most generous people I know. He is *the* funniest. Unfortunately for him, he is also an excellent editor. He read the manuscript twice and wrangled the Zotero citations (which was neither fun nor funny).

My mom and dad, Barbara and Jim Suhay, also read the manuscript and provided suggestions. According to them, the book was ready for publication several incarnations ago (not that they are biased or anything). I am so grateful to them for setting me on a path to be able to write this book. They modelled compassion, earnestness, and intellectual curiosity, provided me with an excellent education and material stability, took my ideas seriously from a young age, and gave me space to follow my own path, which, after some twists and turns, ended up not far from theirs. Mom and Dad met at a political science graduate student mixer at Ohio State University. Dad was on his way out and saw my mom walking in; he immediately did an about face (literally—he was an army guy). Mom went on to teach political science at Henry Ford Community College. Dad got his MBA and worked in finance at Ford Motor Company. It seems appropriate that my first book would focus on Americans' perspectives on politics and economics. This book is dedicated to them.

Introduction

You can make it if you try
You can make it if you try
You'll get what's due you
Everything coming to you
You got to move
If you want to be ahead

     —Sly and the Family Stone, "You Can Make It If You Try" (1969)

THE AMERICAN DREAM—the idea that economic success is available to all who work hard—is one of Americans' most cherished ideals. It has been celebrated by schoolteachers, politicians, business leaders, and artists, such as musicians Sly and the Family Stone in their uplifting (and catchy) song "You Can Make It If You Try." Does the U.S. public believe the nation lives up to this important ideal? For decades, scholars argued that the vast majority of Americans indeed believed the economy to be meritocratic, meaning affluent people earned their riches fair and square and lower income people were primarily responsible for their economic difficulties. Scholars writing in the twentieth century referred to this as the dominant ideology of American political culture.[1] In the twenty-first century, however, faith in the American Dream no longer dominates.[2] Recent surveys indicate economic pessimism has overtaken optimism.[3]

Why the change? One straightforward explanation is that, for most Americans, the economy worsened. It had boomed after the Second World War, and, for several decades, lower-income and middle-class Americans' incomes grew the most. But, beginning in the late 1970s, the U.S. economy slowed and income growth became highly skewed toward the affluent.[4] Today, income inequality in the United States is greater than that of nearly all other advanced industrial democracies,[5] although it no longer appears

https://doi.org/10.7758/trap6910.5640

to be growing.[6] Inequality would be less of a concern if people tended to earn more than their parents had, but upward mobility has declined as well.[7] Americans—along with people around the world—have also experienced several recent, painful economic shocks. The U.S. economy crashed in 2007 in response to a severe housing crisis and recovery thereafter was slow. In 2020, the COVID-19 pandemic caused short-term unemployment and contributed to record inflation. Given these economic trends and events, it would be surprising if faith in the American Dream had not decreased.

Yet, while there is little question that the state of the economy contributes to beliefs about the American Dream,[8] I argue in this book that scholars tend to overlook another important contributing factor: politics. Drawing on representative and near-representative public opinion surveys from more than four decades, I demonstrate in this book that people on the political left—Democrats and liberals—are, on average, more skeptical of the "reality" of the American Dream than those on the political right—Republicans and conservatives. This skepticism increased markedly in the twenty-first century and is primarily responsible for declining faith in the American Dream in the aggregate. By 2022, a Pew Research Center survey showed that Republicans were approximately 30 percentage points more likely than Democrats to say that "most people who want to get ahead can make it if they're willing to work hard." The same year, the General Social Survey found that Democrats were approximately 50 percentage points more likely than Republicans to agree that discrimination was an important cause of unequal economic outcomes between Black and White Americans (see chapter 3). Disagreements over the nature of opportunity in the United States exists across many social divides, including educational and religious ones, but none is greater than that between the political left and right.

The fact that Republicans today have sunnier views than Democrats regarding the abundance and fairness of the U.S. economy may appear strange when set against the backdrop of Donald Trump's populist campaigns for president, during which he often warned that the American Dream was in decline. In this book, I provide an explanation for why these partisan disagreements exist—and why they persist. For most of its history, the Democratic Party has represented individuals and groups of lesser means, generating a policy agenda oriented toward using government to protect workers and redistribute economic resources. The Republican Party's economic agenda, by contrast, has been heavily shaped by affluent and business interests and, thus, oriented toward preserving the current distribution of resources and economic power.[9] The parties have often justified their competing agendas with competing arguments about the American Dream. Arguably the surest method of advocating for the preservation of the current distribution of resources is to argue that it is fair or deserved, and, similarly, the surest method of advocating for redistribution of those resources is to argue that the status quo is unfair or undeserved.[10] For at least a century, the Republican Party has argued that the nation's mostly capitalist economic system produces plentiful and equitably distributed resources. In contrast, the Democratic Party has tended to argue not only that resources are inequitably distributed but also that the nation's plenty is hoarded by the affluent. A related set of arguments relates to whether unequal economic outcomes can be easily addressed: according to Republicans, attempting to ameliorate economic inequalities usually does more harm than good, disrupting the American Dream for the whole; according to Democrats, government is an effective tool to fix deeply rooted structural problems that harm many Americans.

I argue that the parties construct these fact-laden partisan economic ideologies for political purposes, originating with party insiders and the most active and powerful members of party coalitions. However, once such ideologies become part of the party's messaging, they spread far and wide—influencing most of the party faithful and some beyond the party's base. To some degree, these ideologies also attract new like-minded people to the party. This mass persuasion and attraction is not a by-product of policy-making or a quirk associated with partisan psychology—it is the reason for the creation of partisan economic ideologies (and other types of ideologies) in the first place. In democratic nations, citizens vote for candidates who they believe will champion policy agendas that are fair and that will advance their interests. In the final empirical chapter of this book, I demonstrate with survey data just how closely beliefs about the American Dream align with the public's policy preferences. *American Dream skeptics* tend to support redistribution and a wide range of social welfare initiatives, whereas *American Dream believers* do not. These differences persist net of partisanship, left-right ideology, and social prejudice. For example, even within the Republican Party, people who believe economic inequality to be unfair lean in favor of progressive economic policy; within the Democratic Party, people who believe the economy to be relatively fair voice more moderate views on economic policy.

Party coalitions are never static. Slow changes between the two parties over the past several decades have resulted in a Republican coalition that, on average, is no longer more affluent than the Democratic coalition and is much less likely to earn a college degree.[11] Yet, throughout the first two decades of the twenty-first century, Democratic and Republican members of the public did not moderate their beliefs about the American Dream but rather polarized further. Why? Most likely, the influence of party leaders and closely allied interest groups, donors, and activists. From the mid-2000s through the Biden administration, Democratic leaders doubled down on their commitment to progressive taxation and to using government programs to improve lower-earning individuals' and social groups' economic well-being.[12] They likely did so in response to pressure from prominent economic and racial progressives in their coalition, whose arguments grew more urgent after the economic turmoil of the 2000s and Trump's entry into presidential politics in 2015. To publicly justify their more progressive economic agenda, Democratic elites became more insistent that the nation's distribution of job opportunities and economic resources was unfair, with an increasing emphasis on systemic inequalities experienced by racial minorities and, to a lesser extent, women. Republican leaders also sometimes called the American Dream into question during this period; however, hemmed in by staunchly economically conservative and deep-pocketed party allies, Republicans largely avoided serious criticism of the economy. When Trump called attention to job loss due to globalization in the 2016 campaign, he was a lone figure within the Republican Party.[13] And even Trump's economic criticisms have been circumscribed—focusing heavily on trade and immigration and diminishing after the 2016 election. Throughout his time in politics, Trump has also taken a page from Ronald Reagan's playbook, accusing Democrats of ruining the American Dream through their very attempts to use government to address economic disparities.

The partisan rift over the American Dream is a serious one. That said, we should not confuse disagreement over the reality of the American Dream for disagreement over the ideal. The debate over whether the United States delivers on the American Dream is so passionate because most Americans are deeply committed to the idea that the economy should reward hard work with success, and, at the same time, should not allow success without hard work.[14] The accusation that differences in economic status are not the result of meritocracy is offensive to most Americans on the left and right. Some political observers claim that Democrats desire "equal outcomes" regardless of merit, but this does not describe most Democrats. Rather, Democrats who oppose unequal outcomes usually do so because they believe that unequal outcomes are evidence of unequal opportunity. Likewise, some claim that Republicans are committed only to equal treatment before the law and do not care whether people born into disadvantage can access enough opportunity to earn a decent living. This is also incorrect. Republicans tend to believe enough opportunity exists in the nation such that those with grit and determination can climb the ladder of success.[15]

Even when focused on the reality of the American Dream, partisans do not always disagree. A final contribution of this book is a recognition of the limits of polarization over whether the nation's economy provides meritocratic abundance, or equal and ample opportunity. Many of the public's beliefs about the American Dream are scripted according to salient and polarized political rhetoric. In the recent past, public debates over opportunity and inequality have revolved around the difficulties faced by poor people in general, by Black and Latino Americans, and by women. That these are groups that have predominately voted Democratic in recent years is likely not an accident. Many other types of inequality are simply not discussed with any frequency in the political arena. For example, most politicians, with Trump being an important exception, have said much less about economic barriers faced by rural or White Americans. I demonstrate that, outside the well-established "inequality trio" of lower-income people, lower-earning racial minorities, and women, Americans' beliefs about economic fairness are far less polarized and predictable. With this in mind, I argue that the deep partisan and ideological disagreements over the American Dream are likely much more the result of political rhetoric and context than some set of indelible individual characteristics.

Overview of the Book

In the following chapters, I lay out my case that U.S. politics, to a significant degree, revolves around the two parties' distinct economic ideologies that paint the American Dream as either fact or fiction.

Chapter 1, "Debating the American Dream," situates my project within a vast interdisciplinary literature on public beliefs about economic inequality and opportunity and advances a theory as to why such beliefs are often so politicized. I argue that political parties develop policy agendas to advance the interests of the most important and powerful members of their coalitions. These agendas require justificatory arguments that lean heavily on competing factual claims. I refer to each party's bundle of economic policies and supporting arguments as *partisan economic ideologies*, with explanations for economic inequality resting at their center. These ideologies are critical to each party's efforts to persuade as many voters as possible that its agenda is best. To a significant degree, party ideologies are the glue that hold large, heterogeneous coalitions together in American big-tent parties. This perspective helps us to understand a number of puzzles of contemporary American politics—including why partisans disagree over economic policy with genuine conviction, even when their parties' policies do not advance their self-interest, and why redistributive policy is relatively unpopular in the United States compared with other nations.

Chapter 2, "The Politics of the American Dream in Historical Perspective," combines a review of historically oriented scholarship with original data from Democratic and Republican party platforms to describe how American political leaders' views about economic opportunity and inequality have evolved over time. From the nation's earliest days, American politicians seemed to share the goal of national prosperity and at least a limited version of equal opportunity. Over time, expectations regarding the depth and breadth of shared prosperity grew. However, despite many shared ideals, the Democratic and Republican Parties (as well as their forbearers) often clashed over whether the nation's economic ideals were being met. While the United States has long been known as a country committed to the American Dream in both its normative and empirical forms, the role of the Democratic Party as chief critic of the fairness of the economy often goes unrecognized. This Democratic challenge grew in the first two decades of the twenty-first century, especially with respect to racial inequality. The Republican Party under Trump has sometimes mirrored Democrats' pessimism, albeit in a circumscribed way that is careful to avoid calls for redistribution.

Chapter 3, "Americans' Changing Beliefs About Inequality and Opportunity," written with Mark Tenenbaum and Qingya Xu, examines the public's beliefs regarding the American Dream over the past four decades, drawing on publicly available data from the American National Election Study, the General Social Survey, and the Pew Research Center. This chapter demonstrates three general patterns. First, Americans' belief in the reality of the American Dream declined over this period, especially in the past two decades. Americans became more skeptical that low-income people in general, and Black Americans in particular, were responsible for the fact that they earned less than other people. Instead, Americans increasingly blamed society for putting up barriers to success that ultimately harmed these groups. Second, people who identified with either the Democratic or the Republican party polarized during this time. Republicans' beliefs regarding the American Dream remained stable on average, whereas Democrats grew much more pessimistic, especially in the last two decades. This means that the average increasing concern among Americans about economic fairness has been concentrated among Democrats and, to a lesser degree, independents. Third, suggesting a causal link between elite rhetoric and public perception, these and other lay partisan perspectives have tended to reflect the party elite rhetoric described in chapter 2, and this correspondence has been most evident among Americans who pay close attention to politics.

In chapter 4, "How Americans Explain Socioeconomic Inequalities," I introduce two original surveys of the U.S. public conducted in 2016 and 2018 that underlie analyses in the remaining empirical chapters (chapters 5 through 7). My Explanations for Inequality & Politics surveys (EIPS) concern topics similar to those in the public domain but have the advantage of asking about Americans' explanations for multiple types of socioeconomic inequality using parallel-question wording. With this data, we can assess the extent to which Americans' views on the causes of inequality change as they consider more scripted inequalities—poor versus rich, female versus male, and Black and Latino versus White—as compared with less scripted inequalities—rural versus urban, and White versus Asian American. The surveys also probe Americans' beliefs about a wider range of possible causes of economic inequality than is typical in public opinion surveys, including perceived differences in how hard people work, in their access to good schools and jobs, in cultural influences, in discrimination, and in innate talents.

Drawing on this data, chapter 4 provides an overview of Americans' beliefs about the causes of unequal economic outcomes. We see that the nation is not full of people persuaded that the American Dream is available to everyone. This is especially true when survey respondents were asked to consider why, on average, Black and Latino Americans earn less than White

Americans and why women earn less than men. Causal narratives that highlight a lack of access to good jobs and education, as well as discrimination, were popular among respondents. By way of contrast, people doubted that unequal opportunity explains why White Americans, on average, earn less than Asian Americans. We also see that, at the individual level, respondents were relatively consistent in their beliefs about the causes of scripted inequalities, tending to either blame lower-income people or societal inequities for unequal outcomes. However, explanations for less scripted inequalities did not follow an easily interpretable pattern. I also dive into qualitative data collected as a part of the 2018 EIPS—which allowed people to talk about what causes inequality in their own voice. While the open-ended responses mainly mirrored responses to the closed-ended items, they also revealed some novel explanations and normative perspectives.

With chapter 5, "Demographic Divides over Explanations for Socioeconomic Inequality," I begin a two-chapter investigation into the specific factors that might underlie variation in beliefs about unequal economic outcomes. This chapter focuses on demographic characteristics, including a person's age, race, sex, education level, income, religiosity, and rurality. To some degree, experiences and biases associated with social group characteristics appeared to influence people's beliefs about the fairness of the economy. For example, women and Black and Latino Americans were more likely than men and White Americans (respectively) to say that they earned less due to discrimination, and people with low incomes were more likely than those with high incomes to believe that the economy does not give poor people a fair shake. However, in contrast to some conventional wisdom, education levels and religiosity tended to be more consistently associated with people's explanations for economic inequality—with highly religious Americans more likely to see the economy as meritocratic and highly educated people less likely to do so. Together, these demographic findings provide suggestive evidence that cultural socialization shapes beliefs about inequality more so than do direct economic experience or self-serving motivated reasoning.

In chapter 6, "Partisan Divides over Explanations for Socioeconomic Inequality," I examine how lay partisans differ in their understandings of the causes of unequal economic outcomes. I investigate whether evidence exists for partisan economic ideologies in the public, and whether—as expected—these are found mainly in the more scripted domains of inequality by class, race (Black and Latino versus White), and sex. Not surprisingly, given the survey evidence provided in chapter 3, survey respondents who identified with the Democratic Party were more supportive of structural explanations for inequality and less supportive of individual explanations for inequality than Republicans were. Here, however, I am able to show that these belief differences remain after controlling for left–right ideology as well as social prejudice. There were also telling exceptions to the typical Democratic-Republican pattern of beliefs. For example, partisan polarization receded in domains that are less politically scripted (rural versus urban and White versus Asian American inequality), and polarization was also less evident in a comparison survey from 2002 (when party elite narratives about the economy differed less from one another). In sum, partisanship—along with left–right ideology and social prejudice—appears to shape how people think about the causes of inequality. Yet, this is not the same thing as saying politics creates consistent explanatory narratives for economic inequality and opportunity. To some degree, party leaders' rhetoric is flexible and inconsistent as they defend party goals, and lay partisans' views reflect this.

Chapter 7, "Political Preferences and Explanations for Inequality," asks how Americans' explanations for inequality map onto their economic policy and presidential candidate preferences. I focus here on the three causal narratives that are most indicative of whether Americans do or do not believe lower earning people deserve assistance: work ethic, lack of access to good schools and jobs, and discrimination. Overall, survey respondents who held sympathetic beliefs about lower-earning people were much more supportive of redistribution and social welfare than those who held relatively unsympathetic beliefs. These associations diminished but remained robust when holding partisanship, left–right ideology, and social prejudice constant, and they were especially large among independents and Republicans. The foregoing patterns also occurred, although less pronounced, with respect to presidential candidate preferences. A final important point is that the link between Americans' economic narratives and their political attitudes was strongest when they were considering economic inequality in general and, to a lesser extent, difficulties experienced by women and Black and Latino Americans; beliefs about less scripted inequalities did not consistently map to political preferences. This again points to the content and boundaries of partisan economic ideologies—the Democratic Party, in particular, paints its progressive policy agenda as addressing economic inequality writ large as well as the lower earnings of racial minorities and women. Unsurprisingly, Americans do not link difficulties experienced by rural or White Americans to those same policy prescriptions.

I conclude the book with chapter 8, "The American Dream: Belief, Rhetoric, and Reality." I begin by revisiting the book's findings and discussing key limitations. I then discuss its contributions to several scholarly literatures—on causal attributions for inequality, economic inequality and politics, political polarization, and the association between racial prejudice and partisanship.

The remainder of the concluding chapter shifts gears from understanding the politics of Americans' explanations for inequality to providing a brief assessment of the quality of those explanations. The fact that so many people politicize economic narratives does not mean that we cannot, or should not, evaluate those narratives for their truthfulness. I first consider arguments favored by Democrats—that the nation does not provide sufficient educational and job opportunities and that discrimination plays a major role in socioeconomic inequality. I next consider arguments favored by Republicans—that there exists a culture of poverty and that people's work ethics and level of personal responsibility determine their success in life. I find that both parties at least somewhat exaggerate their favored arguments and inappropriately dismiss inconvenient truths. Yet, by the high standards of the American Dream, Democrats are closer to the mark in arguing that the nation is a very long way from distributing its abundance meritocratically. While some readers may disagree with the conclusions I draw from the research literature, more academics, politicians, and members of the public should make good-faith efforts to understand the reasons why so many Americans continue to struggle while others thrive. I conclude the chapter with a speculative look ahead, arguing that, as both parties seek to appeal to working-class Americans, the polarized debate over the American Dream may be receding.

CHAPTER 1

Debating the American Dream

It is clear enough that under certain conditions men respond as powerfully to fictions as they do to realities, and that in many cases they help to create the very fictions to which they respond.

—Walter Lippmann, *Public Opinion* (1922)

WHY ARE AMERICANS' beliefs about economic inequality and opportunity politicized? In this chapter, I provide a theoretical framework that helps to explain why political parties craft and publicize distinct, fact-laden economic messages and how these messages polarize the public along party lines. I also discuss how this framework can help us to understand some perplexing aspects of public opinion and politics.

Partisan Economic Ideologies

Changing Beliefs About the American Dream

Americans have long been committed to the ideal of the American Dream— the idea that economic rewards should be distributed meritocratically, allowing even people born into poverty to enjoy middle-class comfort if they work hard. This commitment can be expressed in a variety of ways. One good measure is the American National Election Studies' long-running survey question that asks whether government should do "everything necessary to ensure equal opportunity."[1] Americans' agreement with this strongly worded statement hovers around 80 percent over time, with even two-thirds of Republicans agreeing.[2] A normative commitment to the American

https://doi.org/10.7758/trap6910.6827

Dream does not necessarily mean one believes it is empirical reality. Yet, public opinion studies carried out in the twentieth century tended to find that most Americans believed the nation met its lofty economic ideals. In perhaps the first representative U.S. survey on beliefs about the causes of income inequality, Joe Feagin found that the most popular explanations for "why there are poor people in this country" consistently attributed poverty to a defect in lower-income individuals.[3] The least popular explanations attributed poverty to societal problems external to the individual. Feagin argued that Americans possess an "ideology of individualism." A decade later, James Kluegel and Eliot Smith replicated these findings in their land-mark *Beliefs About Inequality*.[4] Drawing on data from the International Social Survey Programme from 1987 to 2010, Leslie McCall reported that the top three most popular explanations for "getting ahead in life" reflected confidence in meritocracy: hard work and ambition, having a good education, and natural ability.[5]

Studies updating this rosy picture in more recent years have been few and far between; however, growing evidence suggests that public sentiment is changing. In a follow-up study, McCall finds that, while Americans over-whelmingly believed that hard work was essential to getting ahead, their faith in hard work declined substantially between 2001 and 2012.[6] Further-more, Americans were more likely than people from other industrialized nations to argue that factors external to individuals and not under their control—such as having educated parents, being born into wealth, and knowing the right people—were important to getting ahead. Spencer Pis-ton finds that Americans overwhelmingly believed poor people have less money than they deserve.[7] Siwei Cheng and Fangqui Wen find that Amer-icans underestimated relative upward mobility between generations rather than overestimated it, as scholars often presume.[8]

Why might pessimism about the American economy be growing? The most obvious reason for declining faith in the American Dream is that the U.S. economy has in fact changed for the worse. The publication of the original public opinion studies on beliefs about economic inequality and opportunity happened to coincide with the tail end of the Great Leveling that occurred in the United States from 1910 to 1970, during which income inequality—measured both before and after taxes and transfers—plum-meted and average real family income tripled.[9] It wasn't until the late 1970s that economic growth slowed and inequality began to rise. Given the nationwide trends in income growth and inequality, we could reasonably expect that Americans, in the aggregate, would have become more doubtful about economic opportunity starting in the late 1970s or shortly thereafter. Reinforcing this intuition, some scholars have linked rising and falling economic opportunity in more recent decades to rising and falling public concern over economic inequality and the availability of opportunity.[10] Using an experimental approach, McCall and colleagues find that study participants exposed to information about rising economic inequality in the United States were more likely to blame societal barriers to success for inequality.[11]

However, only a small part of any person's knowledge about the economy stems from direct experience. Knowledge is primarily indirect, deriving from interpersonal communication and media accounts. These communications include assessments of the extent of opportunity and inequality, as well as interpretations of the causes of these economic phenomena—for example, as individual or structural, and thus as deserved or undeserved. The general process by which people come to adopt many of the social views to which they are exposed is called socialization.

The idea that people's beliefs about the extent and origins of inequality are the product of socialization is certainly not new.[12] My argument is somewhat different from previous accounts, however. Most prior work emphasizing social influences on Americans' economic beliefs has emphasized the importance of national culture, whereas I emphasize the distinct political subcultures in which most Americans are embedded. I argue that narratives circulating among Democrats and left-leaning Americans more generally, especially in the past two decades, reinforce the intuition that ordinary Americans' economic prospects have dimmed—or perhaps were never robust in the first place. Democrats tend not to blame lower-earning individuals and social groups, instead arguing that structural inequalities in society have diminished their economic prospects. On the other hand, narratives circulating among Republicans and right-leaning Americans fend off concerns that the market economy no longer rewards effort. Republicans, even today, tend to deny that structural inequalities have much to do with unequal economic outcomes, holding individuals responsible for their relative success or lack thereof.

Party Agendas and Coalitions

The distinct economic ideologies that circulate among Democratic and Republican partisans have not occurred by happenstance. Factual narratives about what underlies variation in economic outcomes—narratives that ultimately paint the American economy as meritocratic or not—are intentionally crafted and disseminated by party elites to justify their policy agendas. Because policy agendas between right and left differ greatly, factual narratives necessarily differ as well.

To get our minds around why Democratic and Republican agendas—and their justifications—take the form they do, we must first understand the inner workings of political parties. Political scientists increasingly believe that a political party's raison d'etre is to champion its diverse coalitions' priorities in government.[13] The reason is simple. People want specific things from government, and they recognize that the political parties' agendas—carried out by elected officials—are the main vehicle for achieving their objectives. Thus, they bargain for a place on the agenda by offering electoral support to a party. As long as they feel their interests are effectively represented, they have an incentive to help the party win through votes, donations, and/or activism. In theory, this conditional offer of electoral support helps to ensure that the political parties remain attentive to their coalitions' desires.

The party coalitions in some respects have changed considerably over time, and in other respects they have retained continuity. The Republican Party has historically represented business owners and the affluent.[14] In earlier eras, the Republican electoral coalition also included industrial workers, Black Americans, and women.[15] In more recent decades, southern and less educated White Americans, Christian conservatives, rural Americans, and men have become overrepresented within the coalition.[16] Since its beginning, the Democratic Party has represented lower income constituencies, initially White farmers and workers. In the mid-to-late twentieth century, the party changed in mirror opposite to Republicans, first gaining more racial minorities and women and losing southern White voters,[17] then trading rural voters for urban voters and less educated White Americans for college educated White Americans.[18]

With respect to income, recent shifts have resulted in a new and unusual parity between the two parties. Figure 1.1 displays the relationship in 2020 between income and three related variables—a seven-point party identification measure, the difference between the proportion of Democrats and Republicans in the population, and the difference between the proportion of Biden and Trump voters. As others have noted, Democrats still have an advantage among low-income households, but they also appear to draw slightly more voters at the upper end of the income continuum.[19] Republicans increasingly enjoy the support of low- and middle-income Americans but retain strong support from the business community and many wealthy individuals.[20] Interestingly, across the income levels, non-White Americans are more likely to identify as and vote for Democrats as income decreases. Among Whites, that correlation is close to zero or, if we consider the seven-point party identification measure (left panel of figure 1.1), reverses direction. In the 2024 presidential election, these economic trends may have deepened. One analysis reveals that voters in the lower third of the income distribution were evenly split between presidential candidates Kamala Harris and Trump, whereas those in the upper third of the income distribution clearly favored Harris.[21] It is too soon to know whether these shifts are ephemeral or enduring, but they raise the question: why is the Democratic Party still so much more economically liberal than the Republican Party?

One contributing factor is that, as coalition members jockey for a piece of their party's agenda, they are not equal. Policy outcomes in the United States skew heavily toward the preferences of wealthy individuals.[22] The influence of campaign donors—who tend to be much more affluent than others[23]—is likely an important cause of this biased outcome.[24] Republicans have tended to receive more campaign donations than Democrats, especially from highly affluent donors.[25]

Organized activist and interest groups also wield disproportionate influence in elections.[26] Organized political groups command many politically relevant resources that they can allocate to candidates in elections, including endorsements, campaign donations, and volunteers. Organizations also cultivate candidates for political office, develop legislative proposals and initiatives, engage in and fund research on political issues, and lobby elected officials.[27] Those representing private-sector businesses and professionals make up the vast majority of interest groups.[28] Although business groups lobby both parties, they are most influential among Republicans.[29] Organized interests advocating for education, health, the public interest (such as environmental or consumer safety groups), or specific social identity

Figure 1.1 Relationship Between Household Income and Partisanship in 2020

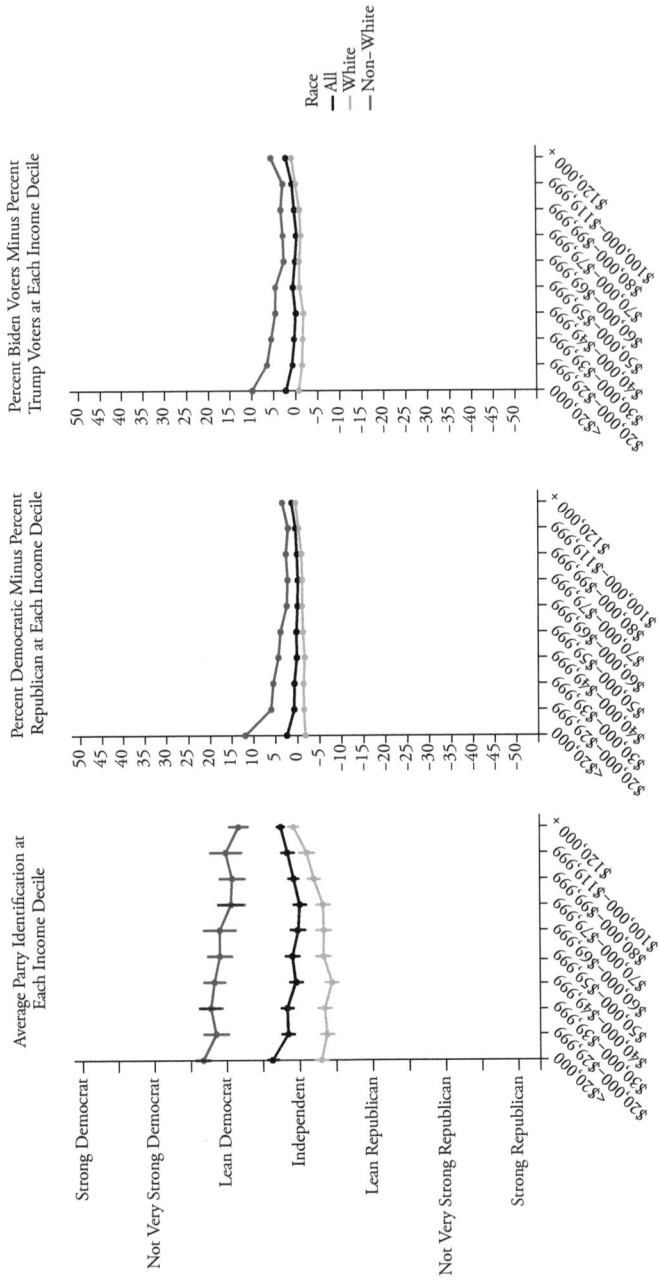

Average Party Identification at
Each Income Decile

Percent Democratic Minus Percent
Republican at Each Income Decile

Percent Biden Voters Minus Percent
Trump Voters at Each Income Decile

Race
— All
— White
— Non–White

Source: Author's calculations using data from the 2020 Cooperative Election Study (Cooperative Election Study 2025).

groups make up a much smaller share of interest groups but are highly influential within the Democratic Party.[30]

These coalitional interests—some with more power than others—are evident in the two parties' agendas. Scholars have described the contemporary Republican agenda as a fusion of economic libertarianism or neoliberalism[31] and moral traditionalism.[32] The party's economic conservatism stretches back further in time than its social conservatism, with a small-government approach evident in presidencies as early as those of Calvin Coolidge and Herbert Hoover, through to those of Ronald Reagan and George W. Bush, although with a notable shift to the center in the mid-twentieth century given the widespread popularity of New Deal economics.[33] For most of this period, the party fought business regulations, workers' ability to unionize, and the progressivism of the income tax. It has consistently sought to scale back social welfare expenditures, at least relative to the Democratic Party. Parties are not necessarily doctrinaire, however. The Republican Party's commitment to the business community is revealed in its frequent support for government subsidies for businesses, ranging from farmers to technology companies.[34] In the Trump era, the party has in some respects pulled back from its commitment to small-government conservatism likely influenced by its changing coalition. Yet, Trump's first presidency was oriented toward traditional conservative economics much more than his rhetoric would suggest.[35] Thus far, Trump's second presidency is considerably more economically unorthodox than the first but retains a strong libertarian streak, as is evident in its commitment to tax cuts and Elon Musk's DOGE initiative.

The Democratic Party's agenda stands opposite that of Republicans, with an emphasis on economic and social liberalism (for the sake of consistency, we might refer to the latter as "social libertarianism" or "social neoliberalism"). Again, the party's economic commitments are older than its social ones. The party's economic agenda has repeatedly challenged concentrated wealth and business interests on behalf of a heterogeneous, and changing, coalition of "have nots." During the Progressive Era, reformers—within and beyond the Democratic Party—turned to the federal government to enact and enforce egalitarian and consumer-oriented policies, ranging from a new income tax to the regulation of food and drugs.[36] In response to the Great Depression, Democrats under President Franklin D. Roosevelt fully embraced a vigorous federal government oriented toward reigning in the power of big business, redistributing wealth, and providing citizens with robust social welfare programs.[37] In the 1960s, with pressure growing among union members and progressive activists and an electoral interest in gaining the votes of Black Americans in particular, Democratic President Lyndon B. Johnson took major steps to advance civil rights, meaning the party sought to ensure that marginalized groups were treated equally by government and the labor market.[38] In the 1990s, the party moderated its economic agenda, even embracing substantial deregulation of business, a shift attributed to the growing power of business in politics and the widespread popularity of neoliberal economics.[39] Beginning in the 2000s, the party moved left again, a change reinforced and amplified by the Great Recession.[40] The Biden administration was particularly notable for its economic progressivism, including its attention to systemic inequalities negatively affecting racial and ethnic minority groups.[41]

The twists and turns of the two parties' histories suggest the interest-driven nature of politics. As Harold Lasswell famously wrote, politics is about "who gets what, when, and how."[42] At any given moment, the two parties are working within two unique and opposing regimes—policy agendas negotiated among coalition members and pursued by party leaders when elected to office.[43] At the same time, we live in a democratic polity in which the expectation come election time is more "right" than "might." Parties must publicly justify their agendas to their members and the broader public with arguments suggesting their plans for the nation will advance widely shared goals.[44]

Agenda Justification

When parties compete in elections, they must put forward appealing visions for the nation that will attract enough voters to win.[45] Some policies are widely popular, but others are more controversial or do not have immediate appeal.[46] These require a persuasive pitch—not only to swing voters and people outside the party but to party regulars too.

Parties overwhelmingly craft their agendas with important members of the party coalition in mind. However, as Kathleen Bawn and colleagues point out, issues of intense interest to a specific subset of a party coalition—for example, reducing taxes on the wealthy or easing unionization in certain industries—tend to be low priorities for others.[47] In some instances, policy proposals may even be opposed by other coalition members. Either way, the party cannot depend on members of its coalition falling into line behind its agenda; it must carefully justify each component to them as well. This crucial step may be especially important to economic agendas today, given that the two parties' coalitions have become so fractured economically. Finally, even policies crafted to appeal to broad swaths of the public benefit from justification—to clarify and emphasize to voters the virtues of a policy in a crowded political marketplace.

Parties justify their agendas in part with salient, shared values. In recent decades, the Republican Party has argued that it stands for freedom, patriotism, and tradition.[48] The value of freedom (or liberty) justifies the party's commitment to a relatively capitalist economy, although at times the party has also evoked patriotism and tradition in defense of the nation's economic system.[49] The Democratic Party has long portrayed itself as the party of economic and political equality, although this commitment was not in fact extended to all Americans until the second half of the twentieth century.[50]

Partisan agendas are not bolstered with appeals to values alone, however. Political observers often fail to appreciate how critical factual arguments are to the act of justifying policy agendas. This practice is quite widespread and extends to all manner of factual claims, ranging from the highly scientific to the more informal and colloquial. In fact, some classic definitions of the term *ideology* include factual claims working in conjunction with value claims.[51] I have argued in prior work that, to be successful in a political debate, a candidate usually must appear to have "the facts" on their side. Where debates are particularly contentious, people are prone to distorting facts by cherry-picking them, relying on dubious sources, or even lying.[52]

Politicians often pair fact and value claims together in political discourse to gain rhetorical advantage. They will argue that a favored value is either not being met or is under threat—and that only their proposals will advance or defend it. These arguments are thick with factual claims: about the state of society and the world and about the effects of government policy. For example, consider the climate change debate. Both political parties value an environment *and* an economy that will enable their constituents to flourish. However, Democrats—who represent environmentalists and wish to aggressively combat climate change—argue that climate change represents a direct threat to people's well-being. Republicans—who represent the oil and gas industry and seek to protect their economic interests—

downplay this harm and instead emphasize the economic harms of transitioning to renewable energy. For years, many Republicans—informed by conservative think tanks and the oil and gas industry—even denied that climate change was occurring.[53]

Politically motivated actors can even more easily present a distorted view of existing evidence on a topic when there is little scholarly consensus, as is often the case in the social sciences and in policy studies.[54] Scholars often wildly disagree over the nature, causes, and consequences of economic inequality.[55] For example, consider the sometimes fierce debate over Thomas Piketty's *Capital in the Twenty-First Century*.[56] This means that political elites on the left can credibly argue that the nation's cherished ideal of robust opportunity for all on equal terms is not being met. And elites on the right can credibly argue that the American Dream, on the whole, is "alive and well" (see figure 1.2).

Factual debates over the American Dream fall along two general lines. The first debate is over the severity of inequality in economic outcomes. Progressive Democratic politicians and allied activists have go-to statistics to illustrate the magnitude of economic inequality in the United States. For example, during his campaigns for the 2016 and 2020 Democratic presidential nomination, Bernie Sanders famously argued that the "top one-tenth of 1 percent owns as much wealth as the bottom 90 percent."[57] Joe Biden claimed at an event in 2019 that "almost half the people in the United States [are] living in poverty." (In fact, 43 percent of Americans at the time were either in poverty or "low-income," meaning they lived in households earning at or below twice the poverty level.)[58] Many progressive Democratic politicians link economic inequality to racial inequality. Elizabeth Warren has highlighted on her website that "the 400 wealthiest Americans currently own more than all Black American households combined."[59] Republicans rarely cite such figures and sometimes accuse Democrats of engaging in "class warfare" when they do. Many Republicans and conservatives also question whether the dire figures oft repeated by Democrats and progressives are in fact accurate. Consider the recent books *The Myth of American Inequality*, cowritten by former Republican Senator Phil Gramm, and *The American Dream Is Not Dead*, by American Enterprise Institute's Michael Strain.[60] Partisans are both biased and probably sincere. In an anonymous survey of lay partisans and local elected officials, Grossmann and colleagues found that Republicans were more optimistic about eco-

Figure 1.2 Image Accompanying *Wall Street Journal* Essay "The American Dream Is Alive and Well"

Source: Strain 2020a. Image by Roberto Parada. Reprinted with permission.

nomic mobility in the United States than economic statistics warranted, and Democrats more pessimistic than warranted.[61]

Although the debate over the severity of inequality has at times been fierce, some degree of consensus exists. While there is disagreement (including among academics) over the precise levels of, and trends in, economic inequality, there is little question that the full spectrum of income and wealth inequality in the United States is extreme—whether one considers it in relation to other democratic nations or its growth over time.[62] One also doesn't need to be an academic to be aware of at least some instances of severe inequality. In most parts of the country, homelessness is impossible to ignore. At the same time, Americans are inundated with images of, and stories about, very rich people, from Elon Musk to Kim Kardashian.

Although Americans often underestimate economic inequality, they reveal in surveys that they are aware of significant economic inequalities as well as over-time trends in inequality.[63] Moreover, many Americans are struggling financially, as Biden pointed out, if in an exaggerated fashion.

The question of the extent of economic inequality is less debated and politicized than the question of whether it is fair. Common debates over economic fairness revolve around equal opportunity.[64] Is the playing field level in the sense that individuals have similar opportunities to develop their skills prior to competing for employment and other positions in society? Further, in any given competition, are all people with relevant attributes included in the pool of applicants, and are those applicants judged only according to relevant attributes? Common conceptions of the American Dream include not only these two components of equal opportunity but also a third: Regardless of the fairness of the competition, is there enough opportunity to go around such that meritorious people can achieve at least a modest standard of living?[65] As in the childhood game of musical chairs, some people will be left without a seat—regardless of merit—if there aren't enough chairs. Disagreements emerge over whether these unfair circumstances exist, how widespread they are, what form they take, and whom they affect.

Republican elites often argue that the fact that the United States is unequal with respect to economic outcomes does not necessarily imply the nation does not offer ample and equal economic opportunity.[66] Paid work is generally available to anyone who wants a job. Americans all have access to public education. Republicans claim that a legally codified equality between individuals and groups has broadly eliminated race and sex discrimination. Following from this perspective, the first Trump administration issued an executive order banning federal entities and contractors from discussing race and sex discrimination (for example, in trainings).[67] On the first day of his second term in 2025, Trump signed an executive order eliminating all "diversity, equity, and inclusion" programs within the federal government.[68] Of course, Republican politicians do not pretend all Americans are born into families with equal resources; however, they often do argue that these differences are relatively inconsequential given the many available opportunities to climb the ladder of success. People who do not climb that ladder—or who fall down it—are generally considered to be personally responsible. For example, Republican Congressman Dusty Johnson made the case for work requirements for food stamp recipients by arguing: "With more than 11 million open jobs, there are plenty of opportunities for SNAP recipients to escape poverty and build a better life."[69] Given widespread and equal opportunity, providing low-income people or groups with generous government resources introduces inequality and undermines meritocracy, according to most Republican leaders.[70] They also tend to argue that such efforts have negative real-world economic effects on individuals, families, and society, as government assistance dampens worker productivity and discourages financial responsibility. John Jost and colleagues refer to this as "fair market ideology."[71]

Democratic elites have tended to take the opposite view, arguing that a market economy, left to its own devices, does not provide ample or equal opportunity.[72] Unfair structural inequalities—ranging from unreasonably low wages in certain sectors to explicit discrimination—lead to very unequal outcomes. We might refer to this as *unfair market ideology*. Consider Hillary Clinton's Growth and Fairness Economy speech in 2015, in which she argued, "Talent is universal; you find it everywhere. But opportunity is not. . . . I firmly believe that the best anti-poverty program is a job but that's hard to say if there aren't enough jobs for people that were trying to help lift themselves out of poverty."[73] Democrats have also insisted that, although job discrimination against racial minorities and women is technically illegal, it occurs nevertheless. In support of a bill to help women retirees, Democratic Congresswomen Lauren Underwood and Patty Murray argued that "the average woman loses more than $400,000 over a forty-year career due to pay inequality."[74] With the American Dream out of reach for many people, Democratic leaders argue that the government should use the many tools at its disposal to remedy the situation.

Although this depiction of Democrats may seem self-evident to those who follow public affairs, documenting it with respect to the contemporary Democratic Party using academic sources is surprisingly difficult. This is partly driven by the fact that the Democratic Party under Bill Clinton, and to a lesser extent Barack Obama, moved to the political center, a shift that has been heavily emphasized among scholars and arguably exaggerated.[75] As I will demonstrate in chapter 2, Democrats never abandoned their insistence that the economic deck is stacked against ordinary Americans; however, in tandem with their economic policy agenda, their rhetoric became more critical of the fairness of the American economy in the early 2000s, hardening in the years following the Great Recession of 2007 to 2009.

In sum: the two parties' baseline economic ideologies are unmistakable. And the parties' distinct explanations for economic inequality—explanations for why some people thrive economically while others fall behind—stand at the center of them. Elements of this framework relate to several important concepts in the social sciences. Frames serve to emphasize or prime preexisting beliefs or values so as to develop or reorient interpretations of an issue or policy.[76] Framing is one tool available to promote and reinforce an economic ideology. Yet, the concept of framing should not be stretched so far as to replace the concepts of argument or justification. The concepts of script and narrative are also relevant. According to Robert Abelson, "a script is a hypothesized cognitive structure that when activated organizes comprehension of event-based situations."[77] Thus, we could consider an explanation for economic inequality as a type of cognitive script. Finally, economists increasingly recognize the importance of economic narratives. Michael Roos and Matthias Reccius argue: "A collective economic narrative is a sense-making story about some economically relevant topic that is shared by members of a group, emerges and proliferates in social interaction, and suggests actions."[78] Narratives are similar to scripts, but the definition emphasizes their communication within groups in service of social needs.

In the next chapter, I provide many examples of such narratives or scripts. Although the specific form they take—and the social inequalities to which they apply—have often changed over time, Democratic skepticism and Republican optimism about the American Dream have been surprisingly consistent throughout American history.

The parties, of course, are not the only ones making these arguments. Party-aligned interest groups and media personalities play an important role in presenting these narratives to the public.[79] Additionally, politically attuned citizens share narratives in conversation and via social media. Cultural institutions, such as schools, religious groups, and entertainment media, join the debate, knowingly and unknowingly.[80] These actors play a role in political socialization. But parties, with their strong incentives to persuade the public and contrasting economic visions for the country, are particularly insistent about their portrait of opportunity in America. The most active party members and leaders coordinate their party's factual narratives about whether the economy rewards merit and spread them through, and as much as possible beyond, the party coalitions, as a part of the general process of partisan socialization.[81]

Partisan Socialization

The best place to find the messages spread via partisan socialization are the two parties' formal platforms, produced every four years just before the presidential nominating conventions. Party platforms are crucial documents for understanding a party's governing intentions and associated rationales.[82] Platforms represent a negotiation among powerful interests within the party coalition—not only those of elected leaders and party functionaries but also those of activists, interest group leaders, and big-dollar donors—regarding how the party should govern if their nominee is elected.[83] Platforms then guide the party in government.[84]

I argue that platforms likely have a second function: they are critical pieces of the parties' communications strategies. This is evident when we consider that platforms are not just lists of policy priorities. They normally include compelling arguments for those priorities—including both fact and value claims. In this way, a platform is a one-stop shop for a party's ideologies. A successful platform is a persuasive document; however, given that few people outside the party core will read that document, it cannot be intended for mass consumption. Rather, it is aimed at the most active party members and allied interest groups and media. A platforms justifies the party's agenda to its heterogeneous coalition members and coordinates messaging, providing arguments to those who wish to persuade others of the party's merits.

Are partisan actors likely to be successful in convincing others that their perspective on the American Dream is correct? Much political science research suggests the answer is "yes" for messages emanating from a party with which a person identifies, but "maybe" or "no" for those messages that do not.

The dominant psychological model of political-opinion formation in the field of political science is roughly as follows. Most people come to identify with one of the two major parties early in life,[85] indeed even during childhood in many cases.[86] This party identification is largely the product of socialization within the family as well as the nearby community.[87] The socialization process also includes a bundle of preferences and values correlated with Democratic or Republican partisanship.[88] These early political viewpoints are not indelible; their stability depends heavily on the similarity or difference of a person's subsequent social environments.[89] Yet, party identification tends to be especially stable and to play an outsize role in influencing subsequent attitudes, beliefs, and perspectives. In their canonical work *The American Voter*, Angus Campbell and colleagues argue that partisanship acts as a perceptual screen biasing one's processing of political information in the direction of the political party.[90]

Arguably the most important implication of the centrality of party identification is that, as elected party leaders change positions over time, Americans who identify with that party—including high-level activists[91]—tend to follow their lead.[92] Party cues, the communication of the party's stands, are influential because they provide a useful informational heuristic regarding what is at stake and because they prime partisan bias.[93] Policy rationales are most influential with respect to people who identify with that particular party; however, rationales that reach people outside the party sometimes persuade them to support a policy if the rationales reflect their preexisting beliefs.[94] Parties are also influential because they structure Americans' information and social environments. People who identify with a particular party are more likely than others to receive information from, and in turn be influenced by, those who share their ideological perspectives.[95] Partisan perspectives are passed from more to less politically attentive individuals in a two-step flow of communication.[96]

While a great deal of political influence is top-down, influence does not flow in only one direction. As I have discussed, political leaders are themselves responsive to powerful interests within their party coalition, ranging from wealthy donors to longstanding interest groups to noisy activists. Their agendas and justifications are formulated in response to (and sometimes directly borrowed from) these coalition members.[97] Party elites then share this information with the broader public. Finally, political socialization also has an important social conformity component, with individuals gravitating toward the views of peers within social identity groups, including their political party.[98] Peer-to-peer influence is probably more common today than in the past given the rise of social media.[99]

While political scientists interested in partisan influence tend to focus on opinion persuasion, the parties also influence people's factual perceptions, resulting in factual belief polarization between lay partisans.[100] We might refer to the distinct bodies of shared knowledge within partisan communities as *partisan common knowledge*, or *partisan knowledge* for short. Political scientists often discuss two other types of partisan polarization—attitudinal or ideological[101] and affective or social.[102] Factual belief polarization is yet a third, underappreciated, type of polarization. This polarization involves many topics, but the subject of this book—explanations for economic inequality—are likely especially implicated given their centrality to parties' economic ideologies. In a series of studies in Denmark, Martin Bisgaard and Rune Slothuus convincingly demonstrate such a partisan influence process over economic beliefs specifically.[103]

Beliefs about the causes of inequality and the nature of opportunity are not just partisan footballs. They likely have an independent influence on people's political preferences, which is why the parties emphasize them. First, they provide an immediate, and probably essential, rationale for a party's policy agenda.[104] Second, once accepted, beliefs about the origins of inequality likely also have downstream effects on policy attitudes. The belief that the American Dream is alive and well logically bolsters the Republican Party's free-market and small-government economic agenda by suggesting that wealthy people and corporations deserve their affluence and market power and that lower income people do not deserve special assistance. For people who might not make these links on their own, Republican politicians and conservative interest groups and media do so for them. Likewise, concern that the American Dream is not a reality for many Americans justifies the Democratic Party's commitment to greater regulation of the economy, redistribution of resources, and robust social welfare. Democratic politicians and progressive allies also make these linkages plain to ensure that they are understood.

An important caveat is in order. I do not mean to argue that partisan communities, even in this polarized day and age, are anywhere near homogeneous in their attitudes and beliefs. The U.S. Congress is far more polarized than the public.[105] Many members of the public don't follow politics closely, meaning political socialization efforts don't consistently reach them. If levels of attention to politics were higher, polarization in the public would be much greater.[106] Furthermore, the two main American political parties are big tents full of people with different political values, demographic characteristics, and organizational affiliations. While the differences between the two party coalitions are unmistakable, "on average" or "most" is not the same thing as "all." Of course, many Americans don't even consider themselves to be partisan—when first asked about party identification, approximately 40 percent say that they are independent (although about two-thirds of those individuals will say they "lean" toward one of the two parties).[107] As a group, independents' political views tend to fall between the two parties on average but are quite varied.

The heterogeneity among partisans and independents turns out to be useful for my purposes. Given that partisanship, policy preferences, and beliefs about inequality are all correlated, it can be difficult to untangle these phenomena to gauge whether factual beliefs about the economy might have an association with policy views independent of partisanship. If I am right that beliefs about the American Dream influence policy preferences, then we should observe a correlation between these factual beliefs and policy preferences *within* political parties (that is, holding partisanship constant), as well as among independents. Within the Democratic Party, American Dream skeptics should be the most likely to champion the economically progressive party line. Within the Republican Party, American Dream believers should be the most likely to champion the economically conservative line. In sum, beliefs about the fairness of the economy may not only increase attitudinal differences between the parties but may also be a source of attitudinal heterogeneity within the parties.

Solving Puzzles

Understanding the two distinct partisan economic ideologies and the grip they have on many Americans psychologically, the goal of this book, helps us to better understand several puzzles of U.S. politics and public opinion.

First, the book helps to explain why Democratic and Republican members of the public disagree over economic policy, often with great conviction. Why are many Republicans opposed to government social services funded by progressive taxation, while many Democrats are in favor? Why are many Democrats supportive of affirmative action, while many Republicans are opposed? While the coalitional makeup of the parties matters to some extent, the answer is not reducible to income or demographics. As we will see, Americans' economic policy views are much more closely aligned with their beliefs about the fairness of the economy than with their personal characteristics. Policy disagreements also cannot be boiled down to partisan differences in values or out-group prejudice (at least, not alone). In sum: if we know whom or what a person blames for economic inequality—individual earners themselves or economic and social inequities over which individuals have little control—we can make a surprisingly accurate guess as to what economic policy views they favor.

Second, this book also helps us to understand why so many Americans remain optimistic about the ability of the market economy to fuel the American Dream without government intervention despite skyrocketing economic inequality in recent decades and slow income growth for most people. Here, to a significant extent, I join a long line of scholars in arguing that this reflects the nation's "dominant ideology."[108] Yet, this book stakes out a somewhat different argument. I argue that this ideology is not a part of some pervasive national culture that everyone absorbs relatively equally. Rather, it is fueled primarily by actors working within and in concert with the Republican Party. Democrats have at times joined in. Yet, the political left at any given moment in modern American politics has been at best lukewarm to the notion that ordinary people receive their just deserts in the market economy.

Third, and relatedly, this book helps us to understand why so many partisans are committed to economic narratives and policies that are out of step with their personal economic circumstances. As shown in figure 1.1., at the individual level, the two parties are at relative parity with respect to income. Republican candidates now consistently win elections among Americans without a college degree, and Democratic candidates win among those with college degrees.[109] At the House district level, Democratic districts are more affluent than Republican districts on average.[110] Yet, in most respects, the party agendas function as if the historical class divide between the two parties was still in place. As the Democratic Party drew more affluent people into its coalition in the 2010s, it actually grew more economically progressive.[111] Although Trump diverged from Republican orthodoxy in some respects, his first-term appointments, decisions, and policy proposals were overwhelmingly in line with conservative economic orthodoxy.[112] With the exception of his tariff policy, Trump in his second term is similarly committed to small-government conservatism so far. Why the disjuncture between party agenda and base? To a significant degree, the parties are

locked into well-defined policy tracks not because of broad voter preferences but because of the ideological commitments of their most influential
members—activists, donors, and interest groups.[113] The parties have, so far,
kept their broader base on board via compelling economic narratives. As a
result, most lay Republicans remain optimistic about the American Dream,
and most lay Democrats remain skeptical.

Fourth, and finally, this book helps us to understand why, for so long,
the United States did not do more to blunt harsh market inequalities. Nations with democratic elections, extreme income and wealth inequality, and
relatively modest redistribution should not exist in theory. If a majority of
citizens would gain from redistribution, as is the case when wealth is highly
concentrated, then we would expect the majority to use their votes to ensure politicians redistribute that wealth.[114] Scholars offer a range of explanations for this, most revolving around the idea that American citizens do
want more redistribution but other elements prevent its political actualiza-
tion.[115] Some argue that the main problem is that politicians, bending to
the will of affluent and business interests, ignore ordinary Americans.[116]
Others argue that Americans may want greater equality in theory but are
confused about policy details, not understanding, for example, that the es-
tate tax only applies to a tiny slice of American families.[117] Still others argue
that many Americans are ambivalent about their electoral choices due to
the limiting nature of the two-party system. They want the government to
redistribute resources, a Democratic position, but they also want socially
conservative policy, a Republican position. Among such conflicted voters,
the latter often takes priority.[118]

Each of these theories has merit. However, I argue that most scholars
underestimate the reservoir of genuine opposition to redistribution and
social welfare among many rank-and-file Republicans. Even in the relatively
populist Trump era, lay Republicans continue to link success to hard work,
and they therefore oppose many redistributive policies.[119] Given that the
U.S. political system, with its many checks and balances, requires bipartisan support for legislation to advance,[120] one party standing against redistribution will usually block reform. My argument adds to those of prior
researchers: competing priorities, a public outmatched by spin, and pluto-
cratic power matter a lot. But a perceptual divide between left and right has
underpinned support for, and opposition to, redistribution. Factual belief

polarization has reinforced, and likely exacerbated, attitudinal polarization and, thus, policy gridlock.

That being said, the era of gridlock could be receding. Bipartisan coalitions passed important economic initiatives—ranging from COVID-19 relief to spending on infrastructure—during both the first Trump and Biden administrations. Could this be linked to shifts in public opinion, especially within the Republican Party? Perhaps. The public opinion data I will discuss shows that Republicans are far from uniform in their insistence that the American Dream is alive and well. Not only is there heterogeneity within the party with respect to the causes of unequal economic outcomes in general, but the party's average faith in hard work also falters when considering women and rural residents' lower incomes. Whether these are exceptions to a more general rule or signs of change to come remains to be seen.

CHAPTER 2

The Politics of the American Dream in Historical Perspective

Equality of opportunity is the right of every American—rich or poor, foreign or native-born, irrespective of faith or color. It is the right of every individual to attain that position in life to which his ability and character entitle him. . . . It is as if we set a race. We, through free and universal education, provide the training of the runners; we give to them an equal start; we provide in the government the umpire of fairness in the race. The winner is he who shows the most conscientious training, the greatest ability, and the greatest character.

—Herbert Hoover nomination acceptance speech (1928)[1]

Poverty is not a trait of character. It is created anew in each generation but not by heredity: by circumstances. Today, millions of American families are caught in circumstances beyond their control. Their children will be compelled to live lives of poverty unless the cycle is broken. President Johnson's war on poverty has this one goal: to provide everyone a chance to grow and make his own way, a chance at education, a chance at training, a chance at a fruitful life.

—Narration from Lyndon Johnson "Poverty" ad (1964)[2]

THE PHRASE *American Dream* can be found in published documents going back to the late 1800s. For decades, the meaning of the term remained in flux, reflecting any given author's or speaker's own ideals. It was used to describe a society committed to democracy, to individual liberty, to moral improvement, and to economic opportunity for all, as it is generally understood today.[3]

https://doi.org/10.7758/trap6910.6313

The American Dream took on a meaning close to its present one in James Truslow Adams's book *The Epic of America*, which popularized the term. Adams crystallized three important tenets of the Dream that remain today. The first tenet is definitional; Adams argued that the American Dream should be understood as relevant to individual upward mobility—advancement with respect to economic achievement, personal development, and, relatedly, social status. The American Dream was

> that dream of a land in which life should be better and richer and fuller for every man, with opportunity for each according to his ability or achievement. . . . It is not a dream of motor cars and high wages merely, but a dream of a social order in which each man and each woman shall be able to attain to the fullest stature of which they are innately capable, and be recognized by others for what they are, regardless of the fortuitous circumstances of birth or position.[4]

The second tenet establishes preconditions for the Dream, giving responsibilities to both the upper and lower classes. Adams writes that "those on top, financially, intellectually, or otherwise, have got to devote themselves to the 'Great Society,' and those who are below in the scale have got to strive to rise, not merely economically, but culturally."[5] Elsewhere he makes clear that the "super-rich" must share their riches, and he laments the era's unfair concentration of wealth and the obvious dearth of economic opportunities available to the poor.[6] The third tenet holds that the American Dream was aspirational and not yet realized, a descriptive assessment reflected in the phrase itself.[7] One could certainly laud the nation for its noble ideals, but one could also—as Adams did—evoke the Dream as a critique of a nation falling short.

The term *American Dream* may be relatively new in the context of the nation's history, but its core ideas seem to have been a part of U.S. culture since the nation's founding. One could argue that Adams and others sought to capture in a single term an ideal they believed had been realized early in the nation's history but was increasingly divorced from reality given the extraordinary inequality of the times—including the broad and deep poverty of the Great Depression. In the country's earliest years, upward mobility for new European immigrants was fairly attainable. Between a seemingly endless frontier and labor shortages, opportunity abounded. Further, with no established aristocracy and a burgeoning democratic culture inherited from England, White newcomers of all classes could engage in economic activity on relatively equal terms.[8] That said, surviving, let alone thriving, as a settler required very hard work.[9] This helped to solidify expectations that Americans worked hard and—at least if they were of European descent—were amply rewarded for their labor.

American political leaders' rhetorical commitment to upward mobility via individual effort has been a constant in the nation's history. Yet, this is not the same thing as saying that all Americans perceive such advancement to be possible. Much political debate has been animated by disagreement over whether they indeed have ample and equal opportunity to get ahead. From its founding in the 1820s, the Democratic Party has tended to advance a narrative questioning the notion that all Americans have sufficient access to economic opportunity. For the first century of its existence, the Democratic Party focused solely on difficulties facing Americans of European descent. In the twentieth century, it would expand its purview to include racial minorities as well. The Republican Party, at least since the late 1800s—when it cemented its ties with industry[10]—has been more likely to argue that the nation has succeeded in providing collective economic opportunity, at least as much as is practically possible. These general narratives have been surprisingly consistent but also come in many permutations. All work to justify the two parties' economic policy agendas as they evolve over time.

In the remainder of this chapter, I first define the related concepts of equal opportunity, meritocracy, and the American Dream. I then provide a chronological examination of partisan rhetoric and policies that touch on these concepts. Throughout, I rely especially on the two parties' platforms to illustrate their thinking about these topics. This is for two reasons. First, party platforms are a negotiation between the presidential nominee and powerful interests within the party. For this reason, a platform likely represents—better than any other single public document—the party's broad goals and policy proposals that it will pursue if elected to office.[11] Second, the platform is a lengthy piece of rhetoric that efficiently sums up not only the party's policy agenda but also its justifications for it. Platforms are a storehouse of the official partisan scripts that provide a rationale for each of their policies. Thus, if we can point to one document to help us understand the substance of partisan ideologies at any given point in time, this is it. I examine platform rhetoric most closely and systematically during the main years of the neoliberal era—beginning in 1980 with Ronald Reagan's election through the 2020 election.[12] This chapter makes clear that devotion to the American Dream and related ideas is a unifying thread in our political history and, at the same time, has long been—and remains—a source of bitter division.

Equal Opportunity, Meritocracy, and the American Dream

Americans love sports metaphors to illustrate their ideals, especially economic equality. Herbert Hoover, as quoted earlier, imagines economic success as the outcome of a fair race. He believed the nation had provided all its athletes (that is, workers) with sufficient training (education) and placed them at the starting line (the job market). In his eyes, winning the race (economic success) was determined by effort and skill alone. Sports metaphors have also been used to illustrate a lack of equality—for example, saying that a person was "born on third base" or that there is "an uneven playing field." This suggests some people inherit resources, connections, or other advantages and, thus, can more easily than others make it to home plate (achieve success).

Elements of fair competition include both meritocracy and equal opportunity. Meritocracy is defined by the combined influence of effort and skill on relative success.[13] In a perfect meritocracy—in which people have been treated fairly and given equal training—economic outcomes are determined solely by the individual's degree of effort and innate talent. That said, an abundance of good opportunities is not a necessary attribute of meritocracy. Opportunities could be awarded meritocratically but also be scarce, necessarily resulting in an impoverished, losing class. On the other end of the economic scale, some so-called opportunities could be associated with gigantic sums of money—such as a CEO's high salary or a business owner's accumulated wealth. Thus, a meritocratic society can, at least in theory, be accompanied by a great deal of income and wealth inequality.[14]

Equal opportunity similarly insists on equal starting conditions and treatment in the marketplace to ensure that any unequal outcomes are the result of differences in effort and skill.[15] In the United States, the main way in which the concept of equal opportunity differs from that of meritocracy, at least in common usage, is its focus on disparities across important social groups in society. The term became popular in the mid-twentieth century as the nation began to seriously address the discrimination against women and racial, ethnic, and religious minorities that kept them from earning as much as others.[16] Thus, people who invoke the importance of equal opportunity are often especially concerned with discrimination linked to a person's ascriptive characteristics (such as race or sex). As with meritocracy, a system with true equality of opportunity can potentially have extreme inequalities in income and wealth. However, inequalities across large and well-defined social groups are more contentious, as people who argue that equal opportunity has been realized also necessarily argue that lower-earning social groups lack effort, skill, or both. In other words, in a society with socioeconomic inequality, if one believes that the society has achieved equal opportunity, one must also believe that some social groups "deserve" to earn less (or more) than others.

The American Dream incorporates most of these ideas. It holds that effort and skill ought to drive success. It tolerates—and even expects—extreme inequality as the especially ambitious and talented accumulate great wealth. However, the Dream differs from the preceding concepts in two key ways. First, it focuses on upward (not downward) mobility, especially for immigrants and people born poor. In other words, it is positive in orientation and does not dwell on the negative. Second, and relatedly, it does not expect scarcity. If the American economy is living up to the American Dream, it will offer equal and ample opportunity. I refer to this as *meritocratic abundance*.[17] The implication is that people who are not uniquely talented but who "work hard and play by the rules" will obtain some reasonable amount of success.[18] The American Dream is a more generous ideal than equal opportunity and meritocracy: We cheer for people who are wildly successful while also celebrating those with more humble achievements—perhaps a simple house with a picket fence. But, as with meritocracy and equal opportunity, the American Dream has a troubling side: unlike Adams, many people have come to see the American Dream not only as an ideal to strive for but also as one that has been reached. If we believe opportunity is abundant and equally available, then one implication is that the poor are morally deficient—lazy or socially deviant.[19] Thus, belief that the Dream is real undercuts some of the most compelling rationales for economic reform.

A critical caveat in this discussion is the fact that each of these concepts have weaker and stronger versions. Some people argue that equal opportunity and meritocracy are constituted only by equal treatment in the marketplace, with laws ensuring that people are hired and promoted solely according to their merit (effort and skill). Others argue that a society that truly offers equal opportunity and meritocracy must either provide people with significant social supports, especially early in life, or must take into account previous disadvantage when making hiring decisions and the like.[20] The notion of what constitutes ample opportunity varies too, with some people believing that low-wage jobs offer an initial foothold in the economy and others believing that such jobs not only provide insufficient wages but also no real path to upward mobility. I argue that, for most Americans, these different definitions do not represent greater or lesser interest in true equality, or greater or lesser tolerance for inequality. Rather, people committed to thinner versions of these ideals often believe, as a matter of fact, that formal equality coupled with abundant low-wage jobs is sufficient to allow nearly all people to advance via hard work and grit. Those who reject this, embracing the thicker versions of these ideals, tend to believe it is unrealistic to expect many, or even most, poor people to "pull themselves up by their bootstraps." In other words, a great deal of debate over equality is factual in nature, or, as social scientists would say, empirical. The quotes that open this chapter demonstrate this: Hoover claims that disparate economic outcomes reflect merit with only equal treatment and free education in place; Johnson argues much more is needed to help poor Americans get to the starting line of the economic race.

The American Dream in Early American Political History

U.S. political culture is best understood as one of multiple traditions.[21] In their book *The American Ethos*, Herbert McClosky and John Zaller argue that capitalism and democracy are the two pillars of America's political tradition.[22] Although many people view these two phenomena as at odds—

with capitalism emphasizing freedom and democracy stressing equality—
these authors argue in favor of a more complementary relationship:

> Capitalism and democracy evolved side by side as part of a common protest
> against the inequities and petty tyrannies of Old World monarchism, mer-
> cantilism, and the remnants of feudalism. Both aimed to free the individual
> from the dead hand of traditional restraints and to limit the power of the
> rich and well-born to exploit the less privileged.[23]

According to McClosky and Zaller, the nation's major ideological conflicts
have taken place within the boundaries of these two powerful traditions.
Rogers Smith adds a critical third tradition.[24] Throughout the nation's history, many people have endorsed ascriptive hierarchies—economic, political, and social inequalities linked to group identities, especially those tied
to race, ethnicity, and sex. The American Dream has drawn formally on the
first two traditions and informally on the third.

Early in U.S. history, the nation's ideals included the freedom to work
in the manner of one's choosing and equal treatment under the law. Relative to most other nations at the time, this normative framework was not
just egalitarian—it was radical.[25] These ideals were reinforced by the United
States' weak class structure relative to those of Europe.[26] And, when combined with labor shortages and the widespread availability of land, they
allowed European men and their families to prosper.[27] Standards of living
for the American working class generally exceeded those in Europe.[28] Furthermore, in Peter Lindert and Jeffrey Williamson's words, "incomes were
more equally distributed in colonial America than in any other place that
can be measured."[29] This early mix of freedom, equality, and prosperity
likely informed the development of the American Dream. This reflects the
sociological argument that ideals often follow experience and practice, not
the other way around.[30]

Yet, by today's standards, the early version of the American Dream was
unreasonably narrow. No system of public education nor any government-
provided social safety net existed. Of course, the Dream was also limited to
men of European descent. Ascriptive racial and ethnic hierarchies forced
most Black Americans into slavery before the Civil War and consigned non-
Whites to inferior jobs more generally. As time passed, a narrow focus on
equal treatment and the freedom to work in a prospering economy would
broaden to include an expectation that children receive an education at the

public's expense and that the government assist people who are unable to provide for themselves. Eventually, these expectations would extend beyond those of European descent to most others. The political parties, representing different interests and jockeying for electoral dominance, would be critical in shaping both Americans' expectations regarding what the nation ought to provide its people and whether it was following through.

The Early Democratic Party

Throughout the 1800s, income inequality sharply rose, to the extent that it rivaled European levels.[31] (Wealth inequality, however, remained less extreme.)[32] Rising inequality would bring the first major political schism over whether the nation was living up to its ideal of widespread economic opportunity for White Americans.

In the 1820s, Andrew Jackson established the Democrats as the first "mass" political party, running populist campaigns and winning votes from many newly enfranchised voters. Jackson won the presidency in 1828, becoming the first Democratic President. He had an enormous influence on the party, catering to Whites with little political power and few resources, especially those in the South and West.[33] Under Jackson, the Democratic Party began to emphasize its coalition's victimhood, an emphasis that would continue into the contemporary era. In pre–Civil War America, this meant protecting ordinary (White) citizens from excessive taxation and battling a federal government perceived as working hand in hand with wealthy northern industrialists.[34] During this period, Democrats, who supported slavery in the South as well as in new territories, were hostile to the interests of Black Americans. As the Civil War unfolded, class conflict took a back seat to racial conflict. Democrats in the South seceded from the United States to protect the institution of slavery. After the war and a brief period of enforced Reconstruction, they unrepentantly established a rigid caste system in the South designed to keep Black Americans in an inferior economic, political, and social position.[35]

Despite their noxious stance on race, Democratic elites pursued economic egalitarian policy on behalf of their coalition even more vociferously after the war. This period would see the rise of the labor and populist movements, both of which forged ties with the party. During the notoriously unequal era of the Gilded Age, Democrats endorsed former socialist Horace

Greeley for president in 1872 and nominated populist Williams Jennings Bryan three times—in 1896, 1900, and 1908.[36]

As economic resources became more concentrated in fewer hands, it was in the interest of the Democrats and their allies, not their Whig and Republican opponents, to problematize it. Bryan famously railed against societal elites in favor of the economic aspirations of the common man.[37] According to him, the concern over concentrations of wealth stemmed from workers and farmers not receiving adequate pay for their toil, in part because capitalists manipulated the system to keep economic gains for themselves. The rich were also idle, reaping gains while doing little work. Consider this passage from Bryan's famous Cross of Gold speech at the 1896 national convention:

> When you come before us and tell us that we shall disturb your business in-
> terests, we reply that you have disturbed our business interests. . . . The man
> who is employed for wages is as much a businessman as his employer. . . .
> The farmer who goes forth in the morning and toils all day, begins in the
> spring and toils all summer, and by the application of brain and muscle to
> the natural resources of this country creates wealth, is as much a businessman
> as the man who goes upon the Board of Trade and bets upon the price of
> grain. The miners who go 1,000 feet into the earth or climb 2,000 feet upon
> the cliffs and bring forth from their hiding places the precious metals to be
> poured in the channels of trade are as much businessmen as the few financial
> magnates who in a backroom corner the money of the world. We come to
> speak for this broader class of businessmen.[38]

Although the Democratic Party's preferred economic policies during this period differed from those of modern Democrats—for example, Bryan advocated for the break-up of monopolies but not for the provision of generous government-provided social welfare—its concern over economic inequality was clear.

The Democratic Party's commitment to economic equality in this early period did not end with Bryan. Many scholars underestimate the extent to which twentieth-century Democratic presidents, including Woodrow Wilson, followed in Bryan's and even Jackson's footsteps. The academic Wilson, president from 1913 to 1921, offered, in John Gerring's words, "Bryanism with a Princeton accent."[39] Wilson's governing philosophy incorporated elements of both agrarian and urban populism. During his administration,

Congress would pass the first income tax (on high-income households), strengthen antitrust law, assist farmers, protect railroad workers, and prohibit the interstate shipment of goods made with child labor. At the same time, reflecting his Southern roots, Wilson actually moved federal policy backward on race, for example, by segregating the federal civil service and firing many Black federal workers.[40]

The Early Republican Party

The Republican Party, emerging from the remnants of the Whig Party, was founded in the 1850s. The new party represented the interests of the industrial sector as well as abolitionists, both concentrated in the northern United States. This mix of interests is surprising to many contemporary Americans. However, it is easily understood when one considers the regional and economic makeup of the two parties. Democrats dominated in the South, where slave plantations powered the economy. Abolitionists had little choice but to join the Republican Party. Southerners' reliance on slave labor also threatened northern industrialists and their workers; by not paying their laborers, southern competitors could produce goods more cheaply, potentially undercutting northern manufacturers and driving down wages.[41]

Republicans' reaction to rising inequality throughout the nineteenth century was quite different from that of Democrats. They argued that what benefited Americans most were national prosperity and wage growth, fueled by business expansion. They also emphasized the dignity of work and the importance of free labor, unrestricted by guilds, unions, or, of course, slavery. With these messages, the party could plausibly refer to itself as the "natural home of the workingman."[42] The Republican Party generally did not impose regulations on big business to ensure fair business practices or improve the treatment of workers, nor did they pursue redistribution or the expansion of social welfare. That said, for a time, the party included a more progressive faction, of which President Theodore Roosevelt (1901 to 1909) was a member. Especially in Roosevelt's second term, he sought to break up monopolies and protect both workers and consumers.[43] Once Roosevelt was out of office, however, Republicans returned to their close alliance with business owners, spurring Roosevelt to run as a Progressive in 1912.

While the Democratic Party took the lead in championing economic equality among Whites, the first appearance of the term *equal opportunity* in a party platform was in the Progressive Party's 1912 platform, when former Republican President Theodore Roosevelt undertook a longshot bid for a third term. Not long after, Republicans—influenced by the Progressives—were talking about equal opportunity too. Consider the following passage from conservative President Herbert Hoover's 1920 nomination acceptance speech (a fuller version of this chapter's opening quote):

> Equality of opportunity is the right of every American—rich or poor, foreign or native-born, irrespective of faith or color. It is the right of every individual to attain that position in life to which his ability and character entitle him. It tolerates no privileged classes or castes or groups who would hold opportunity as their prerogative. . . . It is as if we set a race. We, through free and universal education, provide the training of the runners; we give to them an equal start; we provide in the government the umpire of fairness in the race. The winner is he who shows the most conscientious training, the greatest ability, and the greatest character. . . . Socialism bids all to end the race equally. It holds back the speedy to the pace of the slowest. . . . Equality of opportunity is a fundamental principle of our nation. With it we must test all our policies.[44]

This rhetoric acknowledges a much more expansive definition of equal opportunity than that characteristic of the nation's early years. Here, equal opportunity includes not only equal treatment but also some measure of equal training via a public education system. Hoover also, at least in principle, extends equal opportunity to all social groups. However, equal opportunity here—if achieved—also justifies "small government" conservatism. If the government helps ensure a "fair race," then there is no moral impetus to address the inevitable inequality, even poverty, that results.

This commitment to equal opportunity accompanied the very economically conservative presidencies of Hoover (1929–1933) and, before him, Calvin Coolidge (1923–1929). Republicans lowered the new income tax on high-income earners. Hoover did relatively little to assist the millions of Americans made destitute by the Great Depression.[45] After leaving office, he would reveal how deep his conviction ran that meritocracy inevitably implied unequal economic outcomes. In his 1934 book *The Challenge to Liberty*, Hoover wrote: "No economic equality can survive the working of biological inequality. This is a hard commonplace truth, disappointing as it may be to those who ride upon plans of utopia."[46] Innate explanations for economic inequality suggest not only that inequality is fair but also that there is not much government can do to ameliorate it.[47]

The New Deal Era

Democrats

The Great Depression was a watershed moment in American politics. Republican management of the economy, including a commitment to restrained government, was—at least for a time—repudiated. In 1932, Franklin Delano Roosevelt beat Hoover in a landslide, and Democrats trounced Republicans in congressional elections as well.[48] In response to the Great Depression, Roosevelt and Democrats in Congress would go on to construct and enact the New Deal, which transformed the relationship between government and the economy.

Roosevelt is sometimes considered to have departed from prior Democrats, given his embrace of robust federal intervention in the economy.[49] However, in terms of ultimate goals as opposed to means, his presidency is arguably better thought of as the apex of Democrats' twentieth-century economic populism. The New Deal included many different government policies to assist low-income Americans, ranging from ending anti-union practices among large companies to implementing a minimum wage to building a robust social safety net.[50] Roosevelt's Democratic Party continued to use colorful populist language to justify their policies. For example, its 1936 platform states: "We have begun and shall continue the successful drive to rid our land of kidnappers and bandits. We shall continue to use the powers of government to end the activities of the malefactors of great wealth who defraud and exploit the people."[51] For Democrats, righting these economic wrongs was a moral imperative, and they now argued that government was an appropriate tool to assist in this fight.

Roosevelt's presidency also represented a shift from earlier Democratic presidents when we consider to whom the Democrats' economic progressivism applied. Roosevelt increased government regulation of the economy and introduced new social welfare programs that were helpful to lower-income Americans regardless of racial or ethnic background. Critics correctly point out that the New Deal often put the economic needs of White Americans first, such as a Social Security program that ignored job categories occupied predominantly by Black Americans.[52] Yet, given the extensive assistance the New Deal provided to low-income and working-class Americans, Black Americans—overwhelmingly in these categories—received more material assistance from the government during the Roosevelt Administration than in any prior period. As a result, Black Americans began to gravitate toward the Democratic Party.[53]

The Democratic Party would more fully embrace equal opportunity in the coming decades. These changes were likely the direct result of the fight against a racist Nazi regime during World War II and, not unrelatedly, a pressure campaign within the Democratic Party by labor and civil rights activists to ensure equal opportunity for all Americans.[54] The 1948 Democratic platform under Harry Truman illustrates the party's growing commitment to racial and religious equality with the following text:

> The Democratic Party is responsible for the great civil rights gains made in recent years in eliminating unfair and illegal discrimination based on race, creed or color. The Democratic Party commits itself to continuing its efforts to eradicate all racial, religious and economic discrimination. We again state our belief that racial and religious minorities must have the right to live, the right to work, the right to vote, the full and equal protection of the laws, on a basis of equality with all citizens as guaranteed by the Constitution.[55]

In 1964, President Johnson and Democrats in Congress enacted the Civil Rights Act, a sweeping law outlawing a wide range of discriminatory actions against racial and religious minorities and women.[56] Johnson's Great Society agenda was similar in size and scope to the New Deal—among other things, it launched Medicare, Medicaid, and Head Start and provided assistance to people wishing to buy a home or start a small business. Unlike the New Deal, it placed all Americans on equal footing and prioritized both rural and urban poverty.[57] Although Johnson arguably sought to equalize both opportunities and outcomes, including supporting affirmative action for racial minorities and women, he tended to frame his programs as assisting more with the former than the latter.[58] Yet, as the Johnson ad language at the chapter opening indicates, the more modest goal of equal opportunity still required substantial assistance, "to provide everyone a chance to grow and make his own way, a chance at education, a chance at training, a chance at a fruitful life."

Republicans

During and after World War II, the Republican Party would pivot, softening their economic conservatism. Hoover's minimalist reaction to the Great Depression had not aged well, and Roosevelt's New Deal had been wildly popular among American voters. Furthermore, interest in civil rights for racial minorities was spreading, a reaction to Black American protests as well as the horrors of the Nazi era.[59] Distinct political eras are marked by the dominance of one party's governing ethos and the other party's necessary capitulation. We see this in the mid-to-late twentieth century with Democrats' increasing progressivism and the Republican Party's ideological moderation.[60]

In the 1950s, Rockefeller Republicans, allied with big business and affluent Whites but also supportive of the New Deal and civil rights, ascended. Republican Presidents Dwight Eisenhower and Richard Nixon were popular, but they maintained their popularity by accepting, perhaps reluctantly, that Americans expected substantial government support to ensure a more level playing field.[61] Their economic narratives bolstered these policy choices. For example, the 1968 Republican platform, under Nixon, contains a line that closely mirrors Johnson's language: "Millions of Americans are caught in the cycle of poverty—poor education, unemployment or serious under-employment, and the inability to afford decent housing."[62] Some Republicans went so far as to support a measure of "equality of outcomes." In a speech to the American Business Council, the chairman of both Eisenhower's and Nixon's Council of Economic Advisors, Paul McCracken, stated:

> The optimum toward which society is trying to feel its way here will be neither pure "equality of results" nor just "equality of opportunity." A society organized solely on the principle of equality of opportunity is not acceptable, and one organized solely around the principle of equality of results would not be operational.[63]

President Nixon would bolster Social Security benefits, support programs aimed at helping minority workers and businesses, and even propose guaranteed health care and a minimum income for the poor, placing him firmly in the middle of the ideological spectrum of twentieth-century American

presidents.[64] Yet, Nixon's administration also represented a marked change
with respect to the party's stance on race. As Democrats leaned into civil
rights, Nixon launched his Southern strategy in 1968, seeking to gain more
support from Whites in the South by slowing federal progress on civil rights
and highlighting concerns over race-related crime and disorder.[65]

Bipartisan Support for Equal Opportunity

By the mid-twentieth century, the concept of equal opportunity—broad in
its definition as well as the groups to which it applied—was a centrist idea
on which most Democratic and Republican politicians could agree.[66] Ordinary Americans endorsed this robust equal opportunity ideal too. According to McCloskey and Zaller: "Americans strongly—even overwhelmingly—support the notion that everyone should have the same chance to
'get ahead.'"[67] In 1965, 98 percent of the public agreed with the statement,
"Everyone in America should have equal opportunities to get ahead." With
respect to racial equality specifically, as early as the World War II era, 87
percent of Americans answered "yes" when asked, "Do you think a Negro
doing the same work as a white man should get the same pay?"[68] For a relatively brief moment in time following World War II, both parties also expressed substantial awareness that the nation was falling short of delivering
on the American Dream.

Yet, as the new, more inclusive, equal opportunity ideal solidified in the
American consciousness, partisan disagreement over how to interpret, and
grapple with, inequality remained. In the 1960s and into the 1970s, Democrats' criticisms of the fairness of the American economy grew more stri-
dent, especially with respect to inequality by race and sex. Republicans
remained more optimistic about the fairness of the American economy,
even as they echoed a surprising number of Democratic criticisms. However, as the federal government expanded and criticisms of capitalism became de rigueur, conservatives within the Republican Party mounted a
counteroffensive.

U.S. party politics in the late 1970s shifted from the New Deal Order to
a Neoliberal Order.[69] During this latter period, the Republican Party dominated, retreating from their postwar moderation and becoming much
more economically conservative. They did not retreat from their public
commitment to meritocracy, equal opportunity, and the American Dream;

rather, they argued that these ideals could be met with a smaller government that intervened less in the economy. Republicans increasingly sounded like Hoover: given public education and some minimal guardrails, American capitalism would deliver widespread opportunity. For a period, Democrats would acquiesce and moderate their policy agenda and associated rhetoric, as Republicans had in the New Deal Era.

The Neoliberal Era

Analyzing Party Platforms, 1980–2020

To inform my discussion of this more contemporary period, I incorporate systematic analysis of the two parties' platforms, from 1980 to 2020.[70] With the help of a research assistant, I analyzed all national Democratic and Republican platforms during this period. There are a total of twenty-two platforms—one from each party during each presidential election year, approved at the nominating convention. I accepted as a given that the two parties would embrace the American Dream as an ideal. My main interest is contestation over the reality of the American Dream. Thus, I examine whether—and how—each party used factual claims about the sources of economic and closely related outcomes (such as education and health) to defend its policy prescriptions. A party might make claims about the causes of economic inequality specifically, about why some people are struggling economically, or about why some people are thriving. Narratives suggesting that the nation does not deliver the American Dream argue that some people have less than others because the nation does not have ample nor equal opportunity or that some people have more than others because they have received advantages others do not enjoy. Narratives suggesting that the nation delivers the Dream will argue that the nation does have ample and equal opportunity, implying or stating explicitly that inequalities can be attributed to individual attributes.

Each time one of the political parties sought to explain economic or related inequalities, difficulties, or successes, that assertion received a numerical code.[71] The coding scheme includes six categories. These categories are based on a well-developed scholarly literature on how Americans think about economic fairness, inequality, and opportunity (briefly discussed in chapter 1 and developed more fully in chapter 4) but were augmented after an initial read of a limited set of platforms. Three of the categories hold individuals or social groups responsible for economic (and related) outcomes; these reflect American Dream optimism. Three categories hold society or its institutions responsible for outcomes; these reflect American Dream pessimism (see table 2.1).[72] The three individual-level categories are:

1. individuals' abilities, skills, and personal characteristics;
2. individuals' efforts or sense of responsibility, such as their work ethic; and
3. socialization in the family or community culture.

The three societal-level categories are:

1. societal inequities in opportunity, such as a lack of job opportunities in certain areas or preferential treatment of the wealthy;
2. interindividual or systemic discrimination; and
3. problematic social welfare policies or excessive government.

The final category is unlike the others. A focus on government policy as a cause of inequality simultaneously relieves individuals of blame for their

Table 2.1 Party Platform Coding Scheme

		Description of Code
Individual or group responsibility	Character and ability	Ability, skill, and other personal characteristics lead to success or positive life outcomes (or lack thereof)
	Effort	Effort and personal responsibility determine degree of personal success or failure
	Culture and family	Family or community culture determine degree of personal success or failure
Societal or institutional responsibility	Access to opportunity	Society, its structure, or its institutions directly cause inequality; access to opportunity or barriers to success are unequally distributed
	Discrimination	Explicit mention of inter-individual or systemic discrimination or bias against specific social groups (such as race, sex, or disability) as a cause of inequality
	Excess government	Excess government or badly designed policies indirectly cause inequality

Source: Author's coding scheme.

economic struggles while suggesting that government policy—at least as it currently stands—exacerbates inequality. (In upcoming analyses, I examine this category separately.) After the first round of coding was complete, a second round of coding identified specific groups of Americans, such as racial minorities or workers, to which the platforms applied the attributions (where relevant).

Statements falling into any one of these categories could focus on either end—or both ends—of the ladder of success. A party might applaud the wealthy for business acumen (individual attribute) or argue that people falling behind simply aren't working hard enough (individual effort). It might denigrate the rich as benefiting from nepotism (inequitable access to opportunity) or worry over barriers consistently faced by racial minorities (discrimination).

Figures 2.1, 2.2, and 2.3 summarize the results of these analyses. Figure 2.1 captures how often each party's platform sought to explain economic and related inequality. Because platforms differ in length, sometimes dramatically, this frequency is depicted as a rate—how many explanations are made per 1,000 words in a given platform. Figure 2.2 summarizes the relative occurrence of the main types of explanation within each platform, expressed as a proportion of the total number of explanations provided. Numbers represent, for any given party and year, the sum of the number of times a platform mentioned each type of explanation divided by the total

Figure 2.1 Rate (per 1,000 Words) of Explanations for Economic and Related Inequalities in Party Platforms (1980–2020)

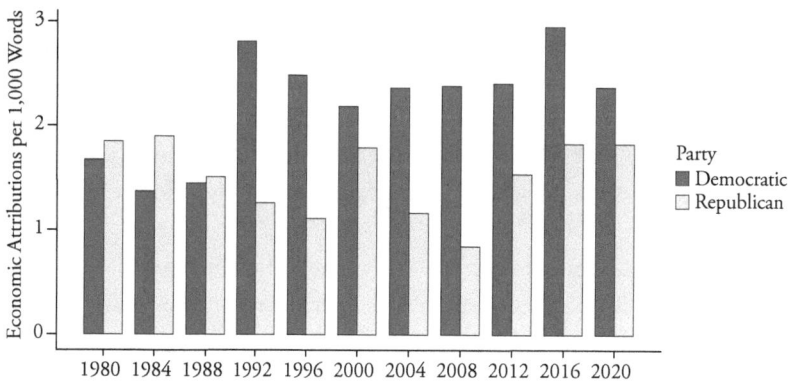

Source: Author's calculations using coded party platform data.

Figure 2.2 Proportion of Three Types of Explanations for Economic and Related Inequalities by Party and Year (1980–2020)

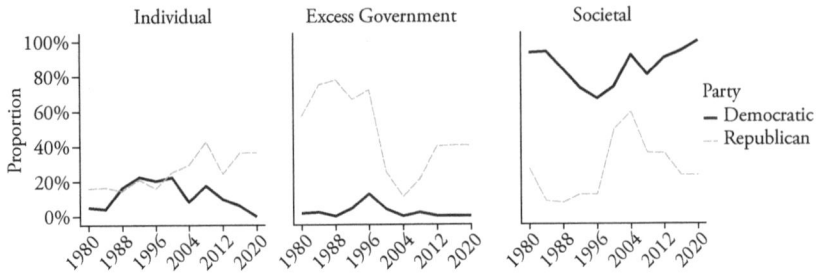

Source: Author's calculations using coded party platform data.

number of explanations in the same platform, producing three proportions for each party in each year that sum to 100. The most common social groups mentioned are presented in figure 2.3. I next resume the examination of historical context, now additionally informed by the party platform content coding represented in these figures.

A Conservative Shift

In response to the rapid growth of the federal government from the Roosevelt through the Johnson era, a coalition of economic conservatives organized and pushed back, eventually pulling the Republican Party rightward.[73] To a significant degree, this shift was economic, in keeping with the party's ties to business; however, a strengthening alliance with Southern conservatives also brought a commitment to religious traditionalism and opposition to federal enforcement of equal rights for racial minorities and women.[74] The first Republican presidential candidate in this new conservative mold, Barry Goldwater, lost badly in 1964. But conservative Republicans finally triumphed with Reagan's election in 1980, partially as a result of Reagan's charisma, as well as a stagnating economy under Democratic President Jimmy Carter.

Reagan's famous quote from his 1981 inaugural address reflected the party's new approach to government: "Government is not the solution to our problems, government *is* the problem." This is both a policy statement and a causal attribution—government is the cause of citizens' problems, including economic inequality and a lack of upward mobility, and should there-

Figure 2.3 Number of Times Specific Social Groups Were Mentioned in Conjunction with Concerns over Unequal Opportunity in Democratic Party Platforms (1980–2020)

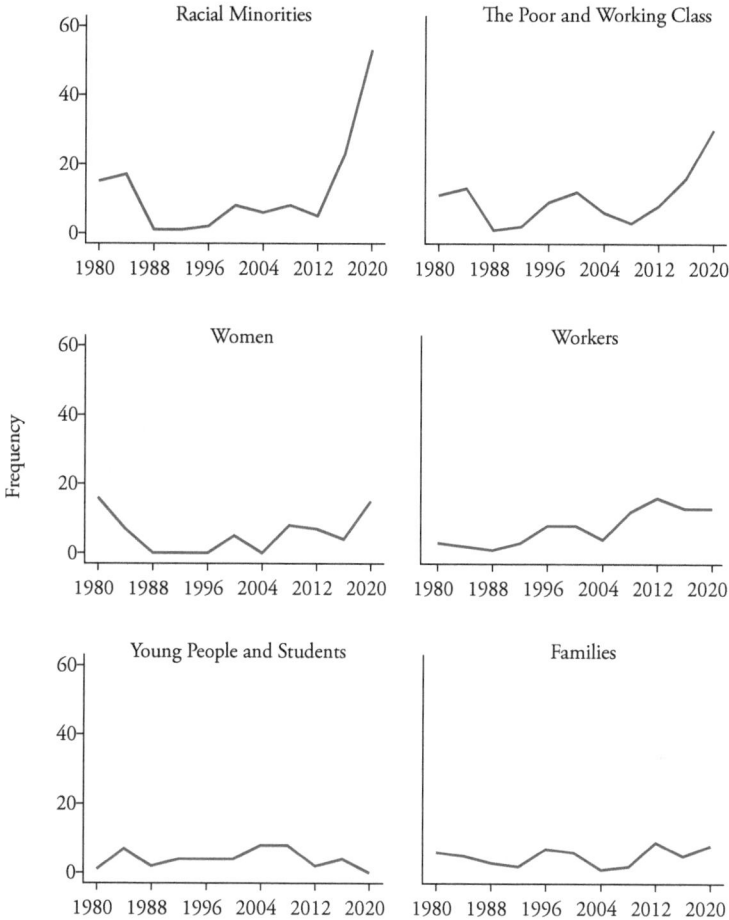

Source: Author's calculations using coded party platform data.

fore be pared back. As we will discuss in chapter 8, this rhetoric likely held some truth; it was also political genius for conservatives wanting a public justification for limited government. They had found a seemingly merito-cratic rationale for opposing government assistance to lower-income indi-viduals and groups; however, their new language did so without explic-itly insulting Americans who were struggling, many of whom were racial minorities. The poor were instead framed as victims of big government. The party stated, again and again, that government social welfare programs, regulations, and tax structures discouraged work. This new rhetoric was accompanied by new policies. Reagan reduced programs intended to assist the poor, pursued deregulation, opposed unions, and made the income tax code less progressive. Although the policy changes under Reagan were not as draconian as conventional wisdom on the political left often suggests,[75] they nevertheless contributed substantially to the sharp increase in economic inequality in the 1980s and thereafter.[76]

Figure 2.1 displays the rate at which the two parties discussed the causes of inequality in the 1980s and thereafter. Although the Democratic Party discussed inequality more often on average over the entire period, Republicans addressed it most during Reagan's presidency. This makes clear that attention to economic disparity is not necessarily accompanied by calls for more government intervention. It is attention to economic inequality in conjunction with the identification of precipitating structural causes in the economy or society that potentially justifies government intervention. Figure 2.2 displays the relative popularity of the three main types of explanations for economic outcomes separately for each party. Explanations that hold individuals or families and communities responsible are in the leftmost panel; explanations that hold society responsible are in the rightmost panel. The Reaganesque big government arguments are represented in the middle panel. Democratic platform language is indicated with the solid line and Republican language with the dashed line. The figure makes clear how much the two parties' official interpretations of economic inequality and opportunity differed throughout this period—Democrats skeptical that Americans are getting a fair shake, and Republicans more confident that any fault rests with individuals or with government's negative influence on them. Note that figure A.1 provides a disaggregated overview of explanations for inequality, displaying the frequency of each specific type of explanation (for example, work ethic or discrimination).

Of course, the explanations also vary over time. This variation matches well-known shifts in the parties' economic agendas. Beginning with the 1980s, Reagan's focus on excess government is plain. This idea received dozens of mentions by Republicans each year in 1980, 1984, and 1988 (when Vice President George H. W. Bush ran to succeed Reagan), making up between 60 and 80 percent of the explanations for economic and related inequalities in any given Republican platform. A typical example of the excess government language—taken from Republicans' 1984 platform—reads: "As part of our effort to reform the tax system, we will reduce disincentives to employment which too often result in a poverty trap for poor Americans." While the party tempered its explicit blame of everyday Americans, these statements implicitly criticized the poor—many were idle due to "disincentives to employment."

Although the Republican Party discussed inequality somewhat less in the 1990s, it continued to hammer the anti–big government theme throughout the era of congressional Republicans' Contract with America. Within the category of individual blame, the party increasingly focused on the importance of families and communities, as opposed to individual effort or skill. For example, the 1988 Republican platform states, in a section on poverty: "Divorce, desertion, and illegitimacy have been responsible for almost all the increase in child poverty in the last 15 years. . . . Strong family life is the most remarkable anti-poverty force in history." By focusing on family structure and individuals' agency in determining it, this argument deflected demands for direct government assistance. It also dovetailed with the party's growing moral conservatism. While many scholars have interpreted these cultural criticisms as explicitly racial,[77] Republicans avoided linking these attributions directly to race in their platforms, perhaps minding norms against explicit racism.[78]

Republicans were not the only ones who shifted to the right in the 1980s. Democrats shifted to the center—and arguably right of center on some issues. The reasons for this shift are varied. Neoliberalism became the dominant theory of political economy among experts and politicians, encouraging Democrats to embrace market-oriented thinking.[79] The business community became more involved in politics, influencing both parties.[80] And, into and through the 1990s, public opinion grew more conservative on economic matters.[81] This rightward movement in the public was likely linked, at least in part, to racism—many White Americans turned against government social welfare programs because they disproportionately benefited Black Americans.[82]

Bill Clinton (president from 1993 to 2001) most exemplified Democrats' relative centrism, explicitly labeling his approach to politics as a "third way." He pledged to "end welfare as we know it" and, indeed, oversaw a major reorganization of social welfare for low-income parents—linking it to work requirements and initiating strict time limits.[83] Clinton also signed into law the Crime Control and Enforcement Act, which toughened federal crime penalties, especially for drug crimes. Interestingly, Democrats in the 1990s did not shy away from talking about inequalities—their rate of discussing inequality doubled relative to the 1980s.

The way Democrats interpreted economic and related inequalities did change, however. Figure 2.2 shows that Democrats' mentions of individual attributions for economic inequality rose sharply from 1980 through 1992— matching Republicans—and then stayed elevated through 2000. And the party's attention to societal causes of inequality declined, falling to its lowest point in the series in 1996. (The party did not significantly adopt Republican complaints about big government, although there is a noticeable upward tick in 1996.) However, throughout the 1990s, approximately 60 percent of Democrats' attributions for economic and related inequality involved unequal access to opportunity, whereas Republicans' hovered near 10 percent. I argue that the Democratic Party's rhetoric around economic inequality reflected its consistent status as the nation's party of the economic left. While Clinton certainly moderated the party's economic policy agenda, his approach to economic policy remained solidly to the left of the Republican Party. For example, he increased tax rates on high-income households and expanded the Earned Income Tax Credit.[84]

In 2000, George W. Bush and Al Gore competed in a famously close election, which ended with Bush's victory. In many respects, Bush's and Gore's campaigns reflected those of their predecessors, including their enthusiasm for privatization that lay at the center of neoliberalism.[85] However, Bush stood out from prior Republicans with his emphasis on "compassionate conservatism," which acknowledged a role for government in helping the vulnerable and addressing societal inequalities.[86] Under Bush, the Reaganesque criticism of big government declined markedly. Attention to societal inequities skyrocketed to its highest point in the Republican series—approximately 60 percent in 2004. That said, much of this attention was given to inequities adjacent to economic inequality—such as disparities in health care and education, which reflected specific proposals the party put forward in these areas (such as Bush's No Child Left Behind legislation).

For Democrats, the pendulum increasingly swung toward progressive rhetoric during the presidency of George W. Bush. Despite campaigning on compassionate conservatism, Bush's policies outside of a few targeted areas were quite conservative in the traditional sense, and often ill-conceived as well.[87] Many policies—including the Iraq War, efforts to privatize Social Security, and resistance to addressing climate change—provoked an intense reaction on the activist left. John Kerry's bid for the presidency in 2004 reflected this. Figure 2.2 reveals a clear rhetorical break from his recent predecessors with respect to (more) concerns over societal inequity and (less) attention to individual responsibility for economic inequalities. Although Kerry did not come close to wining the election, his candidacy was a sign of a changing Democratic Party and nation.

Democrats would take back the House and Senate in 2006. In 2008, Barack Obama was elected president. Although the conventional wisdom is that President Obama largely continued in Bill Clinton's relatively centrist footsteps, in hindsight, Obama's presidency might also, or instead, be considered an on-ramp to a resurgence of economic populism within the Democratic Party. The Great Recession of 2007 to 2009 certainly encouraged this, spawning protests and social movements (for example, Occupy Wall Street) and increasing many Americans' concerns over economic opportunity and fairness. Obama not only signed into law policies grappling with the recession (such as the American Recovery and Reinvestment Act) but also expanded health care via the Affordable Care Act, helped women achieve equal pay, and increased access to Pell Grants. Obama likely would have achieved many more economically progressive aims but for intense opposition from Republicans in Congress.[88]

The Democratic platform under Obama in 2008 seemingly took a step back from the preceding platform's concerns over inequity; other researchers note Obama's embrace of "dominant ideology" rhetoric regarding the importance of hard work and striving.[89] But this shift proved temporary. In 2012, the party focused especially on access to opportunity. Much of this content focused on the Great Recession specifically, including strong language about the damage Republican policies had done to Americans' prosperity and Democrats' course correction. For example, the platform states: "For too long, we've had a financial system that stacked the deck against ordinary Americans. . . . That behavior not only nearly destroyed the financial system, it cost our economy millions of jobs, hurt middle class and poor families, and left taxpayers holding the bill." As we will see, the Democratic Party in the years following Obama would shift into progressive high gear—with respect to both policy and rhetoric.

Some researchers may be tempted to conclude that Obama was reacting to surging economic progressivism across the political spectrum. After all, the Great Recession was to a significant extent caused by loosened financial regulations, and it had a punishing effect on a broad swath of the public. It would make sense for Americans across the board to grow more interested in redistributive programs as well as increased government regulation of wayward industries. Yet, interest in these policies was concentrated among Democratic, and Democratic leaning, Americans. Whereas Democrats responded to the recession as we might expect, by becoming more supportive of progressive economic policy, Republicans reacted by becoming much more critical of progressive policy, accusing the Obama administration of government overreach.[90] As a result of this sizable shift, Americans' policy preferences between 2008 and 2010 on average became more economically conservative.[91]

These trends among the Republican rank and file are closely linked to the actions of Republican leaders, interest groups, and activists. For a surprising length of time, Republican elites reacted to both economic turmoil and electoral defeat by doubling down on small government conservatism and an accompanying ethos of individualism.[92] Activists launched the Tea Party in 2009, helped along considerably by funding and coordination provided by conservative organizations such as FreedomWorks and the Heritage Foundation.[93] The Tea Party argued that government should be less involved in economic affairs and included nativist and racist elements as well.[94] Figure 2.2 shows that, between 2004 and 2012 (when Mitt Romney was the party's presidential nominee), Republican Party platform complaints about excess government doubled and concerns over societal inequities fell. These divergent reactions to the Great Recession demonstrate that the parties often react to the same focal events differently, in keeping with important coalition members' interests and long-standing ideological commitments.

Yet, it would be a mistake to argue that lower- and middle-income Republicans had somehow not noticed rising economic inequality, unemployment, and wage stagnation. After the Great Recession, opinion polls showed growing concern among all Americans with the economy's ability to deliver the American Dream. Some conservative intellectuals concluded that working-class Republicans were growing frustrated with the party's rosy portrait of opportunity and an economic agenda that seemed tilted toward the affluent. These reform-oriented authors largely blamed the Republican "donor class" for ignoring the interests of everyday Americans and feared a coming backlash if the Republican Party did not shift gears. They warned that the party was at risk of being engulfed by xenophobic populism, which was on the rise internationally.[95] In this, these critics were prescient.

The Populist Turn

DONALD TRUMP AND THE CONTEMPORARY REPUBLICAN PARTY

Donald Trump campaigned for the presidency in 2016 as a populist in the Jacksonian mold and even hung a portrait of Jackson in the Oval Office after he became president.[96] From a rhetorical perspective, Trump deserved his reputation as an economic populist after his first presidential campaign. He frequently referred to the American Dream in his speeches, but not to celebrate the American economy, as was typical among Republicans. Trump began his campaign by stating flatly that "the American Dream is dead" and promising to "make America great again."[97] Trump often talked about Americans' economic struggles in dramatic terms. In his inaugural address, he described "American carnage" as follows:

> Mothers and children trapped in poverty in our inner cities; rusted-out factories scattered like tombstones across the landscape of our nation; an education system, flush with cash, but which leaves our young and beautiful students deprived of knowledge; and the crime and gangs and drugs that have stolen too many lives and robbed our country of so much unrealized potential.

But Trump's similarity with the economic progressives of the Democratic Party largely ended with his recognition that the ladder to economic success was broken.

Trump offered a new set of explanations for Americans' economic woes and an accompanying set of new policies.[98] He proposed protectionism, reduced immigration, and modest increases in domestic spending (on infrastructure and bolstering Social Security in particular). Trump critiqued the fairness of the economy, but he largely cast blame beyond the nation's borders. He argued that U.S. trade policy often benefited other nations and their citizens at Americans' expense, implying that free markets were not in fact free but, rather, biased to the advantage of foreigners:

> For many decades, we've enriched foreign industry at the expense of American industry. . . . We've defended other nation's borders while refusing to defend our own. And spent trillions of dollars overseas while America's infrastructure has fallen into disrepair and decay. . . . We've made other countries rich while the wealth, strength, and confidence of our country has disappeared over the horizon. One by one, the factories shuttered and left our shores, with not even a thought about the millions upon millions of American workers left behind. The wealth of our middle class has been ripped from their homes and then redistributed across the entire world.

Throughout the 2016 campaign, Trump consistently derogated immigrants as well, arguing that they caused crime and competed with U.S. workers. In blaming foreigners for ruining the American Dream, Trump also relieved working Americans of responsibility for their economic struggles, challenging the long-standing Republican narrative of individualism.[99]

Trump's willingness to challenge Republican orthodoxy and, in so doing, respond to the economic woes and resentments of working-class Americans is likely the main reason he triumphed in a crowded Republican primary field.[100] At the same time, Trump certainly did not completely abandon Republican economic orthodoxy. Blaming foreigners for economic stagnation provided a justification for nativist economic policy (such as high tariffs and reduced immigration) but did not touch on traditional left-right debates over redistribution. Whether due to his wealth, business background, or perhaps simply deference to party stalwarts, Trump had little interest in greatly expanding social welfare or raising taxes on the affluent or businesses. On the campaign trail, he complained about undeserving people who took advantage of social welfare and warned about affirmative action run amok. In his inaugural address, he emphasized "We will get our people off of welfare and back to work."

The Republicans' 2016 platform includes language reflecting Trump's new approach, as well as long-standing party orthodoxy; yet, the latter dominates the platform more so than in Trump's public statements. Proposed economic reforms in the platform included making the tax code less progressive, reducing regulations on the corporate and financial sectors, and shrinking the welfare state. Platform concessions to the nominee included heavy emphasis on restricting illegal immigration and building a wall on the southern border, some mention of renegotiating trade deals, and a brief mention of concern over corporate welfare. With respect to explanations for socioeconomic inequality, Republicans' platform language overall was the most oriented toward individual responsibility and the least oriented toward societal responsibility in two decades. In its opening section on restoring the American Dream, the 2016 Republican platform states: "Government cannot create prosperity, though government can limit or destroy it." Celebrating individual achievement, the platform says: "Government must give America's innovators the freedom to create and, on their merits, succeed or fail." Later, Republicans argued in favor of an educational reform movement that "affirms higher expectations for all students and rejects the crippling bigotry of low expectations." Echoing the party's long-standing commitment to the traditional family structure and conviction regarding its positive role in children's development, the platform states: "Children raised in a two-parent household tend to be physically and emotionally healthier, more likely to do well in school, less likely to use drugs and alcohol, engage in crime or become pregnant outside of marriage. . . . Moreover, marriage remains the greatest antidote to child poverty." Republicans accused Democrats of "progressive pathology": "Keeping people dependent so that government can redistribute income." While attention to societal inequities fell overall, attention to discrimination, in the form of "reverse" discrimination, increased slightly. For example: "We continue to encourage equality for all citizens and access to the American Dream. Merit and hard work should determine advancement in our society, so we reject unfair preferences, quotas, and set-asides as forms of discrimination."

As is true of past presidential administrations, the Republican Party platform reflected how Trump would govern. Working with Republicans in Congress, the first Trump administration made income taxes less progressive, lowered the corporate tax rate, cut housing subsidies, shifted education toward privatization, weakened the Affordable Care Act, and opened public land to corporate interests, among other things. An analysis of Trump administration budgets indicates that the intended cuts to government were much more dramatic than those ultimately passed by Congress.[101] In short, Trump largely governed not as an economic populist but as a traditional

Republican, at least in part because he was dependent on the Republican Party for advice, personnel, and other resources.[102] Occasional efforts to increase government spending on public goods seemed to run into insurmountable barriers. Trump did achieve several of his priorities in his first term, including significantly limiting immigration, renegotiating various trade deals, and increasing some tariffs. Perhaps most significantly, when COVID-19 wreaked havoc on the nation and its economy, Trump signed into law a generous bipartisan bill to assist American families, businesses, and state and local governments.[103]

The differences between Trump and the Republican establishment—although sometimes exaggerated—were significant and may explain why Republicans failed to write a new platform in 2020. (This is why the 2016 and 2020 data points for Republicans in figure 2.2 are identical.) That said, by 2020, Trump had changed his tune on the economy. He no longer criticized the American economy, and he articulated an "America First" economic ideology that was equal parts nativism and neoliberalism. In his farewell address on January 19, 2021, Trump announced that his policies had fixed the American Dream:

> Together with millions of hardworking patriots across this land, we built the greatest political movement in the history of our country. We also built the greatest economy in the history of the world. It was about "America First" because we all wanted to make America great again. . . . We passed the largest package of tax cuts and reforms in American history. We slashed more job-killing regulations than any administration had ever done before. We fixed our broken trade deals, withdrew from the horrible Trans-Pacific Partnership and the impossible Paris Climate Accord, renegotiated the one-sided South Korea deal, and we replaced NAFTA with the groundbreaking USMCA—that's Mexico and Canada—a deal that's worked out very, very well. Also, and very importantly, we imposed historic and monumental tariffs on China; made a great new deal with China. . . . We reignited America's job creation and achieved record-low unemployment for African Americans, Hispanic Americans, Asian Americans, women—almost everyone. Incomes soared, wages boomed, the American Dream was restored, and millions were lifted from poverty in just a few short years. It was a miracle.

To some degree, this represents an old playbook: criticizing the nation's failure to achieve the American Dream as a political challenger and celebrating its achievement as an incumbent. Yet, just as Trump influenced the Republican Party, it likely influenced him as well. The two parties have unmistakable baseline orientations, with Democrats more skeptical of, and Republicans more confident in, the fairness of the nation's economy. These orientations are closely linked to policy agendas aimed at leveling or preserving the nation's economic hierarchy.

HILLARY CLINTON, JOE BIDEN, AND THE CONTEMPORARY DEMOCRATIC PARTY

Trump beat Hillary Clinton in 2016 in a very close election. While Clinton's campaign focused most of its attention on criticizing the norm-defying Trump—especially his misogyny, racism, and xenophobia—her policy agenda was more economically progressive than Obama's. This shift to the left by a previously moderate Clinton was likely due to growing concerns over economic inequality, particularly among Democratic activists and interest groups, and the related strength of a new crop of charismatic progressive politicians. Clinton agreed to advance some of Senator Elizabeth Warren's economic ideas in the campaign, perhaps in an effort to keep Warren from running against her; however, she still faced the surprisingly popular Democratic Socialist Bernie Sanders in the primary, prompting her to move further left on economic issues.[104]

The 2016 Democratic platform included a long list of economically egalitarian policies. Among other things, it called for creating a $15 minimum wage, helping workers unionize, enacting profit sharing between owners and workers, tightening regulation of Wall Street, and breaking up monopolies. Justifying this shift, the platform discussed the causes of socioeconomic inequality at a rate higher than any other Democratic platform in the series. Just three paragraphs in, the platform reads:

> Too many Americans have been left out and left behind. They are working longer hours with less security. Wages have barely budged and the racial wealth gap remains wide, while the cost of everything from childcare to a college education has continued to rise. And for too many families, the dream of homeownership is out of reach. As working people struggle, the top one percent accrues more wealth and more power. . . . It's no wonder that so many feel like the system is rigged against them.

Democrats did not only talk about inequality more. Figure 2.2 reveals a slight increase in focus on societal inequities and a decrease in emphasis on individual attributions. Language like the earlier quote can be found throughout the platform. This profound criticism of the availability of opportunity in the nation is especially remarkable given Clinton would have replaced a fellow Democrat, Barack Obama, in office.

Democrats' economically populist rhetoric would swell under Biden in 2020. Biden initially ran as a center-left candidate in a crowded primary field. His competition included Sanders, running a second time, as well as the similarly tenacious economic progressive Warren. Whereas Sanders' two campaigns focused on class politics without much attention to race, the 2020 Warren campaign paid close attention to racial disparities in wealth, in addition to economic inequality more generally. Biden won the nomination, but not easily. And, when he did, he faced an active progressive wing of the party that was especially enraged by Trump's presidency and inspired by the left-leaning Sanders and Warren campaigns. He also faced a country roiling from the COVID-19 pandemic and a related economic crisis.[105]

The progressive wing of the party greatly influenced the 2020 Democratic platform, resulting in the most economically progressive platform in decades.[106] The 2020 Democratic platform offered not only modest policy goals such as raising the minimum wage, expanding Medicare, and encouraging unionization, but also far-reaching ones, such as ending poverty and homelessness and seeking large tax increases on the wealthy.

The party justified these policy goals with many arguments about the basic unfairness of the American economy. For example, in the fourth paragraph of the preamble, the platform acknowledges the pandemic but is careful to emphasize that the nation's economic problems had been long-standing: "The COVID-19 pandemic has laid bare deep-seated problems in our society—the fragility of our economy and social safety net, the risks posed by growing inequality, the impacts of racial and economic disparities on health and well-being." According to Democrats, the country was a long way from reaching the American Dream, and, unsurprisingly, they pinned the blame on Republican policies: "We must once again stop another Republican recession from becoming a second Great Depression. President Trump and the Republican Party have rigged the economy in favor of the wealthiest few and the biggest corporations, and left working families and small businesses out in the cold."

The Biden campaign also gave much more attention to racial issues than any Democratic presidential campaign in recent memory, focusing attention on systemic racism in the economy (as well as the criminal justice system). The party promised "a new social and economic contract that at last grapples honestly with America's long and ongoing history of racism and disenfranchisement, of segregation and discrimination, and invests instead in building equity and mobility for the people of color who have been left out and left behind for generations." The party had traveled a long way from Bill Clinton's relatively moderate "third way."

The data in figure 2.1 shows that the 2020 Democratic platform talked about the causes of inequality somewhat less than the 2016 platform did (although it was on par with prior platforms). However, its discourse on inequality changed. The platform does not list any individual- or group-level explanations for economic inequality. It is the only platform analyzed to hold this distinction, and the only platform in the set to exclusively fall on one side of the individual-versus-societal-responsibility divide. In addition, within the societal category, attention to discrimination more than doubled compared to 2016 (see figure A.1).

Of course, the 2020 Democratic platform possibly was not indicative of how Biden intended to govern or of broader party messaging. Yet, despite Biden's long history as a moderate Democrat, some analysts have said that he came to think of his presidency as similar to that of Franklin Delano Roosevelt or Lyndon Johnson—as an opportunity to pass transformative policy in response to a nation in crisis.[107] Biden appointed many progressives to the federal bureaucracy, including those who sought to break up corporate monopolies and strengthen unions. With Democrats initially controlling the House and Senate, he signed into law three major pieces of legislation, all with significant economic components. He enacted the American Rescue Plan, which included direct pandemic-related payments to most Americans as well as anti-poverty measures, such as expanding tax credits for those with and (unusually) those without children. He also enacted the Bipartisan Infrastructure Law, intended to both improve the nation's infrastructure and provide new jobs. In 2022, he signed into law the Inflation Reduction Act, which included progressive tax reforms and reductions in drug prices, as well as significant investments aimed at addressing climate change.[108]

In Biden's State of the Union speech in 2022, he touted his legislative successes and insisted on doing more, including raising the minimum wage, extending child tax credits, reducing health care costs, and increasing education funding. Interestingly, Biden also borrowed some of Trump's nationalist language and goals. He talked about bringing jobs back to the United States, buying American, and leveling the playing field with China. As presidents do, Biden spent some time in the speech engaged in self-congratulation, for example, mentioning that his American Rescue Plan had provided direct economic relief to millions of struggling Americans and spurred job growth. But he also devoted a great deal of attention to unfair economic circumstances in which many Americans continued to find themselves. Given the high inflation rate at the time, he focused especially on prices—the cost of prescription drugs, energy costs, and childcare. He also linked high prices to monopolistic corporations. Finally, he criticized the tax system, alleging that corporations and the wealthy were not paying their fair share. The lack of sufficient progressivism in the tax system drove many problems, according to Biden:

> For the past forty years, we were told that if we gave tax breaks to those at the very top, the benefits would trickle down to everyone else. But that trickle-down theory led to weaker economic growth, lower wages, bigger deficits, and the widest gap between those at the top and everyone else in nearly a century.

From campaigning to governing, the Biden administration's commitment to using the federal government to assist lower income Americans and workers was clear. And, like many Democratic leaders before him, Biden explained the need for his programs and policies by referencing stubborn economic inequities among Americans.

Social Groups on the Agenda

Given Democrats' attention to various disadvantages in society that keep some people from advancing, it is worth asking whom Democrats depict as suffering in this way. Figure 2.3 tallies references to specific social groups in the Democratic Party platforms within both the subcategories of access to opportunity and discrimination (combined into the societal category in figure 2.2). The six most frequently mentioned groups are included—racial minorities, the poor and working class, women, workers, young people and students, and families.[109] The corresponding figure for Republicans is shown in figure A.2. Republicans do not reference the social responsibility categories much and thus mention few groups.

For Democrats, several trends are notable. First, the party mentions many different types of people as facing external barriers to success. However, in 2016 and especially 2020, the party concentrated its attention on racial minorities and the poor and working class, whereas previous platforms spread attention more equally. In 2020, mentions of the poor and working class rose to approximately 30, and mentions of racial minorities skyrocketed to about 50. Women and workers were in a clear second tier in 2020. Attention to families held steady at a slightly lower level, and references to young people and students fell. One final pattern of note in figure 2.3 is that Democrats' attention to class, race, and sex was also elevated in the first two elections in the dataset (1980 and 1984). These election platforms likely reflected a continuity in rhetoric from the relatively progressive 1960s and 1970s.

Platforms rarely mentioned social groups when they employed individual or group-based attributions for inequality. Most likely, designating specific groups as especially meritorious or targeting specific groups for blame (as opposed to sympathy, as when structural attributions were cited) would invite criticism of a party for prejudice. Further, criticizing an entire demographic group is simply electorally unwise, as this would discourage that group from voting for the party. This is something that we do not even see in the Republican 2016 (and 2020) platform.

Conclusion

In this chapter, I have provided a brief, and as such inevitably incomplete, account of U.S. political history with respect to the American Dream and the related ideals of plentiful opportunity and meritocracy. These ideals were imported from England and Western Europe but also reinforced in a new nation that offered settlers from those nations relative equality and prosperity. As time went on, the goal of meritocratic abundance became more socially inclusive, and the notion of an equal playing field would include the expectation of access to publicly provided education and a safety net. By the mid-twentieth century, this expansive notion of the American Dream was one on which both parties agreed.

However, throughout the nation's history, the two parties have often clashed over whether the nation treats its citizens in accord with its ideals. Democrats have a long history of economic populism—arguing vociferously that the economy is unfair. Populist movements are often racially exclusionary, and, throughout its first century of existence, the Democratic Party fit this definition. It defended the interests of White Americans to the detriment of Black Americans, Native Americans, and other racial minorities. Only after a depression, the Second World War, and major coalitional shifts did the party incorporate racial justice and feminism into its agenda. During the New Deal Era, Democrats proposed and enacted policies intended to level the playing field as well as make up for an uneven playing field after the fact via redistribution and affirmative action. Pointed rhetoric defended these policy priorities.

A more systematic study of Democrats since the 1980s reveals a shift to the center and then a return to the left. The party platforms make clear that Bill Clinton's center-left approach to the economy was accompanied by rhetoric that not only criticized long-standing socioeconomic inequities but also emphasized the importance of individual responsibility and highlighted problems associated with government overreach. A progressive evolution since that time—evident under Presidents Obama and Biden, as well as during John Kerry's and Hillary Clinton's runs for the presidency—has been justified with forceful language reminiscent of early Democratic populists, but with a racially inclusive focus. It remains to be seen if Biden's term represents an apex of Democratic economic progressivism in the contemporary era. Vice President Kamala Harris charted a more moderate course in her campaign for the presidency in 2024, likely due to some mix of public perceptions that Democrats had overreached, alongside influence from members of the party's increasingly affluent and corporate coalition.[110]

As for the Republican Party, it has nearly as long of a history of defending the nation's economic system and resisting redistribution and social welfare. There have been moments when Republicans have been pulled to the center, especially during the Progressive Era and after World War II. Republicans also led the way with respect to racial equality for nearly a century, although their racial progressivism was limited to equal treatment and did not address economic disparities between racial groups.[111] From Reagan through George W. Bush, Republicans' policy agenda rested firmly in economically neoliberal territory. Republicans during this period used attributional language oriented toward defending small government and the free market—few fingers pointed at problems in society, and many fingers pointed at individuals, their families, and sometimes the government programs designed to assist them. An important exception is the latter Bush, who spoke about a compassionate conservatism that was evident more in his rhetoric than his governing. Trump's first-term economic agenda moved away from the party's neoliberalism to some degree, emphasizing trade restrictions and reduced immigration in particular. Yet, Trump did not abandon Republicans' commitment to limited regulation of American industry or to limited social welfare. Republicans' 2016 (and 2020) platform justified this with an unusually meritocratic understanding of success. In 2024, Trump chose populist JD Vance as his running mate; yet, at the same time, Trump's 2024 campaign was more pro-business than his earlier campaigns.[112] So far, Trump's second turn at the presidency includes elements that are even more protectionist (high tariffs) and more libertarian (vast reductions in the federal workforce and decreased regulation) than his first.[113]

The two parties' intertwined policy and attributional journeys make for fascinating political history, but it is important not to miss the forest for the trees: Democrats have consistently positioned themselves to the left of Republicans on economic matters—ranging from the regulation of business to redistribution. And both parties have consistently defended their relative positions with factually informed narratives about what drives economic inequality and opportunity. For Democrats, big business and the affluent tend to stack the deck against everyone else, but especially those in their coalition. For Republicans, the healthiest and fairest economy is a lightly regulated one with few government programs propping people up (or holding them back). The two parties' economic ideologies have at times grown closer to one another but, in the 2000s and 2010s, especially diverged. I have argued that these ideologies—captured in the platforms and conveyed via political speeches, media, and word of mouth—both reflect and influence the views of ordinary Americans. We turn to their perspectives next.

CHAPTER 3

Americans' Beliefs About Inequality and Opportunity over Four Decades

With Mark Tenenbaum and Qingya Xu

> The problem is not that voters are necessarily irrational, but that most voters
> have very little real information. . . . Partisanship shapes people's worldviews
> in a deep way, right down to "their own facts."
>
> —Christopher Achen and Larry Bartels,
> *Democracy for Realists* (2016), p. 284[1]

THE PRECEDING CHAPTER traced U.S. political elites' perspectives on
the American Dream throughout the nation's history. From its earliest days,
the United States was said to be the land of opportunity. Early in the nation's history, men of European descent enjoyed relative economic equality,
high standards of living, and upward mobility. This state of affairs for
White men helped to embed the expectation that the United States offered
ample and equal opportunity to its citizens—what I call *meritocratic abundance*. The nation's normative commitment to the American Dream would
eventually deepen to include the provision of public goods oriented toward
leveling the playing field, such as education. And it would eventually extend
to racial and religious minority groups and women. The reality of ample
and equal opportunity, however, has always been contested, especially when
depressions hit or economic inequality rises.

In general, the Democratic and Republican Parties have tended to offer
very different messages about inequality and opportunity to the public.
Democratic leaders usually argue that the American Dream is a goal out of
the reach of many Americans, who struggle economically through no fault
of their own. According to Democrats, the reason for these difficulties lies

https://doi.org/10.7758/trap6910.6570

with inequities and biases that rest in the economy or society more broadly and are outside individuals' control. By contrast, Republican leaders tend to emphasize the high frequency with which Americans achieve the American Dream, lauding successful Americans' efforts and ingenuity and—sometimes explicitly but more often implicitly—casting blame on the individuals, families, and social groups who fall behind.

These diverging factual assertions provide both moral and pragmatic justification for very different policy agendas. Republican politicians tend to argue that the government cannot or should not do much about inequality. Incomes and wealth tend to reflect merit, and—to the extent they do not—government programs do not necessarily provide a straightforward solution. Democratic politicians generally argue that current income distributions are both unfair and fairly easily remedied via government action.

That said, the parties also vary over time in what they say about the causes of inequality. The systematic platform analyses in the last chapter began with platforms from 1980, the approximate starting point of the neoliberal era.[2] This was the year Americans elected Ronald Reagan, running on an agenda to reduce the size and scope of government, to the presidency. Republicans' messages about inequality changed markedly in this era, from accepting that society bore some of the blame for inequality to placing blame onto the government and citizens themselves. Reacting to this popular conservative turn, Democratic leaders moved toward the center. Republicans also tacked to the center, at least rhetorically, under George W. Bush. In the 2010s, the two parties polarized again, driven mainly by renewed Democratic criticisms of the economy.

In this chapter, we refocus our lens on the American public by examining data from major national surveys. We examine trends in the public's beliefs about equality and opportunity—both for the public overall and separately among Democrats and Republicans. (Independents' views closely track the average trends.) This allows us to evaluate whether Americans generally believe in the American Dream, and how this may have changed over time. Our analysis also allows us to see whether lay partisans' views reflect party elite rhetoric.

The data examined in this chapter comes from three national surveys that have examined Americans' beliefs about opportunity and equality since approximately 1980. (Note that, prior to this period, high-quality survey data on this topic is rare.) We specifically examine answers to survey questions about equal opportunity, the relationship between a person's work ethic and success, and why markers of economic success among Black Americans are lower than among White Americans on average. To ease comparisons over time, we only analyze trends for survey questions that were asked using the same question wording and that were asked over at least two decades.

Overall, four clear findings emerge. First, for most of the series, survey respondents were ambivalent about the reality of the American Dream, and, in the last two decades, faith in the Dream declined. Second, Democratic and Republican respondents tended to profoundly disagree over whether the nation provides ample and equal opportunity, with Democrats much more pessimistic than Republicans. Third, the timing and extent of partisan polarization tended to mirror elite rhetoric discussed in the previous chapter. Fourth, and finally, recent declines in faith in the American Dream have been concentrated among Democrats. Despite the economic difficulties Americans have faced in recent decades and the Republican Party's increasingly working-class base, Republicans have mostly resisted becoming more pessimistic about the nature of opportunity in America.

A Nation of Blamers?

Before examining the data, we take a step back and consider prior scholarship about ordinary Americans' faith in the American Dream. Robert Lane carried out one of the first academic studies to address this topic.[3] Interviewing a small group of White, male, mostly working-class voters, Lane notes that nearly all his respondents believed that the United States offered something approximating equal opportunity and that, therefore, a person's income reflected their merit. According to Lane, these perceptions often led the men to experience emotional distress. Rather than suffer the angst of injustice, they further justified the system and their place within it.[4] While insightful, Lane's findings from his small group of interlocutors could not be generalized to the entire nation. But interest in the topic of inequality among survey researchers would soon blossom, likely encouraged by what Michael Harrington describes as the "rediscovery" of poverty, as well as by social movements supporting the poor, racial minorities, and women.[5]

In work carried out in 1969, Joe Feagin conducted what appears to be the first representative nationwide survey devoted to understanding beliefs and attitudes about poverty and welfare.[6] He argues that Americans possess a clear "ideology of individualism." Of a list of eleven possible explanations for "why there are poor people in this country," the five most popular explanations attributed poverty to a defect in poor individuals. These included (in order of popularity) "lack of thrift and proper money management," "lack of effort," "lack of ability and talent," "loose morals and drunkenness," and "sickness and physical handicaps." The least popular explanations all attributed poverty to causes external to the individual, most of them identifiable societal problems. Those explanations, in order of popularity, were: "low wages in some businesses and industries," "failure of society to provide good schools for many Americans," "prejudice and discrimination," "failure of private industry to provide enough jobs," "being taken advantage of by rich people," and, finally, "just bad luck."[7] In 1980, James Kluegel and Eliot Smith conducted a comprehensive survey of the U.S. public on explanations for inequality and related attitudes, resulting in their landmark study *Beliefs about Inequality*.[8] Their findings significantly mirror those of Feagin: Kluegel and Smith find a great deal of optimism about the United States as the land of opportunity and, presenting the same explanations for poverty to their survey respondents as Feagin had, nearly replicate his findings. Although these findings are now decades old, more recent scholarship reports similar evidence. Leslie McCall comes to similar conclusions regarding Americans' continued faith in hard work, meritocracy, and the like.[9] Drawing on qualitative data, Meghan Condon and Amber Wichowsky, as well as Enobong Hannah Branch and Caroline Hanley, find a persistent faith in meritocracy and the promise of hard work.[10] Finally, at least two recent studies find that Americans overestimate the extent of upward mobility.[11]

Americans' average beliefs about inequality stand in contrast to those of people in many other countries. For example, drawing on World Values Survey data, Alberto Alesina and George-Marios Angeletos report that Americans were twice as likely as Europeans to say that the poor could become rich if only they tried harder.[12] When asked whether luck and connections or hard work bring success, Americans were among the strongest believers in hard work when compared with citizens of dozens of other nations around the world. In a more recent study of sixty countries, Ingvild Almås and colleagues find that Americans are much more interested in financially rewarding people they consider meritorious (and withholding such rewards from those perceived as unmeritorious) and less interested in using government to reduce economic inequality than are citizens of other nations.[13]

Shifting to explanations for unequal economic outcomes across social groups, much scholarship suggests that Americans' criticisms of low-income people—and an accompanying defense of the nation's economic system—grow even more common when the subject is racial or ethnic inequality. Kluegel and Smith report on American National Election Studies data from the 1970s that depicts the public as overwhelmingly blaming Black Americans for their economic difficulties and correspondingly denying that discrimination is a problem.[14] Martin Gilens presents nationally representative survey data indicating that White Americans were three times as likely to say that Black Americans (39 percent) as opposed to White Americans (13 percent) were lazy.[15] Americans who thought that most welfare recipients were Black were 50 percent more likely to say that lack of effort led to people going on welfare.[16] Donald Kinder and Lynn Sanders find that White Americans had high levels of racial resentment—a belief that Black Americans earn less due to lack of effort and an accompanying resentful belief that Black people request and receive benefits they don't deserve.[17] More recently, Branch and Hanley find that White study participants largely denied the negative impacts of structural racism on Black Americans and were most concerned about the negative effects of affirmative action on White Americans.[18] While these meritocratic views historically have been most common among White Americans,[19] Matthew Hunt and Branch and Hanley find that they have become more common among non-White Americans over time.[20]

The evidence so far presents what we might consider to be the stereotypical view of Americans' beliefs about inequality: in believing that the American Dream is real, Americans implicitly (and sometimes explicitly) blame individuals and groups who fall behind as responsible for their struggles. However, some research finds evidence of substantial skepticism, even decades ago, of the notion that the U.S. economy provides just deserts.

One of the most well-known early studies of beliefs about inequality is Joan Huber and William Form's 1966 to 1967 survey of residents of Muskegan, Michigan.[21] The researchers interviewed several hundred people, drawing a representative sample of the community and oversampling the wealthy and the poor. They find that the wealthy were much more likely than others to believe that the United States provides equal opportunity and to blame poor people for their lower incomes. Middle- and low-income people often doubted claims of equal opportunity, especially if they were Black. Huber and Form refer to the set of beliefs championed by the rich as "the dominant ideology," because these beliefs represented the views of those at the top of the socioeconomic hierarchy and were therefore culturally predominant.

Of course, Americans sometimes have mixed feelings about the American Dream. In an interview study reminiscent of Lane's, Jennifer Hochschild characterizes Americans' views on economic inequality as ambivalent in many respects.[22] She finds that people generally accept the normative view that the economic system ought to differentiate among people according to merit and that most believe to some degree that the economy's rewards are in fact fair—that is, people are being rewarded according to merit. Yet, most of Hochschild's interviewees also identified and criticized specific instances of unequal opportunity in their own lives or among those they knew. Thus, "people are ambivalent because they are torn between general differentiating beliefs that they have been taught and specific egalitarian beliefs that they derive from experience."[23]

Although Huber and Form and Hochschild did not interview representative samples of Americans, representative surveys from the same era uncover similar patterns. Kluegel and Smith find that lower-income people, Black Americans, and women were considerably more likely than others to believe that societal structure, as opposed to individuals, created inequality.[24] In response to a question about why people get rich, Americans in general believed that inherited wealth was just as determinative in getting ahead as a person's drive to succeed. These authors also find considerable sympathy for women with respect to their problematic treatment in the workplace, among both male and female respondents. Similar to Hochschild, Kluegel and Smith argue that their survey respondents were often ambivalent—justifying the status quo distribution of resources while simultaneously admitting to important injustices.[25] Finally, Herbert McClosky and John Zaller unexpectedly find that nearly 50 percent of respondents often declined to choose between two stark explanatory statements, such as (in answer to why the poor are poor) "the wealthy and powerful keep them poor" versus "they don't try hard enough to get ahead."[26] This may similarly reflect ambivalence, uncertainty, or perhaps simply the belief that both individual and structural factors contribute to economic inequality.

There is further reason to be cautious in accepting the notion that Americans are overwhelmingly optimistic about opportunity in the country. Specific question wording employed in publicly available datasets may bias findings. Alesina and colleagues discuss a frequently used World Values Survey item that contrasts "luck" with "hard work."[27] "Luck" is a common and colloquial explanation for inequality in Europe. Yet, as we saw in Feagin's study (replicated by Kluegel and Smith), "luck" is a uniquely unpopular perspective in the United States. This is not to say that Americans reject all factors beyond people's control, but rather, as McCall writes, "luck may be masquerading under different, more vernacular guises."[28] Many explanations for inequality that criticize society and cast a sympathetic light on poor people receive much more support from the American public: low wages, lack of good schools, prejudice, lack of jobs, and exploitation by rich people.[29] Providing "luck" as the key contrast to "hard work" will bias answers in favor of the latter. Another commonly used type of question may also bias survey results in the direction of optimism about the American Dream—questions that ask people about why some people "get ahead" or what causes "success." Not only do these questions leave out any mention of inequality or low-income people, they also may spur motivational thinking on the part of respondents. McCall worries that these "bootstraps opportunity" beliefs are more aspirational than factual. She writes: "Even if [Americans] feel less optimistic about their chances for upward mobility, they may still profess an allegiance to the only way they know how to survive."[30] McCall argues that questions asking about inequality—as opposed to "getting ahead" or "success"—will uncover more criticism of the economy.

Finally, we can consider whether the most recent academic studies on this topic tend to tell a different story compared with those conducted in the mid-to-late twentieth century. McCall finds high but declining faith in the ability to get ahead via hard work between 2001 and 2012, as well as surprising cynicism about certain unfair advantages in society, such as being born into wealth or knowing the right people.[31] Siwei Cheng and Fangqi Wen, as well as Spencer Piston, find considerable pessimism among Americans regarding lower-income people's economic prospects.[32]

Causes of Opinion Change

Thus far, we have discussed findings from survey research that depict Americans as—on balance—committed to the notion that the American Dream is alive and well. At the same time, we have observed that the most persuasive studies making this case are decades old. We have also discussed skepticism and ambivalence among the public regarding economic equality and opportunity, the possibility that question wording skewed responses toward greater apparent optimism, and, finally, some recent survey evidence of growing skepticism about the American Dream.

Let's consider why beliefs about the causes of inequality might have changed in recent decades. The most obvious reason to expect declining faith in the American Dream is that the U.S. economy has changed, especially in comparison with the 1960s and 1970s, when researchers conducted the foundational studies of beliefs about inequality. The publication of these studies happened to coincide with the tail end of the Great Leveling that occurred from 1910 to 1970 in the United States, during which income inequality—measured both before and after taxes and transfers—plummeted and average real family income tripled.[33] Beginning in the late 1970s, inequality began to rise, and it rose more sharply in the United States than in other nations.[34] Rising inequality was accompanied by declining (until recently) real wages for men without a college degree,[35] and declining absolute mobility—the likelihood of earning more than one's parents.[36] Black–White economic inequality improved from 1940 into the 1970s but, for decades thereafter, either remained stable or worsened, depending on how it is measured.[37] The only bright spot in the inequality picture is the fact that wage differentials between men and women have declined substantially in recent decades.[38]

A number of studies indicate that these troubling economic circumstances have likely influenced Americans' beliefs about the economy. Jennifer Wolak and David Peterson find that, from 1973 to 2018, Americans were more pessimistic about the American Dream during periods when inequality was higher and social mobility and homeownership lower.[39] McCall likewise finds that public concern about the economy rose when economic inequality was especially great.[40] Using an experimental approach, McCall and colleagues find that exposure to information about rising economic inequality increased study participants' skepticism about economic opportunity.[41]

In sum, evidence suggests that economic circumstances influence Americans' beliefs about the economy in a straightforward fashion. With this in mind, reactions to salient economic events should be apparent in the survey data we examine. Negative economic events include the following:

- Throughout most of the period under study, economic inequality rose, and wages for men without a college degree stagnated.
- In 2008 and 2009, the United States experienced the Great Recession, and recovery thereafter was sluggish.
- In 2020, the United States experienced the COVID-19 pandemic and a sudden and serious recession. The recession was blunted by generous government assistance signed into law by Presidents Trump and Biden; however, in 2022, the country experienced unusually high inflation.

Not all of the economic news is bad news. The 1990s, in particular, had periods of strong wage growth. Since the Great Recession, economic inequality has plateaued and, if considering government transfers, lessened somewhat.[42]

Of course, economic realities are not experienced in a vacuum. Any given individual's knowledge about inequality and opportunity beyond their direct experience comes from communication with others and exposure to media. The extent to which journalists and others recognize fluctuations in economic opportunity and inequality will influence public beliefs in a corresponding fashion.[43] Perhaps more important is how economic outcomes are interpreted—as deserved or undeserved, fair or unfair.[44] People may have firsthand experience of economic unfairness; however, this does not necessarily translate into a belief that economic outcomes in general are undeserved.[45] The sense-making stories people share about the economy, especially within social groups, are important.[46]

As described in the previous chapter, the two political parties offer distinct economic narratives. All else equal, Democratic leaders and activists tend to posit more economic difficulty and disparity than do Republicans, and they tend to argue that those disparities are more unfair. Republican leaders and other elites paint a more optimistic, and therefore less problematized, economic picture. But the parties' economic ideologies have also fluctuated over time. We can draw on the analyses in chapter 2 to take stock of salient patterns and trends in the parties' economic ideologies as they relate to economic inequality and opportunity since the 1980s:

- Democrats have tended to problematize economic outcomes, emphasizing a lack of opportunity for lower-income people overall as well as inequities linked to historically marginalized groups, especially Black Americans and women. Republicans have tended to celebrate Americans' ability to succeed, most often ascribing success to hard work. At least in its formal communications, the Republican Party has often avoided denigrating lower-earning individuals or groups, instead faulting the design of government social welfare programs or emphasizing the promise of traditional families and strong communities.
- In the mid-1990s, the Democratic Party moderated its economic agenda and rhetoric. During this period, the party argued that unequal outcomes stemmed from not only societal inequalities but also characteristics of individuals. In the 2000s, the Republican Party increased its emphasis on societal barriers to success and decreased its criticisms of wasteful government programs.
- This partisan détente was brief. Democrats reverted to their usual criticism of economic fairness in the mid-2000s, turning up the volume after the Great Recession. In the 2020 election, the Democratic Party paid particular attention to structural inequalities linked to race. Republicans reverted to neoliberal rhetoric after George W. Bush's presidency.
- The Republican Party under Trump has sent mixed messages. Its party platform in 2016 (repeated in 2020) was undeniably individualistic. During the 2016 campaign, Trump often criticized the state of economic opportunity, especially a lack of good jobs; however, in 2020, he said that his administration had restored the American Dream.

The parties would of course prefer their narratives to be broadly influential. Yet, prior research in political science suggests that any given party's persuasive powers are most effective among the party identifiers who make up its coalition.

Within-party influence tends to be profound, often leading to sharp partisan differences in the public, including over economic beliefs.[47] As discussed in chapter 1, partisan influence occurs for a number of reasons: people are motivated to stay in line with their party, they trust information from their party and co-partisans, and they simply are exposed to more information associated with their party than with the other. There is a positive, although not always linear, correlation between how much people's views align with those of their party and how closely they follow politics. This is likely because those who pay attention to political discussions are exposed to more relevant information and have greater ability to recognize party cues that they believe they ought to follow.[48] Of course, as previously noted, Americans' relationship with the political parties is not a one-way street. To a limited extent, people's partisan affiliations will change when they see one party as more attractive than another—because a party has performed better or espouses more congenial points of view.[49]

In the next section, we dive into Americans' beliefs about the American Dream—assessing their optimism and pessimism—over time and by political persuasion. Considering the likelihood that question wording influences the nature of survey responses, we examine a variety of different question types in this chapter. We expect to see declining faith in the Dream in the aggregate—due to increases in economic inequality and decreases in wage growth, as well as greater criticism of the nation's economy among politicians and in the media. We also expect to observe trends that reflect changes in party elite rhetoric, especially amid growing partisan polarization over the past two decades. While we focus on economic trends in conjunction with partisan rhetoric, we must acknowledge that other factors likely influence public opinion on this topic as well. For example, partisans are somewhat more optimistic about the American Dream when a president from their party is in office (and, similarly, somewhat more pessimistic when a president from the opposition party holds office). Major changes to government policy and to prominent social movements also likely influence average trends. We remark on such additional factors where they seem relevant.

Americans' Beliefs over Time

To examine trends in Americans' beliefs about ample and equal opportunity in the United States, we draw on answers to questions asked by three prominent and long-standing series of surveys of American economic and political perspectives: the American National Election Study (ANES), the General Social Survey (GSS), and surveys by the Pew Research Center (referred to as Pew).[50] These are gold-standard surveyors of the U.S. population that have been in operation for decades. Each survey we use interviewed respondents selected via probability sampling and provided survey weights, which we utilize. This means that the trends discussed are reflective of the general U.S. adult population.

We identified relevant questions by conducting keyword searches of terms associated with equal opportunity and explanations for economic inequality on each survey provider's website. Given the focus in this chapter on trends over time, we only use data from questions asked over at least two decades. We include all questions that met these criteria in this analysis with one exception: we deliberately set aside questions that forced a choice between "luck" and "hard work," determining that these questions include too much measurement error (given the lack of popularity of "luck" in the U.S. context). We also considered but ultimately excluded questions on the causes of inequality asked by the International Social Survey Programme. These items have been asked only a few times, and they are also framed in terms of "getting ahead," without reference to inequality or low-income individuals.[51]

Throughout the analyses that follow, we examine respondents in the aggregate (designated by *all*) and by partisan identification (Democratic or Republican). Partisan leaners—those who initially deny any partisan affiliation but who later say they lean toward the Democratic or Republican Party—are grouped with the relevant partisans, following common practice in political science. Each estimate represents a proportion and appears with a 95 percent confidence interval. True independents (usually around 10 percent of the population) are not depicted; trends for independents are very similar to aggregate trends.

Hard Work and Opportunity

We start with two questions periodically asked by Pew. The first, asked between 1999 and 2022, asks respondents to choose between two statements: "Most people who want to get ahead can make it if they're willing to work hard" or "Hard work and determination are no guarantee of success for most people." Figure 3.1 shows the proportion of Americans who chose the initial, more optimistic, statement. In 1999, more than 75 percent

Figure 3.1 Americans Who Agree That Most People Can Make It If They Work Hard

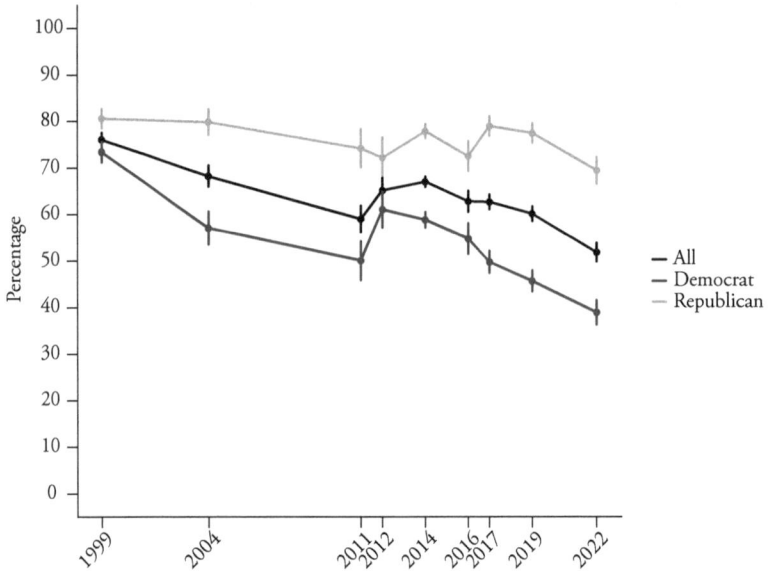

Source: Author's calculations using weighted Pew Research Center data (Pew Research Center 2025).
Note: Figure displays proportion of all Americans, Democrats, and Republicans who choose the statement "most people who want to get ahead can make it if they're willing to work hard" (versus "hard work and determination are no guarantee of success for most people"). *N*s range from 1,480 to 9,718 depending on year.

of Americans believed that most people can make it. By 2022, only about 50 percent of Americans agreed.

The trend masks enormous differences between the two parties; however, polarization is only apparent over time. In 1999, the tail end of Clinton's presidency, 73 percent of Democrats and 81 percent of Republicans agreed that hard work usually led to success. Soon after, differences emerged, driven by growing Democratic skepticism. By 2004, fewer than 60 percent of Democrats agreed with this statement. Between 2004 and 2011, a period that includes the Great Recession, both Democrats and Republicans became less likely to say that hardworking people can get ahead. Democrats' views surprisingly rebounded in the summer of 2012. This is not in keeping with the economically pessimistic party platform the Democratic Party would campaign on in the fall. Democrats' temporary rebound may have stemmed from optimism surrounding Barack Obama's reelection campaign as well as a recovering economy (for which Democrats took credit). Growing pessimism soon returned, however. After 2012, Democrats' belief that most people can make it consistently fell through 2022, ending at 40 percent. During this final decade of data, Republican beliefs rebounded somewhat, only falling again after 2019. Given incomplete data, we cannot know whether this final downward trend among Republicans was a reaction to Biden assuming the presidency or to inflation; however, survey analyses of Americans' views of economic conditions in general suggest that both factors likely contributed.[52] In any case, Republicans' recent skepticism only modestly reduced the partisan gap. An 8 point difference between the two parties in 1999 became an approximately 30 point difference by 2022.

This question is a useful way to assess the public's views on the fairness of the American economy for most people; however, the wording leaves uncertain what people believe about poor people. Are poor people included in "most people"—with access to opportunity they don't take advantage of—or are poor people an unfortunate exception—a minority facing unique difficulties? The second Pew measure gets at this question, albeit imperfectly, by asking respondents to choose between the following two statements: "Poor people today have it easy because they can get government benefits without doing anything in return" or "Poor people have hard lives because government benefits don't go far enough to help them live decently." This question was asked from 1997 to 2019. These two options are not perfectly parallel, and their colloquial phrasing works a bit circuitously. The first implies that government benefits are generous and that recipients are lazy; the second suggests that benefits are inadequate and that this insubstantial support is the cause of poor people's problems. The proportion of those selecting the first option is depicted in figure 3.2.

Americans in the aggregate begin the series a few points above the 50 percent mark (in 1997) and end just below it (in 2019). Perhaps because this question mixes ideas about both poor people's behavior and government programs, it generates some of the largest partisan differences we see. In 1997, nearly 70 percent of Republicans agreed that poor people have it easy, while just over 40 percent of Democrats chose this answer. Thereafter, the share of respondents in all groups who agreed with the statement trended downward; this decline may reflect widespread knowledge of welfare reform under Clinton and the two parties' increasing attention to economic unfairness. Although the data is sparse in the years immediately after 2004,

Figure 3.2 Americans Who Agree That Poor People Have It Easy Because of Government Benefits

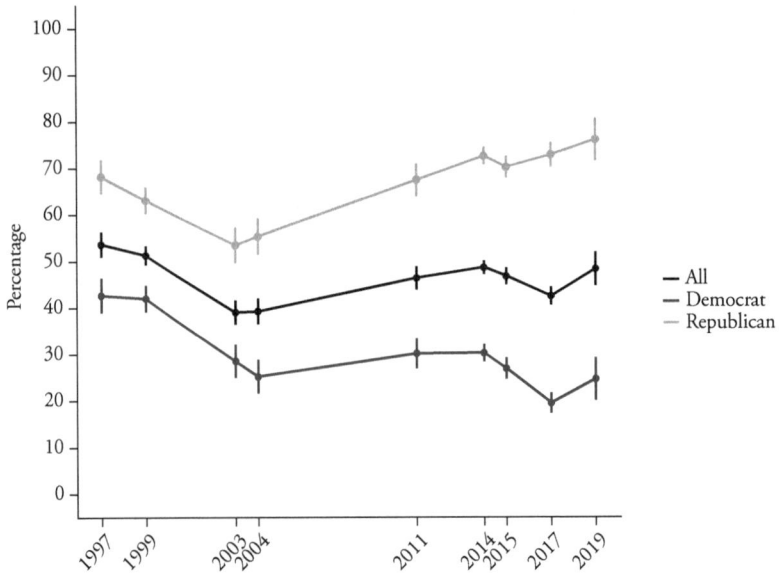

Source: Author's calculations using weighted Pew Research Center data (Pew Research Center 2025).

Note: Figure displays proportion of all Americans, Democrats, and Republicans who choose the statement "poor people today have it easy because they can get government benefits without doing anything in return" (as opposed to "poor people have hard lives because government benefits don't go far enough to help them live decently"). *N*s range from 1,572 to 8,939 depending on year.

this period appears to be a turning point for lay Republicans, just as it was for Republican leaders. By 2019, more than 75 percent of Republicans said the poor have it easy. Democrats fell to only 25 percent agreement in 2004, noticeably trended downward between 2014 and 2017, and then ended the series back at 25 percent in 2019. At the end of the series, the between-party difference is 50 percentage points.

Equal Opportunity and Racial Inequality

Thus far, we have examined questions about inequality and opportunity in the U.S. in general. However, economic inequality often overlaps with social group membership. Black Americans have especially low levels of income and wealth relative to White Americans. In recent years, Black American workers have made approximately 80 percent of what White American workers made.[53] Although poverty rates among Black Americans have diminished, they remain about double those of White Americans.[54] Wealth disparities are even greater. The net worth of a typical White family is more than six times greater than that of a typical Black family. As a result of these economic differences, White Americans are more than 50 percent more likely than Black Americans to own a home, an important symbolic marker of the American Dream.[55]

In the next series of questions, we consider trends in beliefs related to equal opportunity across social groups. We begin with a general question asked by the ANES from 1984 to 2012. The survey asked respondents whether they agreed or disagreed that "one of the big problems in this country is that we don't give everyone an equal chance." In figure 3.3, we indicate the percentage of respondents who agreed or strongly agreed with the statement, in contrast to those who disagreed, strongly disagreed, or selected the neutral option. The wording of this question is unfortunately double barreled, in that those who agree with the statement are indicating that societal inequities not only exist but also are a big problem. Even so, the combination meaningfully captures the perceived seriousness of unequal opportunity in terms of its raw magnitude and implications.

We see that Americans on average have oscillated around the 50 percent mark when answering this question, indicating substantial concern about the fairness of the American economy and mirroring the considerable recognition of unfairness found in the prior two analyses. Americans' concerns about a lack of equality drifted upward throughout the 1980s, peaking in 1992, when Clinton was elected president. This upward trend does not reflect trends in the two parties' platforms and may instead reflect recognition that government assistance to lower-income people and groups rapidly diminished under Presidents Reagan and George H. W. Bush. This elevated concern did not endure, however; agreement declined substantially from 1992 through 2000. This decline likely reflects Republican politicians' noisy opposition to Clinton's early progressive agenda (including their Contract with America in 1994), as well as Clinton's later criticisms of social welfare and promise to "end welfare as we know it."

Again, the average responses hide much disagreement. Democrats and Republicans have disagreed substantially about the existence of unequal

Figure 3.3 Americans Who Agree That We Don't Give Everyone an Equal Chance

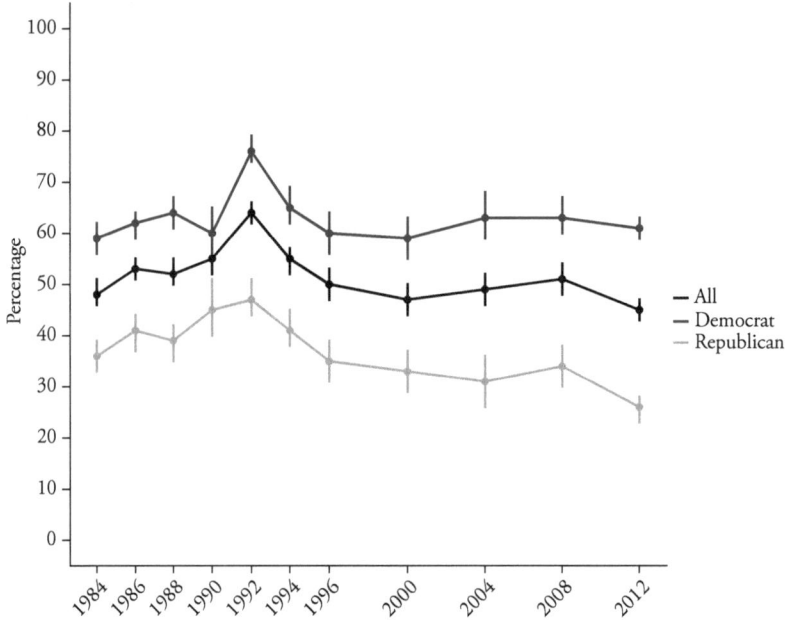

Source: Author's calculations using weighted ANES data (American National Election Studies 2025).

Note: Figure displays proportion of all Americans, Democrats, and Republicans who agree with the statement, "One of the big problems in this country is that we don't give everyone an equal chance." *Ns* range from 984 to 5,499 depending on year.

opportunity since at least the 1980s, when partisans were separated by more than 20 percentage points. Democrats' responses remained mostly stable at 60 percent agreement throughout the series, with a sharp spike upward in 1992 that we conjecture is linked to the acquittal of police officers in the famous Rodney King case and accompanying riots. Republicans trended upward through 1992 and then steadily downward from 1994 through 2012. By that final point in the series, only approximately 25 percent of Republicans believed unequal opportunity was a big problem, thus creating a 35 point partisan difference. Unfortunately, we do not have more recent data for this particular question; we might note that partisan polarization accelerated beginning shortly after 2012 according to the other measures analyzed in this chapter.

Next, we turn to a series of GSS questions on Americans' beliefs about the causes of Black–White economic inequality specifically, asked from 1977 to 2022. This battery of questions begins with the statement: "On the average, African-Americans [or Black Americans] have worse jobs, income, and housing than white people." This is then followed by the question stem, "Do you think these differences are . . ." and a series of explanations. Two of the explanations blame society, not Black Americans: "because most African-Americans don't have the chance for education that it takes to rise out of poverty?" and "mainly due to discrimination?" Two very different explanations locate the cause of racial inequality in Black Americans themselves: "because most African-Americans just don't have the motivation or will power to pull themselves up out of poverty?" and "because most African-Americans have less in-born ability to learn?" These questions are among the most controversial we examine. In fact, scholars generally agree that answering the final question in the affirmative is synonymous with biological or scientific racism.[56] Many scholars argue that the question on motivation is indicative of racial prejudice as well.[57]

We begin by examining trends for the two explanations that are critical of society as opposed to Black Americans: a lack of access to education and the presence of discrimination. See figures 3.4 and 3.5. Note that the percentages in the figures represent the proportion of Americans who answered "yes" to each specific question, agreeing with the explanation provided.

Approximately 50 percent of Americans indicated that lack of access to education contributed to Black Americans' economic difficulties in 1977. Approximately 40 percent said that discrimination played an important role. These numbers remained relatively stable into the early 1990s but then dropped throughout the decade, into the early 2000s. This downward trend corresponds with the Clinton era, when Republicans tacked further to the right, and Democrats followed them. The trend for education then reversed, increasing through the present day (with a brief drop in 2012 and 2014 during the Obama era). Belief that discrimination held Black Americans back remained stable until 2014 and then began a precipitous rise. By the end of the series in 2022, between 50 and 60 percent of Americans said lack of access to education and discrimination played an important role in racial economic inequality. For education, this represents a return to the original level of belief found at the beginning of the series; for discrimination, this represents a significant increase in concern over a lack of racial equality since that early period.

Figure 3.4 Americans Who Agree That African Americans Have Worse Jobs, Income, and Housing Due to Lack of Access to Education

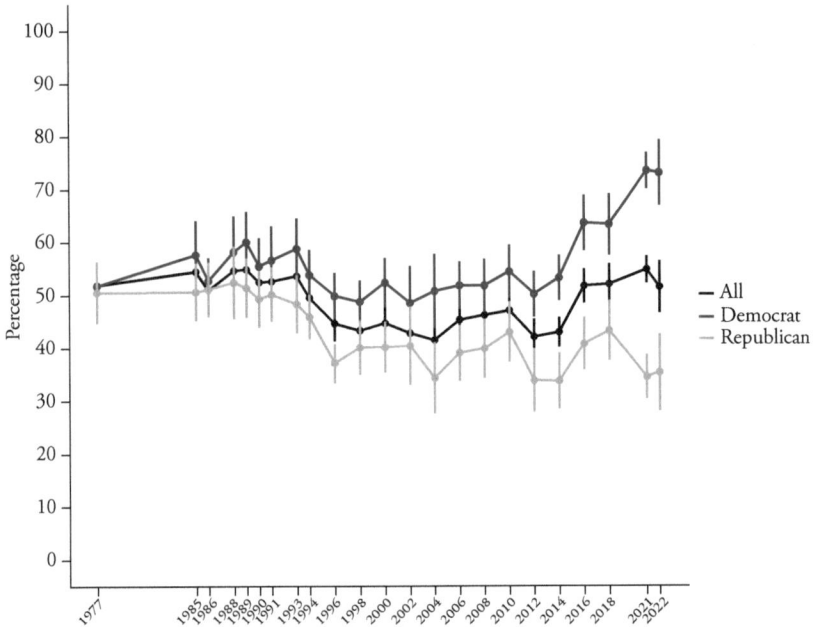

Source: Author's calculations using weighted GSS data (General Social Survey 2025).
Note: Figure displays proportion of all Americans, Democrats, and Republicans who, when asked about the causes of Black–White economic inequality, agree with the explanation that such differences are "because most African-Americans don't have the chance for education that it takes to rise out of poverty." Ns range from 873 to 2,673 depending on year.

Even more so than the preceding questions, these average trends are not very meaningful without considering growing partisan polarization over time. At the beginning of the series, partisans agreed at the same rate (for education) or nearly the same rate (for discrimination) with one another, but their opinions diverged soon after. The 1990s saw an approximately 10 percentage point partisan gap for the education explanation and a 20 point gap for the discrimination explanation. By 2022, there was an approximately 40 point gap with respect to education and an approximately 50 point gap for discrimination. We can certainly attribute some of this partisan divergence to the fact that White Americans with racially prejudiced views left the Democratic Party for the Republican Party in the 1960s and 1970s. Yet, this shift was mostly complete by the 1980s, meaning further

Figure 3.5 Americans Who Agree That African Americans Have Worse Jobs, Income, and Housing Due to Discrimination

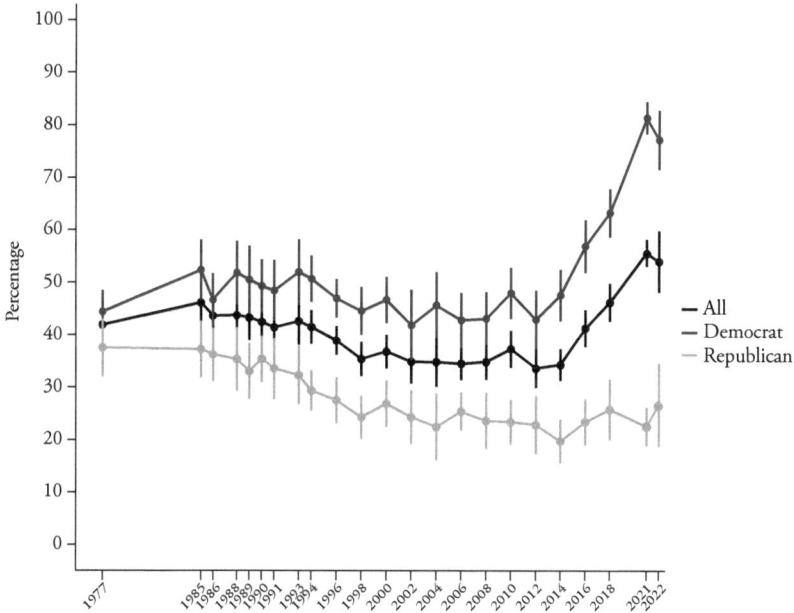

Source: Author's calculations using weighted GSS data (General Social Survey 2025).
Note: Figure displays proportion of all Americans, Democrats, and Republicans who, when asked about the causes of Black–White economic inequality, agree with the explanation that such differences are "mainly due to discrimination." Ns range from 866 to 2,681 depending on year.

changes were happening among preexisting partisans.[58] Both parties, but especially Republicans, became less concerned about structural barriers to advancement for Black Americans in the 1990s. Republicans then stabilized, landing at 30-40 percent for education and 20–25 percent for discrimination. However, Democrats' belief that access to education is an important cause of racial inequality climbed from 50 percent in 2012 to more than 70 percent in 2022, and their belief that discrimination is important went from approximately 45 percent in 2012 to roughly 75 percent in 2022 (falling from a peak of more than 80 percent in 2021). We see particularly large increases for Democrats around the 2016 and 2020 elections. In the end, what began as national ambivalence among all partisans in the late 1970s became a textbook case of extreme partisan polarization by 2021.

Finally, we discuss the two explanations for racial inequality that locate

Figure 3.6 Americans Who Agree That African Americans Have Worse Jobs, Income, and Housing Due to a Lack of Will

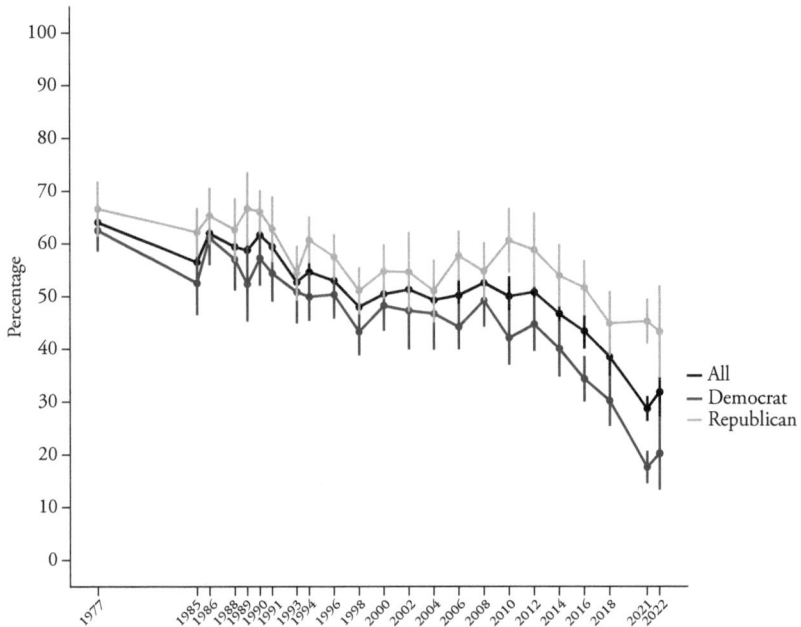

Source: Author's calculations using weighted GSS data (General Social Survey 2025).
Note: Figure displays proportion of all Americans, Democrats, and Republicans who, when asked about the causes of Black–White economic inequality, agree with the explanation that these differences are "because most African-Americans just don't have the motivation or will power to pull themselves up out of poverty." *N*s range from 857 to 2,666 depending on year.

the causes of Black Americans' economic difficulties in Black Americans' characteristics or abilities. See figures 3.6 and 3.7. We begin with the "lack of will" explanation. At the beginning of the series, approximately 65% of Americans endorsed this explanation. By the end of the series, fewer than 30% of Americans agreed. In short, this represents another instance of Americans, in the aggregate, becoming increasingly doubtful that the nation offers its people plentiful opportunity that some simply fail to take advantage of. In between the end points of the time series, there is a lot of movement. In the aggregate, the trend slopes downward in the 1990s during the Clinton presidency and then stabilizes in the 2000s, in the George W. Bush era. Support for this idea then falls again substantially beginning in 2014.

Figure 3.7 Americans Who Agree That African Americans Have Worse Jobs, Income, and Housing Due to a Lesser Ability to Learn

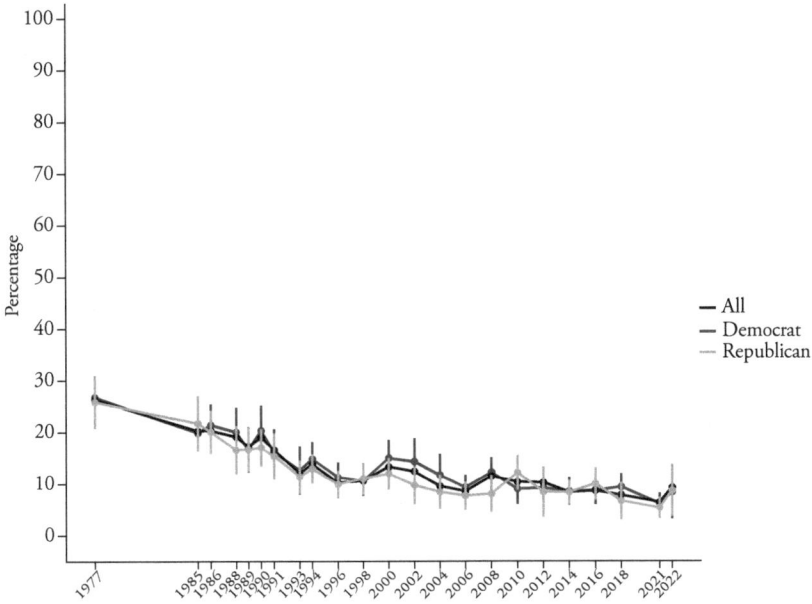

Source: Author's calculations using weighted GSS data (General Social Survey 2025).
Note: Figure displays proportion of all Americans, Democrats, and Republicans who, when asked about the causes of Black–White economic inequality, agree with the explanation that these differences are "because most African-Americans have less in-born ability to learn." *N*s range from 884 to 2,689 depending on year.

In contrast to the prior two questions about structural inequalities, increasing hesitation to blame Black Americans can be found among people in both parties and in two different eras. This may reflect the influence of broad racially progressive social movements, such as Black Lives Matter, in more recent years. Regarding the bipartisan nature of the trends, the platform rhetoric discussed in the previous chapter largely avoided casting explicit blame on individuals and, especially, social groups who fell behind. In other words, at least in the most formal of their communications, partisan elites were not very differentiated on the question of "lack of will" (that is, laziness). Even so, across the series, the declines among Democrats were relatively greater, especially in the final decade of data. This resulted in a significant partisan gap in 2022. What began as an inconsequential difference in 1977 became an approximately 20 percentage point gap (with Republicans just above 40 percent and Democrats at 20 percent).

The last question is the most controversial—whether there are innate differences in intelligence between Black and White Americans that can explain different economic outcomes for the two groups. This racially essentialist claim has been rejected by most scientists since the mid-twentieth century,[59] and it has been excluded from mainstream political discourse for decades,[60] although Trump at points has arguably signaled his belief in this idea in public statements. Support for this claim is low and has declined over time, reflecting changing norms. In 1977, approximately 25 percent of Americans agreed with this explanation; today, approximately 10 percent do. The fact that there is no discernable partisan polarization in response to this question is at once remarkable given polarization of the other explanations yet also expected given the relative absence of biological racism from mainstream party politics during the study period. Note that polarization does not even emerge in the early period of the series when many racially prejudiced Whites moved from the Democratic to the Republican Party.[61]

This final set of findings on beliefs about the origins of racial economic inequality may raise a question for some readers: When partisan differences emerge, to what extent are they driven by the fact that Democratic partisans are much more likely to be Black and Republican partisans to be White? The answer is: almost not at all. If we examine answers given only by White survey respondents, the trends are nearly identical to those displayed here. In fact, in related work conducted with Mark Tenenbaum and Austin Bartola, we found that restricting the sample to White survey takers often reveals party polarization that is greater than in the full sample.[62]

Suspicion that something other than partisanship may be driving results extends to other demographic factors as well. Could the reported partisan differences throughout this chapter be driven by education, income, or religiosity, for example? In the appendix (see figures A.3 through A.9), we display predicted probabilities for Democrats and Republicans generated from logit regression models that control for age, race, sex, education, and income.[63] The findings are similar to those already discussed, suggesting that some form of partisan ideology—and not partisans' demographic characteristics—underlies the observed partisan differences in economic belief.

Partisan Differences by Level of Political Interest

The findings discussed thus far provide suggestive evidence that rhetoric emanating from the two major parties influences their rank-and-file members, as prior research in political science would suggest. Yet, the observed patterns could also be the result of party elite responsiveness to lay partisans or could represent elite and lay partisans responding in tandem to shifting events. Do we have any evidence that Americans exposed to political rhetoric are actually following political leaders? One simple method of answering this question is to measure Americans' attentiveness to politics and then assess whether partisans who are most attentive are also most likely to hold views that are similar to party elites.[64] We would not expect inattentive Democrats and Republicans to differ much at all, as they are unlikely to be aware of the economic beliefs of their party. To be clear, we also would not expect any partisans to differ, no matter how attentive, if political elites in both parties did not disagree with one another.

In the analyses that follow, we display predicted probabilities and 95 percent confidence intervals for Democrats and Republicans generated from logit regression models in which the various beliefs about inequality and opportunity were regressed onto partisanship (Democrat or Republican), interacted with political interest and controlling for age, race, sex, income, and education. (Note that we are unable to analyze the two questions from Pew due to lack of a suitable variable measuring political attention or interest.)

We first analyze the ANES question asking whether survey respondents agreed that "one of the big problems in this country is that we don't give everyone an equal chance." We grouped respondents into low, moderate, and high interest categories according to their responses to the following question: "Some people don't pay much attention to political campaigns. How about you, would you say that you have been/were very much interested, somewhat interested, or not much interested in the political campaign (so far) this year?"

Results are shown in figure 3.8. The left-most panel represents the predicted probability of saying that "we don't give everyone an equal chance" among those who were not much interested in the political campaign. Although on balance Democrats in this group were usually more likely to agree with this statement than comparable Republicans, most of the differences are relatively small and not statistically significant ($p < .05$). Partisans who were somewhat interested, in the middle panel, demonstrate a strikingly different pattern. Democrats in this group were consistently and substantially more likely than Republicans to express concern about equal opportunity, and this difference grew over time. All such partisan differences are statistically significant. Finally, among those who were very much interested (in the right-most panel), partisan differences were even larger, and again expanded over time, with an especially large gap in 2012, the final year of data. In short, figure 3.8 indicates that, as we would expect, partisans with moderate and high political interests drove the polarization patterns observed in figure 3.3.

We next analyze the series on racial beliefs from the GSS. In the GSS, respondents were asked, "How interested would you say you personally are in politics?" Respondents were, again, categorized as low, moderate, or high interest. Given that the GSS included more than three response options to this question that varied slightly over time, we coded responses so as to create three categories that were equivalent in size to the ANES categories.[65] Results for the first two outcome variables—belief that lack of access to

Figure 3.8 Partisans' Beliefs That We Don't Give Everyone an Equal Chance by Level of Political Interest

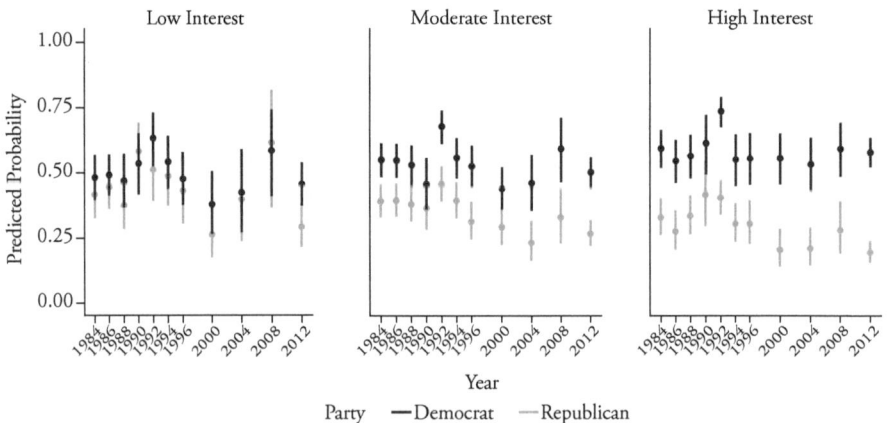

Source: Author's calculations using weighted ANES data (American National Election Studies 2025).
Note: Each panel displays predicted probabilities from logit regressions for Democrats and Republicans, allowing coefficients to vary by interest level and controlling for demographic characteristics (age, sex, race, income, and education). Outcome variable is agreement (versus disagreement) that "we don't give everyone an equal chance."

education or discrimination cause racial inequality—are depicted in figure 3.9. Results are similar to those in the prior analysis. Partisan differences were negligible among those categorized as low interest. They were greater among those in the moderate interest category and then greater still in the high interest category. In these latter two groups, we also observe a clear

Figure 3.9 Partisans' Beliefs That Lack of Access to Education and Discrimination Cause Racial Inequality by Level of Political Interest

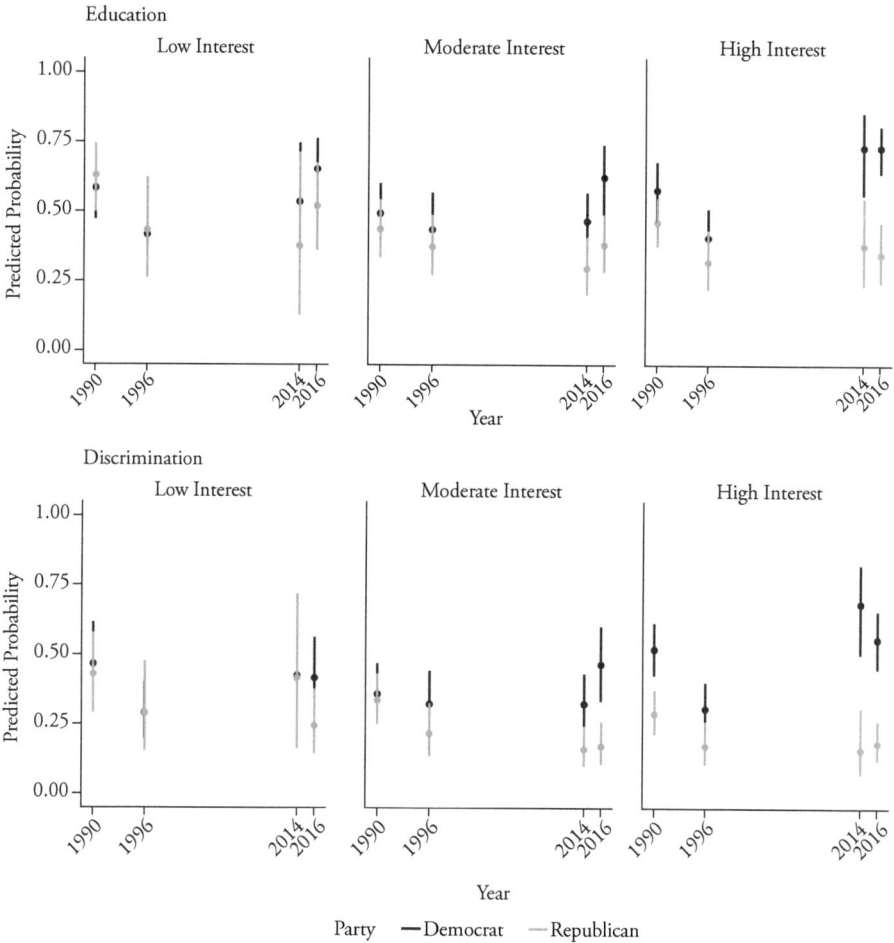

Source: Author's calculations using weighted GSS data (General Social Survey 2025).
Note: Each panel displays predicted probabilities from logit regressions for Democrats and Republicans, allowing coefficients to vary by interest level and controlling for demographic characteristics (age, sex, race, income, and education). Outcome variables are agreement (versus disagreement) that access to education (top) and discrimination (bottom) cause racial inequality.

pattern in time, with partisan differences much greater toward the end of the series than the beginning of the series.

Figure 3.10 displays results for the final two outcome variables that blame Black Americans for achieving less economic success than White Ameri-

Figure 3.10 Partisans' Beliefs That Lack of Will and Inborn Ability to Learn Cause Racial Inequality by Level of Political Interest

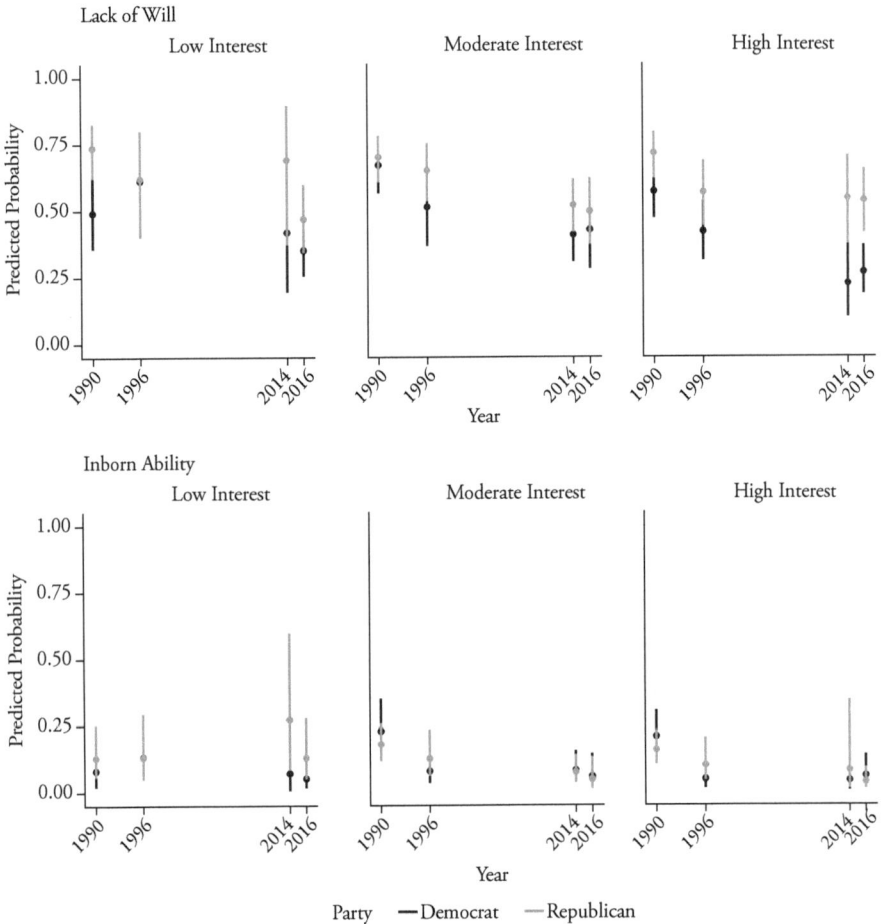

Source: Author's calculations using weighted GSS data (General Social Survey 2025).
Note: Each panel displays predicted probabilities from logit regressions for Democrats and Republicans, allowing coefficients to vary by interest level and controlling for demographic characteristics (age, sex, race, income, and education). Outcome variables are agreement (versus disagreement) that lack of will (top) and inborn ability (bottom) cause racial inequality.

cans. In this first instance ("lack of will"), a consistent Democratic–Republican difference, and one that became larger over time, is only evident among those with high interest. Overall, partisans did not differ as much as when considering structural explanations for racial inequality (in the prior two analyses), perhaps reflecting the fact that this narrative for Black–White inequality has not been as salient a part of formal party communications in recent decades. The final set of analyses ("inborn ability") show no appreciable partisan difference in any years or at any interest level, again likely reflecting the fact that this narrative has been largely absent from formal partisan discourse.

Conclusion

The survey data provides a thorough look at trends in Americans' beliefs about the availability of the American Dream over four decades. It reveals several notable patterns in the public's views. The first is that Americans are not as convinced of the reality of the American Dream as many observers suggest. To a significant extent, we might describe them as ambivalent, at least in the aggregate. Furthermore, they have become more pessimistic over time according to most of the questions examined herewith. Americans have become substantially less likely to say that hard work leads to success. They have become much more likely to reject the notion that Black Americans have insufficient will power to succeed and to embrace the idea that Black Americans suffer economically due to discrimination.

In the aggregate, the trends give the impression of a public responding to growing economic inequality and lessening upward mobility in recent decades. However, the substantial disagreements between the political parties throws this into doubt. Throughout the period under study, Americans who identified as Democrats and Republicans have often sharply disagreed over the extent to which economic opportunities are available to all Americans and are equitably distributed. (The small number of true independents in the electorate, not depicted in the figures, have tended to split the difference between the two partisan camps.) Partisan differences have also increased over time, leading to gaps of up to 50 percentage points. The size of these gaps rival those for more widely acknowledged topics of controversy, such as climate change and abortion.[66]

Changes among both Democrats and Republicans have contributed to polarization over time; however, such shifts have generally been greater among Democrats, especially in the 2000s and 2010s. Democratic citizens began to move in a direction more critical of the national economy during George W. Bush's presidency. Their skepticism picked up steam under the Obama administration and accelerated thereafter, as the Democratic Party became more outspoken in its concerns over a rigged economy. Democrats' belief that societal barriers to success harm Black Americans in particular has skyrocketed in recent years. Among Democrats, belief that discrimination contributes to economic inequality between Black and White Americans went from about 45 percent in 2012 to more than 80 percent in 2021 (thereafter falling slightly). This timing reflects Democratic elites' embrace of racially egalitarian rhetoric in their party platforms, as well as increased social activism among Black Americans. It also overlaps with Trump's entry into politics in 2015. Likely all of these phenomena, interacting with one another, mattered. Republican views have been somewhat more stable than those of Democrats, defying economic downturns in particular. This comparable stability has one main exception. In recent years, Republicans have become considerably more likely to say that poor people "have it easy." This tracks with Republican elites' greater rhetorical emphasis on personal responsibility, as well as their return to Reaganesque language about wasteful anti-poverty programs in the Obama years and thereafter.

There is just one question over which partisan differences do not arise: the mostly rejected idea that those who earn less (in this case, Black Americans) are innately less capable than others. It is worth noting that "character and ability" was the least-common attribution offered in the party platforms surveyed in chapter 2, and even these mentions tended to celebrate individual success instead of denigrating the unsuccessful. None of the party platforms attributed lack of ability or skill to innate, or in-born, factors. Such insulting explanations for inequality are apparently anathema in formal party communications. While politicians may be paying lip service to norms of equality, their avoidance of such language may well influence broader debate and public opinion in a positive direction.

The evidence we have provided for the influence of a party's rhetoric on lay partisans is admittedly circumstantial. It strengthens our case that those partisan identifiers who said that they were interested in, and presumably follow, politics were considerably more polarized over politicized narratives than their non-interested counterparts. As we would expect if they were

responding to party cues, Democrats and Republicans who were most interested in politics became more polarized than others over time as well,
especially during the most recent two decades of data. Our tentative conclusion that these patterns reflect elite persuasion also reflects the careful
empirical research of many scholars who have found persuasive causal evidence for the parties' ability to influence lay partisans' ideological commitments.[67] Yet, to some degree, what politicians say also reflects popular narratives circulating among influential coalition members. Whether party
elites persuade or are persuaded, elite and lay co-partisans exhibit a shared
partisan common knowledge regarding the American Dream.

Finally, some analysts might argue that the similarity between party elite
and lay partisans is driven by a third phenomenon: Americans changing
parties to find a more accommodating ideological home. Yet, while some
of the early polarization observed in this chapter—especially in the series
of questions about racial inequality—may have been due to conservatives
moving from the Democratic to the Republican Party (and vice versa),[68]
such shifts became more modest beginning in the 1980s.[69] Further, some
of the changes in public beliefs are just too large to be attributed to party
switching, such as Democrats' 30 point rise in support of discrimination as
an explanation for Black–White inequality between 2012 and 2022. In sum,
the evidence for some type of within-party influence is much better than
that for "rational" party updating.

Setting aside the question of what has caused these trends, we are certain
about their existence. The fact that we find relatively similar patterns of polarization and trends over time while drawing on data from a variety of
questions asked by three different survey providers gives us confidence in
the trends' validity. Yet, assembling data from different sources results in an
important weakness. The use of different questions and different samples
prevents straightforward comparisons between them. Do differences
emerge between beliefs about the poor and about Black Americans—the
latter seeming somewhat more sympathetic than the former—because of
different question wording or because of the different groups being considered? A further weakness is that the questions examined herein, while varied, do not cover many different types of inequality. Do the patterns we
discovered extend to other demographic inequalities, such as those between
women and men or between rural and urban Americans?

In chapter 4, I introduce two original surveys that systematically vary a core set of questions about the causes of five different types of inequality. The findings are interesting in and of themselves. However, as I discuss in later chapters, they also can help us to understand how parties may influence, and capitalize on, polarization over beliefs about the American Dream, meritocracy, and equal opportunity.

CHAPTER 4

How Americans Explain Socioeconomic Inequalities

It is still a White boys club in this country. But it's changing. . . . It's slipping out of their hands. Sadly they are going to fight it all the way it appears instead of cooperating.

> —EIPS survey respondent on why women tend
> to earn less than men

I spent three years in the mountains of Western North Carolina. Jobs are scarce. Temporary layoffs are not uncommon. I remember hearing my boss tell me "You're not fired but you get no more hours until April."

> —EIPS survey respondent on why rural residents tend
> to earn less than urban residents

IN THE LAST chapter, we saw that beliefs about the American Dream in the aggregate are less optimistic—and beliefs about low-income people and groups less critical—than much scholarly conventional wisdom suggests. However, we also discovered that Democrats and Republicans tend to view the economy quite differently. Over time, Republicans have been much more likely than Democrats to indicate that they believe people can get ahead via hard work, and Democrats have been much more likely than Republicans to express concern over societal barriers to advancement. Because Democrats and Republicans exist in relatively equal numbers, the American citizenry on the whole appears ambivalent; in fact, a sharp divide exists between these distinct political subgroups.

We also saw that Americans' viewpoints have shifted over time. On average, skepticism regarding the nation's provision of meritocratic abundance has increased over the past two decades. However, this skepticism has

https://doi.org/10.7758/trap6910.3722

mainly taken hold among Democrats. Republicans' economic optimism shows some evidence of decline, but not enough to close the gap with Democrats.

While the publicly available survey data examined in the last chapter is rich and informative, it also is limiting in certain respects. Survey organizations have asked respondents many different types of questions that relate to the American Dream. The similar partisan patterns that emerge reassure us that these patterns are robust. Yet, the varied question wording also prevents systematic comparison across questions addressing different domains of economic inequality—for example, beliefs about the causes of disparate economic outcomes in general versus between Black and White Americans. Further, survey organizations have inquired about a surprisingly limited number of domains of inequality. For example, they have often asked about racial inequality but rarely about geographic inequality. These two limitations together prevent us from carefully comparing people's beliefs as they assess multiple domains of inequality.

As we compare Americans' explanations for unequal economic outcomes between different groups, we also want to capture a wide range of their possible explanations for those inequalities. In the prior chapter, only the question series on the causes of Black–White differences captured multiple reasons why some people might earn less than others—educational access, discrimination, motivation, and ability. This type of inquiry reveals more nuanced beliefs about inequality, including whether people associate specific narratives with specific domains of socioeconomic inequality.

In this chapter, I introduce two original surveys of Americans' beliefs about the economy. Although the wording does not specifically evoke the American Dream, it assesses the Dream's core meaning by asking about the causes of inequalities between individuals and groups. If the nation provides meritocratic abundance, then inequalities can be traced to individual characteristics. If it does not, then inequalities can be attributed to specific barriers in people's way. In an initial survey from 2016, I asked Americans several questions: why some people earn less than others in general; why Black and Latino Americans earn less than White Americans (on average); and why women earn less than men (on average). In a second survey from 2018, I focused strictly on socioeconomic inequalities, repeating the race and sex comparisons and adding two question series: why rural residents earn less than urban residents (on average); and why White Americans earn less than Asian Americans (on average).[1] These latter comparisons allow for investigation of Americans' beliefs about a set of inequalities that are substantial but nevertheless differ in important ways from the preceding set: such inequalities are less often discussed in the political sphere; they map to the political party coalitions differently; and, in the case of the White–Asian American contrast, they involve two above-median income groups. For each comparison, I asked survey respondents to consider five possible reasons why some individuals or group members are less successful economically than others: a lack of educational or job opportunities, discrimination, a failure to work hard, family or community culture, and innately low intelligence.

In analyzing the quantitative data, I come to several conclusions. Consistent with findings in the last chapter, respondents did not overwhelmingly blame lower-earning people and social groups for inequalities. Respondents expressed considerable sympathy for lower-earning social groups in particular (with the exception of White Americans). There is also a great deal of meaningful complexity underneath the surface. American Dream optimists were more likely to agree with causal narratives that emphasize personal responsibility (but not inherent ability), and American Dream skeptics were more likely to say that both discrimination and a lack of education or job opportunity were the rule. This pattern grew stronger or weaker as different inequalities came into view. It was most evident when people were asked about poor versus rich Americans and Black and Latino versus White Americans. It was weaker when people were asked to compare female versus male Americans. The pattern nearly disappeared when people were asked about rural versus urban Americans and disappeared completely for the White versus Asian American comparison. In short, the two novel comparisons scrambled typical response patterns.

A final innovation in my study is the addition of open-ended questions probing what else—beyond the five standard explanations provided—a person believed contributes to economic inequality in various social domains. These open-ended items gave respondents the opportunity to share alternate explanations for unequal economic outcomes as well as to speak about inequality in their own words. The qualitative data provides a helpful supplement to the quantitative data. From a methodological perspective, they are reassuring in that relatively few respondents voiced alternative explanations for economic inequality unrelated to the five explanations provided in the closed-ended portion of the survey. However, the open-ended responses also provide rich additional information about Americans' beliefs about economic inequality and opportunity that the closed-ended responses cannot provide.

Explanations for Unequal Economic Outcomes

Before examining the survey results, I first situate my investigation within the relevant scholarly literature. I have focused heretofore on the American Dream. Belief in the reality of the American Dream involves the perception widespread opportunities to get ahead exist and that these opportunities are awarded according to merit—chiefly hard work and, to a lesser extent, ingenuity and skill. Doubt, alternatively, involves the perception that these attributes do not reliably lead to success. Due to lack of opportunity overall or inequity in who receives available opportunities, some people fall behind due to no fault of their own. Belief in the American Dream involves assigning causes to economic outcomes that suggest the successful are meritorious and the unsuccessful are not. A lack of faith in the American Dream involves the belief that many of the economically unsuccessful are in fact meritorious and many of the successful are not as meritorious as they appear.

Beliefs such as these are relevant far beyond U.S. borders. Psychologically oriented social scientists refer to the set of beliefs I am studying as *causal attributions* or *explanations* for economic and other outcomes.[2] Causal attributions rest beneath an even broader theoretical umbrella of *lay theories* or *epistemologies*—ordinary people's (as opposed to scientists') perceptions of what is true about the world.[3] Social scientists pay so much attention to causal attributions because they are ubiquitous and are thought to influence a wide range of other beliefs, attitudes, and behaviors.[4]

Scholars have offered a variety of frameworks that organize common attributions into typologies. Most emphasize a straightforward division between causal factors that are internal and those that are external to the individual.[5] Some focus on the closely related dichotomies of differentiating individual from societal factors,[6] or distinguishing between dispositional and situational ones.[7] Many scholars believe this dichotomous categorization is too simplistic to capture all of the important features of causal attributions, however. Feagin argues that one must consider who, if anyone, is responsible for inequality. He offers a three-part framework:

(1) *Individualistic explanations*, which place the responsibility for poverty primarily on the poor themselves; (2) *structural explanations*, which blame external social and economic forces; and (3) *fatalistic explanations*, which cite such factors as bad luck, illness, and the like.[8]

Wim van Oorschot and Loek Halman suggest a slightly different organization: preserving the internal versus external distinction and locating blame and fate within each side of that divide. The result is a four-part scheme: individual blame (such as the poor don't work hard), individual fate (the poor are innately less talented or unlucky), social blame (society doesn't provide equal access to high-quality schools), and social fate (uncontrollable economic forces lead to poverty).[9] This is also in accord with work by Bernard Weiner. In psychological terms, whether someone is responsible for an outcome boils down to whether they are in control of it.[10] This two-by-two conceptual matrix is a helpful way to organize the key types of causal attributions for unequal economic outcomes. See Table 4.1.

Table 4.1 Typology and Examples of Causal Attributions for Economic Outcomes

	Internal, Individual, or Dispositional	External, Societal, or Situational
Blame, responsibility, or control	"Poor people are lazier than rich people."	"Poor people do not have access to the good jobs that others enjoy." "Poor people suffer from discrimination."
Lack of blame, responsibility, or control	"Poor people have inborn traits (such as disabilities) that hold them back relative to others." "Poor people suffer from worse luck than others."	"Poor people are victims of economic forces outside of anyone's control, such as economic depressions."

Source: Author's summary of typologies provided by van Oorschot and Halman 2000 and Weiner 1995.

This typology is a satisfying beginning point, but it leaves out several complications. First, because democratic politics involves a great deal of blame, the most common narratives in the political arena tend to fall into the individual and social blame quadrants of van Oorschot's typology. Second, not all attributions can fit neatly into one category or another. Cultural explanations fall in between individual and societal ones, as they often point to the influence of a person's local community or even family on their behavior.[11] This explanation places some blame on social groups or families but also exonerates individuals, assuming they act under the influence of cultural norms they cannot control. Third and finally, the typology leaves out a sometimes significant aspect of causal explanation: the perceived stability or permanence of a causal force.[12] The most salient example is when a person is thought to have a genetically determined trait.[13] Such traits relieve individuals of blame, but people perceive them to be unavoidable and permanent.[14]

In sum, blame-oriented internal and external attributions are most relevant to politics. To these, we should add culture as an important in-between category of explanation, as well as (perceived) innate factors. While innate explanations for unequal economic outcomes do not blame in the traditional sense, their assumed permanence is politically significant.

How does the American Dream fit into this expanded typology? Those who believe in the American Dream do not locate the causes of unequal economic outcomes in society. To them, opportunity is plentiful and equally available. Thus, inequalities must rest within individuals. The power of hard work and personal responsibility should play the starring role in their belief systems, given its emphasis in American culture as well as Republican Party rhetoric, although they may be open to other individual-level explanations, such as innate ones. Optimists may also view subcultures as important contributors to inequality, given common rhetorical linkages between cultural socialization and economically adaptive or maladaptive behavior. American Dream skeptics, however, in large part believe that unequal economic outcomes originate in an American economic system that does not provide ample and equal opportunities. They are likely to point fingers at societal practices and institutions and to have little patience for any explanation that locates causes of inequality within lower-earning individuals or social groups.

Finally, the various types of causal attributions for economic inequality carry with them important moral and political implications. People thought to be responsible for their success and those thought to be guiltless for some difficulty tend to be judged positively and considered deserving—of their success or of assistance, respectively. Those perceived as responsible for their problems and those believed to be enjoying unearned success are more likely to be judged negatively and considered undeserving. I discuss how these implications play out politically in detail in chapter 7.

Explanatory Consistency and Inconsistency

In providing this conceptual overview, I do not intend to argue that all people have carefully elaborated and neatly organized attributional theories that line up with a belief that the United States does, or does not, provide its people with the American Dream. Thinking about the origins of inequality is an ordinary part of human psychology, but that does not necessarily imply that people give their explanations for inequality a lot of thought. Even among those who have considered this topic at length, few hold views that can be organized neatly into the cells of table 4.1 or located at one or the other end of the individual–societal blame continuum. Views are also likely to shift as people consider different domains of inequality.

There is surprisingly little explicit attention in the scholarly literature to the consistency of people's explanations for inequality under different conditions. Some scholars do argue in favor of at least somewhat consistent attributional styles among people. Psychologists have established that people are often consistent in their causal interpretations of events in their own lives. For example, people with low self-esteem are less likely to give themselves credit for their accomplishments.[15] Scholars interested in psychological essentialism have also argued that some people are consistently more likely than others to view human differences as innate—with important consequences for other beliefs.[16] Researchers who study international differences in attributional tendencies have found that Americans tend to use individual or dispositional explanations more than people in other places such as Europe and China.[17]

Much of the scholarship asserting that people have consistent attributional tendencies when thinking about social inequality has a political flavor. Some scholars argue that American conservatives consistently champion personal responsibility, whereas liberals consistently emphasize societal causes of inequalities.[18] In an article by G. Scott Morgan, Elizabeth Mullen, and Linda J. Skitka, the authors write that the research literature has accumulated such a long record of conservatives blaming people and groups for problematic behaviors—and liberals exonerating them—that the finding deserves a name: the ideo-attribution effect.[19] This would accord with the data discussed in the prior chapter.[20]

A number of scholars argue in favor of a more complicated picture of causal attributions, however. Jennifer Hochschild, as well as Kluegel and Smith, emphasize that many individuals hold inconsistent views—endorsing both individual and structural explanations.[21] Kluegel and Smith's comprehensive study finds these two dimensions are largely uncorrelated.[22] In a review article, Matthew Hunt and Heather Bullock indicate that many studies have documented this phenomenon, referring to it alternately as "dual consciousness," "split consciousness," and a tendency to believe "compromise" explanations.[23] Individuals may be even more inconsistent than this, for example, changing their mind over time or as they consider different social groups.

There are numerous reasons for such disorganization in people's attributions. First is the possibility that many people are simply ambivalent. Dominant cultural explanations may conflict with individuals' personal experiences,[24] or people may simply be attuned to a noisy marketplace of ideas.[25] In addition, as discussed earlier, many attributions have mixed moral and political implications. Innate explanations imply that people are not responsible for their behaviors and yet also suggest that their behaviors are unlikely to change, stigmatizing them and undercutting some arguments for reform.[26] Cultural explanations likewise imply that individuals are not responsible for their behavior but largely blame entire subgroups of people for social problems while deflecting blame from the broader society.[27] These mixed implications may simultaneously draw and repel people with specific intuitions about responsibility and reform.

A second reason for disorganization may be that there are so many domains of economic disparity to consider: between poor and rich, between the sexes, between racial and religious groups, between geographic groups, and many more. Some people may believe the American Dream is available—or not available—to all people in equal measure; however, others may differentiate between some or all domains of social inequality. A given person's response pattern may be informed by (negative and positive) stereotypes about the unequal groups in combination with the individual's own social identities or political attachments. To provide some examples: Americans have, in the past, expressed beliefs about the causes of women's lower average incomes that were more sympathetic than their beliefs about Black Americans' lower average incomes, an outcome likely driven by negative stereotypes about and prejudice toward Black Americans.[28] Michael Hughes and Steven Tuch delve into response patterns by race and ethnicity.[29] They find that Black respondents used individualizing attributions most when considering the reasons for economic difficulties among Asian Americans; Asian Americans were a mirror image, using individualizing attributions most when thinking about Black inequality. In sum, there are many reasons to expect that Americans hold complicated beliefs about the origins of socioeconomic inequality.

Explanations for Inequality & Politics Surveys

In the pages that follow, I answer questions about how Americans explain unequal economic outcomes across individuals as well as social groups. Which explanations are most popular, and which least popular? How do survey respondents' perspectives change—if at all—as different socioeconomic inequalities come into view? Are attributions organized as the previously discussed typologies suggest they would be?

I draw on data from two surveys I designed—the Explanations for Inequality & Politics surveys (EIPS)—administered by YouGov in 2016 and 2018.[30] YouGov is an industry leader in obtaining near-representative samples from opt-in panelists.[31] One comprehensive analysis ranked YouGov fourth in quality out of more than 300 pollsters.[32] YouGov approximates representativeness of the U.S. adult population in three steps: randomly selecting from their nearly two million U.S. panelists combined and oversampling those with a lower propensity to respond; matching respondents to a sampling frame constructed from the 2016 American Community Survey (conducted by the U.S. Census Bureau) on age, education, race, and sex; and, finally, constructing population weights using the same four variables as well as 2016 presidential vote choice.

YouGov conducted the 2016 survey as a module within the Cooperative Congressional Election Study[33] and fielded it in two waves—before the general election (in September and October) and afterward (November).

The preelection survey measured respondents' explanations for unequal economic outcomes and candidate preferences. The postelection survey measured attitudes about economics and government policy. YouGov collected most of the demographic variables prior to the study. The N for the preelection sample is 2,000, and the panel N—those who took part in both the preelection and postelection surveys (discussed primarily in chapter 7)—is approximately 1,700. All analyses use weights that YouGov provided to improve representativeness.

In 2018, I contracted with YouGov directly to conduct a second study of American adults in July of that year. Although the original sample was 1,000 respondents, the survey had a split-sample design, and YouGov administered the survey questions discussed herein to approximately 500 individuals.[34] The implementation of this survey was similar to the previous, with the main difference being that the later study was standalone and conducted several months prior to the fall elections. This second survey addresses limitations in the first by including a number of new question types, described shortly and in the coming chapters. It also has the advantage of being conducted in a non-presidential election year, which helps ensure that my conclusions are not biased by the especially dramatic 2016 presidential election.

The attributes of the samples from the preelection wave of the 2016 survey can be found in table 4.2 and those of the 2018 survey can be found in table 4.3. I include unweighted and weighted sample statistics as well as comparable statistics from gold-standard probability-based surveys with similar demographic measures. Overall, my surveys' statistics match those of the major probability surveys, especially when the data is weighted. (Thus, I use population weights throughout.) There are two important caveats to this. Even with weights, the 2016 sample includes too many White-identifying Americans and too few Hispanic-identifying Americans.[35] In both years, the weighted samples include slightly too many Democrats and too few Republicans, a bias common to surveys during this period. The latter bias is potentially most problematic given Democrats' and Republicans' diverging viewpoints on the topic of economic inequality; however, the bias is so small that it does not impact my conclusions (and is potentially relevant only on the rare occasions when I do not statistically control for partisanship, as in the aggregate statistics in this chapter).

Table 4.2 Characteristics of 2016 EIPS Sample

Variable	Unweighted (%)	Weighted (%)	Benchmark (%)	Reference Survey
Sex				
Male	929 (46)	964 (48)	1,990 (48)	Pew American Trends
Female	1,071 (54)	1,036 (52)	2,193 (52)	(2016)
Race				
White	1,459 (73)	1,476 (74)	2,674 (64)	
Black	253 (13)	252 (13)	485 (12)	Pew American Trends
Hispanic	145 (7)	140 (7)	627 (15)	(2016)
Asian American	63 (3)	60 (3.0)	151 (4)	
Other	80 (4.0)	73 (4)	246 (6)	
Age (median)	49	47	47	GSS (2016)
Education				
No high school degree	53 (3)	221 (11)	431 (10)	
High school graduate	507 (25)	589 (29)	1,134 (27)	Pew American Trends
Some college or two-year degree	697 (35)	657 (33)	1,369 (32)	(2016)
Four-year college degree	486 (24)	345 (17)	751 (18)	
Postgrad	257 (13)	188 (9)	496 (12)	
Religion				
Protestant	719 (36)	745 (37)	1,761 (42)	
Roman Catholic	433 (22)	379 (19)	756 (18)	
Jewish	48 (2.4)	41 (2)	39 (2)	Pew American Trends
Agnostic, atheist, or none	614 (31)	649 (32)	1,171 (28)	(2016)
Other	184 (9)	183 (9)	416 (10)	
Party ID				
Democrat	796 (40)	762 (38)	1,449 (35)	
Republican	476 (24)	509 (25)	1,229 (28)	ANES (2016)
Independent or other	728 (37)	729 (37)	1,569 (37)	

Source: Author's calculations using data from 2016 EIPS as well as Pew Research Center 2025, General Social Survey 2025, and American National Election Studies 2025.

Causal Attribution Questions

In this chapter and those ahead, I discuss five general narratives for unequal economic outcomes: access to good schools and jobs, exposure to discrimination, hard work, cultural norms, and innate intelligence. While the most thorough study would ask Americans about more explanations for inequal-

Table 4.3 Characteristics of 2018 EIPS Sample

Variable	Unweighted (%)	Weighted (%)	Benchmark (%)	Reference Survey
Sex				
Male	232 (45)	256 (49)	1,215 (48)	Pew American Trends
Female	283 (55)	262 (51)	1,308 (52)	(2018)
Race				
White	351 (68)	337 (65)	1,601 (63)	
Black	59 (11)	63 (12)	298 (12)	Pew American Trends
Hispanic	67 (13)	81 (16)	380 (15)	(2018)
Asian American	15 (3)	16 (3)	83 (3)	
Other	23 (5)	21 (4)	162 (6)	
Age (median)	50	48	45	GSS (2018)
Education				
No high school degree	30 (6)	39 (8)	260 (10)	
High school graduate	172 (33)	182 (35)	714 (28)	Pew American Trends
Some college or two-year degree	170 (33)	163 (31)	782 (31)	(2018)
Four-year college degree	86 (17)	86 (16)	432 (17)	
Postgrad	57 (11)	50 (10)	324 (13)	
Religion				
Protestant	203 (39)	201 (39)	978 (39)	
Roman Catholic	91 (18)	96 (19)	476 (19)	Pew American Trends
Jewish	10 (2)	10 (2)	43 (2)	(2018)
Agnostic, atheist, or none	165 (32)	162 (31)	865 (34)	
Other	46 (9)	49 (10)	163 (6)	
Party ID				
Democrat	200 (39)	204 (39)	1,449 (35)	
Republican	127 (25)	136 (26)	1,229 (28)	ANES (2016)
Independent or other	188 (36)	178 (35)	1,596 (37)	

Source: Author's calculations using data from 2016 EIPS as well as Pew Research Center 2025, General Social Survey 2025, and American National Election Studies 2025.

ity, survey researchers crafting closed-ended questions must economize to keep surveys to a reasonable length. I used a variety of criteria to choose these five narratives. First, it was critical that the survey include key explanations in the literature that rest both "inside the person" and "outside the person," as emphasized by prior researchers, such as Feagin and Kluegel and Smith.[36] For the sake of efficiency, I let go of explanations found to be relatively unpopular among Americans in prior research, such as references to luck, fate, or God.[37] I combined similar explanations in one instance: access to good schools and jobs are asked about together. I also set aside the idea of big government encouraging idleness, as this is captured to a significant degree by the hard-work question, as well as the discussion of policy attitudes in chapter 7. Finally, I added a question on community culture that is intended to reflect "culture of poverty" arguments that have not been well-represented in the survey literature on causal attributions for inequality.

One oversight was failing to ask survey respondents about the importance of inherited wealth. This is less relevant in the 2016 survey, which focused on explanations for why people occupied better and worse jobs and earned higher and lower incomes, but it is more relevant in the 2018 survey, which included language about wealth disparities between individuals and groups. As I began this study, this narrative simply was not as common in political debate as it is today. Future research should incorporate this narrative, especially given rising wealth inequality.

I modeled question wording on a question appearing in the 2002 ANES (similar to the GSS questions discussed in the last chapter). It asked people: "In America today, some people have worse jobs and lower incomes than others do. Why do you think that is – why do some Americans have worse jobs and lower incomes than others do?" The ANES included nearly identical attributional questions on unequal economic outcomes in general, between Black and White Americans, and between women and men. It asked people to rate a number of explanations for these inequalities in terms of importance.

Figure 4.1 provides an overview of the relevant 2002 ANES explanations for inequality. The data reveals that Americans embraced a mix of explanations for inequality but, overall, were more oriented toward structural explanations than individual ones. When considering economic inequality in general, education was most popular, followed by hard work, inborn ability, and, finally, discrimination. In the group domains, society-blaming explanations (such as discrimination or access to education) were more popular than individual-blaming ones (hard work or inborn ability). When comparing women and men, discrimination was much more popular than access to education. When comparing Black to White Americans, discrimination and education were equally popular.

Figure 4.1 Explanations for Economic Inequalities, 2002 ANES

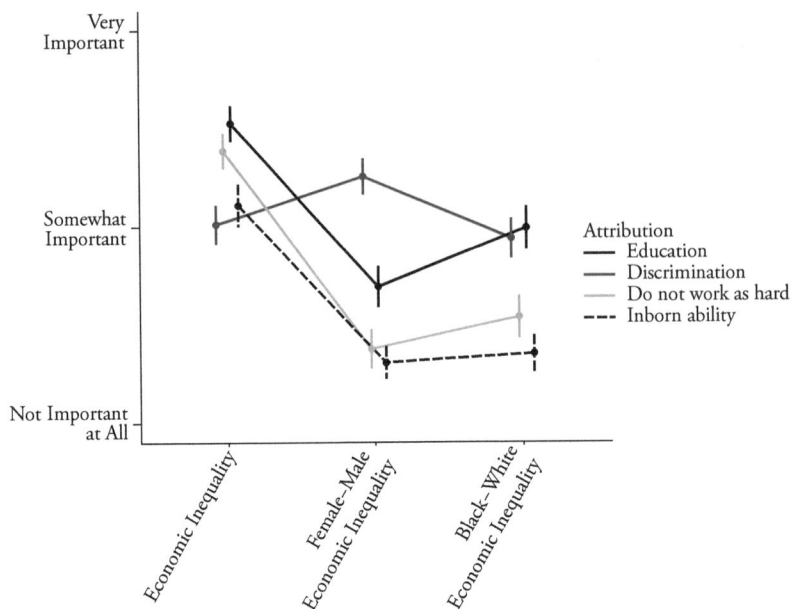

Source: Author's calculations using 2002 ANES data (American National Election Studies 2025).

In 2016, I asked respondents: "Why do you think it is that, in America today, some people have worse jobs and lower incomes than others? Please respond to this question by indicating your level of agreement or disagreement with each of the explanations below."[38] I presented them with five possible explanations (which were randomly ordered for each participant): "because some people don't have access to high quality schools and jobs," "because discrimination holds some people back," "because there is a culture of low expectations in some communities," "because some people choose not to work as hard," and "because some people have less in-born ability to learn." In response to each explanation, respondents chose from among six possible answers: strongly disagree, disagree, slightly disagree, slightly agree, agree, or strongly agree.

When asked about poverty or inequality, Americans inevitably have heterogeneous exemplars in mind, which influences their responses; the goal of my questions on economic inequality in general is to average this heterogeneity to generate a summary set of explanations for economic inequality. However, similar to the ANES, I followed this battery with two variations. First, I asked respondents why "Blacks and Latinos tend to have worse jobs and lower incomes than Whites."[39] I included Black and Latino Americans together due to space constraints. Note that Hughes and Tuch find that explanations for lower incomes among Black and Hispanic Americans tend to be similar.[40] Next, I asked respondents why "women tend to have worse jobs and lower incomes than men." To reflect some of the uniqueness of economic inequality by sex—while also keeping question wording relatively uniform—I replaced "high quality schools and jobs" with "child care for their children." I edited the wording within each explanation type as appropriate, such as replacing "some people" with "women" or "Blacks and Latinos."

The 2018 EIPS included nearly identical items, with some changes. First, I improved question wording by replacing the term "worse jobs" with "less wealth" and randomly assigning respondents to receive the Black versus White or Latino versus White comparison.[41] Second, and most important, I also inquired about a wider range of economic inequalities, adding a rural versus urban comparison and a White versus Asian American comparison (with rural people and White Americans in the lower earning position).

National politics often ignores these inequalities, but they are considerable. By a variety of measures, geographic income inequality is high, even adjusting for cost of living. A U.S. Department of Commerce report states:

> On average, larger metropolitan areas have higher incomes than smaller places, even after adjusting for the cost of living, which also is higher in larger metros. This gap is large: incomes are 24% higher in large metropolitan areas than in smaller metropolitan areas, 39% higher than in micropolitan areas, and 51% higher than in counties outside of metropolitan and micropolitan areas. Many of the lowest-income communities are in rural America.[42]

Geographic inequality also rose a great deal between 1980 and 2020. Average incomes grew throughout the United States during this period, but the highest-performing places grew at a rate of 172 percent, compared with 55 percent in the lowest-performing places.[43] Widespread job and population loss in particular drove economic problems in rural areas.[44]

While White Americans tend to fair well economically compared with the nation as a whole, they earn considerably less than Asian Americans on average. A U.S. census report on 2021 household income data indicates that median household income for Asian Americans was approximately

$101,000, whereas non-Hispanic White households earned approximately $80,000 at the median. This is followed by median Hispanic American households earning $58,000 and Black American households earning $48,000.[45] The report summarizes these inequalities as follows:

> The real median incomes of different groups can be compared by calculating the ratio of the median income of a specific group to the median income of non-Hispanic White households. For 2021, the ratio of Asian to non-Hispanic White household income was 1.30. In other words, the median Asian household had a household income 1.30 times greater than that of the median non-Hispanic White household. The ratio of Black to non-Hispanic White household income was 0.62, while the ratio of Hispanic to non-Hispanic White household income was 0.74. None of these ratios were statistically different from 2020.[46]

In sum, rural–urban and White–Asian American income gaps—perhaps surprisingly—rival the size of Latino–White and even Black–White gaps. This is not to suggest that all of these gaps are of equal normative concern, especially when we consider White Americans, whose average and median incomes are higher than the national average and median. Yet, these statistics make clear that more substantial inequalities exist beyond those frequently talked about in politics. They are worthy of inquiry. Americans may or may not perceive them as fair, and Americans' beliefs about these inequalities may or may not have clear political implications.

The 2018 survey included one final addition to each attribution question battery: the opportunity for survey respondents to state in their own words whether the survey had missed any important explanations for inequality. The specific question wording was: "In your view, is there any other reason why [women; Black/Latino Americans; people in rural areas; White Americans] tend to have lower incomes and less wealth than [men; White Americans; people in urban areas; Asian Americans]?" As will be discussed later in the chapter, very few responses included a brand-new causal attribution. Rather, respondents tended to expand on one or more of the explanations already provided in the closed-ended portion.

To make room for the various additions to the 2018 survey, I removed the questions on unequal economic outcomes in general. Finally, I randomized the order in which the four group contrasts appeared for each survey respondent.

How Americans Explain Inequality

On average, what explanations for unequal economic outcomes are most popular relative to others? How does this comparison change as people consider different types of economic inequality? Figure 4.2 provides average responses (with 95 percent confidence intervals) in 2016 for the five explanations for economic inequality in general, between women and men, and between Black and Latino Americans and White Americans. This figure makes clear that causal attributions that are outside the person on balance were more popular in 2016 than those inside the person. Although the different samples and question wording do not allow for strict comparison, the aggregate responses appear to be more critical of economic fairness across all domains when compared to the 2002 ANES data.

Regarding explanations for unequal economic outcomes in general, the populace on the whole blamed poor individuals and society in relatively equal measure. The sympathetic "schools and jobs" attribution, the more

Figure 4.2 Explanations for Economic Inequalities (2016)

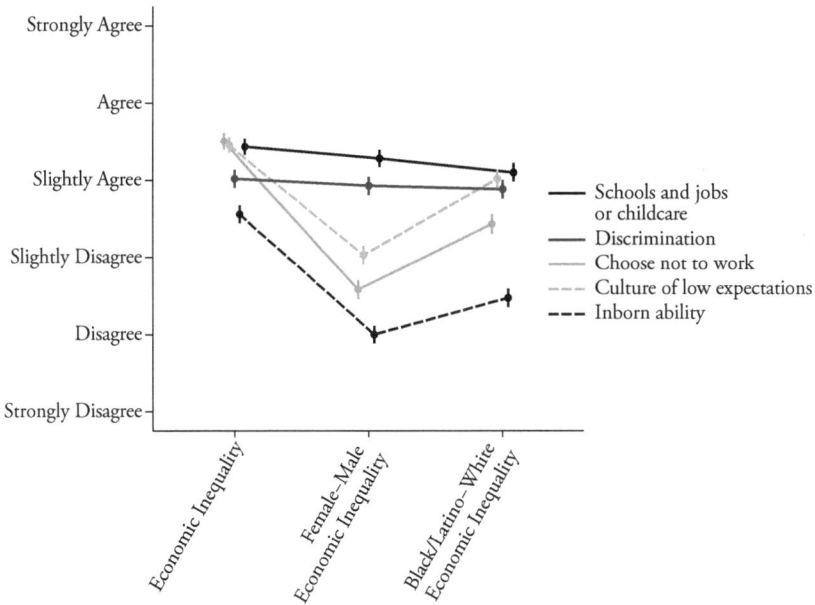

Source: Author's calculations using 2016 EIPS data.

complex "culture" attribution, and the blame-oriented "hard work" attribution were approximately equally popular, with discrimination a half-step behind. Inborn ability was the least popular explanation for economic inequality in general, landing in-between "slightly agree" and "slightly disagree." This preference for forces outside the person was even greater when people considered sex-based inequalities. Here, a lack of childcare was the most popular explanation, followed closely by discrimination. On balance, respondents disagreed that a culture of low expectations, choosing not to work hard, or (especially) innate inferior intelligence caused disparate economic outcomes between women and men. Finally, the patterns for racial inequality rested in between those for inequality in general and between the sexes. Here, schools and jobs, discrimination, and culture were about equally popular (hovering near "slightly agree"). On average, respondents were ambivalent about the relevance of work ethic when considering racial inequality and dismissed innate ability, although not quite as resolutely as in the case of women and men.

Next, we turn to the more varied set of explanations for inequality in the 2018 survey. Recall that this survey asked respondents not only about the average lower earnings and wealth of women and Black and Latino Americans, but also about the lower earnings and wealth of rural residents (compared with urban residents) and White Americans (compared with Asian Americans). This survey allows us to differentiate between beliefs about Black–White as opposed to Latino–White inequality. Is the somewhat surprising tendency for survey respondents to blame society for socioeconomic inequality specific to inequalities involving women and Black and Latino Americans? Is it specific to any social group earning below-median income? Or is the tendency to blame society something people do when considering any inequality between social groups at all?

Figure 4.3 provides mean responses focused on female versus male, Black versus White, Latino versus White, rural versus urban, and White versus Asian American inequality. The most important pattern to note is that, in the aggregate, Americans were much more likely to cast blame on society, and not the individual, with respect to the average lower incomes and wealth of women, Black and Latino Americans, and rural Americans. Among the below-median income groups, all four were perceived similarly with respect to lack of access to good schools and jobs (or childcare); however, elsewhere, differences emerged. Respondents recognized Black and

Figure 4.3 Explanations for Economic Inequalities (2018)

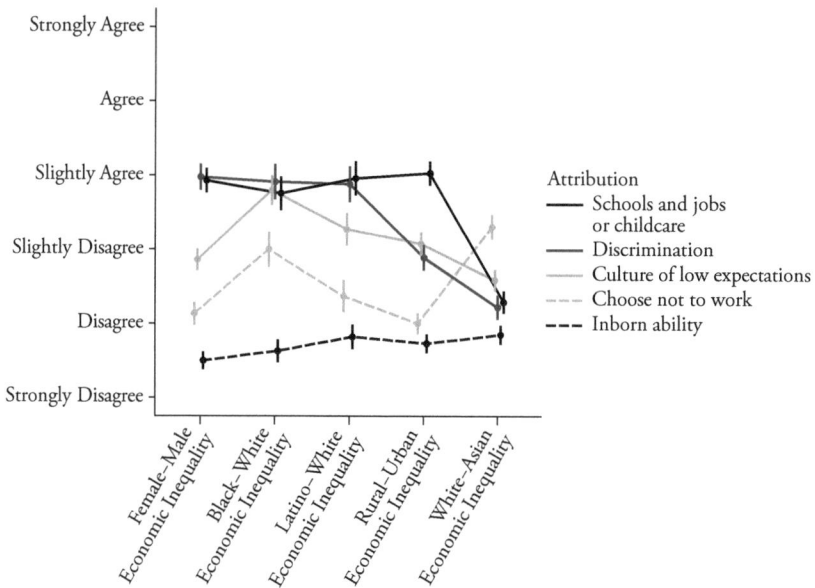

Source: Author's calculations using 2018 EIPS data.

Latino Americans and women as suffering from discrimination more so than rural residents. They applied culture, the next-most popular explanation, most strongly to Black people, then Latino people, followed by rural residents, and, finally, women. Lack of hard work was a relatively unpopular cause of inequality, but respondents attributed it more to Black Americans than other below-median income groups. References to inborn ability were uniquely unpopular across the board.

Responses differed considerably when comparing White and Asian Americans. Here, respondents were most likely to attribute inequality to variation in work ethic. Culture, discrimination, and schools/jobs clustered together and were much less popular. Similar to the prior domains of inequality, inborn ability was least popular.

In sum, survey respondents provided uniquely sympathetic beliefs about women and uniquely unsympathetic beliefs about White Americans (when contrasted with Asian Americans). The other groups rested in-between. There was some blame cast on Black and Latino Americans but also acknowledgement that they face discrimination that others don't.

How much may the Democratic bias in the sample have influenced these results? As we will discuss in chapter 6, Democrats and Republicans especially disagreed on three specific explanations for inequality: discrimination (Democrats prefer), access to education and jobs (Democrats prefer), and hard work (Republicans prefer). The largest average difference (for discrimination) was nearly two points on the six-point answer scale. Such large differences were only observed for the most politically salient inequalities (inequality in general, between women and men, and between Black and Latino Americans and White Americans)—that is, those depicted in figure 4.2. If we were to switch the responses of the 3 percent of the sample who represent excess Democrats from the typical Democratic to the typical Republican response, the aggregate response would shift by less than 0.1 of a point on the six-point scale. This would be noticeable only where two average responses are at parity and is not enough of a shift to change the aforementioned conclusions.

Response Patterns in the American Public

Average responses across the public are important, but they tell us little about what is going on at the individual level. For example, "schools and jobs" and "choose not to work hard" were both popular explanations for unequal economic outcomes in general. But who exactly advocated for these ideas? Did the explanations have similar levels of support because the same group of Americans supported both of them? Or were different groups of Americans agreeing with each of these contrasting explanations for inequality? The answer matters a great deal. Among other things, if the same individuals held a mix of blaming and excusing views, this indicates that individual-level ambivalence was the norm. As Hochschild and others have argued, perhaps many people were persuaded by the American ethos of hard work but also formed views that were more sympathetic toward lower-income people due to personal knowledge of hardship. Other people may have doubted the American Dream but simultaneously held negative views of poor people's behavior. Alternatively, if we see some people supporting individual explanations for inequality and others supporting societal explanations, then the mixed beliefs about inequality in the aggregate were due not to ambivalent individuals but rather a heterogeneous public. In other words, this would signal that consistent social or political attributional divides existed among Americans. Of course, we observed divides by party in chapter 3, but only for a relatively limited set of comparisons.

With the various types of socioeconomic inequalities in mind, aggregate patterns may or may not reflect individual-level patterns in another important respect. We have seen that Americans on average emphasized external barriers to success more than any internal ones when considering the fact that women, racial minorities, and people living in rural areas have fewer resources than others; however, when considering the fact that White Americans tend to earn less and have less wealth than Asian Americans, the hard work explanation was relatively more popular than the others. We can ask the same question as before from a slightly different angle: What is underneath these average similarities and differences across the various domains of socioeconomic inequality? Did significant numbers of people consistently offer society-wide explanations for lower-income groups but individual-level reasons for White Americans? Or was the average pattern of results perhaps due to more subtle shifts across the entire sample?

In sum, attributions may be patterned at the individual level in three ways: (1) most people hold a mix of views about the causes of unequal outcomes, endorsing a range of popular narratives even if they point to opposite conclusions (for example, "hard work" and "discrimination"); (2) some people consistently locate the causes of inequality in the person (or in the group) whereas others consistently locate the causes of inequality in society; and (3) people's tendency to locate the causes of inequality in the person/ group or in society depends on whose inequality is being considered. In other words, people may prefer to locate the causes of inequalities between some groups in the person and between other groups in society.

We can begin to answer these questions by examining Pearson correlations among the different explanations for inequality in the two surveys. Theoretically, correlations range from –1 to 1, indicating the direction and strength of the covariance between two variables. A positive correlation indicates that high values on one variable tend to co-occur with high values on the other variable. A negative correlation indicates that high values on one variable tend to co-occur with low values on the other variable. A zero correlation indicates no pattern of covariance whatsoever. We'll begin with associations among different explanations for inequality within the same domain of socioeconomic inequality, and then we'll consider associations among the same explanations across different domains.

In figure 4.4, we see patterns of association among explanations for economic inequality in general—that is, beliefs about why some people earn much less than others. There is some order to the data suggesting a blame-individual-versus-society dichotomy. Respondents who were more likely than others to say schools and jobs are an important explanation for unequal economic outcomes were also more likely to say discrimination is important ($r = .56$) and less likely to say choosing not to work hard is important ($r = -.19$). Those who said discrimination is important were also less likely to say hard work is important ($r = -.29$). This interconnected group of three attributions also clearly emerged as the first factor in an exploratory factor analysis.

A trio of interrelated attributions exclusively locates the causes of inequality within individuals—culture, hard work, and inborn ability. Those who said some people choose not to work as hard as others were more likely to emphasize culture ($r = .34$) and innate ability ($r = .30$). People who favored culture also tended to favor innate ability ($r = .27$). However, notice that culture and innate ability were also positively correlated with schools/jobs and discrimination. These not-easily-explained associations suggest respondent answers may have been influenced to some degree by

Figure 4.4 Correlations Among Explanations for Economic Inequality (2016)

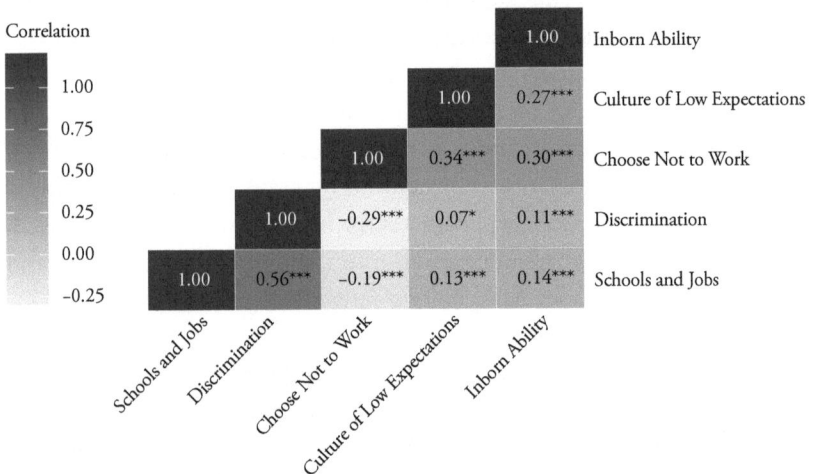

Source: Author's calculations using 2016 EIPS data.
Note: Pearson correlations for causal attributions for economic inequality between low- and high-income people.
* $p < .05$; ** $p < .01$; *** $p < .001$

response bias—the tendency to answer questions in a similar fashion across topics. The likelihood of response bias makes the negative correlations between hard work and the structural explanations all the more significant.

Do these specific patterns reappear when we examine other economic inequalities? The appendix includes correlations among the various explanations for inequality within all domains in the 2018 survey (see figure A.10). For the Black/Latino–White and female–male comparisons, the personal versus societal responsibility cluster (hard work negatively correlated with schools/jobs and discrimination) is evident in both cases. Patterns are different for the more novel inequalities—rural versus urban, and White versus Asian American—explored in the 2018 survey. Discrimination and schools/jobs were positively correlated, although not as strongly, and hard work was no longer negatively correlated with discrimination or schools/jobs.[47]

What happens when we consider correlations between the same explanation—for example, the importance of hard work—across different domains of inequality? Generally, we see much more consistency. People tended to stick with one or more attributions as they moved across inequality domains. Focusing on respondents' explanations for unequal outcomes in general, between women and men, and between Black/Latino and White Americans (assessed in 2016), the correlations for any one explanation across domains were always positive. Correlations for discrimination were highest, ranging from .61 to .79. Correlations were lowest and most variable (but still positive) for culture.

In the 2018 survey, correlations remained positive on balance but lower overall, especially as people moved between consideration of the more salient (women, Black/Latino) and less salient (rural, White) inequalities. Interestingly, the innate intelligence items had the most consistent pattern of responses in the 2018 survey. The correlations were always positive (ranging from .36 to .55), despite the range of groups discussed. In short, whatever respondents thought about inborn intelligence, they tended to stick with that view regardless of the groups under consideration. Discrimination had the least consistent correlations in 2018. Respondents who agreed that discrimination explains Black/Latino versus White inequality and female versus male inequality ($r = .67$) were somewhat less likely than others to say that discrimination explains White versus Asian American inequality.

Summary of Response Patterns

We can sum up patterns of response within and across specific domains of economic inequality in the following way. First, with respect to beliefs about economic inequality in general, between women and men, and between Black and Latino and White Americans, respondents loosely fit into two groups: those who gravitated toward unequal-opportunity explanations and rejected individual-responsibility attributions, and those who exhibited the opposite configuration of beliefs. People who believed in individual responsibility also tended to express belief in the importance of innate ability and cultural influences. These patterns weakened, however, when people considered rural versus urban and, especially, White versus Asian American inequality. In addition to observing these attributional patterns in the data, there is also a certain stickiness with respect to any given causal attribution—if people agreed with something once, they likely agreed with it again. However, this tendency was less evident in 2018 as people sought to explain four very different types of socioeconomic inequality.

Where does this leave us with respect to whether people are mostly consistent attributional reasoners, mostly inconsistent attributional reasoners, or consistent contingent on the domain of inequality? In some respects, there was obviously a great deal of consistency. Yet, the patterns in the data underwent a shift as people switched between the classic class-race-sex trio of inequalities and the more novel rural–urban and White–Asian comparisons. In the latter two instances, we do not see a clear divide between unequal opportunity and individual responsibility.

One possible reason for this difference is that the political parties communicate about—and argue over—some inequalities more than others. The Democratic Party, whose coalition in recent decades has disproportionately included poor people, women, and Black and Latino Americans, has long focused its criticisms of the economy on these groups' difficulties in particular, especially in recent years. Once the party of rural and White America, the Democratic Party has said little in recent decades about economic problems facing these former constituencies. The Republican Party has become the natural home for discussion of rural and White Americans' economic stagnation. Yet, as the party of hard work and small government, Republicans also have said relatively little in recent years about structural problems facing some members of their coalition. Some signs indicate that this is changing under Trump's leadership of the party, but individualism remains the rule and structural critiques the exception. As a result, the more familiar inequality domains of class, race, and sex are more scripted than the rural versus urban and White versus Asian American inequality domains.

These various inequalities do not only differ from one another according to their relationship to the political arena. Poor versus rich reflects interindividual, not intergroup, inequality and is an empirical constant. Female versus male and Black/Latino versus White inequalities are long-standing and, in earlier eras, were indisputably driven by legal and social inequalities. Rural versus urban and White versus Asian American inequality have become more noticeable recently, as urban areas have outpaced rural areas in economic growth and as the Asian American population has grown. Finally, of course, White Americans on average earn more than other racial groups. For all of these reasons, Americans' views may be more crystallized in the older inequality domains than the newer ones, leading to more predictable patterns. Acknowledging this, I argue that the evidence is also compatible with the idea that partisan scripts explain differences in the public's beliefs across these domains. I return to this in chapter 6.

Explanations for Inequality in Respondents' Own Words

I have, so far, investigated responses to the closed-ended explanations for economic inequality—the five concrete narratives that respondents evaluated across multiple domains of inequality. Meaningful patterns and some perplexing disorganization have emerged. In this final section, I consider how respondents talk about unequal economic outcomes in their own words. Examining people's views expressed exactly as they want to express them is helpful in several respects.

First, open-ended responses offer a window into whether the set of five narratives provided to survey respondents successfully reflected the most common types of causal attributions for inequality. There would be little reason for concern if the survey excluded a specific explanation for inequality that is closely related to a provided explanation. For example, a concern about lack of transportation in rural areas is usually another way of expressing a concern that people in the area do not have access to employment.

There are too many specific explanations for one survey to cover; some narratives must be left to the side. However, it would be more concerning if the survey excluded major types of explanation—such as luck—that are (unexpectedly) popular.

Second, we can use the responses to assess the salience of some explanations relative to others. Open-ended survey questions are taxing, forcing respondents to rely on information recall as opposed to the simple recognition needed to answer a closed-ended question. Thus, the open-ended items more accurately capture a person's thoughts at the time of the survey interview.[48]

Third, in qualitative responses, people can provide more detail and complexity, which may reveal meaning and interpretation not evident from the closed-ended items alone. What details or caveats might the person have added if given the chance? Was the question understood and evaluated in the way the researcher assumes? These detailed answers may also shed some light on whether respondents were at points engaging in acquiescence bias (agreeing with questions, regardless of content)[49] or socially desirable responding (agreeing with answers that paint them in a favorable light or disagreeing with answers likely to be frowned upon).[50]

Taken together, these investigations are likely to also shed light on why we observe the patterns (and lack of patterns) we do in the closed-ended data.

Measuring Respondents' Beliefs via Open-Ended Questions

The 2018 EIPS included open-ended questions. After indicating their level of agreement or disagreement with the five standard explanations for a given socioeconomic inequality, respondents were asked: "In your view, is there any other reason why [X group] tend to have lower incomes and less wealth than [Y group]?" With four kinds of economic inequality discussed, there were four related open-ended questions.

Once the data was collected, two students—who were not aware of this project's research questions or arguments—read and systematically coded the open-ended responses. Given that the purpose of these questions was to thoroughly canvas and summarize respondents' additional viewpoints, we employed a more inductive approach to interpreting these data.[51] Before creating the coding scheme, the two coders first read all the responses.

I asked them to provide me with the main emergent themes they detected. After considerable discussion, we organized most of these themes into five parent categories that included the five standard narratives but could accommodate related ones.

Those categories are as follows:

1. Access to opportunity: The key to this category was lack of access to opportunities, whether due to a dearth of available opportunity or barriers to that opportunity. Opportunities were primarily conceptualized as high-quality education, jobs, and job training. This category included references to economic depression in an area, lack of transportation, and lack of childcare.

2. Discrimination: Answers in this category referred to bias against a salient social category of people that results in them having fewer resources than others. Relevant answers could refer to the harmful effects of stereotypes or other prejudices, interpersonal discrimination, or institutionally embedded biases (such as structural racism or sexism).

3. People's choices or effort: These answers suggested that people are autonomous agents and make choices, have preferences, and do or don't exert effort or try hard to succeed. Generally, these answers seated responsibility—for success or failure—with individuals. Unlike the intrinsic characteristics category, these answers tended to be more behavior oriented, as opposed to focused on a person's characteristics.

4. Culture or socialization: These answers emphasized cultural influences on the individual—including family, community, and broader societal influences. This category included explicit references to people's values and morals.

5. Intrinsic characteristics: These answers argued that economic inequality is driven by individuals' intrinsic (essential, natural, or unchanging) characteristics. They tended to describe people with adjectives or stereotypes. They did not need to explicitly employ "innate" language (and very few did).

Three additional categories were added to these five standard categories. Answers in the *policy and politics* category placed blame for inequality on some aspect of the political system. This could include policies enacted (or not enacted) by government/elected officials. For example, a respondent might complain about the failures of trickle-down economics or, alternatively, a bloated welfare system. These answers could also include references to political actors (individuals or groups, such as conservatives or liberals) or processes (such as elections). Beyond this new category, the remaining uncategorized, substantive answers reflected many idiosyncratic themes. Thus, we added an *other* category to capture responses that did not fit any of the previous six categories. Finally, we added a category for responses that *rejected the question or survey*. In these interesting nonanswers, the respondent did not answer the question and instead criticized either the question or sometimes the entire survey. These rejections most commonly took the form of respondents doubting the veracity of the inequality mentioned in the question stem, which happened most often when assessing the relatively novel inequalities.

Once the coding scheme was completed, the coders applied it to the data. We followed a thorough process intended to reduce coder error and inconsistency. Each coder first independently read and coded each answer with respect to a particular type of socioeconomic inequality (such as Black or Latino versus White). Answers could be coded into as many categories as relevant (indicated by 1s and 0s in a spreadsheet); in practice, most answers were coded into just one or two categories.[52] The two coders then met and discussed any disagreements, forming a consensus and flagging borderline cases. I reviewed those cases, and we decided on final changes by consensus. After completing answers for one type of socioeconomic inequality, we moved on to the next. As such, codes assigned to any given answer in response to one domain of inequality could not be influenced by codes assigned in another domain.

Are the Five Standard Causal Narratives Sufficient?

I use this data to first determine whether the five original categories represented by the closed-ended questions appear to capture the main causal attributions participants believe are important. For the most part, they did. A detailed breakdown of the percentage of respondents in each category in response to each inequality contrast is presented in table 4.4.

First, approximately one-third of respondents (depending on the specific type of socioeconomic inequality) left their answer blank or explicitly indicated that they could not think of a reason why an inequality existed be-

Table 4.4 Open-Ended Explanations for Four Types of Socioeconomic Inequality (2018)

Explanation	Female–Male	Black/ Latino–White	Rural–Urban	White–Asian American
			Type of Socioeconomic Inequality	
Access to opportunity	10%	16%	39%	6%
	(53)	(79)	(201)	(29)
Discrimination	30%	21%	2%	4%
	(155)	(107)	(8)	(18)
Choices / effort	15%	15%	9%	20%
	(74)	(78)	(48)	(104)
Culture / socialization	10%	13%	5%	21%
	(49)	(67)	(26)	(105
Intrinsic traits	6%	5%	3%	10%
	(31)	(26)	(14)	(52)
Policy / politics	2%	6%	3%	4%
	(10)	(28)	(16)	(18)
Other	3%	3%	3%	3%
	(14)	(15)	(15)	(13)
Rejects	3%	2%	6%	5%
	(17)	(10)	(29)	(25)
No answer / don't know	32%	34%	35%	37%
	(161)	(175)	(178)	(187)
Uninterpretable	2%	1%	2%	1%
	(8)	(7)	(12)	(7)

Source: Author's calculations using 2018 EIPS data.
Note: Cells list proportion of sample, rounded to the nearest whole number, and number of people, listed in parentheses, coded into a specific category for any given contrast. Because comments could be coded into multiple categories of explanation, proportions in each column do not add to 100.

yond those stated in the survey. To some degree, this is good news, in that many survey takers appeared satisfied with the closed-ended explanations. That said, given that open-ended questions require more time and energy to complete, respondents tend to skip them more often than they would closed-ended questions on surveys. Thus, we cannot assume that all nonanswers represent respondent satisfaction with the provided narratives.

The vast majority of the approximately two-thirds of respondents who did provide another perspective offered answers that closely mapped to, or were even synonymous with, one of the closed-ended explanations. I provide examples that revolve around the theme of discrimination from among explanations for Black and Latino versus White inequality. Here, the straightforward terms *discrimination* and *racial discrimination* (and similar phrases) were common responses. In these cases, I surmise that individuals were using the open-ended responses to indicate what they believed to be the most important cause of a given socioeconomic inequality. Others provided a response that mirrored one of the five standard narratives but used different wording. For example, "They don't have the same advantages as whites." Still others used the opportunity to enrich the closed-ended response with interesting and sometimes impressive detail. One person wrote: "Historic obvious and blatant oppression until the Great Society programs under LBJ [Lyndon B. Johnson]. Followed by more subliminal racism, and covert discrimination."

A nontrivial minority of people had something new to say. Across the four kinds of socioeconomic inequality, up to 9 percent of participants offered at least one explanation that did not fit into the five original buckets—even generously defined, as I have done. About 3 percent of answers were placed in the catchall other category. For example, in response to the question about rural versus urban inequality, one person wrote: "Rural areas have cheaper rent. So people with lower incomes tend to go where rent is cheap." This is a legitimate causal explanation but does not fit within any major causal category. Depending on the domain of inequality, 2 to 6 percent of responses were coded as paying attention to politics or policy. Most often, and not surprisingly, narratives coded as being about policy or politics circled around a consistent theme: generous social welfare policies encourage dependence. For example, one person wrote: "Government policies give too much of an incentive to not try to advance." These answers resemble those that invoke hard work; they differ only in that they stipulate government as a preceding cause. Other political answers cast various aspersions on the survey respondent's political opposition.[53]

In sum, survey respondents' answers to the open-ended probes suggest the original five narratives reflect major categories of explanations for inequality used by the public. Some might argue that the survey—in locating these probes immediately after the closed-ended explanations—biased responses in favor of close correspondence between closed- and open-ended responses. In other words, if I had asked people to provide their explanations for inequality in open-ended form before the closed-ended battery of questions, they would have provided much more heterogeneous responses.

While I agree that such bias may be a concern, the survey question wording explicitly asked people to provide alternate explanations ("In your view, is there any other reason") and relatively few did so. While this method is not foolproof in detecting alternate explanations for inequality, it provides some measure of reassurance that the five narratives provided covered the bases.

Open-Ended Answers and the Salience of Specific Explanations for Inequality

We can also use the open-ended responses to investigate variation in the salience, or importance, of specific explanations for inequality that goes undetected in the closed-ended portion of the survey. To do this, we can compare the pattern of frequencies in table 4.4 with the patterns of relative agreement or disagreement in figure 4.3. How similar are the distributions?

In many respects, the relative popularity of the various types of causal explanation are similar. For example, when people were thinking about the lower earnings of women and Black and Latino Americans, discrimination was the most popular explanation in the open-ended answers and was among the most popular of the closed-ended ones. The same is true for access to opportunity in the rural–urban domain. Unpopular closed-ended explanations, especially individual traits, remained unpopular in the open-ended portion, for the most part. Yet, clear differences also emerged. When considering the lower earnings of women and rural people, the choices and effort category loomed larger in the open-ended question series than it did in the closed-ended one. With respect to White versus Asian American inequality, culture and socialization emerged as a leading explanation in the open-ended portion but not the closed-ended one.

In some cases, relative rankings among the various explanations remained the same, but there was a great deal of variation in how many people subscribed to each one. For inequality between women and men, respondents mentioned discrimination in the open-ended portion three times as often as the next most popular category. In the instance of rural inequality, access to opportunity was approximately four times as popular as the next-most popular category. For the comparison between White Americans and Asian Americans, respondents mentioned personal effort (as well as culture) four times as often as the two societal explanations. These high frequencies when respondents were able to answer in their own words suggest that they felt so strongly that a favored explanation bore repeating—and, in some cases, elaboration. Answers to the closed-ended questions did not reflect this emphasis.

Variations on a Theme

Finally, I overview the ways in which survey respondents interpreted the five major categories of explanation in the open-ended section. I focus on expected and unexpected interpretations in the most popular categories, as well as sizable clusters of similar responses that emerge elsewhere.

Regarding unequal economic outcomes between women and men, discrimination was by far the most popular response (30 percent of responses in this domain were coded as discrimination). Most of the answers talked about discrimination and prejudice in familiar ways, although many of the responses were unusually detailed and nuanced. Some participants noted unequal pay by companies, sometimes adding that this was practiced because companies could "get away with it." Some observed that men tend to be in powerful positions (such as "the people paying the wages are men"), leaving implicit the notion that discrimination against women would follow. Some located discrimination largely in the past, indicating that contemporary women are still "playing catch-up." Many discussed deeply entrenched societal prejudices, ranging from the notion that women should stay home to stereotypes of lesser skills to sexual objectification. As one person said: "There are those that feel women should be at home instead of in the workplace. Also they assume women have a husband helping with finances. Some think women aren't strong enough, smart enough, capable of doing the same job as a man." Answers in the barriers to opportunity category also reflected the closed-ended version. These answers were overwhelmingly dominated by references to the time spent to raise children ("They have to take more time off for pregnancy and raising kids") and the lack of childcare ("child care is hard to find and cost a ton of money").

There were two places where survey respondents conveyed alternate ideas in their open-ended responses—themes not adequately captured by the closed-ended questions. First, open-ended responses coded as culture focused not on low expectations among women but, rather, on cultural expectations (among men as well) that women ought to devote their time to caring for children or that men should dominate in the economic sphere. Second, in the choice category, many respondents stated matter-of-factly, and sometimes defensively, that women choose to stay home with children. One annoyed respondent said: "Maybe they like to be stay at home Mom's raising their own children. What a concept." Still other choice responses suggested that women knowingly select into lower-earning fields for a variety of reasons.

Turning to unequal economic outcomes between Black and Latino Americans and White Americans, discrimination was again the most popular category (21 percent of all answers in this domain), although these answers were not as heterogeneous or detailed as those in response to female–male inequality. Many participants simply wrote "racism," "prejudice," or "discrimination." Respondents thinking about racial inequality conveyed more unusual and varied answers within the also popular access to opportunity, choices, and culture categories. With respect to choices or effort level, one of the most common themes was the belief that many Latinos and/or Hispanics refuse to assimilate or learn English. In the culture and socialization category, many people wrote that single-parent homes or a lack of strong role models holds young people back, especially in Black households. Finally, in the access to opportunity category, a number of respondents mentioned the importance of being born into poverty or affluence. While all of these responses were coded into one of the five standard categories of explanation, they make clear how substantively varied causal attributions can be when people speak in their own voice.

Next, let us consider rural versus urban inequality. Here, survey respondents overwhelmingly mentioned a lack of access to opportunity. In fact, this was the single most frequent type of response in the entire open-ended section, with a remarkable 39 percent of the sample mentioning it. Most of these answers were similar to the relevant closed-ended narrative: the vast majority of individuals said that rural areas did not have enough jobs, or at least not enough well-paying ones, and a smaller proportion mentioned poor schools. There was a close corollary in specific mentions of a lack of transportation options available to rural residents. These answers make clear that many Americans recognize and are concerned about geographic inequality.

That said, a sizable minority of the open-ended explanations for rural–

urban inequality included unexpected content. These responses were united in pushing back against the negative implications of designating rural people as low income. Over twenty respondents rejected the premise of the rural–urban inequality question by pointing out that, because the cost of living was lower in rural areas, income differences with urban areas were inconsequential. Elsewhere, some reinterpreted the normative upshot of the Protestant work ethic: nearly half of respondents who argued that differences in people's choices or work ethic explained rural–urban inequality put a positive spin on this attribution. Many said that some people chose to live in rural areas because they preferred a less stressful environment, even if well-paying jobs were fewer. Others argued that rural people rejected materialism or placed a greater emphasis on family or community. As one respondent wrote: "People in rural areas are not as obsessed with money and keeping up with the Jones. They are more down to earth and family oriented." This positive spin mirrored some respondents' defense of women's average lower incomes. Note that these creative reevaluations of some Americans' lower earnings were not found in discussions of Black and Latino Americans' resources.

Qualitative explanations for White versus Asian American inequality were even more distinctive. Across the categories of explanation, respondents were much more likely than elsewhere to focus on the higher-achieving group: Asian Americans. Throughout, people focused on the perception that Asian Americans are smarter, or at least more skilled in high-paying industries, and are harder working than White Americans. (Mention of intrinsic traits was most common in this domain of economic inequality.) Many respondents argued that Asian American culture, especially as inculcated within families, encouraged achievement in school and hard work in general, helping Asian Americans get ahead. For example, one person wrote: "Asian American family culture tends to expect perfection and high achievement out of their children, so the kids work harder than their white counterparts." Other responses rooted an orientation toward achievement and hard work in either personal choices or characteristics. One choice-oriented answer reads as follows: "Because Asians dedicate themselves to learning and actually work hard to make there life better." A small portion of respondents did not hold back from criticizing White Americans. Some of those criticisms simply inverted the praise given elsewhere to Asian Americans, such as this comment about White Americans:

"Lazier and not as smart!" A notable subtheme indicated that White Americanss were falling behind because they felt "entitled"—this exact word, or variants of it, was used by ten respondents. Although not a well-established aspect of partisan rhetoric, at least at present, these comments reflect a common belief among survey respondents that, whether due to culture, hard work, or skill, Asian Americans are a model minority.[54]

These substantive responses can help us interpret findings from the prior section on salience. They may explain why explanations related to choices and effort emerged more often in the open-ended responses than in the closed-ended ones. In short, many respondents employed this narrative in a neutral or even positive manner in their open-ended comments, in opposition to the more derogatory wording of the closed-ended item about work ethics. The qualitative responses also help explain why culture and socialization was a more popular narrative for White–Asian American inequality in the open-ended portion than in the closed-ended one. In this instance, the narrow wording of the closed-ended explanation (about cultures with "low expectations") did not capture many respondents' positive ideas about Asian American culture.

Conclusion

While the bulk of scholarship on Americans' beliefs about economic inequality has advanced the perspective that the United States is a nation committed to believing the American Dream is real, the data from the two original surveys introduced in this chapter tells a different story: when thinking about unequal economic outcomes in general, explanations that blamed society were just as popular as those that blamed individuals (and were considerably more popular if we consider the unpopular innate intelligence narrative). Skepticism about the American Dream grew when people were asked about Black and Latino Americans' and women's lower average earnings and wealth. Although scholars have for some time noted broadly sympathetic views toward women in the workplace, past scholarship has almost uniformly found much more derogatory beliefs about Black Americans. The received wisdom that Americans tend to be not only hard on the poor but also especially hard on racial minorities appears to be out of date. The belief that a lower-earning social group does not work as hard as others—and faces few external barriers to success—was most common when people considered why White Americans earned less than Asian Americans.

These aggregate results are not the end of the story, however. There is a lot going on beneath the hood. Some prior scholars have suggested that many people hold consistent attributional styles. Others have argued that individuals are often ambivalent, holding multiple conflicting beliefs simultaneously. I find evidence for both points of view. Someone with an unusually strong commitment to a particular causal explanation in one circumstance tends to be unusually committed to that same belief in a different circumstance. We observe a different kind of consistency when examining families of attributions. The clearest such pattern is a positive correlation among societal explanations for inequality (access to high-quality schools and jobs or discrimination) and a negative correlation between these explanations and a belief in the importance of hard work. Or, at least, this is true when survey respondents considered economic inequality in general, between women and men, or between Black and Latino Americans and White Americans. When rural or White Americans' lower earnings were in view, responses did not fall along a clear personal responsibility versus unequal opportunity continuum. The reason for this patterning and un-patterning may stem from the fact that political leaders, especially in the Democratic Party, have frequently discussed the more salient inequalities in a consistent and stylized way and ignored the less salient inequalities.

Finally, as many survey methodologists counsel, qualitative evidence often helps to better understand the quantitative evidence. The qualitative data discussed in this chapter—free responses to four open-ended questions—bears this out. This data mostly reassures us that the five closed-ended explanatory statements on which I rely provide a reasonable summary of common American explanations for inequality. Most respondents indicated they could not think of alternate explanations or doubled down on those already provided. One possible oversight is omitting a policy and politics category in the closed-ended responses; however, open-ended answers related to this theme bore much resemblance to the hard work category. The open-ended responses also provided reassurance that answers to the closed-ended items reflected true points of view, as opposed to acquiescence or social desirability, because the relative popularity of the main categories of explanation tended to be similar whether respondents were answering a closed- or open-ended question.

That said, the open-ended responses were by no means redundant with the closed-ended ones. First, the qualitative responses conveyed the complexity and occasional differentiation of responses even within defined categories. For example, mentions of discrimination ranged from historical to present day examples, and from individual to cultural to institutional levels. Problems with access to opportunity might involve a lack of jobs in an area, transportation difficulties, or a lack of money to pay for education. The culture category, perhaps not surprisingly, was especially varied. Respondents pointed to the importance of cultural expectations, norms, and biases within families, social groups, and society at large. Sometimes open-ended responses differed enough in theme or tone relative to the closed-ended item that they conveyed opposite normative or political implications. For example, respondents who attributed inequality between the sexes and between geographic areas to the choices people make or to their effort often interpreted these things as normatively benign and even positive. With respect to unequal economic outcomes between White and Asian Americans, cultural narratives overwhelmingly complimented the higher-earning group as opposed to disparaging the lower-earning group. For this reason, there is a particular mismatch between the closed- and open-ended versions of this narrative.

Finally, the open-ended portion also provides us with a test of the salience, or importance, of the individual narratives. Among the qualitative responses, discrimination stood out as especially dominant when people considered the reasons for female–male inequality. Similarly, lack of access to opportunities drew an overwhelming number of responses regarding rural–urban inequality. Compared with the closed-ended responses, the open-ended responses suggest that people may differentiate much more among the various attributions in terms of strength of feeling.

There is much more to explore as we seek to understand Americans' heterogeneous beliefs about what drives economic inequality. In the next two chapters, I explore demographic and political divides underlying Americans' causal attributions, especially those that hold society or individuals responsible for economic inequality.

CHAPTER 5

Demographic Divides over Explanations for Socioeconomic Inequality

> I learned to cry at all funerals, and I didn't know who was dead. I had been inculcated with the idea that something very valuable has passed. . . . Someone has gone. You'd hear people say: He could have been this or she could have been this if she just had a chance.
>
> —Vernon Jarrett, from Studs Terkel's *American Dreams* (1980)

IN THE PREVIOUS chapter, we examined how the public in general explains unequal economic outcomes. Americans are far from persuaded that the American Dream is real. Survey respondents ascribed inequalities to differences in individual effort but also to discrimination and a lack of educational and job opportunities. We also saw that people tended to individualize inequality when considering economic inequality in general but did so considerably less when they sought to explain unequal economic outcomes across social groups. Innate explanations were especially unpopular.

However, this on-average portrait masks major divisions within the public. Chapter 4 also demonstrated that many people have attributional styles when it comes to explanations for economic inequality. Those who endorsed one type of explanation in one instance were more likely than others to use that same explanation again, even in quite different circumstances. We also saw that Americans can be grouped according to their general tendency to view economic inequality as the result of unequal opportunities or variation in personal responsibility. American Dream believers emphasize the importance of work ethic and deny that external barriers—like discrimination or a lack of access to education and jobs—hold people back. American Dream skeptics worry about discrimination or access to educa-

https://doi.org/10.7758/trap6910.4798

tion and do not believe that work ethics have much of an impact on inequality. These patterns were evident when I asked respondents to explain economic inequality in general, inequality between Black and Latino and White Americans, and inequality between women and men. These patterns were missing, however, when people considered why rural residents earn less than urban ones or why White Americans earn less than Asian Americans. In these instances, beliefs about socioeconomic inequality were less organized at the individual level.

The general question raised in this chapter is whether attributional styles vary systematically with individuals' demographic characteristics. I consider people's age, education level, level of religiosity, place of residence (rural or urban), income, racial or ethnic identity, and sex. I consider these characteristics before partisanship—discussed in the next chapter—for several reasons. First, for decades, social scientists have given demographic variables the most attention in their studies of explanations for inequality. Any systematic study of this topic should engage seriously with such research, including the theoretical frameworks that seek to explain why demographic traits may influence economic narratives. Second, demographic variables are useful to establish a kind of baseline for what typical effect sizes look like as we explore possible causes of Americans' beliefs about inequality and opportunity. Third, every demographic characteristic analyzed, except perhaps income, is at least moderately correlated with either Democratic or Republican partisan identification.[1] We must take stock of these relationships in conjunction with a study of partisan differences.

Demographic factors could influence people's explanations for economic inequality for at least three reasons. First, as referenced in the opening quote from Studs Terkel's *American Dreams*, these characteristics could signal distinct subcultures into which a person has been socialized. Culture is, of course, not a monolith. Any nation's culture is heterogeneous and sometimes internally contradictory. The specific cultural elements with which a person becomes familiar will vary according to their social context. Although people tend to know a lot about a nation's heterogeneous culture, they tend to use or act on only those elements with which they are intimately familiar and, therefore, comfortable.[2] These pieces of culture, represented as scripts or schemas in people's minds, affect how they interpret the world, including inequality.[3] Another way of looking at this is through the lens of within-group influence or social network theory—peer-to-peer influence within social groups and networks is deeply influential on attitudes and beliefs.[4]

Second, a person's demographic characteristics will reflect different experiences in the world that may influence their beliefs about inequality.[5] To state the obvious, people with low incomes or who are a part of lower-income groups observe economic hardship and external barriers to success firsthand. Those who are high income or who are a part of higher-income groups observe less economic hardship and fewer barriers, especially given increasing social isolation among the affluent.[6] This may lead to divergent views about the causes and fairness of inequality, with greater affluence associated with more optimism about the American Dream.[7]

Third, research in psychology on the origins of people's causal attributions has found evidence for a variety of psychological biases underlying them. Generally speaking, people are more likely to voice explanations for inequalities that reflect well on themselves and the groups to which they belong, and that reflect comparatively poorly on others, especially out-groups.[8] For example, people are prone to attribute internal causes (such as ability) to in-group success and external causes (like assistance from others) to out-group success. A related framework, social dominance theory, argues that dominant groups—for example, White people, men, and those with high incomes—are consistently more likely to blame individuals and groups with few resources for their economic and other difficulties.[9] That being said, marginalized groups do not always react in kind (by excusing their own difficulties or by arguing that dominant groups do not deserve their success). This may be due to an internalization of negative societal judgments,[10] or as system justification theory asserts, a coping mechanism to reduce anxiety stemming from the belief that the world is unjust.[11]

Any—or all—of these three mechanisms could contribute to a body of common knowledge within a social group about the causes of disparate economic outcomes.

In this chapter, I develop these expectations further, drawing on literature from across the social sciences. Then, with data from the two Explanations for Inequality & Politics surveys, I examine how differences emerge. In the end, I conclude two key things about demographic divides over inequality. First, among the characteristics considered in this chapter, educational attainment and religiosity have the most consistent associations with the outcome variables—in opposite directions. These findings suggest that cultural scripts associated with major societal institutions play an important part in shaping Americans' beliefs about inequality. Second, race, ethnicity, and sex are also associated with beliefs about inequality. Response patterns reveal particular sensitivity to identity-relevant inequalities, suggesting the influence of the unique experiences of social groups or some form of biased cognition or prejudice in these instances.

Demographic Divides

Age

Economic beliefs are likely to vary according to age for many reasons. Parents appear to have the most influence over young people's political and social views.[12] At the same time, a person's birth cohort or generation also has an impact.[13] Teenagers and young adults are especially influenced by the events in their daily lives, be it a recession, social movements, war, or charismatic political figures.[14] As with any social group, people of a similar age also tend to influence one another via peer influence, especially if they recognize themselves as a distinct generation.[15]

Recent economic and political events suggest that younger Americans today are more skeptical than older Americans that the economy is meritocratic. Economic inequality has reached historic highs in recent years. The United States experienced a very serious recession in 2008 and 2009.[16] At the time my surveys were conducted, millennial Americans (born between 1981 and 1996, aged twenty to thirty-five in 2016) earned less, had accumulated less wealth, and were less likely to own a home than prior generations at similar ages.[17] The millennial and Gen Z (born between 1997 and 2012) generations have also come of age during a time of political tumult and salient protest. Although some recent political movements have been conservative (such as the Tea Party), most have leaned left (for example, Occupy Wall Street or Black Lives Matter). These and a range of other factors—including the presidency of Donald Trump and the racial and ethnic diversity among younger cohorts—led young people to favor the Democratic Party over the Republican Party by a substantial margin, at least through the 2000s and 2010s.[18]

Life-cycle effects may also influence people's causal attributions, with people changing in predictable ways as they age.[19] A common saying (perhaps falsely attributed to Winston Churchill) is, "If you're not a liberal at twenty, you have no heart. If you're not a conservative at forty, you have no brain." Researchers have confirmed that people tend to become more conservative as they age, although the general rule favors stability over change.[20] In a rare study of causal attributions by age, Freda Blanchard-Fields finds that older people were somewhat more inclined than younger people to employ dispositional attributions—the belief that a person's characteristics, as opposed to circumstances, lead to an outcome.[21]

Overall, I expect younger Americans interviewed in 2016 and 2018 for the two EIPS to be more skeptical than older Americans of the reality of the American Dream.

Education

Educational differences represent another possible influence on people's explanations for inequality. Educational institutions are, first and foremost, a site of cultural socialization.[22] Schools provide direct instruction to students, and instructors model and enforce norms of behavior. In a more informal socialization process, students likewise bring their perspectives to schools and share them with others.[23] While early research on political socialization in educational institutions produced mixed results,[24] evidence of the powerful effects that attending school has on political attitudes has accumulated over time. However, to state the obvious, education is most influential with respect to fact perceptions—as opposed to values or policy preferences—as schools are designed primarily for the purpose of sharing knowledge.[25]

Most of the evidence for politically relevant socialization comes from studies of higher education. But in which direction should we expect influence? Do schools encourage belief in, or skepticism of, meritocracy? On the one hand, the notion of a liberal arts education, championed by many colleges and universities, is premised on the idea of open-minded consideration of diverse ideas and tolerance, a perspective associated with

social liberalism.[26] Several empirical studies support the idea of a liberalizing influence of higher education,[27] especially surrounding equal opportunity and criticism of discrimination.[28] Such liberalizing effects of
attending college may have grown in the United States in recent years, as
college and university faculties have become more liberal and Democratic.[29] Socializing effects may continue beyond university walls, as beliefs popular among academics spread among the "Brahmin left"—highly
educated liberals.[30]

That said, the effects of education are not so straightforward. Consider
that schools, by their nature, emphasize meritocracy. They encourage students to work hard and obey the rules and often track them according to
perceived ability. Private schools are especially likely to champion meritocracy—as an important societal value that has been attained and ought to
be maintained.[31] An emphasis on meritocracy, especially among highly
selective colleges, is likely driven in part by colleges' desire to justify their
societal function of sorting young people into visible levels of achievement
that are predictive of future success.[32] Thus, studies that have found a con-
servatizing effect of education unsurprisingly have found it in the economic
domain. In her study of the UK education system, Paula Surridge finds that
increasing education tends to influence students in a more economically
conservative direction, increasing their belief that economic inequality is
fair.[33] Tali Mendelberg and colleagues find that college campuses with a
concentration of affluent students tend to influence students' economic
attitudes in a conservative direction.[34]

We might observe different beliefs about inequality by level of education
for reasons other than socialization. On balance, people with more education will be more capable intellectually, more driven, and more interested
in learning than others.[35] (Of course, many other factors play a role in educational achievement in the United States, most notably whether one can
afford college.) These traits conceivably push in opposite directions: those
who are more capable and driven may be inclined to see the world in meritocratic terms;[36] however, greater curiosity and the better grasp of complexity that comes with learning are likely associated with a relative preference for external (societal) over internal (dispositional) attributions.

In sum, prior research on the association between education levels and
people's beliefs about meritocracy points in opposite directions.

Religion and Religiosity

Scholars have long recognized the relevance of religion and religiosity to how a person thinks about the causes of material success and inequalities in economic outcomes. In *The Protestant Ethic and the Spirit of Capitalism*, Max Weber argues that early Protestantism encouraged the values of hard work and self-discipline.[37] Despite this history, evidence linking religious denominations to attributional beliefs is mixed.[38] In the U.S. context, null results may stem from the fact that a Protestant belief system was established early in the nation's history and adopted by newcomers, regardless of their religious background. Indeed, Weber argues that such spreading of Protestant beliefs and ideals within nations was common, ultimately doing more to create differences between nations than within them.

A second way to consider the relevance of religion is to deemphasize individual denominations in favor of commonalities across all religions, such as the tendency to be more (or less) fundamentalist.[39] Matthew Hunt finds that religious fundamentalists are more inclined toward meritocratic explanations for Black–White differences in economic success.[40] On a related note, the degree of religiosity, or religious commitment,[41] may spur attributional differences between people. Frederick Solt and colleagues find that the most economically unequal nations are also the most deeply religious.[42] And Kenneth Scheve and David Stasavage find that highly religious people are more opposed to redistributive spending than others.[43] At least two possible reasons underlie these associations. The first is that religion may dampen criticism of the prevailing socioeconomic order. Karl Marx famously proclaimed that "religion is the opium of the people."[44] Some contemporary scholars argue that religion comforts individuals experiencing distress, providing them with psychic rewards, including knowledge of a happy afterlife.[45] A second interpretation, at least in the U.S. context, is an explicit marriage between Christianity and capitalism encouraged by the Republican Party.[46] The long-standing popularity of the prosperity gospel within Protestantism, a motivational belief system similar to that described by Weber arguing that God rewards the righteous, may have encouraged this fusion.[47]

For these reasons, religious faith, at least in the United States, is likely associated with a faith in a meritocratic economy and the American Dream.

Rurality

For many years, political scientists studying U.S. politics considered geographic regions to be very important in influencing a person's political views, especially if one lived in the South. However, this view has given way to recognition of the relatively greater differences in political attitudes between rural and urban dwellers, with the former being much more conservative and Republican than the latter.[48]

What aspects of rural life might draw a person to the political right? Some scholars argue that rural areas are culturally distinct for reasons related to their low population density and distance from city centers; this may foster personal autonomy.[49] Rural residents with more progressive values, or who have identity characteristics that put them out-of-step with rural norms (such as being LGBTQ), often leave rural areas for urban ones.[50] Other scholars argue—somewhat counterintuitively—that rural areas reject generous government-sponsored social welfare because they see it as siphoning off tax dollars to the advantage of those in urban areas,[51] or as providing assistance to the undeserving.[52]

In short, despite rural America's declining economic fortunes, prior research suggests that residents of rural areas may be more likely to embrace the notion that the economy is meritocratic. However, this of course may not be the case when respondents are specifically asked about the reasons for rural–urban inequality.

Dominant and Marginalized Groups: Income or Wealth, Race, and Sex

Scholars have long argued that people with power and wealth in a society will be more likely than others to say that the societal status quo is fair.[53] Should this be true, the reason is not mysterious: individuals and groups at the top of societal hierarchies gain materially, psychologically, and socially from the justification of existing inequalities. If they can persuade themselves that the status quo is fair, this enables a satisfying sense of superiority. If they can persuade others that the status quo is fair, then they are more likely to be respected and less likely to face calls for the redistribution of wealth or power. Many studies offer empirical support for the idea that highly affluent people are more likely to say the economic system is meritocratic.[54] Dominant groups—especially men and White Americans—

are more likely than others to favor meritocratic explanations for inequality as well.[55]

Given the great attention social science scholars pay to this subject, we should spend some time to understand its theorized underpinnings. Jim Sidanius and Felicia Pratto argue that social hierarchies are enforced via discrimination buttressed by "legitimizing myths," which "provide moral and intellectual justification for the social practices that distribute social value within the social system."[56] Legitimizing myths are "hierarchy en-hancing" (HE-LM) if they justify the current social order. According to Sidanius and Pratto:

> In contemporary U.S. and Western cultures, among the most important of HE-LMs are the notions of individual responsibility, the Protestant work ethic, internal attributions of the misfortunes of the poor, and the set of ideas and assumptions collectively referred to as "political conservatism." What all these ideas and doctrines have in common is the notion that each individual occupies that position along the social status continuum that he or she has earned and therefore deserves. From these perspectives then, particular con-figurations of the hierarchical social system are fair, legitimate, natural, and perhaps even inevitable.[57]

Notice the overlap between meritocratic causal attributions for socioeco-nomic inequality—both effort and innate characteristics—and what these authors consider to be the "most important" of the hierarchy-enhancing legitimizing myths.[58] Although these myths are often widely embraced in highly unequal societies, they are expected to be especially popular among dominant groups for self-interested reasons.

Sidanius and Pratto build their theory in part on an older theoretical framework called social identity theory, associated most closely with the research of Henri Tajfel and John Turner.[59] A person's social identity is both a sense of belonging to a group and a sense that the group forms a part of the individual's personal identity.[60] Tajfel and Turner famously demon-strate that most people are consistently biased in favor of the groups with which they identify. At root, social identities are powerful because they are linked to self-esteem. People are strongly motivated to see themselves, and therefore the social groups intimately linked to the self, in a positive light. Given this, we would expect people to tend to adopt causal attributions that reflect well on themselves as individuals—for example, attributing personal or in-group failures to external causes and others' failures to internal ones.[61] Social identity theory suggests that this bias will occur to some degree regardless of whether one is in a dominant or subordinate societal position.[62]

Not all scholars see people's beliefs about inequality as self-serving, at least in the straightforward senses previously described. System justification theory suggests that disadvantaged groups will, counterintuitively, be drawn to meritocracy. John Jost and coauthors argue that seeing the world as inherently unfair is deeply stressful.[63] Thus, marginalized people may be motivated more than others, or at least more than one would expect, to believe in a just world.[64] This tendency is likely greater in countries with a meritocratic culture because the relevant narratives are readily available.[65]

Finally, while scholars tend to posit group differences in causal attributions as stemming from some combination of culture and cognitive biases, they possibly stem from a direct and unbiased rendering of different economic and social experiences. Affluent individuals and groups will necessarily observe less economic struggle and fewer hurdles to success, such as low-quality schools, than those with low incomes. Racial minorities and women will have more direct experience with discrimination than White people and men. Black and Native Americans have been especially harmed by historical discrimination. Jennifer Hochschild finds that Black Americans were far more pessimistic than White Americans about the fairness of the economy.[66]

The foregoing points to two possible patterns of belief with respect to income, race, and sex. A social dominance perspective suggests that these characteristics will be consistently linked to explanations for unequal economic outcomes—with more privileged groups tending to be American Dream believers—regardless of what inequality is under consideration. The social identity and experiential perspectives suggest that clear explanatory patterns emerge only when people are considering economic inequalities linked to their own social group.

Investigating Demographic Divides over the Causes of Inequality

In the remainder of the chapter, I investigate associations between these demographic characteristics and specific explanations for unequal economic outcomes in five domains: economic inequality in general, between women and men, between Black and Latino and White Americans, between White Americans and Asian Americans, and between rural and urban residents.

Most of my focus is on three narratives: lack of access to education and jobs, discrimination, and lack of work ethic. These explanations for inequality are most clearly linked to judgments of personal or societal responsibility (that is, unequal opportunities). They are also commonly found in political debate. And, as seen in the last chapter, they are consistently correlated with one another, at least in more politically scripted domains of inequality. Finally, these items have the advantage of being "signed" in opposite directions, with the first two blaming society and the third blaming individuals. This helps to address possible survey response bias.

At points, I examine these attributional beliefs one by one; more often, I rely on a measurement index original to this study that I call the *responsibility–unequal opportunity index*. This index averages survey respondents' beliefs about access to schools and jobs,[67] discrimination, and lack of hard work (reverse scored). I present three different versions of the index derived from the 2016 data, one for each of the three inequality domains: unequal economic opportunity (for lower earners in general), unequal economic opportunity for women, and unequal economic opportunity for Black and Latino Americans.[68] The latter two indexes are also available in the 2018 survey. Because individuals' responses regarding less politically salient inequalities (that is, rural–urban and White–Asian American disparities) were less organized along these lines, I do not use the summary index when analyzing beliefs about these inequalities.

The distributions for the three indexes from 2016 are available in figure 5.1. Values range from 1 (someone who strongly agreed that some people don't work as hard and strongly disagreed that discrimination and access to education or jobs matter) to 6 (someone who strongly disagreed that some people don't work as hard and strongly agreed that discrimination and access to education or jobs matter). The distribution for the unequal opportunity index is close to symmetrical around its mean (3.6). However, the other indexes are clearly skewed toward the belief that opportunity is unequal, especially when considering unequal outcomes between women and men. The means are 4.2 for unequal opportunity for women and 3.8 for unequal opportunity for Black and Latino Americans.

Figure 5.1 Frequency Distributions of the Three Unequal Economic Opportunity Indexes (2016)

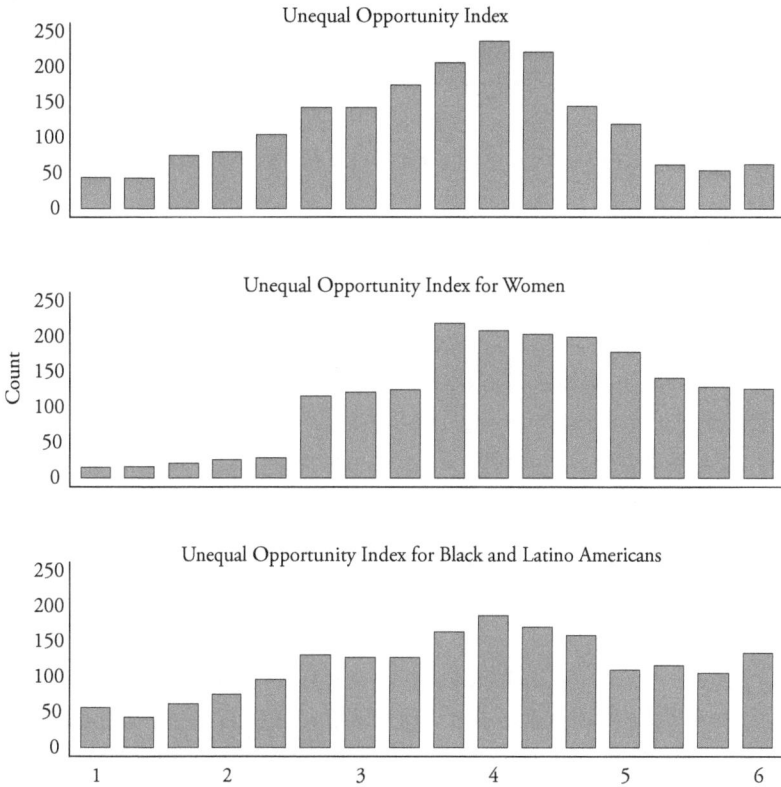

Source: Author's calculations using 2016 EIPS data.

I examine patterns of attributional beliefs according to household income, sex, race and ethnicity, rurality, religiosity, highest level of education, and age. All variables were self-reported except for rurality. The original survey question on income asked respondents to report their approximate income by identifying the income range into which their household income fell (for example, $30,000–$40,000 or $120,000–$140,000). To create a near-continuous variable, I then grouped respondents by approximate income decile within the sample, with the final variable including ten levels to denote each decile.[69] Respondent sex was provided by YouGov and is the respondent's answer to the question: "Are you male or female?" Race or ethnicity, also provided by YouGov, is the respondent's answer to the question: "What racial or ethnic group best describes you?" Options included White, Black, Hispanic, Asian, Native American, Middle Eastern, mixed, and other.[70] Given small sample sizes of racial and ethnic minorities, I focus these analyses on Black, Hispanic, and White Americans. The rurality variable is a measure of population density within the respondent's zip code, with lack of density scoring highest.[71] Jonathan Rodden argues that density is the best method of distinguishing rural from urban areas.[72] I measured religious commitment by taking the average of the following three items, made available by YouGov: How important is religion in your life? Aside from weddings and funerals, how often do you attend religious services? And, outside of attending religious services, how often do you pray? This index is similar to that used by Robert Putnam and David Campbell.[73] Highest level of education is a five-level variable: no high school degree, high school degree, some college or two-year college degree, four-year college degree, and graduate degree. YouGov recorded age at the time of the survey based on respondents' year of birth.

Examining Demographic Differences in Beliefs

We analyze these relationships with the assistance of multiple linear regression. This allows us to assess the association between explanations for inequality and each of the demographic variables independently—holding the others constant. Statistical controls are important because many of these demographic groups overlap considerably. One of the best examples of this is the relationship between education and income. On average, Americans with a college degree earn much more than those with only a high school degree, and those with an advanced degree earn even more.[74] While we might be interested in the views of highly educated people in general, when interpreting the meaning of differences in beliefs between more- and less-educated people, we must keep in mind the association between education and income. If people who have graduated from college or received advanced degrees have unique views on inequality, it may be due to either their education level or their greater income or wealth. In this example, income is what is known as a potential confounder. Because it is associated with both the predictor (education) and the outcome variable (beliefs about inequality), we cannot be certain whether a correlation between education and beliefs about inequality stems from education itself or from income. To understand better the unique influence of education on people's beliefs about the origins of inequality, we must control income, or hold it constant, removing its influence. The same goes for the influence of income as well— to understand its unique association with beliefs about inequality, we must control for education.

Other such examples abound. Rural Americans are disproportionately older, religious, and White. White Americans tend to have higher incomes and are more likely to go to college than Black and Latino Americans. Older people tend to earn more simply by virtue of being employed longer, etcetera. By controlling for various demographic variables, we can better isolate patterns of beliefs associated with specific social groups and characteristics, as opposed to correlated phenomena. That said, we might be interested in assessing patterns without statistical controls to understand patterns among whole groups of people, with all their diversity and complexity. I note where bivariate associations between a particular demographic variable and beliefs about inequality diverge from the regression findings reported herein.

Figure 5.2 displays results from three statistical models. The three unequal opportunity indexes were regressed onto income, sex (female), racial and ethnic identification (Black and Hispanic versus White), rurality, religiosity, education, and age. (Table A.1 displays the precise regression estimates.) The coefficients and 95 percent confidence intervals from these regressions are indicated. All explanatory variables have been placed on the 0 to 1 interval to ease interpretation and comparison. The outcome variables range from 1 to 6, reflecting the fact that each of the three questions in each measurement index includes six possible responses (strongly agree, agree, slightly agree, slightly disagree, disagree, strongly disagree). The coefficients to the right of the vertical line (at 0) represent positive relationships between the explanatory (demographic) and outcome (explanations for inequality) variables. The coefficients to the left of the vertical line represent negative relationships. Coefficients with confidence intervals that cross the vertical line are not statistically significant at conventional levels ($p < .05$). A coefficient of 1 would mean that respondents with characteristics that place them at the top (1) of the explanatory variable score higher than those at the bottom (0) of the variable on the outcome variable by one full answer level (for example, agree versus slightly agree). A coefficient of −1 would mean that

Figure 5.2 Coefficient Plot of Unequal Opportunity Indexes Regressed onto Demographic Characteristics (2016)

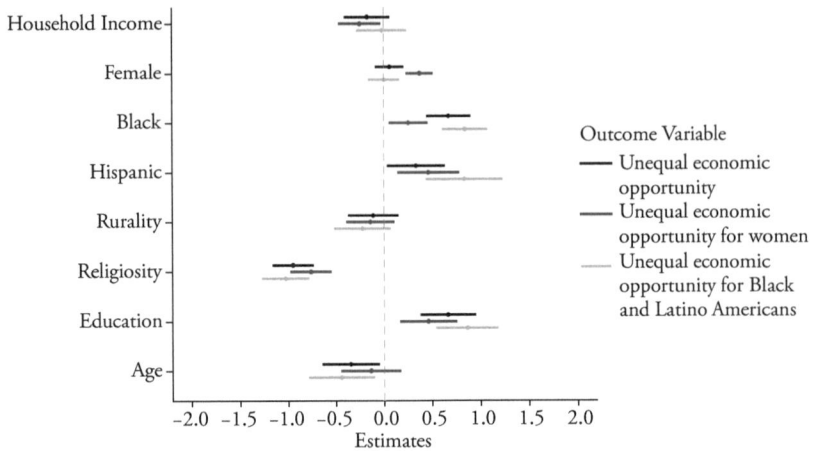

Source: Author's calculations using 2016 EIPS data.
Note: Coefficient plots with estimates from three separate linear regressions, with unequal economic opportunity, unequal economic opportunity for women, and unequal economic opportunity for Black and Latino Americans as outcome variables. Explanatory variables are scored 0 to 1 and outcome variables are scored 1 to 6.

respondents at the top of an explanatory variable score lower than those at the bottom of the variable on the outcome by one level. These differences are on-average and hold the other explanatory variables constant.

Beginning with income: respondents with higher incomes scored lower on the unequal opportunity indexes for economic and sex inequality (but not racial inequality), although only the latter is statistically significant. These associations are surprisingly small given the many reasons why higher-income people are less likely than others to say that they perceive unequal opportunity and in light of prior research on the topic. When the unequal economic opportunity index is disaggregated into its component parts, income is most strongly associated with the belief that hard work leads to economic success. One limitation of these analyses is that the data does not allow for analysis of the highly affluent, given few such individuals will be captured in a representative survey of the American public. Turning to differences between men and women, an association arises only for beliefs regarding sex inequality; women were considerably more likely than men to say that women face unequal opportunity. The fact that this pattern appears only for female–male economic inequality suggests that respondent experiences or identities linked to their sex have influenced their responses. The pattern for Black and Hispanic respondents is somewhat different: these two groups were more likely than White respondents to see unequal opportunity across the board; however, differences were sharpest when considering unequal opportunity for Black and Latino Americans specifically, for which coefficients are close to 1.

Those living in rural areas scored somewhat lower on the unequal economic inequality indexes than others, but the coefficients do not reach the standard level of statistical significance. (This is one clear dimension for which results change in the multiple regression analysis; rurality is more strongly, negatively, associated with belief in unequal opportunity when assessed alone, without controls.) Religiosity was strongly associated with lower scores on the indexes. Those who expressed the most religiosity were approximately one level lower than the least religious on the unequal opportunity indexes. Education also appeared to be influential, in the other direction, with coefficients ranging from .5 to close to 1. Finally, older people scored lower (and young people higher) on the unequal opportunity indexes overall, especially when considering unequal outcomes in general and between racial groups.

For those interested in examining differences between the coefficients for these indexes more precisely, see appendix figure A.11. In this figure, each person's score on the unequal economic opportunity index is subtracted from their score on the unequal opportunity for women index and, separately, the unequal opportunity for Black and Latino Americans index. This generates two variables that indicate whether a person is more or less likely to blame society (versus individuals) when considering inequality by sex and race as opposed to economic inequality throughout the population. Here, women stand out as more concerned about female–male economic inequality than economic inequality in general (and, alternatively, men less concerned). This approach also makes clear that Hispanic Americans, not Black Americans, were unusually pessimistic about racial and ethnic inequality compared to economic inequality generally. Black Americans, on the other hand, were unusually unconcerned about women earning less than men. More-educated people stand out as seeing Black and Latino Americans as facing more barriers to success than lower-income people in general and as seeing women as facing fewer obstacles than others. Finally,

Figure 5.3 Coefficient Plots of Explanations for Inequality Regressed onto Demographic Characteristics (2018)

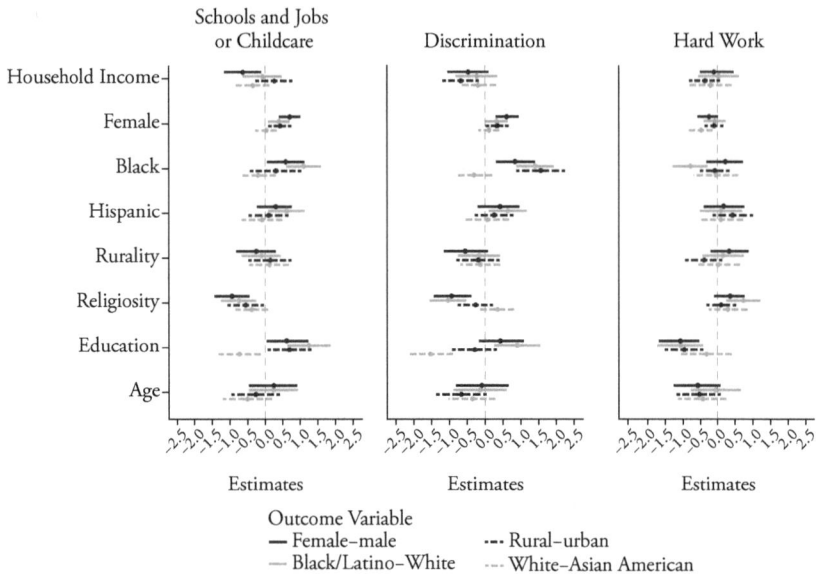

Source: Author's calculations using 2018 EIPS data.

relative to young people, older Americans were uniquely concerned about women's opportunity compared to lower income people in general.

It is useful to expand the analysis in two ways. First, we can examine specific explanations for inequality (as opposed to the indexes) to check for consistency, or inconsistency, across index components. Second, we can incorporate the two new domains of inequality introduced in the second survey: rural versus urban and White versus Asian American inequality. Figure 5.3 displays results for the schools and jobs (or childcare), discrimination, and hard work explanations regressed onto the demographic variables, this time for four separate inequality domains (indicated in the key). Note that confidence intervals are necessarily wider in these analyses because the outcome variables are single items, not indexes, and the sample size of the 2018 survey is much smaller.

Overall, there is much continuity with the prior analysis. Black, female, and more-educated Americans were more likely to embrace the idea that societal inequalities (discrimination or access to education, jobs, or child-care) negatively affect lower-earning groups, and religious people were more likely to reject this idea. For the most part, these differences emerged as people considered rural–urban inequality. These patterns, however, disappear or reverse when people were asked about White versus Asian American inequality. Highly educated people (relative to the less educated) stand out for their belief that White Americans do not face discrimination or lack access to good schools and jobs.

When survey respondents considered whether different work ethics may play a role in inequality, differences were much more muted. There are two exceptions. Black Americans were less likely (and White Americans more likely) to evoke hard work for unequal outcomes between Black and Latino and White Americans, and highly educated people were also less likely to do so for all inequalities except the White–Asian American comparison (for which the finding is null).

Figure 5.4 conveys patterns for the innate ability and culture explanations. Beginning with innate explanations, highly educated and older respondents were consistently likely to reject innate explanations for inequality, meaning the less-educated and younger respondents were more likely to make these claims. The education trend likely reflects the fact that scholars today generally reject the notion that average genetic differences between the types of social groups discussed in this study contribute to differences in economic outcomes.[75] The age trend is perhaps more surprising. It may reflect growing enthusiasm for biological narratives in our genomic era, narratives that have been increasingly used to argue in favor of social equality.[76] Beyond these two sets of findings, patterns are less robust and without clear explanation: high-income people, women, Hispanics, and rural residents were somewhat less likely to agree that innate ability matters much, and Black and religious Americans were somewhat more likely to agree with this explanation. There are few clear relationships with respect to culture, although one strong result stands out—Black Americans were more likely than White Americans to say that a culture of low expectations among women holds them back economically. High-income people were also less likely (and low-income people more likely) to say this. These may be chance findings; however, if they are meaningful, they may reflect the many different interpretations survey respondents attached to the culture

Figure 5.4 Coefficient Plots of Additional Explanations for Inequality Regressed onto Demographic Characteristics (2018)

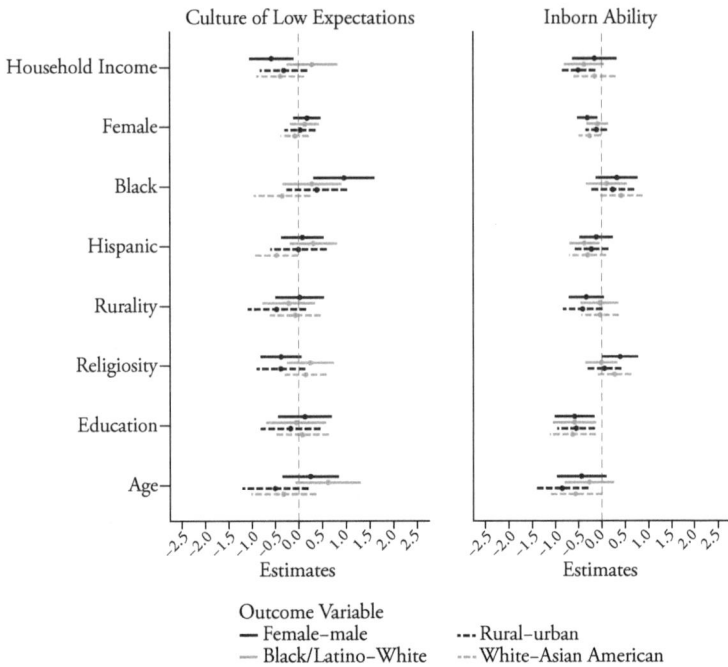

Source: Authors' calculations using 2018 EIPS data.

category (see chapter 4). Evoking culture was sometimes done in sympathy with lower-earning groups and need not be disparaging.

Conclusion

In this chapter, we have considered whether the U.S. population is divided along demographic lines over the subject of what causes inequality and, by extension, whether the nation has realized the American Dream. People from different walks of life may disagree with one another for at least three reasons: because their personal experiences relating to inequality have differed; because of self-interest, even if only psychological, in viewing the world in a way that reflects well on their in-group; or because they have been exposed to distinct cultural narratives about why unequal economic outcomes occur.

The most consistent differences were found between the more and less religious and the more and less educated. The patterns for religion and education, which push in opposite directions—with highly educated people more likely to blame society for economic inequality and highly religious people more likely to blame individuals—suggest that culture influences people's beliefs. The religiosity result was expected; however, the education result was not, given higher education's role in providing the credentials that often justify higher incomes. This finding indicates that economically progressive narratives have taken root among people with postsecondary degrees. This complicates the emerging Brahmin left thesis—that the dominance of the highly educated on the political left dampens the left's attention to economic inequality and promotes attention to social issues instead.[77] The results in this chapter indicate that education is strongly associated with endorsing structural explanations for inequality, albeit in a somewhat qualified fashion—White Americans were singled out by respondents with high levels of education as being unaffected by structural barriers to success.

We also observed differences between demographic groups that may be driven by different economic experiences and interests or, alternatively, biases associated with one's social identity. There was little support for the notion that dominant groups were more likely than marginalized groups to individualize inequality and reject structural explanations across the board. Black and Hispanic respondents (compared to White respondents) were more concerned about unequal opportunity for lower-earning groups in general but especially so for Black and Latino Americans. Female respondents were somewhat more pessimistic than men about opportunity for women specifically but not for other groups. High-income people were slightly more optimistic about the American Dream in general and for women but not for Black and Latino Americans. Younger respondents were more pessimistic about the fairness of the U.S. economy in general and for Black and Latino Americans but not for women. An important demographic exception is rural and urban respondents, who differed little from one another, at least in the regression models.

This is not the end of our investigation into societal divides over beliefs about what causes unequal economic outcomes. In the next chapter, we push into political terrain, asking how much—and in what way—partisan and other political predispositions may influence respondents' beliefs about the American Dream. Investigating demographic and political characteristics simultaneously will allow comparison of these two sets of influences. It will also allow us to see whether the demographic divides found in this chapter are an artifact of the different characteristics of the American left and right today or, rather, stand on their own as independent influences on Americans' explanations for economic inequality.

CHAPTER 6

Partisan Divides over Explanations for Socioeconomic Inequality

When you've got a government, when you've got an economy that does great for those with money and isn't doing great for everyone else, that is corruption, pure and simple. . . . We need to make structural change in our government, in our economy, and in our country.

> —Senator Elizabeth Warren at first 2020 Democratic
> presidential debate (NBC News transcript 2019)

I think it's sad that the previous administration was willing to admit that we couldn't get better than 1.9 percent growth....That assumes a pessimism about America, about the economy, about its people, about its culture that we're simply refusing to accept....We need people to go to work. If you're on food stamps, and you're able-bodied, we need you to go to work. If you're on disability insurance and you're not supposed to be—if you're not truly disabled, we need you to go back to work.

> —Mick Mulvaney, Trump administration White House budget
> director, in press briefing about 2018 presidential budget

IN THE PREVIOUS chapter, I investigated how Americans' demographic characteristics relate to their explanations for economic inequality. Conventional wisdom suggests that people tend to be acutely sensitive to their own economic circumstances—arguing that the system is meritocratic when they and the people they know are faring well and arguing that it is not meritocratic when they or many of the people they know face economic difficulties. These perceptual differences may stem from honest appraisals of disparate circumstances, psychological biases linked to self-esteem maintenance, or some combination. The data provided some evidence that race,

https://doi.org/10.7758/trap6910.8799

ethnicity, sex, and, to a lesser extent, income are associated with beliefs about whether the nation provides meritocratic abundance, in line with conventional wisdom.

That said, these associations were often substantively weak, leaving room for many other influences on beliefs about the American Dream, such as education and religiosity. Respondents with college degrees were more likely than others to be skeptical of the fairness of the economy. The highly religious were more likely than others to believe the economy to be fair. These patterns were consistent when respondents considered the reasons for unequal economic outcomes in general, as well as between women and men and Black and Latino Americans and White Americans. However, these differences diminished when people considered other socioeconomic inequalities, especially between White Americans and Asian Americans.

The findings for educational and religious differences suggest that explanations for inequality are rooted in cultural socialization at least as much as personal economic experiences or biases. I continue this line of inquiry in this chapter, investigating the relationship between Americans' partisan identifications and their explanations for inequality. Do partisan groups share distinct bodies of common knowledge about the causes of unequal economic outcomes? How varied are these causal beliefs, and do they change as different domains of economic inequality come into view?

A person's partisan identification (or *party ID* or *partisanship*) is their feeling of attachment, or belonging, to a political party.[1] In the United States, that party will nearly always be the Democratic or Republican Party. We already observed in chapter 3 that Republicans are much more likely than Democrats to believe that the U.S. economy delivers the American Dream. Democrats not only are consistently more skeptical of the fairness of the economy but also have become more skeptical in recent years. This partisan belief polarization roughly maps to changing rhetoric found within the Democratic and Republican platforms, suggesting ongoing influence between elite and lay partisans.

Yet, the data in chapter 3 does not allow us to thoroughly investigate lay partisans' explanations for unequal economic outcomes. First, they cannot tell us how consistently Democrats and Republicans disagree over whether the U.S. economy is meritocratic. We might observe at least three different patterns as we consider partisans' explanations for a wide range of inequalities. One pattern is meritocratic consistency, in which Republicans always locate the causes of inequality in people (individual explanations), and

Democrats always locate the causes of inequality in society (structural explanations), no matter the specific explanation or type of inequality in view. Much prior scholarship seems to assume consistency. Another pattern is intergroup bias, treating partisanship as one would any other social identity. Within this framework, partisans tend to locate the causes of unequal outcomes within individuals when members of their party coalition are faring well (and the out-party coalition is faring poorly) and in society when members of their coalition are faring poorly (and the out-party coalition is faring well). A final possible pattern is partisan economic ideology, a more variegated pattern that reflects specific narratives within each party and is likely generated via socialization by partisan leaders and peers. This pattern should be most evident among the most attentive partisans. They are more familiar with "what goes with what" in contemporary politics, bringing their beliefs about inequality into line with their partisanship or (more rarely) abandoning one party for the other because it better reflects their views.

Second, the data in chapter 3 sheds no light on whether the observed associations between partisanship and beliefs about the fairness of the economy are possibly driven by phenomena closely related to, but distinguishable from, partisanship. Partisans also share what political scientists call symbolic ideology, or a tendency to identify as conservatives or liberals. At least in the contemporary era, self-identified ideology tends to differentiate people according to their interest in combating socioeconomic inequality (liberalism) versus accepting it (conservatism).[2] Party identifiers also differ at least somewhat in their average levels of racial prejudice and sexism, with Republicans tending to be more prejudiced. Prior scholarship has identified racial prejudice in particular as a driver of causal attributions for socioeconomic inequality.[3]

Drawing on data from the two Explanations for Inequality & Politics surveys, I come to several conclusions about the relationship between partisanship and explanations for unequal economic outcomes. First, the findings here replicate and extend those in chapter 3. Republicans tended to be American Dream believers and Democrats American Dream skeptics. These differences emerged when people sought to explain class, race, and sex inequality and were very large, much larger than the demographic differences discussed in the prior chapter. These differences became larger over time and at higher levels of political engagement, especially beliefs about structural inequality. Yet again, whereas structural explanations for inequality were especially polarized by party, innate explanations were not. Second, drawing on the measurement of beliefs regarding additional domains of inequality, partisan differences were smaller and less consistent outside of the classic class-race-sex trio, disappearing completely when partisans considered why Asian Americans earn more and are wealthier than White Americans on average. Third, incorporating left–right ideology and social prejudice into the analyses yielded expected findings, in that respondents who were conservative and prejudiced were more likely than their counterparts to attribute inequalities to meritocratic processes. However, holding these variables constant still left substantial partisan disagreement over the causes of socioeconomic inequalities.

Each of these findings is interesting in and of itself; together, they provide further evidence that partisan rhetoric likely shapes Americans' beliefs about socioeconomic inequality. Across time and at high levels of political engagement, partisan survey respondents expressed beliefs about socioeconomic inequality that mirrored those of their party's elites. Where party elites were silent, polarization among lay partisans diminished.

Partisan Disagreements over the Causes of Inequality

An enormous amount of scholarship examines the associations between explanations for inequality and partisanship, ideology, and related concepts. The scholarly literature provides evidence for each of the three patterns of partisan disagreement over the causes of inequality described earlier: meritocratic consistency, intergroup bias, and partisan ideology. However, most studies of causal attributions suggest that partisan or ideological divisions tend to reflect meritocratic consistency: conservatives and Republicans are always more likely than others to ascribe inequality to individuals' choices and characteristics and liberals and Democrats to ascribe inequality to larger societal forces outside of individuals' control.

Meritocratic consistency assumes that people have attributional styles that they use time and again to interpret the social world.[4] Many scholars provide evidence that conservatives and liberals—defined in a variety of ways, including as symbolic ideology—have distinct attributional styles. A belief that meritocracy tends to prevail characterizes Americans on the right, and doubt about the prevalence of meritocracy characterizes those on the left.[5] This is the aforementioned ideo-attribution effect.[6] That Democrats tend to be liberal and Republicans conservative could explain why the parties differ in their beliefs about inequality. This could also in part explain the parties' growing divide over inequality: as Democrats and Republicans became increasingly sorted by ideology during the twentieth century,[7] the former grew more skeptical of the American Dream and the latter more certain of it.

The possible reasons for meritocratic consistency among conservatives and liberals are many. Some scholars argue that personality differences play a key role in shaping conservative and liberal styles of thinking. Conservatives may be less tolerant of ambiguity and more cognitively rigid and liberals more open-minded and flexible.[8] As a result, conservatives may be more attracted to simple explanations for inequality (individual as cause) and liberals may be more attracted to complex ones (factors beyond the individual as cause).[9] Or those on the left may be more empathic than those on the right.[10] As George Lakoff suggests, they may be more forgiving of mistakes, having grown up in "nurturing mother" as opposed to "strict father" homes.[11] Some scholars argue that left–right disagreements over the causes of inequality stem from ideologically motivated reasoning. Liberals may be motivated to adopt structural explanations for economic inequality as a way of justifying their interest in using government to achieve equality of outcomes for all social groups in society, and conservatives may be motivated to adopt individualizing explanations to justify their opposition to governmental redistribution and regulation.[12] Whatever the origins of ideological difference, the result— according to this line of thinking—is two rigid sets of beliefs about the origins of inequality that are strongly associated with the two major political parties.

But not all scholars find a consistent left–right divide in the public's causal attributions.[13] If people on the left and right differ in attributional style, then they should tend to evaluate various types of inequality similarly: as the result of a meritocratic system in which internal causes—effort or talents—drive inequality or as the result of an unmeritocratic system in which external causes—discrimination or unequal access to opportunity— do. Scholars possibly have created the impression of consistency, because they tend to study exactly those inequalities on which Democrats and liberals on one hand and Republicans and conservatives on the other consistently disagree—for example, why some people end up poor and others rich, or why Black Americans earn less on average than White Americans. Would this consistency disappear if scholars studied other types of inequality? Some existing scholarly evidence supports this idea. Erin Cooley and colleagues find that liberals were more likely to blame poor White people for being poor (but not poor Black people) after reading about White privilege.[14] Morgan and colleagues similarly document reversals of the ideo-attribution effect when asking people to explain problematic behavior by conservative-leaning individuals or groups.[15]

A second, less rigid, partisan pattern of attribution, intergroup bias, is contingent on whose inequality people consider. The Democratic and Republican coalitions differ significantly in demographic composition. Poor people, racial and religious minorities, and women are disproportionately likely to identify with the Democratic Party. White people, men, and rural residents are disproportionately likely to identify with the Republican Party.[16] Political scientists increasingly note that these groups are central to the formation of people's partisan identities. However, partisanship is not simply a matter of people joining the party that represents their group.[17] Rather, people's partisanship is strongly associated with their feelings of closeness to, and evaluations of, those groups they believe the parties represent. As John Kane and colleagues write: "Partisanship is not solely reliant on decisions about which party contains 'people like me.' . . . Citizens also care about which party contains 'people I like.'"[18] Feelings toward social groups are similarly associated with people's ideological identifications, conservative or liberal.[19] Ultimately, these coalition-related evaluations and identifications—positive for in-party groups and negative for out-party groups—likely play a role in affective and social polarization between the two parties.[20]

Given partisan polarization, we might expect partisans to defend groups perceived to be part of their coalition by endorsing narratives for their success or failure that reflect well on them and to be critical of groups perceived to be part of the other party's coalition. This would be a partisan version of a well-known bias that Miles Hewstone refers to as intergroup attributional bias, whereby Democrats and Republicans blame individuals or society in equal measure, depending on the demographics of the inequality they are considering.[21] For example, Republicans might blame Black and Latino Americans for earning less than other racial and ethnic groups but refuse to blame rural Americans for their relatively low incomes, instead endorsing structural explanations. Democrats might endorse structural explanations for Black and Latino Americans' lower earnings but refuse to do so for rural Americans, instead arguing that they have fallen behind due to lack of innate talent or work ethic. To be clear, this particular set of hypotheses is not linked to elite-level politics—we already saw, in chapter 2's coverage of party platforms, that the Republican Party does not invoke structural explanations to defend members of its coalition nor does the Democratic Party argue that many rural and White Americans have fallen behind others due to their own inadequacies. In this chapter, we investigate whether lay Democrats and Republicans share mirror-image prejudices—expressed via economic narratives—in favor of their own coalition and against the opposition's coalition.

A third and final pattern, partisan economic ideology, assumes that narratives that justify each party's economic policy agenda, whether emanating from political elites or others, heavily shape lay partisans' explanations for inequality. Thus, the observed patterns should not be as consistent as in the prior two examples—a simple internal–external or in-group–out-group dichotomy. Rather, Americans who identify with or lean toward a party ought to follow readily available political narratives that their party provides. Although few scholars have directly investigated the social spread of narratives about the causes of inequality, many assume that these beliefs are rooted in national cultures.[22] By way of contrast, in their canonical work on beliefs about economic inequality, Kluegel and Smith argue that changing explanations for inequality in the 1960s and 1970s were rooted not in a shifting national conversation but, rather, in changing beliefs among progressive politicians and activists.[23] Here, I follow and expand on this intuition about the importance of thought leaders within political groups.

The two parties' economic ideologies have long been two sides of a coin. Democrats have been the more economically populist party, seeking to level economic inequality. Republicans have been the party seeking to preserve and defend status quo economic differences. However, underneath this general description is considerable variation. First, the parties have increased and decreased their level of critique or justification over time. In recent years, the Democratic Party increased its criticism of the fairness of the economy. Second, many particular explanations for inequality come and go, as a result of changing economic circumstances and social trends. Since the mid-twentieth century, innate explanations for inequality—especially group differences—have fallen out of favor.[24] Thus, they are left out of most partisan debate. Lately, structural explanations, especially among Democrats, have gained favor. Third, for political reasons, parties debate, and thus choreograph, certain domains of inequality more often than others at any given time. As the leveling party, the Democratic Party critiques economic inequality more, but it does so with an eye toward economic difficulties faced by members of its own coalition. A century ago, this coalition was almost entirely White and disproportionately male; today, it is disproportionately non-White and female. The Republican Party, meanwhile, favors the economic status quo. It tends to resist these specific critiques and be slow to critique the economic system on behalf of lower-earning members of its own coalition.

Analytically, we can disaggregate each party's economic ideology into individual scripts, each with a particular explanation (for example, discrimination) and a referent (the particular economic inequality being explained, such as female–male inequality).[25] Yet, such complexity does not make for compelling persuasion. The parties knit these scripts together into a more general, and memorable, logic. The Republican Party champions a responsibility narrative that is relevant to all Americans. It locates the causes of inequality primarily in choices and work ethic. The Democratic Party presses an unequal opportunity narrative that locates the causes of inequality in structural barriers and suggests that higher-earning people and White Americans take more than their fair share of economic rewards. As we saw in chapter 2, partisan debate over these narratives has increased in the past two decades.

It is one thing to argue that party elites and peers influence people's policy positions. It is another to argue that people's factual beliefs about the origins of economic inequality may hinge in large part on their party identification. Why is party socialization so often successful in shaping these beliefs? First, people are extremely reliant on others for information. Unless they are social scientists (or read social science research closely), people do not have access to data and analysis on the causes of broad societal inequalities. They can extrapolate from their day-to-day experiences and firsthand observations but, otherwise, must learn these beliefs secondhand. Differentiating true from false claims is far more difficult than academics sometimes assume, especially because many politically relevant facts are highly contested.[26]

As discussed in chapter 1, scholars describe a two-step flow of information and persuasion, whereby more informed citizens absorb political information directly from media and other sources and then spread these views to their peers in informal conversation as well as via social media.[27] Given that people are more likely to pay attention to information sources that align with their ideological and partisan identities, a phenomenon known as selective attention,[28] this two-step flow will be infected by political bias. Even if people avoid information bubbles, for a variety of reasons, they are more likely to adopt the positions of their ideological and partisan allies and to counterargue those of their opponents.[29] These patterns are strongest among those most interested in, and attentive to, politics.[30] Alexander Coppock counsels us to not overstate the extent to which the public filters information according to political biases. People tend to be open-minded to new information when it is not accompanied by a clear ideological or party cue.[31] Yet, much information these days is accompanied by such cues. And, political cue or not, the information to which people are exposed is heavily shaped by the ideological and partisan lean of their social networks.

Symbolic Ideology and Social Prejudice

One of the challenges in understanding the dynamics underlying people's reasoning about socioeconomic inequality is that partisanship is interwoven with important individual characteristics. Left–right ideology and social prejudice are both correlated with partisanship and causal attributions for economic inequality. If we find that ordinary citizens who identify with different parties explain inequality differently, could it simply be that different kinds of people are drawn to the Democratic and Republican Parties? In other words, could it be the case that parties don't change people's minds about inequality but rather pull like-minded people into the party fold?

The short answer is yes. Acknowledging that debates over the meaning and prevalence of political ideology are ongoing in political science,[32] left or right and liberal or conservative are meaningful ways of dividing the U.S. public. Yet, these terms signal three overlapping and entangled commitments: interest in using government to combat economic inequality versus allowing economic differentiation according to individual behavior and market dynamics (economic liberalism–conservatism), interest in allowing individuals to live as they please versus encouraging or enforcing traditional social mores, often religious (social liberalism–conservatism), and, along different lines, a commitment to the specific Democratic or Republican policy agenda.[33] People vary in their understandings of the terms liberal and conservative and, thus, how they use them to define themselves—political scientists refer to these varied self-identifications as symbolic ideology.[34] For some people, their self-description as conservative or liberal maps to social conservatism or liberalism. For many people, the terms are basically redundant with Democratic or Republican partisanship. Yet, for some, conservative and liberal map to economic conservatism or liberalism, representing those who have long-standing libertarian or egalitarian value commitments that likely influence their beliefs about inequality, independent of party. Thus, I control for symbolic ideology in some upcoming analyses.[35]

A second competing theory explaining the parties' differing inequality narratives is rooted in the finding that Republicans today are more racially prejudiced than Democrats on average.[36] Variation in racial prejudice ought to be most relevant to Americans' beliefs about the causes of racial inequality specifically. In accordance with the psychological theory introduced in chapter 5, people who are biased against Black Americans, Latino Americans, or people of color in general tend to blame them for just about any difficulty they face. We can follow the same logic when thinking about the relationship between sexism and beliefs about the causes of female–male resource gaps. Controlling for racism and sexism will help to account for their role in shaping Americans' explanations for race and sex inequality in particular.

Yet, some scholars argue that racism in particular is the most important driver of not only attributions for unequal economic outcomes by race but also economic inequality in general. The argument runs as follows. Because low-income people are disproportionately non-White, and especially disproportionately Black, when Americans think about a typical poor person, they usually call to mind a person of color, often a Black person.[37] Racist Americans therefore extend their negative bias to poor people in general, blaming them for their economic difficulties. According to this line of argument, partisan differences in explanations for economic inequality— with Republicans more likely than Democrats to blame poor people—are largely derivative of greater racism among Republicans.

I argue that this line of thinking probably overstates the role of racism in shaping Americans' beliefs about the causes of economic inequality in the contemporary United States. The argument rests heavily on the uncertain assumption that Americans today imagining a poor person overwhelmingly think of a person of color. Yet, one recent study suggests that Americans who call to mind a prototypical poor person are about as likely to think of a White person as a person of color.[38] Further, White Americans— those most likely to harbor anti-Black prejudice—are more likely than

Black Americans to view White people as poor.[39] This is not to say that poverty was not heavily racialized in the past; rather, economic changes—especially increased inequality among White Americans and fewer Black Americans in poverty—may have revised perceptions of who is poor today.

We also should not overstate Republicans' greater racial prejudice relative to Democrats. For example, Spencer Piston finds that, in 2008, 67 percent of White Republicans scored above the midpoint of a negative racial stereotype measure, but so did 54 percent of Democrats.[40] In 2016, I measured explicit racial-ethnic bias with two social distance items: "Imagine for a moment that you are moving to another community. In deciding where to live, how important would it be to you to live in a place where most people were of the same race and ethnicity as you?" ("Not important at all, A little important, Moderately important, Very important, Extremely important") and "How do you think you would react if a member of your family told you they were going to marry a person who was of a different race or ethnicity? Would you be . . . Very happy, Somewhat happy, Somewhat unhappy, Very unhappy?" On average, White Democrats scored at the midpoint, whereas White Republicans scored higher by approximately one level on each of the scales.

Investigating Partisan Divides in the Public

The survey data allows us to investigate the relationship between partisanship, related phenomena such as symbolic ideology, and Americans' explanations for unequal economic outcomes. As a reminder, the two EIPS asked representative samples of Americans in 2016 and 2018 to indicate their level of agreement with various explanations for economic inequality between different kinds of people: economic inequality among Americans generally, between Black and Latino Americans and White Americans, between women and men, between rural and urban residents, and between White Americans and Asian Americans. Survey respondents rated their level of agreement or disagreement (six possible answers, from strongly agree to strongly disagree) with five provided explanations for inequality: varying levels of access to good schools and jobs (or, for women, lack of access to childcare), discrimination experienced by some more than others, variation in people's work ethics, socialization into different subcultures, and differences in innate intelligence.

At times, I use these items independently in the statistical analyses. I also use the three unequal economic opportunity indexes. As a reminder, each index is made up of three items measuring the extent to which respondents believed the lack of resources in a lower-earning group is driven by discrimination and lack of access to educational and job opportunities and is not driven by a deficient work ethic.[41] The indexes are scored from 1 to 6, in keeping with the six answer options of strongly agree to strongly disagree for each scale item. Again, I used the unequal opportunity indexes only in the more politically scripted domains of class, sex, and race (Black and Latino versus White), because response patterns for the less scripted domains are not organized neatly along the responsibility–unequal opportunity continuum.

Each of the two surveys followed standard practice in measuring partisan identification. First, people were asked: "Generally speaking, do you think of yourself as a ... " The answer choices were "Democrat," "Republican," "Independent," "Other," and "Not sure." This question was followed with a probe to tease out a person's strength of partisanship. A person who chose Democrat was asked whether they were a "Strong Democrat" or "Not very strong Democrat." Someone who chose Republican was asked whether they were a "Strong Republican" or "Not very strong Republican." Finally, those who chose one of the other answers were asked whether they leaned toward the Democratic or the Republican Party. These probes allow for the creation of a seven-point measure of partisanship: strong Democrat, not strong Democrat, Democratic leaner, true independent, Republican leaner, not strong Republican, and strong Republican.[42]

We also examine symbolic ideology and social prejudice. For symbolic ideology, respondents were asked to place themselves on a five-point ideology continuum, from "Very liberal" to "Very conservative" (with "Moderate" in the middle). I measure racial prejudice with the two items described earlier that capture a desire for social distance from racial and ethnic outgroups (when a person is choosing a new community in which to live or considering how they feel about a family member marrying a person of a different race or ethnicity). These items have the advantage of uncovering prejudice among White as well as non-White Americans. I conceptualize sexism as a commitment to traditional gender roles and separate spheres for men and women, measuring it with the following two items: "It is much better for everyone involved if the man is the achiever outside the home and the woman takes care of the home and family," and, reverse-scored, "It's fine for a husband to stay home to take care of home and family instead of working outside the home."[43]

Partisan Disagreements over Scripted Inequalities

We begin by examining beliefs about the causes of economic inequality generally speaking, as measured by the generic unequal economic opportunity index. See figure 6.1, which displays the number of survey respondents (in 2016) at each level of the index by partisanship (or lack thereof). This figure establishes three patterns of note. First, as expected, Democrats scored higher on the index than Republicans (and independents rest in between). The very bottom of the index had very few Democrats, and the top had even fewer Republicans. Second, although the partisan patterns are unmistakable, there was also quite a bit of variance within each party (as well as among independents). Third, relatively few people rested at the extremes of the index.

Next, we turn to a more systematic analysis of partisan differences in explanations for socioeconomic inequality. In the previous chapter, I regressed the three unequal opportunity indexes onto demographic variables: income, sex, race, rurality, religiosity, education, and age. I repeat these analyses here, adding partisanship as an explanatory variable (scored such that "strong Republican" takes on the highest value) and then additional control variables.

Figure 6.2 plots the regression coefficients for three models that include partisanship and the demographic variables. (Supporting tables for this and other figures can be found in the appendix. See tables A.2, A.3, and A.4.) As in chapter 5, all explanatory variables are scored from 0 to 1, while the outcome variables range from 1 to 6. The results reveal large partisan divides. They are all in the same direction, although there is some variation in the size of the partisan gaps. Partisans differed most over explanations for Black/Latino–White inequality and differed least over explanations for female–male inequality. These divides were much greater than the demographic ones. Strong Democrats and strong Republicans differed by 1 to 1.5 points on the outcome variables (17 to 25 percent of their range). These differences were approximately two to three times the effect sizes of the two most important demographic variables—education and religiosity. Not surprisingly, the inclusion of partisanship also reduced the associations between many of the demographic variables and the unequal opportunity

Figure 6.1 Frequency Distributions of the Unequal Economic Opportunity Index for Democrats, Independents, and Republicans (2016)

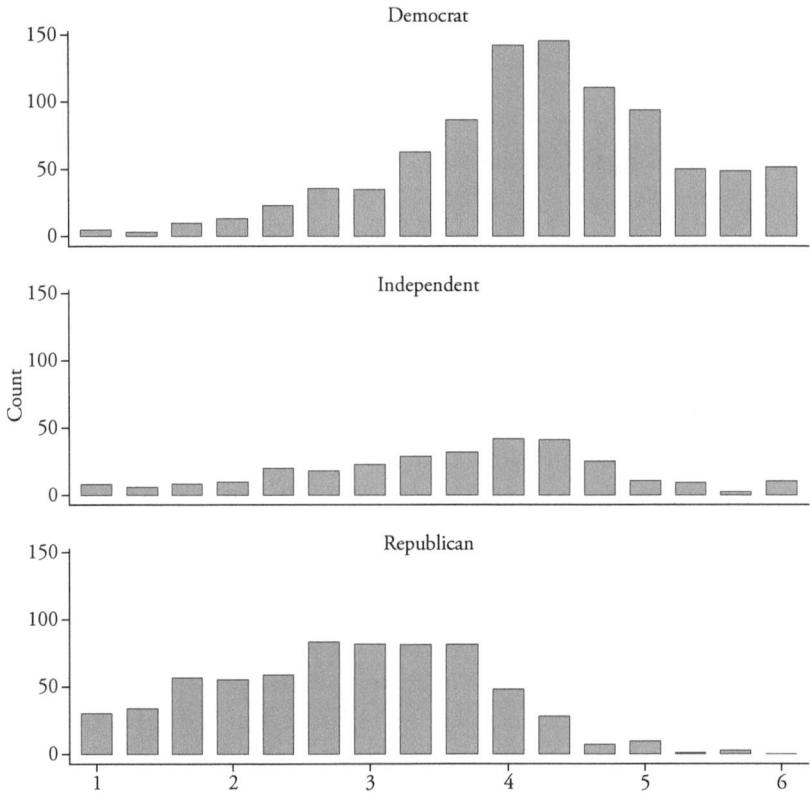

Source: Author's calculations using 2016 EIPS data.

indexes, especially race, rurality, religiosity, and education. This suggests that some of the findings in chapter 5 were due to the partisan leanings of demographic groups. That said, clear demographic associations remain after accounting for partisanship. Women were more likely than men to say that women experience unequal opportunity. Likewise, Black and Hispanic Americans were more likely to say that Black and Latino Americans as well as other groups face unequal opportunity. As before, religious people were less likely to believe unequal opportunity is a problem, and educated people more likely.

Some people may be skeptical that the schism is uniquely linked to partisanship as opposed to some correlated phenomenon. Perhaps this divide

Figure 6.2 Coefficient Plot of Unequal Opportunity Indexes Regressed onto Partisanship and Demographic Variables (2016)

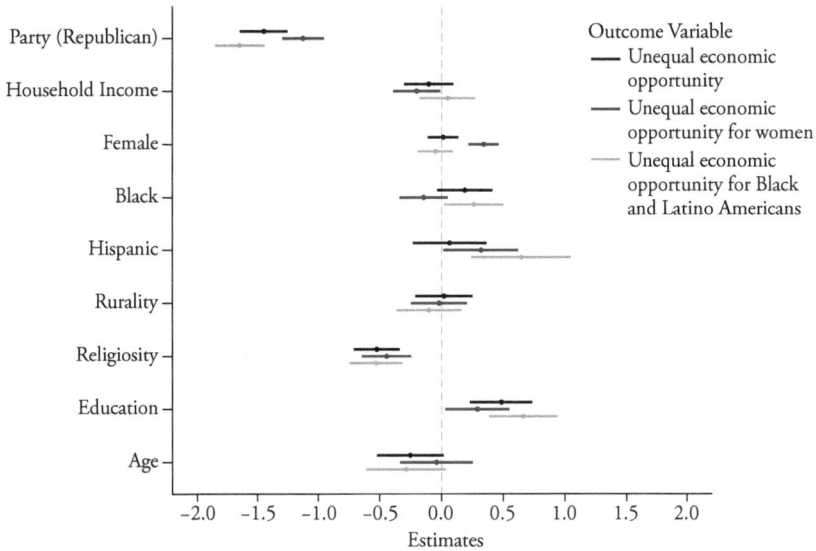

Source: Author's calculations using 2016 EIPS data.
Note: Coefficient plot depicts estimates from three separate linear regressions, with unequal economic opportunity, unequal economic opportunity for women, and unequal economic opportunity for Black and Latino Americans as outcome variables. Explanatory variables are scored 0 to 1 and outcome variables are scored 1 to 6. Models also control for additional racial categories (not shown).

is more accurately considered ideological, in the sense that symbolic liberal–conservative ideology represents a psychological or political phenomenon distinct from partisanship. Or perhaps it can be boiled down to variation in social prejudice between the parties.

Figure 6.3 displays results from the same set of regressions but with the addition of symbolic ideology (with relative conservatism taking on higher values) and social prejudice. Survey respondents' symbolic ideologies were associated with the outcome variables in almost exactly the same manner as partisanship, with a slightly stronger set of associations. This is not surprising given that symbolic ideology reflects not only people's preferences for economic policy but also their commitment to the Democratic or Republican agenda (partisanship and ideology correlate at .64). Racism was also negatively associated with the three indexes, especially the unequal economic opportunity for Black and Latino Americans index. Interestingly, the sexism measure was about equally associated with beliefs about economic opportunity for women and for Black and Latino Americans, suggesting that this measure tapped respondents' lack of concern for historically marginalized groups in general. As a result of adding these additional explanatory variables, the coefficient for partisanship was reduced by approximately 35 to 40 percent. It remains large by social scientific standards. In short, the association between partisanship and the unequal economic opportunity indexes in the 2016 survey was robust to the inclusion of several competing phenomena also correlated with Americans' explanations for socioeconomic inequality.

The evidence so far suggests that Republicans may be consistent American Dream believers and Democrats consistent American Dream skeptics. These differences are rooted primarily in partisanship and its sibling, conservative–liberal ideology, with racism and sexism also contributing. Yet,

Figure 6.3 Coefficient Plot of Unequal Opportunity Indexes Regressed onto Partisanship, Ideology, and Prejudice (2016)

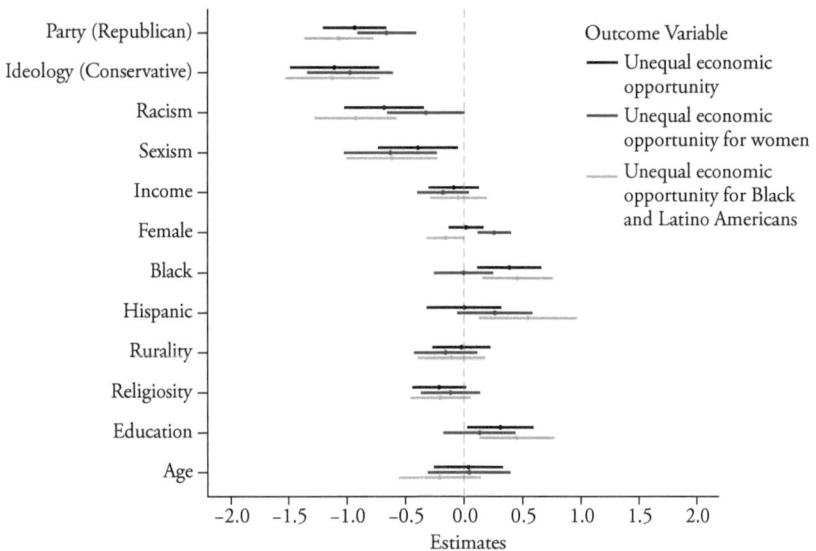

Source: Author's calculations using 2016 EIPS data.
Note: Coefficient plot depicts estimates from three separate linear regressions, with unequal economic opportunity, unequal economic opportunity for women, and unequal economic opportunity for Black and Latino Americans as outcome variables. Explanatory variables are scored 0 to 1 and outcome variables are scored 1 to 6. Models also control for additional racial categories (not shown).

we have examined beliefs regarding a relatively limited number of socioeconomic inequalities and with one snapshot in time. To better understand the landscape of explanations for inequality and what might be driving them, we must examine whether (and how) partisans shift gears over time and as other explanations and inequalities come into view.

How Partisans Explain Many Inequalities

In the analyses that follow, I examine the association between partisanship and each unique explanation for inequality, one by one and across all five domains of economic inequality. Incorporating data from the 2002 ANES,[44] as well as the two EIPS, I draw some tentative conclusions regarding the changes in relationships between partisanship and economic narratives over time. Recall that chapters 2 and 3 suggested that the recent era of extreme polarization in elite and lay economic narratives began in the mid-2000s, with arguments over class inequality diverging first and arguments over racial inequality diverging in the 2010s. Here, we ought to observe more dramatic partisan differences, especially around race, in the latter period than the former. Incorporating the additional inequality domains involving rural and Asian Americans, I can also investigate whether partisan differences fall away, as expected, when partisan scripts are less available.

Figure 6.4 displays structural explanations for economic inequality by level of partisanship across the three surveys. The top panel focuses on lack of access to education and jobs.[45] The bottom panel focuses on discrimination. First, across all years, Democrats were more likely to advance structural explanations than Republicans. Second, this pattern is sharpest when considering the more politically scripted class-race-sex trio. In the 2018 survey, the partisan trend weakened in the case of rural–urban inequality and discrimination, was close to null in the case of White–Asian American inequality and education and jobs, and reversed with respect to White–Asian American inequality and discrimination. Democrats drove these changes, whereas Republicans consistently disagreed across inequality domains. Third, partisan response patterns in the heavily scripted inequality domains became more similar—in terms of means and slopes—between the 2002 and 2016 or 2018 surveys.

Figure 6.5 displays the relationships between partisanship and individual (or meritocratic) explanations for inequality. Interestingly, the partisan trends overall are weaker and far more varied. In the analysis of data from

Figure 6.4 Associations Between Partisanship and Societal Explanations for Socioeconomic Inequality

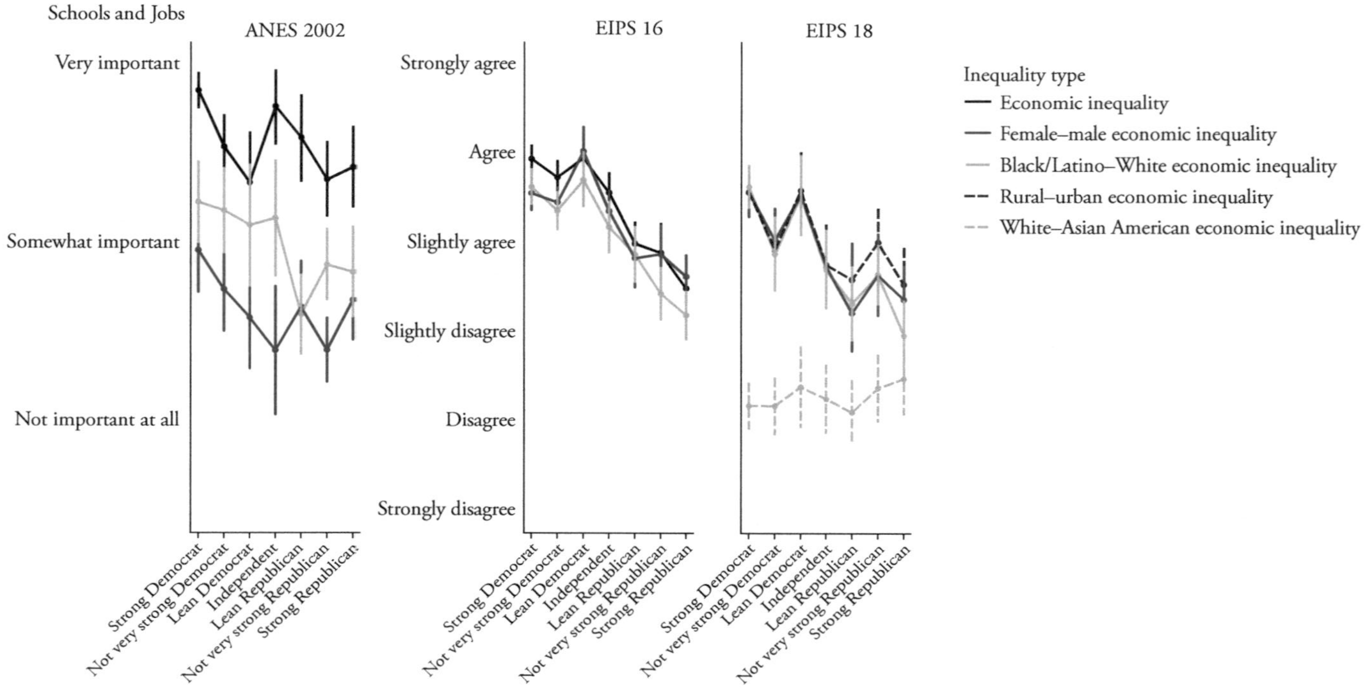

Inequality type
— Economic inequality
— Female–male economic inequality
— Black/Latino–White economic inequality
-- Rural–urban economic inequality
-- White–Asian American economic inequality

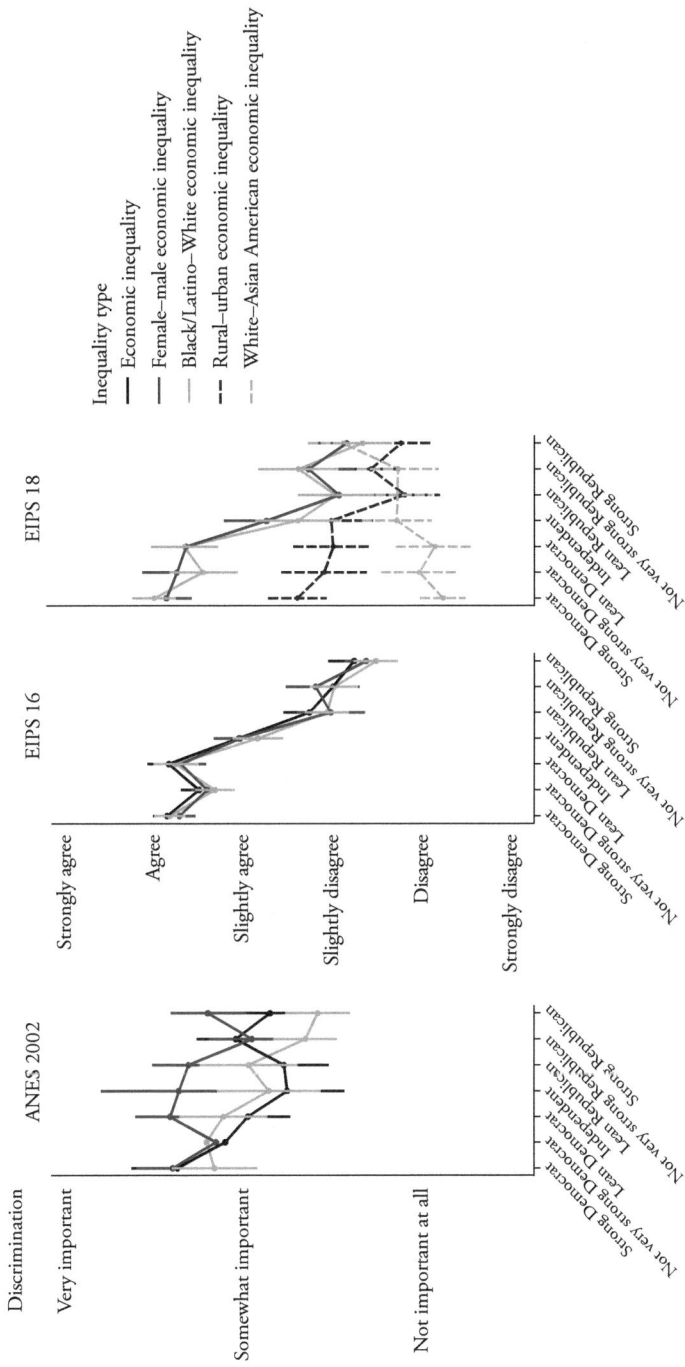

Source: Author's calculations using data from 2016 and 2018 EIPS as well as 2002 ANES (American National Election Studies 2025).

Figure 6.5 Associations Between Partisanship and Individual Explanations for Socioeconomic Inequality

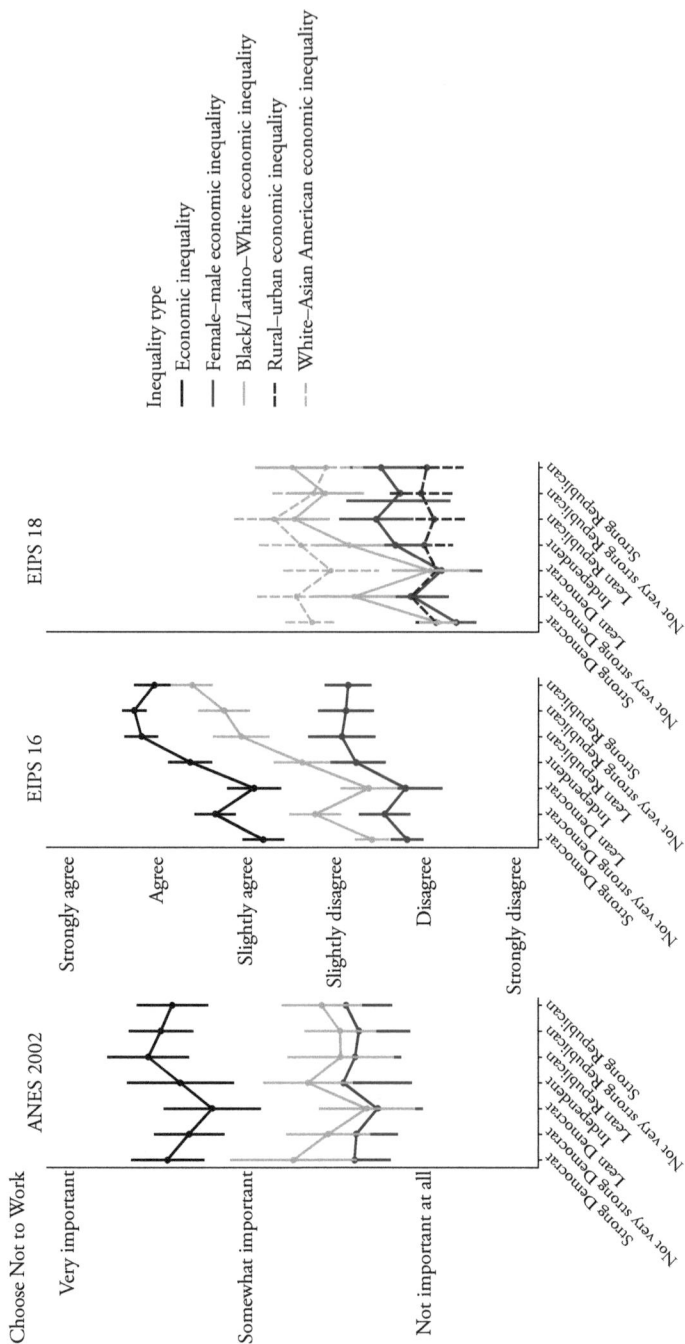

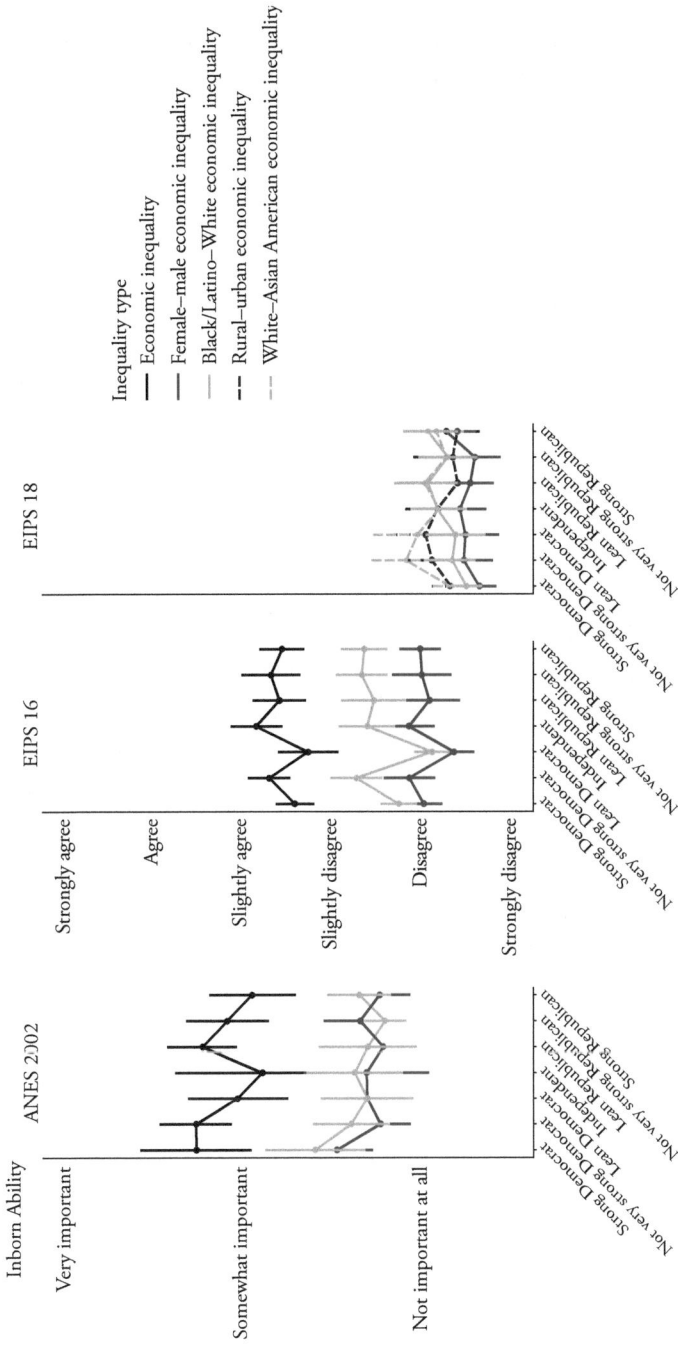

Source: Author's calculations using data from 2016 and 2018 EIPS as well as 2002 ANES (American National Election Studies 2025).

2002, partisan patterns are null or, surprisingly, have Democrats somewhat more likely than Republicans to argue that work ethic and innate ability drive inequality. By 2016, Republicans were much more likely than Democrats to say that economic inequality in general, and between Black and Latino Americans and White Americans, were driven by differences in how hard people work. Notice that, in both 2016 and 2018, Republicans employed the hard work explanation much less in the case of both women and rural Americans. On the other hand, Republicans said that hard work matters for Black Americans and White Americans (when they earn less) at about equal rates. In 2016 and 2018, innate explanations did not differ across the partisan spectrum.[46]

The appendix includes additional analyses of interest. See figure A.12. There, I include partisan trends for cultural explanations, which are not included here because there is no ANES corollary. In 2016 and 2018, Republicans were more likely to employ a cultural explanation for unequal economic outcomes in general and between lower earning racial minorities and White Americans, but this is not true for the other three domains of inequality (female–male, rural–urban, and White–Asian American). I also include linear regression analyses with the five distinct explanations for inequality in general regressed onto partisanship and the full set of demographic controls. The coefficients on partisanship are largest and relatively similar in size for schools and jobs ($b = -1.2$), discrimination ($b = -1.8$), and work ethic ($b = 1.25$).

Evidence from Open-Ended Responses

One final way of thinking about the relationship between respondent partisanship and their explanations for unequal outcomes is to return to the open-ended responses discussed in chapter 4. Recall that, after each question about the causes of a particular inequality in the 2018 EIPS, respondents were asked whether they thought any other cause accounted for the inequality. While some respondents took the opportunity to offer a new explanation, most doubled down or expanded on an explanation already included in the survey. These open-ended responses were then coded into expanded versions of the five standard categories of explanation (access to opportunity, discrimination, choices/effort, culture, or intrinsic characteristics) or two additional categories (politics or other, not discussed here).

Responses that mentioned a particular type of explanation were coded 1 for that explanation category, and those that didn't mention it were coded 0 for that category. This coding allows for statistical analysis.

Table 6.1 displays the results of twenty unique logit regression analyses whereby each indicator variable for a given open-ended response category (for example, discrimination) within each domain of inequality (for example, women versus men) was regressed onto the seven-point partisanship measure (with strong Republican assigned the highest value of 1 and strong Democrat assigned the lowest value of 0) and the standard demographic control variables. The number in each cell represents the coefficient on partisanship, transformed into an odds ratio. Ratios above 1 indicate that Republicans were more likely than Democrats to mention a particular explanation for a particular inequality, and ratios below 1 indicate that Democrats were more likely than Republicans to mention that explanation for that inequality. I next focus on relationships that reach standard thresholds of significance ($p < .05$).

Beginning with the top row, strong Republicans were approximately one-third as likely as strong Democrats to mention access to opportunity (education and jobs, or childcare) when considering Black and Latino versus White inequality, but findings for access to opportunity were otherwise

Table 6.1 Republican Versus Democratic Odds of Mentioning Five Explanations for Four Types of Inequality, Results from Twenty Independent Logit Regressions (2018)

| | Type of Socioeconomic Inequality | | | |
| | | Black/ | | White–Asian |
Explanation	Female–Male	Latino–White	Rural–Urban	American
Access	1.739	0.328**	0.692	0.473
Discrimination	0.243***	0.108***	0.245	2.534
Choices/effort	3.437***	5.420***	1.535	0.718
Culture/socialization	0.408	1.627	0.926	1.132
Intrinsic traits	1.104	1.305	1.629	1.382

Source: Author's calculations using 2018 EIPS data.

Note: Each cell represents the partisanship odds ratio from an independent logistic regression. Each open-ended explanation (access, discrimination, choices/effort, culture/socialization, or intrinsic traits), scored 1 or 0, for a particular domain of inequality (female–male, Black/Latino–White, rural–urban, or White–Asian American) was regressed onto partisanship and standard demographic control variables (not shown).

* $p < .1$; ** $p < .05$; *** $p < .01$

null. Strong Republicans were even less likely to mention discrimination compared with strong Democrats for the female–male and Black/Latino–White contrasts. On the other hand, strong Republicans were more than three times as likely to say that people's choices or effort levels played a role in female–male inequality and more than five times as likely to say the same for Black/Latino–White inequality. The results elsewhere did not reach standard levels of statistical significance ($p < .05$), although some of the co-efficients were substantively large.[47] Overall, these findings echo the prior analyses and, in fact, suggest larger differences between Democratic and Republican partisans. When given the opportunity to say whatever was on their mind, partisans were even more likely to turn to tried-and-true scripts common within their party.

Do Politically Attentive Partisans Explain Inequality Differently?

Political scientists have established that Americans who follow politics closely differ in important ways from others. One important difference is their greater tendency to mirror the political views of political leaders who share their partisanship and ideology. While people occasionally switch parties as a result of changes in parties' agendas, party switching is much less common than toeing the party line. Examples abound of partisan or ideological polarization over fact claims increasing with higher levels of attentiveness or exposure to relevant political rhetoric.[48]

In chapter 3, we saw evidence that politically attentive partisans were more likely to subscribe to their party's economic narratives for inequalities by class and race (Black versus White inequality). In this chapter, we can conduct a more systematic analysis, examining partisan explanations for two types of racial inequality, sex inequality, and geographic inequality, all measured with nearly identical question wording. I measured political attention with the following question: "Some people seem to follow what's going on in government and public affairs most of the time, whether there's an election going on or not. Others aren't that interested. Would you say you follow what's going on in government and public affairs . . . Most of the time, Some of the time, Only now and then, Hardly at all."[49] In the upcoming figures, the final two categories were combined due to low frequencies (in the last category in particular).

Figure 6.6 displays Democratic and Republican respondents' average explanations for the more scripted inequalities—Black and Latino Americans earning less than White Americans, and women earning less than men—by level of attention. I display actual, as opposed to predicted, means mainly to avoid assuming linearity.[50] Similar findings emerge from linear regressions that include demographic control variables, as well as when I take into account partisan intensity.

For the explanations for Black/Latino–White and female–male inequality, findings are entirely as expected for beliefs regarding barriers to opportunity (schools and jobs or childcare, and discrimination). Partisans disagreed with one another on average, but these disagreements were larger among those who said that they follow politics "most of the time." Patterns for belief in hard work are mixed: Democrats were less likely to voice this point of view at higher levels of political attention, as expected; however, among Republicans, those who were low in political attention were especially likely to say that a lack of hard work holds women and Black and Latino Americans back. For culture, partisan differences increase in the expected direction for Black/Latino-White inequality with higher levels of attention; however, this is not true for female-male inequality (where the most politically attentive Republicans are less likely to evoke culture). As expected, no clear partisan differences emerge for innate inequality.

We would not expect the same level of polarization according to political interest for the less scripted domains of inequality. Figure 6.7 displays partisans' explanations for rural–urban and White–Asian American inequality. The only patterns that resemble those in figure 6.6 are for structural explanations for rural–urban inequality, for which partisans differ in the expected direction only at higher levels of political attention. Other intriguing patterns emerge but do not reflect any discernable party ideology. For example, with higher levels of attention, Republicans were more likely than Democrats to disagree that cultural differences contribute to rural–urban inequality; attentive Republicans were again less likely than their inattentive counterparts to argue in favor of work ethic. For White–Asian American inequality, there is nothing systematic to report beyond the already observed tendency for Democrats to be somewhat less likely than Republicans to say that discrimination plays a role in White Americans' lower earnings and wealth.

Figure 6.6 Explanations for Race and Sex Inequality by Level of Political Attention and Partisanship (2018)

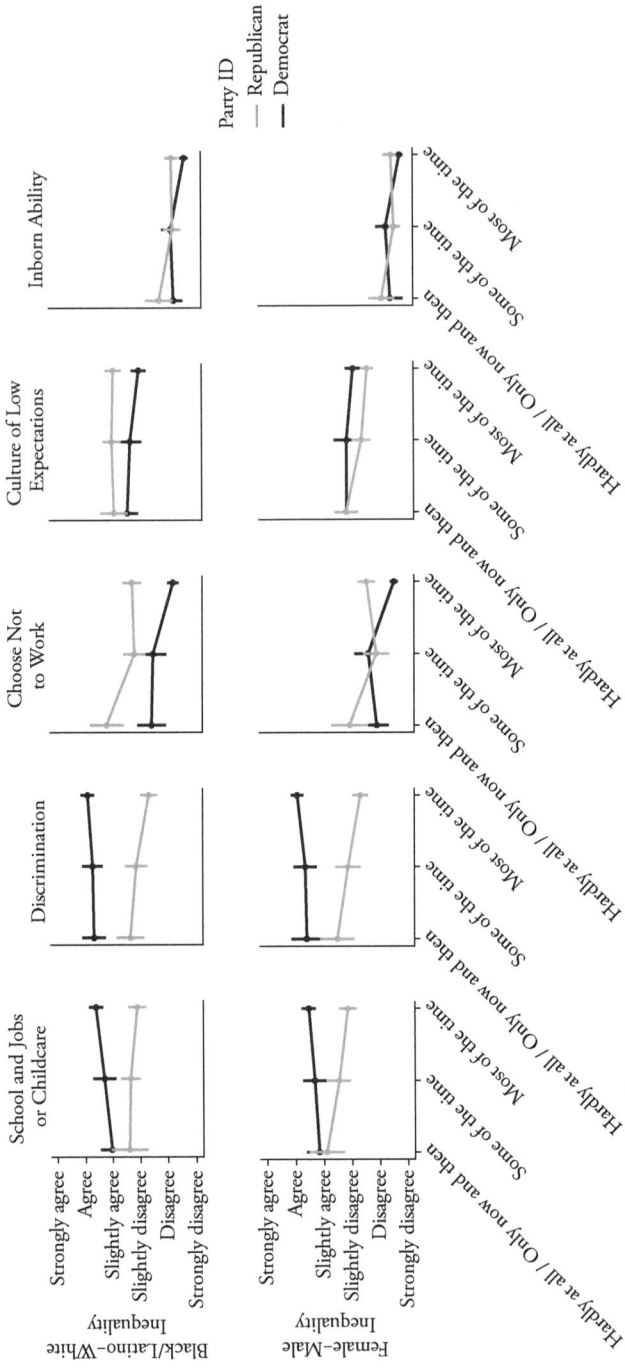

Source: Author's calculations using 2018 EIPS data.

Note: Each panel displays means for one type of explanation for socioeconomic inequality (Black/Latino–White in the top row and female–male in the bottom row) among partisans at varying levels of political attentiveness.

Figure 6.7 Explanations for Rural-Urban and White-Asian American Inequality by Level of Political Attention and Partisanship (2018)

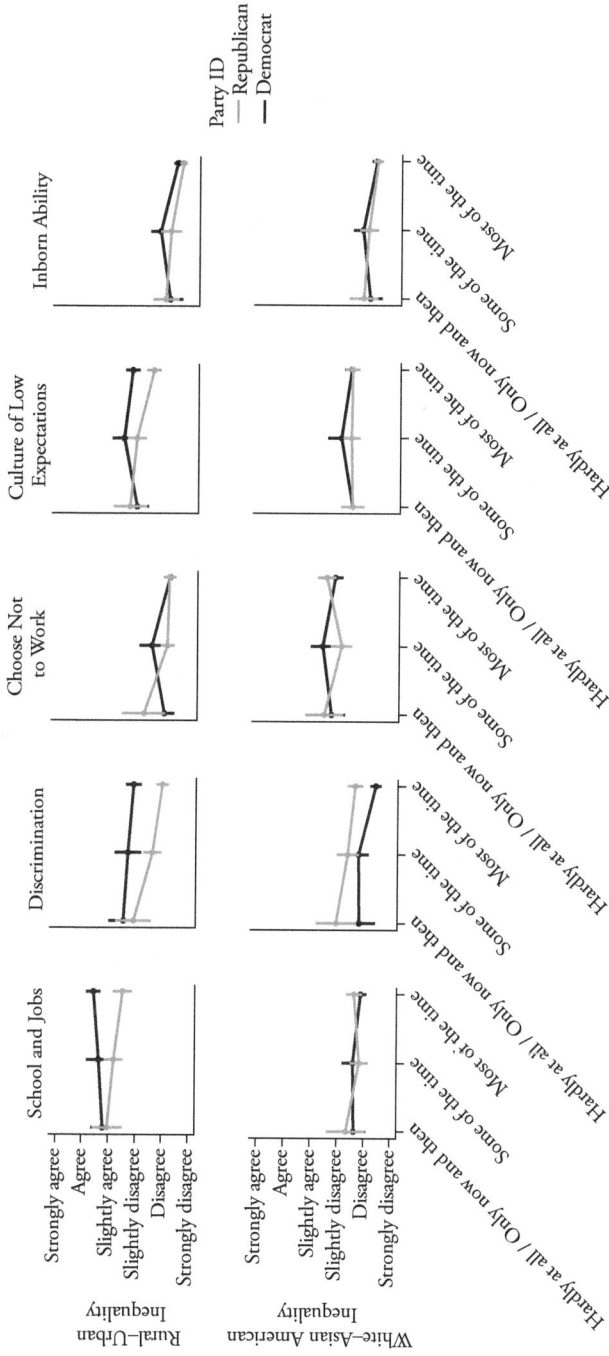

Source: Author's calculations using 2018 EIPS data.
Note: Each panel displays means for one type of explanation for socioeconomic inequality (rural-urban in the top row and White-Asian American in the bottom row) among partisans at varying levels of political attentiveness.

Conclusion

In this chapter, we have considered whether lay Democrats and Republicans disagree over explanations for inequality and, by extension, whether the American economy rewards merit. While many scholars understand that the two partisan camps think about inequality differently, prior research has pointed to many different patterns of, and reasons for, disagreement. The three main possibilities are as follows: Democrats and Republicans have rigid attributional styles in which Republicans stubbornly insist that every inequality is legitimate and that Democrats likewise protest each and every one; Democrats and Republicans express biased attributions in order to cast their own coalition in a positive light and the other party's coalition in a negative light (because women and Americans of color are disproportionately Democratic, this hypothesis incorporates the idea that Republicans' explanations for inequality reflect racism and sexism); and Democratic and Republican coalitions develop flexible partisan economic ideologies that incorporate some of the previous elements but in service of bolstering their policy agendas.

The analyses in this chapter allow me to draw some firm conclusions as well as some more tentative ones. First and foremost, at the time of my original surveys, Democrats and Republicans disagreed over the reasons for economic inequalities often discussed in the public sphere—economic inequality in general, between women and men, and between Black/Latino Americans and White Americans. Democrats endorsed structural explanations for these inequalities, and Republicans argued in favor of personal responsibility. This is true over and above the influence of demographic, ideological, and other differences between the party coalitions. Yet, at the same time, we must reject the idea that partisans have a rigid attributional style. Partisan disagreement was less evident in 2002, in the politically less scripted domains of rural–urban and White–Asian American inequality, and when people considered innate attributions.

Despite the fact that partisan polarization was sharpest over economic inequality in general and racial inequality (Black and Latino Americans earning less than White Americans), the evidence also revealed that partisans were not consistently motivated to defend members of their partisan coalition or criticize members of the other party's coalition. Republicans blamed White Americans for falling behind Asian Americans about as much as they blamed Black and Latino Americans for earning less than White Americans. Republicans hesitated to blame rural Americans for earning less than others, but they did the same for women. For their part, Democrats took care to differentiate between rural and White Americans— the former were thought to be victims of structural inequality to some degree, whereas the latter were not. I do not mean to argue that racism and sexism are irrelevant to debates over the origins of economic inequality; in fact, the statistical analyses make clear that these predispositions matter a great deal. The point is that we cannot boil down partisan economic disagreements, even broadly understood, to prejudice only.

Taking a step back, the patterns in the data are most supportive of the partisan economic ideology thesis. Each party has their preferred overarching narrative for economic inequality: Democrats tend to see structural inequalities as dividing lower-earning people and below–median income groups from higher-earning ones. According to most Democrats, individual attributions are simply not relevant to socioeconomic inequality, period. Republicans tend to deny structural inequality across the board and to believe that hard work differentiates the rich from the poor and higher-earning racial and ethnic groups from lower-earning ones (not only White Americans relative to Black and Latino Americans but also Asian Americans relative to White Americans). Republicans also turn to cultural explanations, but these are reserved for lower-income people in general as well as Black and Latino Americans. Partisans in both camps tend to reject innate explanations, especially for unequal outcomes across groups. Focusing on the most talked about inequalities—class, sex, and race (Black and Latino versus White)—lay partisans became more similar to their co-partisans and more different from out-party members between 2002 and 2016, in line with party polarization at the elite level. We see a similar polarization pattern in Democratic and Republican respondents' explanations for structural inequalities (although not work ethic) across levels of political attention.[51]

In the next chapter, I consider whether explanations for inequality might matter to Americans' electoral and policy preferences, above and beyond party identification and associated phenomena. We have learned that Americans have heterogeneous and highly politicized ideas about what drives economic inequality, especially the oft-discussed inequalities between the poor and the rich, Black and Latino and White Americans, and women and men. Are these narratives simply symbols of societal division and disagreement that are themselves of little consequence? Or, as the two parties and other political actors seem to intend, do they play a role in shaping people's public policy and voting preferences?

CHAPTER 7

Political Preferences and Explanations for Inequality

> Vincent is stymied. He is certain of only one thing, namely, that some people are so wrongly and wretchedly poor that "they'd be better off dead." But since he cannot pinpoint the blame for this tragedy, he cannot decide how to solve it.
>
> —Jennifer Hochschild, *What's Fair?* (1981)[1]

IN THE LAST chapter, we learned that Americans' partisan identities and symbolic ideologies strongly correlate with their causal attributions for frequently debated inequalities: poor versus rich, female versus male, and Black and Latino versus White. Survey respondents with more Republican and conservative commitments were more likely to say that people themselves are responsible for their economic circumstances. Likewise, those with Democratic and liberal commitments were more likely to say that unequal opportunities cause economic outcomes to diverge. In the preceding chapters, I have provided suggestive evidence that political communication shared by party leaders and their political allies drives much of this relationship. Political elites on the left and right construct and promulgate partisan economic ideologies that bolster their policy agendas. Where the parties publicly disagree about the origins of economic inequality, the public divides along similar lines. Where the parties do not publicly disagree, divisions in the public are minimal or nonexistent. While party leaders do not invent these narratives from whole cloth—in fact, they are influenced themselves by powerful coalition members—they likely play an important role in spreading narratives among the party faithful. For political actors interested in justifying a conservative or liberal economic policy agenda,

https://doi.org/10.7758/trap6910.4841

explanations for inequality are intended to shore up support for that agenda among loyal followers and persuade as many others as possible of its merits.

The main question I ask in this chapter is whether Americans' explanations for more scripted inequalities—those associated with class, race (Black and Latino versus White), and sex—influence their political preferences in the way political elites intend them to do. Democratic politicians wish to use government policy to combat inequality, at least more so than Republicans. They justify this effort to the public by arguing that real equal opportunity has not been achieved. Are people who subscribe to the Democratic Party's American Dream skepticism more likely to support economically progressive policy and Democratic political candidates? Republican politicians, relative to Democrats, want to limit the amount of government assistance to people with fewer resources and the taxes on those with greater resources that must fund it. In support of this approach, they tend to argue that inequality does not represent a problem that needs solving: there is plenty of economic opportunity to go around, and the economic difficulties individuals experience stem from their own lack of effort and, thus, are best addressed by individuals themselves. Are those who subscribe to the Republican Party's American Dream optimism more likely to support economically conservative policy and Republican political candidates?

I also seek to answer several more nuanced questions about the relationship between people's beliefs about socioeconomic inequality and their political views that much prior scholarship has overlooked. For example, does the explanation-attitude relationship differ when we compare Democrats, Republicans, and independents? What about Black, Hispanic, and White Americans? Further, in which domains of inequality are causal attributions most relevant to Americans' political preferences?

I draw on the two Explanations for Inequality & Politics surveys to answer these questions. For most of the analyses, I focus on the association between respondents' scores on the responsibility–unequal opportunity indexes and support for government-sponsored social welfare broadly understood, ranging from public schools to guaranteed jobs. I also investigate whether the opportunity indexes are associated with respondents' views on redistribution, affirmative action, and support for Democratic and Republican presidential candidates. Overall, I find that survey respondents who were pessimistic about the American Dream expressed substantially more progressive political views and were more likely to support the Democratic presidential candidate at the time of the relevant survey (Hillary Clinton). Citizens who were optimistic about the American Dream expressed more conservative views, including support for the Republican presidential candidate at the time (Donald Trump). These relationships were robust—they persisted when potentially confounding predispositions, including partisanship and symbolic ideology, were held constant.

These associations varied considerably across domains of inequality, however. Overall, people's explanations for economic inequality in general were reliably most closely associated with their public policy preferences. When it came to presidential preferences, however, explanations for racial inequality were most important. Beliefs about less scripted domains of inequality—rural versus urban, and White versus Asian American—were not associated with political preferences. Associations also varied between population subgroups. Among Latino and White Americans, and among independents and Republicans, political preferences were especially closely associated with beliefs about the causes of inequality.

The evidence in this chapter suggests that political leaders' persuasive efforts regarding the causes of inequality are not done in vain. It also helps us to understand why people can say that they believe in equal opportunity yet oppose policies designed to enhance it—something scholars have referred to as the principles–implementation gap.[2] Many people who believe in the American Dream as an ideal simply believe it has been reached.

In the next section, I discuss some of the extant scholarly literature on the associations between how people think about economic inequality and opportunity on one hand, and their political candidate and policy preferences on the other. Prior scholarship has covered a lot of ground already and is especially helpful to this project in lending credence to my argument in favor of a causal interpretation of the associations discussed herein: beliefs about inequality influence political views. The scholarly research literature also helps to flesh out why beliefs about economic inequality are so politically powerful. I contribute to this work by providing a thorough examination of the belief-preference relationship that considers multiple explanations for five different types of inequality while also comparing associations across political and social groups.

The Relationship Between Explanations for Inequality and Political Attitudes

It makes intuitive sense that people's beliefs about the economy will influence their political attitudes. As *The New York Times* argued in a 2020 editorial, "The importance of rewriting our stories about the way that the economy works is that they frame our policy debates. Our beliefs about economics determine what seems viable and worthwhile."[3] That said, I argued in chapter 6 that a different kind of relationship exists between these phenomena: political predispositions influence people's causal narratives surrounding inequality. People find a partisan home early on—often literally in the home, as young people tend to take on the political identities of their parents. Many then absorb a package of associated beliefs, including salient policy prescriptions, favored politicians, and factual narratives. This conclusion reflects work by socialization researchers,[4] as well as by scholars who emphasize the power of elite cues over Americans' views on a wide range of topics.[5] If politics influences people's politically relevant factual beliefs, are we ruling out the possibility that these same factual beliefs can also influence their politics? Not necessarily.

Denying a role for beliefs about the American Dream in influencing people's political attitudes would suggest that the persuasive efforts of political elites have no purpose. Why do so many political actors—including party leaders, activists, and media pundits—spend so much time and energy insisting that their preferred set of facts on the economy (not to mention other controversial topics) is right? For one reason, they believe that these facts are critical to persuading people to support their policy agendas. Fact claims provided by political leaders and allies likely influence people's political preferences in two ways. First, compelling justifications for a policy agenda maximize persuasion in the moment. Lay partisans are admittedly motivated to support their party no matter what; however, they wish to do so for fact-based, logical reasons, not on emotional grounds.[6] And persuading independents or out-party members will depend even more on the specific arguments they make. Second, factual rationales probably have downstream effects as people encounter new, relevant policy decisions at later points in time. In short, a party may provide a factual narrative to rationalize its current agenda, but once absorbed, that factual narrative will likely influence other policy views down the road.[7]

What kinds of political preferences are associated with causal explanations for economic inequality? According to scholars, quite a few. In their comprehensive study of Americans' beliefs about inequality, Kluegel and Smith demonstrate a consistent link between the belief that unequal economic outcomes stem from structural inequality (that is, societal inequities) and support for welfare and affirmative action.[8] In a large, although not U.S. representative sample, Shanto Iyengar examines a wide range of topics and finds that people who blamed society for poverty were more likely than others to support social welfare, and that people who blamed society for racial inequality were more likely to support government assistance and spending to help Black Americans specifically.[9] In both domains, people who held society responsible for social problems also evaluated Republican President Ronald Reagan more negatively. Hunt and Bullock's review of the literature on this topic provides further support for such findings.[10] Scholars have also found many of these relationships outside the United States. In a study of people in thirty-four countries, Paul Piff and colleagues find that societal (rather than individual) attributions for poverty were consistently associated with greater opposition to income inequality and more support for redistribution.[11] Focusing on aggregate differences between nations, Alesina and Angeletos find that the belief that good or bad luck (rather than hard work) drives success in life was positively associated with actual social spending across approximately thirty nations.[12]

Most of this work is strictly correlational. Controlled experiments provide better evidence for causation by randomly assigning relevant informational treatments to research subjects and assessing their effects. Researchers have carried out numerous experimental studies on this topic and demonstrate just such an effect. Lauren Appelbaum finds that study participants experimentally assigned to read vignettes about people who were poor through no fault of their own were more likely than others to support liberal policy views at the end of the experiment.[13] Piff and colleagues find that subjects who played a game about the various challenges of experiencing poverty were more likely to endorse societal explanations for poverty and became more supportive of redistribution, an effect mediated by shifting explanations for poverty.[14] Finally, in a series of articles based on experimental data, Petersen and colleagues provide evidence of an automatic "deservingness heuristic."[15] The heuristic was triggered when study participants learned about people facing difficulties who are (or are not) trying to help themselves and leads to a desire for more (or less) government assistance.[16] These authors also demonstrate that this heuristic can operate independently of political ideology and values.[17]

Many scholars see deservingness as the key to understanding why causal attributions for inequalities appear to be so influential. In short, perceiving someone to be deserving generates positive evaluations and, if that person is experiencing some difficulty, a motivation to assist them.[18] In the context of hardship, the perception of deservingness stems primarily from the belief that people or groups are not responsible for the problem they experience; those believed to be causing their problem are perceived as undeserving. Deservingness is closely associated with moral ideas of fairness.[19] A final step in this process is emotion. As Bernard Weiner and colleagues argue: "Emotions are hypothesized to provide the bridge between causal thoughts and behaviors."[20] Perceived deservingness generates compassion, which motivates assistance.[21] For example, Shahrzad Goudarzi and colleagues demonstrate across several experimental studies that people who tend to see inequality as deserved experience less emotional distress when observing homelessness.[22] Belief that a person experiencing some difficulty is undeserving of assistance can even lead to anger, motivating not only a refusal of assistance but also retribution.[23]

Some explanations for economic inequality (and other social problems) have a straightforward relationship to deservingness. People often hold lower-income people and groups responsible for inequality if they believe that those groups are not putting in enough effort; they tend to excuse people's circumstances if they believe that external forces, such as access to opportunities or discrimination, are holding those people back. This is how we locate people's beliefs about economic inequality on the responsibility–unequal opportunity continuum. However, not all causal attributions for inequality have a straightforward relationship with perceived responsibility and, thus, helping behavior. There are two in-between categories: cultural and innate explanations.

First, many researchers examine the importance of culture and familial socialization to poverty and inequality in nuanced ways that do not place blame on individuals. For example, some scholars argue that cultural forces are powerful and largely beyond any given individual's control and, further, that many of the resulting traits that some call problematic—such as prioritizing "street smarts" over "book smarts"—are in fact adaptive responses to the difficulties of resource-deprived contexts.[24] However, in American political debate, people point to culture as an important cause of inequality often to blame an entire group of individuals for negative life outcomes (see chapter 2). The term *culture of poverty* especially carries this connotation for poor people,[25] and often poor Black Americans specifically.[26] In short, attributing inequalities to culture may not always be associated with blame; however, in public debate, these explanations have been linked to blaming poor and Black Americans specifically.

The second type of causal attribution with an ambiguous relationship to responsibility and deservingness is innate explanation—arguing that some people are held back due to characteristics with which they were born, such as a handicap or a learning disability. Innate characteristics, by definition, are within individuals, not society; yet, many people would argue that it is wrong to blame people for characteristics and related outcomes they cannot control. Some researchers argue that someone who believes that another person's difficulty stems from innate factors will tend to consider that person as deserving of assistance.[27] According to this perspective, even people who aren't very smart or who don't work very hard may be met with sympathy if these traits are perceived as being inborn.[28] This perspective is not uniform among researchers, however. We have already discussed the fact that inborn characteristics are part of a traditional meritocratic framework. Scholars working in the essentialism tradition argue that innate explanations are most often constructed as justifications for economic inequality, not reasons to level it.[29] These authors emphasize that notions of responsibility are less important than the fact that innate differences are perceived as natural—and, therefore, legitimate—as well as impossible to change.[30]

Deservingness, Social Groups, and Social Welfare Preferences

Americans often make very different assumptions about the deservingness of individuals and groups based on minimal context cues. For example, Appelbaum demonstrates that people view poor single mothers as less deserving than poor widowed mothers, and poor able-bodied people less deserving than poor people with physical disabilities.[31] Americans also often perceive people receiving welfare as undeserving, presumably because they assume that welfare recipients are not working.[32] Much research argues that negative stereotypes of Black Americans and other racial minorities paint them as less deserving than others (although the findings presented in chapter 4 call this into question, at least on average and in the contemporary era).[33] These findings suggest that the public will be less supportive of social welfare for some groups because they consider those groups to be undeserving.

However, this research often overlooks the fact that—as we have seen—Americans often fiercely disagree over whether a particular individual or group is deserving. In this chapter, I ask which of these disagreements are most politically potent. Political leaders could play an important role not only in linking explanations for inequality in general to policy prescriptions but also in determining which socioeconomic inequalities are linked to which prescriptions. In recent years, Democratic Party rhetoric has argued that its agenda addresses structural barriers faced by lower-income and working-class people, women, and racial minorities most of all. The Republican Party, in opposing the Democratic agenda, has tended to argue that these inequalities are not normatively problematic. In the period leading up to my surveys, the parties had few policy initiatives—and little accompanying rhetoric—aimed at rural Americans. Republicans have been more likely to discuss economic difficulties experienced by White Americans. Yet, the Republican Party often implies that White Americans don't benefit from government assistance. Perhaps the most salient policy solution offered by the Republican Party is the rolling back of affirmative action and diversity, equity, and inclusion programs. In short, many Americans, and maybe Republicans in particular, see economic struggles among rural and White people as disconnected from government policies to assist low-income people.[34]

Important differences may exist among the domains of inequality most often discussed by Democrats as well. Some scholarship argues that Americans' beliefs about why Black Americans tend to earn less than others are especially influential over their social welfare preferences. The primary reason for this is thought to be the common assumption that Black Americans make up an overwhelming number of welfare recipients.[35] In recent years, the Democratic Party may have inadvertently encouraged this stereotype by especially highlighting Black–White economic inequality and emphasizing the ways in which its policy agenda addresses systemic racism. Gilens finds that study participants' stereotypes of Black mothers receiving welfare were twice as predictive of their welfare support than stereotypes of White welfare mothers.[36] Gilens, as well as Thomas Nelson, also finds that explanations for low incomes among Black Americans were approximately as predictive of welfare attitudes as explanations for why poor people in general earn less than others.[37]

Few studies carefully compare the effects of the perceived deservingness of various social groups on support for generous social welfare; those that do focus on explanations for economic inequality in general or between Black and White Americans. None to my knowledge consider the relative effects of the perceived deservingness of women, rural residents, and White Americans on political attitudes. Prior research as well as my theory of partisan communication suggests we will find, to use Philip Converse's term, "constraint" linking explanations for inequality to political attitudes in more politically scripted inequality domains (the classic class-race-sex trio), but not in the less politically scripted domains (rural–urban and White–Asian American inequality).[38] Whether beliefs about Black and Latino versus White economic inequality are the most politically potent of all is an open question.

Investigating the Association Between Explanations for Inequality and Political Attitudes

Political Attitudes

In the pages that follow, I investigate various political attitudes as outcome variables. I rely most heavily on a battery of five questions that measure support for government-sponsored social welfare policy. Participants received the following prompt: "For each of the following questions, please indicate on a scale from 1 to 7 how much responsibility you think governments should have."[39] This was followed by five domains of social welfare, broadly understood, in which a government might be involved: "To ensure a job for everyone who wants one?," "To ensure adequate health care?," "To ensure that all children can go to good schools?," "To ensure a reasonable standard of living for the unemployed?," and "To ensure a college education for everyone who wants one?" (Question order was randomized across survey respondents.) These five statements were averaged to create a government responsibility for social welfare measurement scale.[40] In addition, the surveys included two questions even more directly linked to redistribution that asked respondents whether they agreed with the following statements: "Differences in incomes in the U.S. are too large," and "The wealthy should pay more in taxes than they do currently." The first statement gauged whether respondents believed income differentials ought to be smaller, and the second statement provided a mechanism for decreasing income inequality. Answer choices here ranged from strongly disagree to strongly agree. These items were also averaged to create a measurement index (referred to as the decrease economic inequality index).[41]

Distributions for these variables are available in figures 7.1 and 7.2. In figure 7.1, we see that answers to the questions about the provision of health care and K–12 education were skewed toward endorsing government responsibility in these areas. In other words, the policy goals of government-guaranteed health care and high-quality schools accessible to all children were quite popular. Responses to the other three items making up the government social welfare scale (guaranteed job, reasonable standard of living,

Figure 7.1 Distributions of Items in Government Responsibility for Social Welfare Index (2016)

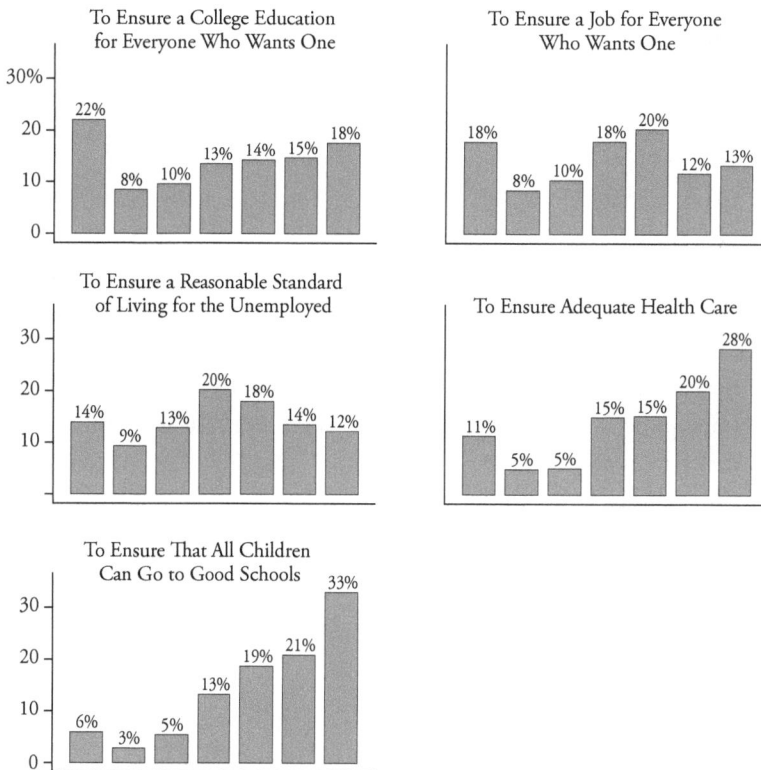

Source: Author's calculations using 2016 EIPS data.

Note: 1 = not government responsibility at all; 7 = entirely government responsibility.

Figure 7.2 Distributions of Items in Decrease Economic Inequality Index (2016)

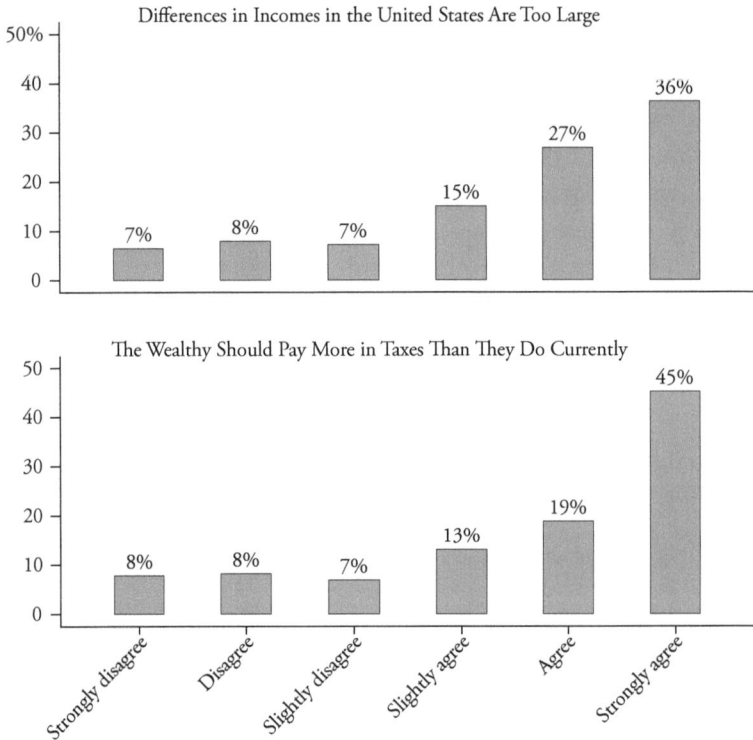

Differences in Incomes in the United States Are Too Large

The Wealthy Should Pay More in Taxes Than They Do Currently

Source: Author's calculations using 2016 EIPS data.

and college education) were distributed relatively equally. Turning to Figure 7.2, respondents tended to agree with the statements about income differences being too large and the wealthy paying more in taxes. Only 22 to 23 percent of respondents disagreed.

I also included two questions on the 2018 survey about affirmative action policies. Respondents were presented with the statements: "Employers and universities should use gender-based affirmative action to help women get ahead," and "Employers and universities should use race-based affirmative action to help people of color get ahead." Answer choices here ranged from strongly disagree to strongly agree. The distributions are available in figure 7.3. The strongly disagree option was especially popular (with approximately 30 percent of respondents strongly disagreeing), but otherwise, responses were fairly evenly distributed across the answer categories.

Figure 7.3 Distributions of Affirmative Action Items (2018)

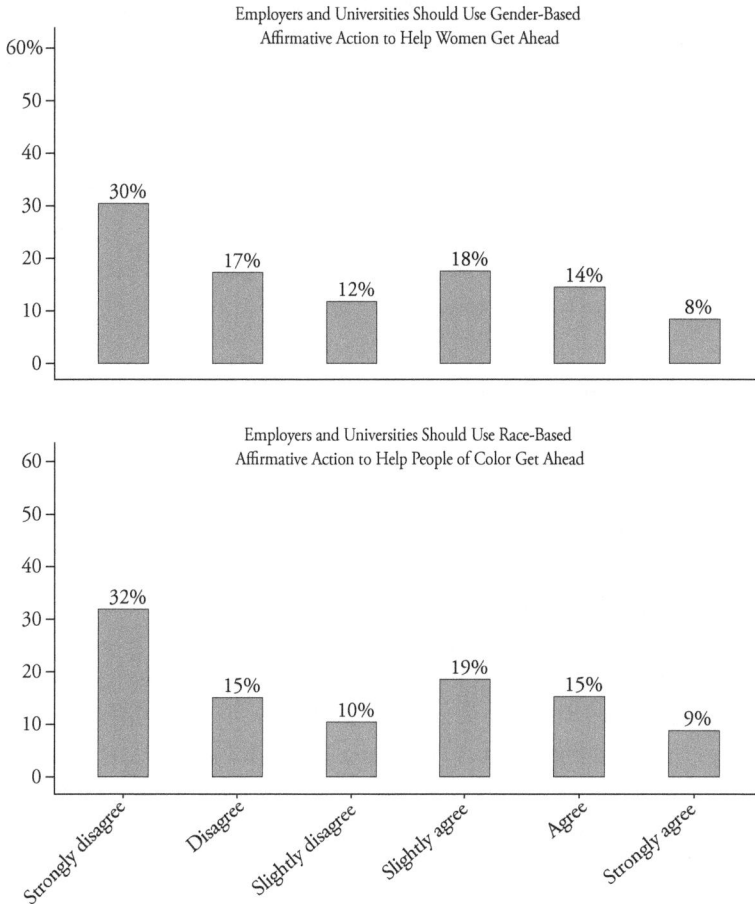

Source: Author's calculations using 2018 EIPS data.

Finally, I measured presidential candidate preferences using feeling thermometers, a common measurement technique that is closely linked to people's electoral choices. Respondents were asked: "How do you feel about Hillary Clinton?" (and, separately, about Donald Trump and Bernie Sanders). For each candidate, they were shown an image of a thermometer which they could use to locate the temperature anywhere from 0 (very cold) to 100 (very warm). Distributions for these variables are available in appendix figure A.13. For purposes of the analyses, I created two comparative measures: I subtracted feelings about Trump from feelings about Clinton, and, in a separate variable, I subtracted feelings about Sanders from feelings about Clinton, such that the final measures (from –100 to 100) reflect a relative preference for Clinton.[42] While scholarly work linking causal attributions to presidential preferences is not uncommon, I am not aware of any prior studies examining whether Americans' causal attributions are associated with their candidate preferences as between those running for the same party's nomination. Given that Sanders' politics were more progressive than those of Clinton, we would expect respondents doubting the American Dream to feel more warmly toward him than toward her.

Explanations for Inequality

In this chapter, I use the same inequality attribution questions as in chapters 4, 5, and 6; however, I rely mostly on the responsibility–unequal opportunity indexes for economic inequality in general, between women and men, and between Black and Latino Americans and White Americans. Politicians link these inequalities most reliably to policy prescriptions. Again, those indexes take the average of respondents' beliefs about the importance of unequal access to schools and jobs (or, for women, childcare), discrimination, and hard work (this item is reverse-scored) in determining inequality. The three indexes are referred to as unequal economic opportunity, unequal economic opportunity for women, and unequal economic opportunity for Black and Latino Americans.

Additional Variables to Control for Possible Confounds

To understand the relationship between explanations for inequality and people's political preferences—and especially to give any such relationship a causal interpretation—we must take into account those factors that may be causes of both factual beliefs about inequality and political attitudes. Such variables include the demographic characteristics discussed in chapter 5 and partisanship, ideology, and social prejudice, discussed in chapter 6. I also consider the impact of social dominance orientation, which can be interpreted as a preference for inequality (or, at the low end of the measurement scale, a desire for equality). As discussed in chapter 5, social dominance orientation is thought to be higher in socially dominant groups; however, it is also a characteristic that can vary within groups. Given that it is likely closely associated both with people's explanations for inequality and their political views, I control for it in some of the analyses in this chapter. Finally, one variable I do not include as a control in the analyses presented in this chapter is the level of inequality people perceive exists in the United States. As discussed early in the book, how people interpret economic inequality is much more politically consequential than their beliefs about how much inequality exists. In line with these expectations, preliminary analyses employing a measure of perceived inequality revealed a weak and inconsistent relationship with the outcome variables examined herein.[43]

The Unequal Economic Opportunity Index and Political Attitudes

In figure 7.4, we begin with a bivariate look—without any control variables—at the relationship between the unequal economic opportunity index and policy-oriented views encapsulated by the government social welfare and decrease economic inequality scales (top row) and presidential candidate preferences (bottom row). Given that different patterns emerge among racial and ethnic groups, relationships among Black, Hispanic, and White survey respondents are displayed separately. (Other racial and ethnic categories are excluded due to small sample sizes.) The y-axis on the left side gives the full range of the political attitude variables on a common scale (0 to 1 for the policy views and −100 to 100 for the feeling thermometer variables).

Beginning with the top row of figure 7.4, first, the relationships between explanations for inequality and the two attitude indexes were remarkably similar (within racial groups), despite the different objects in view and different question types. This suggests a tight cluster of attitudes about inequality related in the same way to beliefs about the origins of inequality. Second, for White Americans, the magnitude of both relationships is very large, covering approximately half of the political attitude response range. For Hispanic Americans, the magnitude of the relationship for the government social welfare index in particular is enormous, although noisily estimated given the smaller sample size. On average, Hispanics who were most optimistic about the American Dream (low on the unequal opportunity index) appeared to reject a role for government in social welfare, and those most cynical about the American Dream (high on the index)

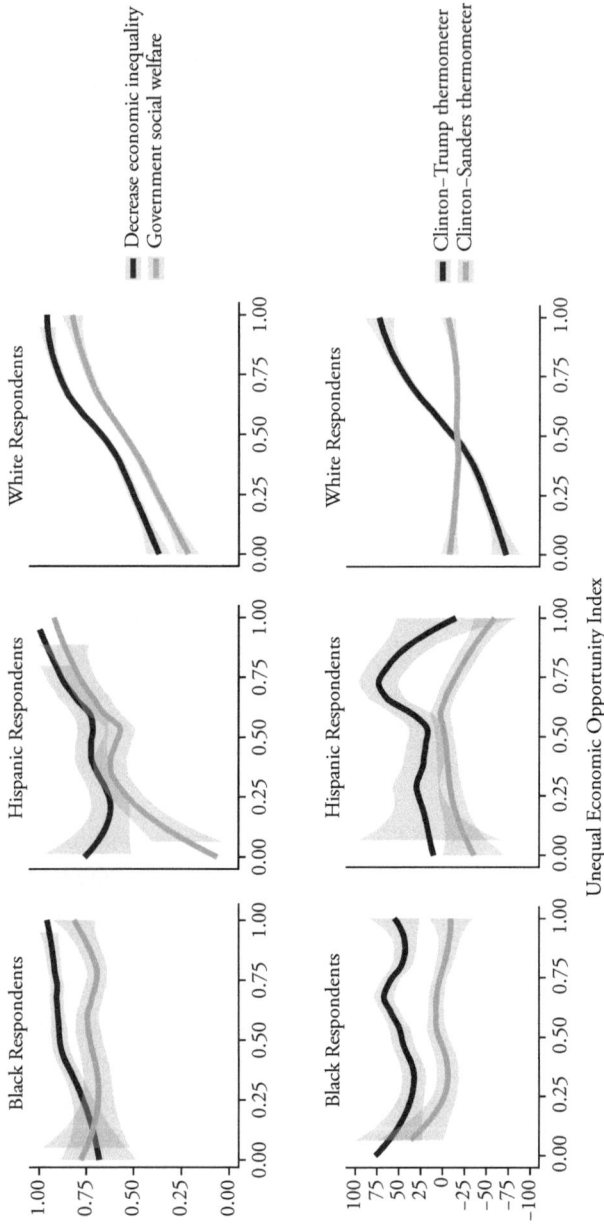

Figure 7.4 Relationship Between the Unequal Economic Opportunity Index and Political Attitudes (2016)

Source: Author's calculations using 2016 EIPS data.

Note: Figure depicts the relationship between the unequal economic opportunity index and policy-relevant attitudes (top row) and presidential preferences (bottom row). Localized regression with 95 percent confidence intervals. Estimates for racial and ethnic minority groups are necessarily less precisely estimated because sample sizes are much smaller.

fully embraced it. Patterns among Black Americans differed considerably—there was only a weak relationship between the unequal opportunity index and political attitudes. That said, this may be the case due to ceiling effects among Black Americans; their economic policy attitudes were quite progressive across the board.

The survey findings linking causal attributions for inequality to presidential candidate preferences differed in some important ways. Among White Americans, the relationship between the unequal economic opportunity index and feelings toward Clinton as compared with Trump was similar to that for the policy-relevant items. On average, respondents who believed that the economy is meritocratic rated Trump 50 points warmer than Clinton, and those who believed that the economy is not meritocratic rated Clinton 50 points warmer than Trump. However, the relationship was weak for Black and Hispanic Americans. While the weak effect among Black Americans may again be due to ceiling effects, the similar finding among Hispanic Americans raises the question of whether members of these groups simply did not perceive Clinton as the more economically progressive candidate relative to Trump. Finally, the relationship between survey respondents' explanations for inequality and their preference for Clinton over Sanders was negligible, although it trended negative (as expected).

While some of the trends were weaker for members of racial and ethnic minorities, the relationship between the unequal economic opportunity index and political preferences tended to be quite large. Of course, without the inclusion of statistical controls, these figures almost certainly overstate the size of the unique relationship between explanations for unequal economic outcomes and political preferences. Recall especially the argument from earlier chapters that explanations stem in part from a person's partisan identification and related political predispositions. Because partisanship in particular overlaps so strongly with policy views and vote choice, a bivariate look at explanations for economic inequality and political attitudes like this one will exaggerate their relationship because partisanship is likely a hidden driver of both phenomena.

In the next set of analyses, I examine the relationship between respondents' explanations for inequality and their political attitudes while taking into account possible confounding factors. See figure 7.5.[44] Each coefficient

Figure 7.5 Associations Between the Unequal Opportunity Index and Political Attitudes Holding Potential Confounders Constant (2016)

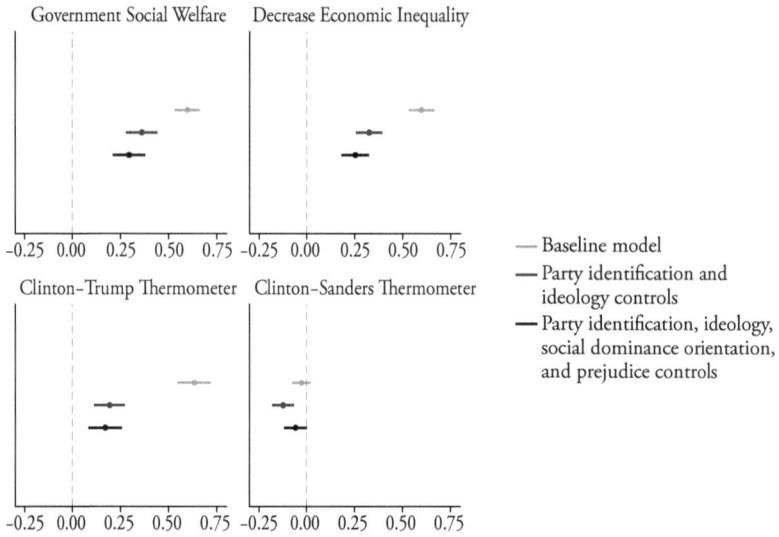

Government Social Welfare   Decrease Economic Inequality

-0.25 0.00   0.25   0.50   0.75 -0.25 0.00   0.25   0.50   0.75

Clinton–Trump Thermometer   Clinton–Sanders Thermometer

— Baseline model
— Party identification and ideology controls
— Party identification, ideology, social dominance orientation, and prejudice controls

-0.25 0.00   0.25   0.50   0.75 -0.25 0.00   0.25   0.50   0.75

Source: Author's calculations using 2016 EIPS data.
Note: Each coefficient depicted is from an independent linear regression with the unequal economic opportunity index as the key predictor and control variables included as indicated in the key. The baseline model includes income, sex, race, rurality, religiosity, education, and age. All variables are coded 0 to 1.

represents the association between the unequal economic opportunity index and one of the political attitude outcome variables. Note that all variables have been re-coded to range from 0 to 1 for ease of interpretation. Policy-relevant attitudes are on the top and presidential candidate preferences are on the bottom. The baseline model includes the unequal economic opportunity index and demographic variables as controls, and then partisanship and ideology are added, followed by a model including all of these control variables as well as social dominance orientation, racism, and sexism. (The coefficients for the control variables are not displayed; full results are in appendix tables A.5 and A.6.) The fuller models risk overcontrolling in the sense that ideology, social dominance, and perhaps prejudice too are in part shaped by a person's beliefs about the origins of inequality (and not only vice versa, as this analysis assumes). However, my goal is to demonstrate the robustness of a unique explanation–attitude relationship, even with stringent controls.

We see that coefficients are large—and quite similar in size—in the analyses predicting support for social welfare and redistribution. In both cases, the coefficients are close to .6 (more than half of the outcome variable's range) in the baseline model and remain greater than .25 (25 percent of the outcome variable's range) with the many control variables added. The relationship between the unequal economic opportunity index and a preference for Clinton over Trump is even stronger in the baseline model but more diminished (.17) with the addition of the control variables, especially partisanship. This reflects the long-standing, very close relationship between partisanship and presidential vote choice.

The only weak association emerged when comparing Clinton to Sanders. The relationship between the opportunity index and a preference for Clinton varied depending on which control variables were included; it was null in the baseline model but negative (as expected) when removing the effects of partisanship. In hindsight, these marginal results may not be surprising given that we are investigating variation in candidate support at the primary stage. Such candidates are less known to voters, and candidates in the same primary tend to have broadly similar policy agendas. Reflecting my findings here, Larry Bartels finds that Clinton and Sanders supporters were quite similar in their economic policy views and that the two candidates' patterns of support were most unique in that Clinton performed well among Democratic partisans whereas Sanders attracted many independents.[45]

Before moving on, let me comment on the political relevance of the two attributions for inequality that were not a part of the unequal economic opportunity index—beliefs about culture and innate intelligence. When regressing the policy and Clinton–Trump feeling thermometer variables onto these two attributions (separately), cultural explanations were associated with more conservative policy views and a preference for Trump, and innate intelligence explanations were associated with a preference for Trump (the policy attitude analysis yields a null result). Overall, the relationships were smaller than for the other explanations. (See appendix figure A.14.) These smaller (and null) associations may have stemmed from the unclear moral implications of these narratives, as discussed in chapter 4. Further, innate explanations for inequality in particular have not been salient in political debates for some time, meaning people simply might not connect these beliefs to their economic policy preferences.

One final question to ask is whether the sizable association between the unequal economic opportunity index and these political attitudes is found among Democrats, Republicans, and independents approximately equally. From a statistical perspective, we can obtain a large coefficient on an explanatory variable in a linear regression even if the effects are concentrated among one subgroup of respondents. If this occurs, the average coefficient is real, but it is not typical of survey respondents or consistent across subgroups.

Figure 7.6 displays results from four linear regressions that allowed the coefficient on the unequal economic opportunity index to vary according to partisanship (or independence). (Full results are available in appendix table A.7.) Demographic control variables were included and held at their means in the figure. The findings are reassuring in that the unequal economic opportunity index was associated with relatively left-leaning views regardless of respondents' party identification or lack thereof. However, the size of the slopes vary considerably. As in the case of Black Americans, Democrats held relatively left-leaning views on policy and presidential candidates across the board and, thus, had less room to move up the index as they became more pessimistic about the American economy. Beliefs about the origins of unequal economic outcomes appeared to be much more influential over independents' and Republicans' policy views. As they neared the top of the unequal opportunity index, independents' and Republicans' policy views grew surprisingly similar to those of Democrats. Scores on the unequal opportunity index were also strongly associated with independents' preferences for Clinton over Trump. Finally, the index had a modest association with a preference for Sanders over Clinton across all groups.

Given that Republicans were much less likely than Democrats to score highly on the unequal opportunity index,[46] are the regression estimates for Republicans reliable? On a related note, there is reason to be concerned that linearity assumptions have produced misleading results. In figure 7.7, I include bivariate localized regression results that assess the relationship between the unequal economic opportunity index and the four political attitude variables among Democrats, Republicans, and independents separately. These figures include density plots along the x-axis. These analyses complement those in figure 7.6 and confirm relatively small relationships among Democrats and large ones among independents and Republicans; however, trends toward the very high end of the unequal opportunity index are not reliable among Republicans.

Figure 7.6 Association Between the Unequal Opportunity Index and Political Attitudes by Respondent Party Identification (2016)

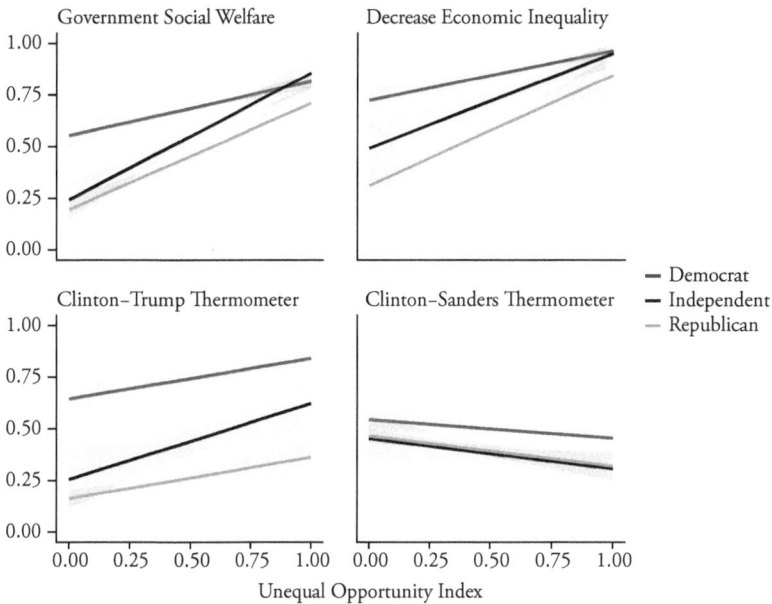

Source: Author's calculations using 2016 EIPS data.
Note: Figure represents predicted values from linear regressions with four political attitude outcome measures. Models allow the coefficient on the unequal economic opportunity index to vary by partisanship. Demographic controls are held at their means with 95 percent confidence intervals.

Political Attitudes and Explanations for Different Kinds of Socioeconomic Inequality

Throughout the chapter thus far, I have analyzed the association between the unequal economic opportunity index, which asks about the causes of economic inequality in general, and various political attitude measures. However, there are two more indexes to consider: unequal economic opportunity for women and unequal economic opportunity for Black and Latino Americans. I have not shown analyses including these variables because the patterns are nearly identical to those for the unequal economic opportunity index. The magnitudes of the effects are slightly larger for the general opportunity index than the opportunity for women index, and slightly larger for the opportunity for women index than the opportunity for Black and Latino Americans index. However, the overall similarity suggests that an underlying responsibility–unequal opportunity orientation

Figure 7.7 Relationship Between the Unequal Opportunity Index and Political Attitudes by Partisanship (2016)

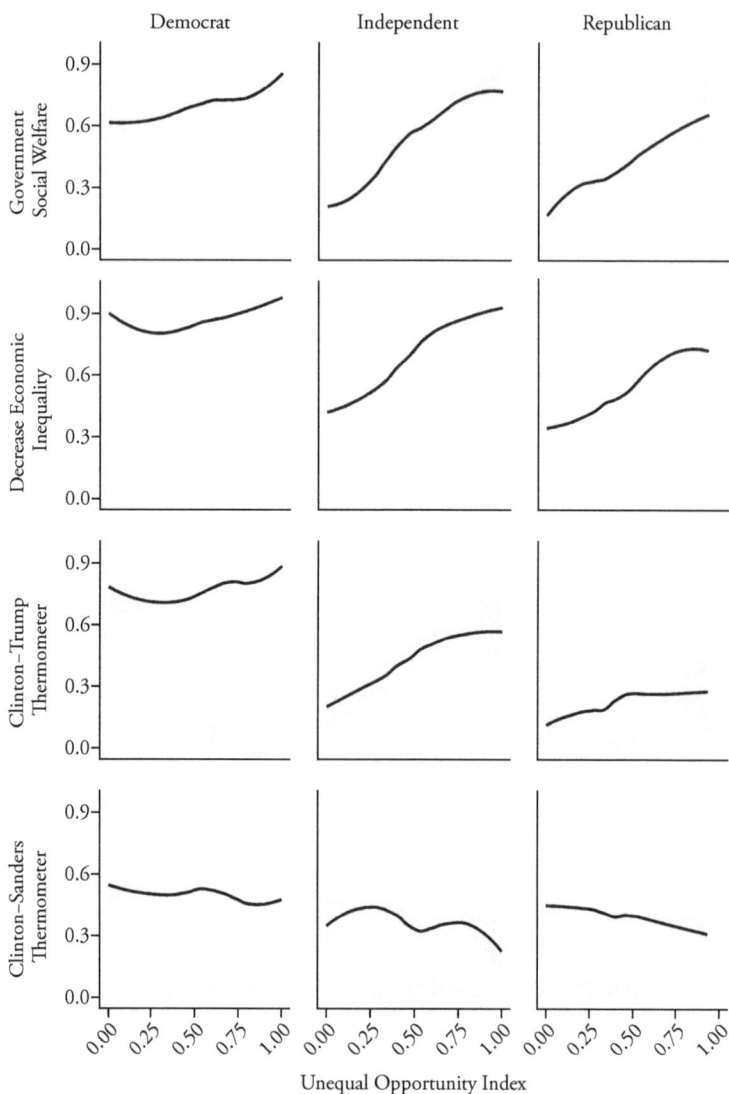

Source: Author's calculations using 2016 EIPS data.

Note: Figure depicts the relationship between the unequal economic opportunity index and four political attitudes by political party (or independence). Localized regression with 95 percent confidence intervals.

among participants may be driving all results. While this implies that we might consider combining the indexes into one measurement index, such a summary measure would hide any meaningful differences among them, such as those noted by Gilens and Nelson.[47]

In the next set of analyses, I include each of the three indexes as explanatory variables together in each model. These indexes are admittedly highly correlated with one another (from .64 to .81). This indicates that multicollinearity may be a concern; however, the variance inflation factors for the three unequal opportunity indexes are in the range of 2 to 3, signaling that the coefficients are meaningful representations of the relationship between each index and the outcome variable while holding the other two indexes constant.[48] As before, I also control for demographic variables and partisanship but don't display the coefficients.

The results, in figure 7.8, contradict the conventional scholarly wisdom that explanations for racial inequality are most closely associated with social welfare attitudes. In the two panels on the left, the coefficients indicate that scores on the generic economic opportunity index were strongly associated with progressive economic policy attitudes. The sex economic inequality items also were associated with these outcome measures, although to a lesser extent. However, holding these variables constant, variation in people's beliefs about the origins of inequality between Black and Latino Americans and White Americans was not associated with attitudes on social welfare or redistribution.[49] The appendix includes the full regression results (see table A.8) as well as results broken out by race, revealing that this pattern was driven primarily by views among White Americans (see figure A.16).

These patterns reverse with respect to support for Clinton over Trump, however. Believing that Black and Latino Americans face unfair barriers to success—and should not be blamed for earning less than others on average—was associated with support for Clinton over Trump. Controlling for these beliefs, explanations for female–male inequality contributed little to variation in support for Clinton and explanations for generic inequality did not contribute at all.

At face value, these patterns may reflect new political realities as well as the specific context of the 2016 presidential election. A straightforward rendering of the policy results in figure 7.8 is that, at least for White Americans, the decision to support or oppose government assistance and redistribution for the benefit of lower-income Americans in general stemmed from

Figure 7.8 Coefficient Plots of Political Attitudes Regressed onto Three Unequal Opportunity Indexes (2016)

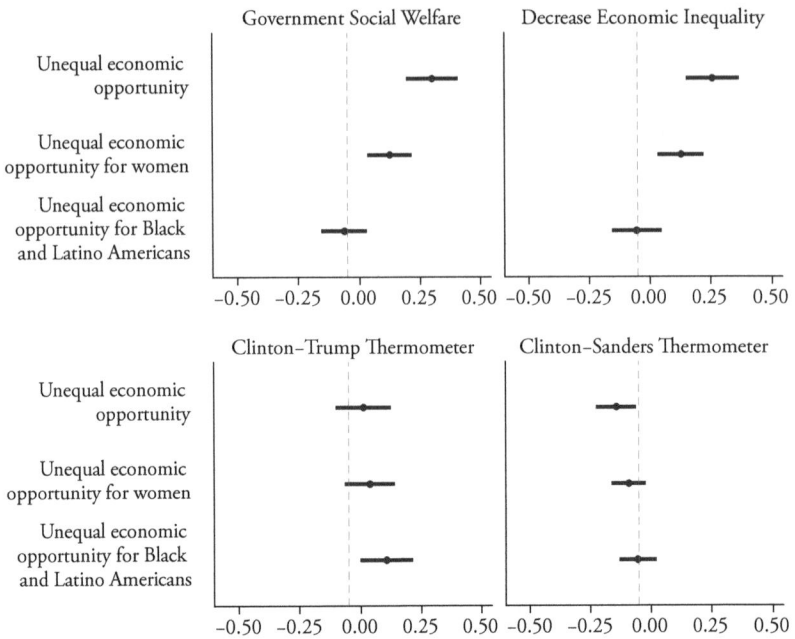

Source: Author's calculations using 2016 EIPS data.
Note: Each panel displays results from one linear regression that includes three indexes as predictors: unequal economic opportunity, unequal economic opportunity for women, and unequal economic opportunity for Black and Latino Americans. Partisanship and demographic variables are included as control variables.

their beliefs about the origins of unequal economic outcomes in general, not their beliefs about the origins of racial inequality.[50] Assuming that this indeed represents a change from similar analyses carried out two decades ago,[51] we might conclude that beliefs about the beneficiaries of government assistance are not as racialized as they were in the past.

A similarly straightforward interpretation of the presidential preference findings is that Clinton—at least relative to an allegedly populist Trump—was perceived as interested in assisting historically marginalized racial groups but not lower-income people in general. This reflects some current critiques of the Democratic Party. Some analysts argue that the Democratic Party has become consumed with issues linked to social identity—most unrelated to economics—and, for both normative and pragmatic reasons, should reorient toward a platform catering to the economic interests of low- and middle-income Americans.[52] Although I have argued that the Democratic Party has in recent elections returned to its economic populist origins, its attention to social identity at times has overshadowed this message. This may have been especially true of Clinton's campaign, as she sought to defeat a Republican opponent who by all appearances was unusually socially prejudiced.

Yet, two aspects of the patterns we have observed suggest that this is not the full story. One is the fact that the sharp differences among the index coefficients arose among White Americans but not others. The second is the surprising null result for the Black and Latino index in the policy opinion analyses. We might consider whether some White Americans responded to the race index questions in what has become known as a performative manner—stating their concerns about structural inequalities and denying individual-level causes of unequal outcomes to align themselves with the racial-justice ethos popular at the time. Performative concern over racial inequality may have been associated with support for Clinton but not for economically progressive policy, as we see in figure 7.8. Note that this explanation is similar, but not identical, to social desirability bias. Social desirability bias is thought to be confined largely to the survey response, whereas efforts to subscribe to reigning social norms can be found in everyday behavior, not only the survey context.[53]

In the final statistical analysis in this section, let us examine whether responses measured by the unequal economic opportunity for women and unequal economic opportunity for Black and Latino Americans indexes were more closely related to outcome variables specifically linked to race and sex inequality. Figure 7.9 (see also appendix table A.9) depicts findings from two linear regressions with preferences on affirmative action as the outcome variables. (These data are drawn from the 2018 survey; unfortunately, the general unequal economic opportunity index is not available to assess its added explanatory value.) In the affirmative action for women model, both indexes were positively associated with the outcome variable, but the coefficient on unequal opportunity for women was larger than that for unequal opportunity for Black and Latino Americans, as we would expect. With respect to support for affirmative action for Black and Latino Americans, the coefficients on both the sex and race opportunity indexes were large and of approximately equal size. The underperformance of the race inequality index relative to the sex inequality index again raises suspicions about the integrity of at least some respondents' answers on the for-

Figure 7.9 Coefficient Plots of Affirmative Action Support Regressed onto Two Unequal Opportunity Indexes (2018)

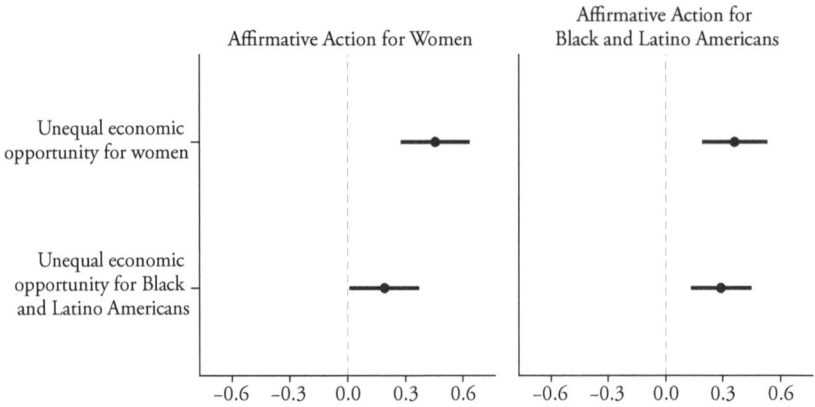

Source: Author's calculations using 2016 EIPS data.
Note: Each panel displays results from one linear regression that includes two indexes as predictors: unequal economic opportunity for women and unequal economic opportunity for Black and Latino Americans. Partisanship and demographic variables are included as control variables.

mer. Some respondents may have had a performative concern for structural inequality among racial minorities that did not relate to their views on affirmative action.

Less Scripted Inequalities and Political Attitudes

In a final set of analyses, I consider the relationship between people's beliefs about the origins of two less salient inequalities and their political attitudes. Recall that, in the 2018 survey, I asked survey respondents to explain not only unequal economic outcomes between women and men and between Black and Latino Americans and White Americans but also unequal outcomes between rural and urban Americans, and between White and Asian Americans. At least theoretically, skepticism about the American Dream for any social group ought to be associated with progressive views on economic policy—both means-tested and broad-based economic policies assist people regardless of their social identity. Yet, given the complicated politics of inequality in the heterogeneous and polarized United States, all is not equal.

Figure 7.10 includes regression coefficients for all five causal narratives for the four different domains of socioeconomic inequality captured in the

2018 survey. Each panel represents a coefficient from a separate linear regression (with partisanship and demographic controls included but not shown); the outcome variable in each is the government social welfare index. For the more scripted inequalities (the two columns on the left), coefficients for the three explanations that make up the unequal opportunity

Figure 7.10 Coefficient Plots of Social Welfare Support Regressed onto Specific Explanations for More and Less Scripted Inequalities (2018)

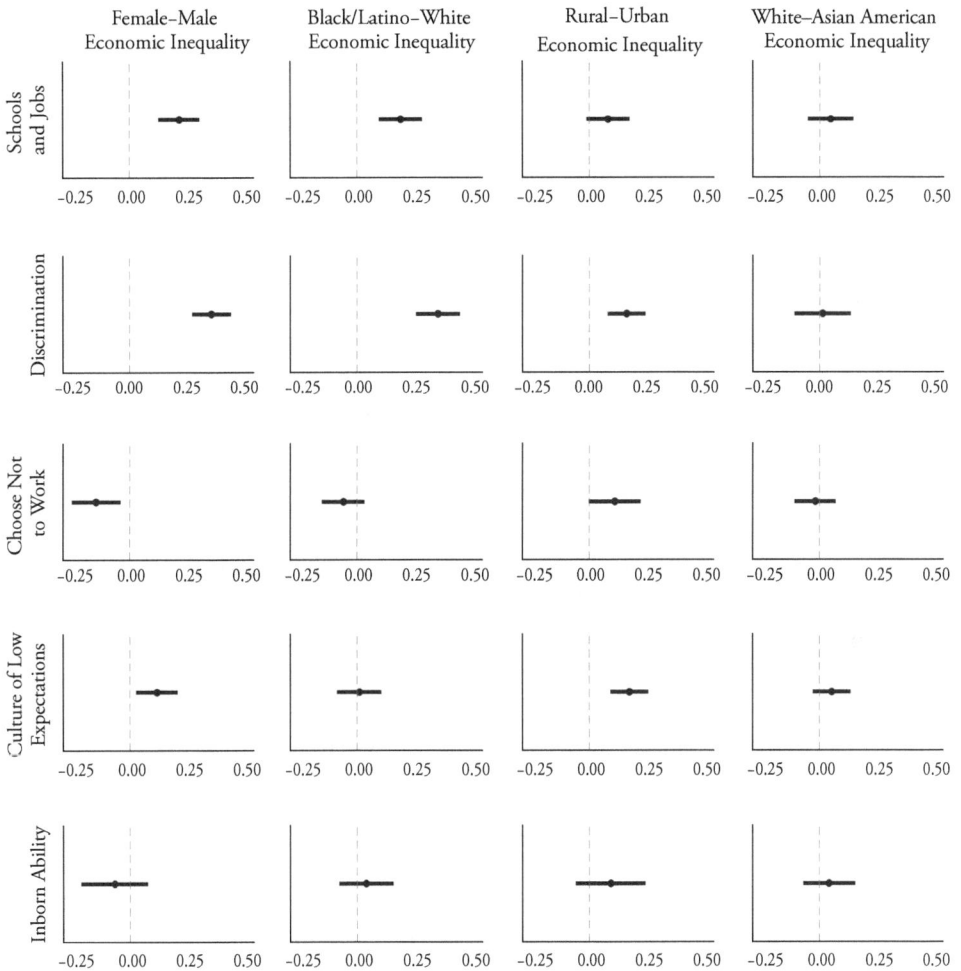

Source: Author's calculations using 2018 EIPS data.
Note: Each panel displays coefficient for indicated explanation for female–male, Black/Latino–White, rural–urban, or White–Asian American inequality. Outcome variable is the government responsibility for social welfare index. Partisanship and demographic variables are included as control variables.

indexes are as expected: believing in discrimination and lack of access to schools and jobs (or childcare) was associated with support for government social welfare; believing people choose not to work was associated with opposition to it (although the coefficient is not statistically significant in the Black/Latino–White model). For the less scripted inequalities (the two columns on the right), findings in the rural–urban model are confusing: all explanations were associated with support for social welfare (even those arguing that rural Americans do not work hard or are socialized into a culture with low expectations). On the other hand, in the White–Asian American domain of inequality, all of the findings were null. These patterns were almost identical when the outcome variable was support for redistribution. Analyses predicting presidential preferences yielded similar results in the more scripted inequality domains and mostly null results in the less scripted domains.[54]

Conclusion

This chapter has argued that faith in the American Dream, or lack thereof, likely influences Americans' political candidate and policy preferences. Survey respondents who viewed unequal outcomes as the product of unequal opportunity—rather than individual behavioral choice—were more likely than others to favor Democratic and progressive presidential candidates, generous government-provided social welfare, tax increases on the rich to reduce inequality, and affirmative action for women and Black and Latino Americans. Most of these associations were substantial, even controlling for partisanship, symbolic ideology, social dominance orientation, social prejudice, and a range of demographic variables. The list of policy preferences strongly associated with beliefs about the origins of inequality is potentially much longer, limited here by available survey measures.

That said, these associations varied across social groups. They were less evident among Black Americans and Democrats; these groups already held quite progressive views, even when they conveyed that they thought the economy is fair. The associations were often quite large among independents and Republicans, and among Hispanic and White Americans. These findings help us to understand why so many people—especially on the political right—say that they value equal opportunity but at the same time oppose economically progressive policy: they simply believe that the U.S. economy has achieved equal opportunity.

We also examined whether beliefs about some types of economic inequality were more aligned with people's political views than others. Do Americans' explanations for economic inequality in general influence their political views? Or is it possible that their explanations for racial economic inequality are the underlying causes of those views? In the past, scholars have found evidence that causal attributions for Black Americans' economic difficulties were especially politically potent.[55] Do explanations for less salient inequalities matter at all politically?

Results from my analyses converge in some respects with these prior analyses and diverge in others. My results converge in the sense that Americans' beliefs about the causes of Black–White inequality were much more closely associated with policy preferences than beliefs about inequalities explicitly or implicitly involving lower–income White people. However, the findings in this chapter diverge from prior work in that explanations for Black–White inequality were not associated with policy preferences over and above the influence of explanations for economic inequality in general. Political correctness could have clouded these analyses, making responses to the Black–White inequality measures insincere. In addition, after decades of growing economic inequality for all Americans accompanied by more broad-based government assistance, social welfare possibly may have become less racialized.

We must consider two important caveats. First, because I draw on cross-sectional survey evidence, I cannot be certain that Americans' beliefs about the origins of economic inequality causally influence their political opinions. My analyses may leave out important confounding variables, or political opinions could be what shape people's economic narratives about inequality and not vice versa. In addition, people may have simply learned the "correct" partisan explanations for inequality and policy prescriptions together as a bundle, meaning that the explanations for inequality play no functional role in bolstering related policy prescriptions or the candidates who champion them. My model and these counterarguments both merit testing with methods better oriented toward causal inference.

Second, the political outcome variables I examined were limited primarily to redistributive government programs designed to respond after the fact to unequal labor market inequalities, such as providing health care to low-income people, guaranteeing incomes for the unemployed, or taxing the rich at higher rates. However, government as well as private sector actors can also work to reduce labor market inequality directly, for example, by setting minimum wages, curbing executive compensation, or boosting employee benefits.[56] The explanations for economic inequality that I examine herein are likely also associated with opinion on such policies. For example, scores on the unequal economic opportunity index were strongly associated with a measure of support for raising the minimum wage (available in the 2016 Cooperative Election Study). On a related note, Trump has focused Americans' attention on international trade (a focus adopted to a lesser extent by the Biden administration as well), arguing in favor of new trade deals and tariffs to counter the trade practices of other countries that harm some American workers. The politics surrounding such arguments and related patterns in public opinion are important to explore in future work.[57]

CHAPTER 8

The American Dream: Belief, Rhetoric, and Reality

> The real problem…is that not only does your side already say more false and
> misleading things than you'd like to admit, but they are almost certainly say-
> ing more false and misleading things than you realize. That's because your
> side is much better at misleading *you* than they are at misleading people out-
> side of your ideological camp, and this kind of own-team deception creates
> huge tactical and strategic problems.
>
> —Matthew Yglesias in Substack article "Misinformation
> Mostly Confuses Your Own Side" (2025)

DEBATES OVER THE American Dream are central to U.S. politics. Nearly
all Americans believe the nation's economy ought to provide hard-working
citizens the opportunity to earn a good wage and live a comfortable life.
However, Democrats and Republicans tend to disagree as to whether that
dream is reality. These disagreements fuel opposing policy prescriptions.
In this concluding chapter, I summarize the book's theoretical framework
and empirical evidence, consider key limitations thereof, and discuss its
contributions to several lines of social scientific research. I then turn my
attention to a question that has been lurking since the opening pages: How
accurate are the two parties' factual claims about economic inequality and
opportunity? Is the American Dream only a dream, or is it reality?

Partisan debates over the American Dream have animated U.S. politics
since the nation's founding, and they have resembled their current form for
at least a century. The Republican Party has tended to argue that the nation
has achieved the American Dream. The notion that anyone who works hard
will thrive suggests that existing economic disparities represent either just
deserts or only temporary inequalities. Conversely, the Democratic Party
has tended to argue that the Dream has not been achieved. According to

https://doi.org/10.7758/trap6910.7022

Democrats, economic disparities exist because there are not enough good opportunities to go around and because many people are treated unfairly. Many observers of U.S. politics have argued that the nation's individualistic dominant ideology consistently justifies high levels of economic inequality, underplaying this persistent Democratic protest. Jacksonian, Gilded Age, New Deal, Johnson era, and contemporary Democratic leaders have all made this claim. Republican leaders have sometimes voiced the concern too—most recently (although inconsistently) by Donald Trump—but this is a much rarer occurrence.

These factual narratives serve a purpose: they are intended to justify each party's policy agenda and persuade citizens inside and outside the party of its merits. Throughout its history, the Democratic Party has tended to represent working class and lower-income Americans. Thus, they have been the leveling party, seeking ways to equalize economic resources and power. For nearly a century, this effort has focused on empowering the federal government to rein in business power, implement progressive taxation, and design generous social welfare programs. The Republican Party has historically represented business interests and higher-income Americans. Thus, they have tended to defend existing economic arrangements. For at least a century, this has meant opposing restrictive government regulation on business, progressive taxation, and redistributive policy. I have referred to the parties' packages of policy proposals and factual justifications as partisan economic ideologies. Coalitional shifts, changing power dynamics within parties, and electoral pressures have often altered these modal tendencies— at points moderating them or forcing changes in emphasis. However, these political dynamics have not changed the overall character of the two parties' economic narratives about inequality and opportunity, at least not yet. Even today, with relative income parity between the parties' members, Republicans continue to be relative believers and Democrats relative skeptics of the American Dream.

A party's ideas tend to be absorbed by its supporters. Assuming that messages remain fairly consistent, they become embedded in partisan communities, eventually becoming common knowledge therein. While party leaders have great influence over what becomes partisan knowledge, they themselves are influenced by powerful coalitional interests when formulating their rhetoric and, further, become limited by the party's common knowledge once it is entrenched. Acknowledging a role for parties is also not meant to suggest that nothing else influences Americans' beliefs about economic inequality and opportunity. Other influences include people's personal economic situations, their experiences and biases associated with their social identities, and other socializing institutions, such as religious communities, schools, and entertainment media.[1] However, parties have the most incentive to persuade citizens. Their raison d'être is to enact their policy agenda by winning elections. To do so, they must persuade the public that their agenda is the right one. They also have great ability to persuade, given that most Americans psychologically identify with one of the two major parties and, increasingly, obtain information about politics from partisan sources.

The extensive survey data that I have presented herein supports this theoretical framework. Persistent and substantial disagreements exist between Democratic and Republican identifiers in the public over whether the nation provides ample and equal opportunity. Between 1980 and 2020, small partisan gaps became chasms. On balance, Republicans' views on the American Dream did not change much over these years; however, Democrats became much more pessimistic. Fluctuations in the public's beliefs over time—especially the politically attentive public—mirrored party leaders.

When asked to explain unequal economic outcomes in general and by race and sex, contemporary Democrats and Republicans often held dramatically different views. Democratic survey respondents were much more likely to point to underlying structural inequalities and Republican respondents to differences in work ethic. These partisan disagreements were much larger than those associated with demographic factors: they were approximately three times larger than those associated with survey respondents' education and religiosity, and generally at least five times larger than differences by respondent age, income, race or ethnicity, and sex. The only factors as divisive as party were also political. Symbolic political ideology—whether people refer to themselves as conservative or liberal—was also strongly associated with a person's beliefs about the American Dream. Social prejudice also mattered. However, racial prejudice and sexism were not as strongly associated with people's explanations for inequality as partisanship or symbolic ideology.

The recent survey data also conveyed telling complexity. Lay Democrats and Republicans disagreed most when the official party lines differed most—when economic inequality is more scripted by politicians and other influential political actors. They disagreed over the relevance of hard work to getting ahead or falling behind, the availability of good jobs and schools, and discrimination. (They also differed somewhat over the relevance of culture, mainly when they were trying to explain the origins of racial inequality.) Democrats and Republicans barely differed over the relevance of innate traits to economic inequality, a narrative that mostly fell out of mainstream political debate decades ago (although it has increasingly surfaced during the Trump era, unfortunately).

Partisan gaps were also most evident when people were trying to explain differences between the poor and the rich, women and men, and Black and Latino and White Americans. When the less scripted inequalities of rural versus urban and White versus Asian Americans were considered—not coincidentally, inequalities with members of the Republican coalition in the losing position—polarization was less evident. Partisans did not change sides in these instances. Rather, each side backed away from their usual narrative for inequality but refused to take up stock narratives favored by the other side.

Finally, I have demonstrated that beliefs about the American Dream—at least with respect to class, sex, and race (Black and Latino versus White)—tend to be closely associated with Americans' public policy and presidential candidate preferences. Importantly, this is true even controlling for partisanship, symbolic ideology, social prejudice, and egalitarian values. The most fervent American Dream believers conveyed much more conservative policy opinions than the biggest skeptics on average. Differences between believers and skeptics were nearly as large for presidential preferences—in this case, Trump versus Clinton. These patterns varied across different groups of survey respondents, however. American Dream beliefs appeared to matter less for Black Americans' and Democrats' policy views. By way of contrast, they appeared to be very consequential among independents and Republicans, and among Hispanic and non-Hispanic White Americans.

In sum, these empirical findings demonstrate that Americans who identify as Democratic or Republican, and liberal or conservative, tend to believe very different things about why lower-income people and lower-earning social groups earn less than others. These beliefs are closely linked to political preferences. Polarization is not all pervasive, however. Once we step outside well-worn public debates and inquire about more novel inequalities and narratives, partisans are more likely to see eye to eye. The predictable presence, and absence, of politicization supports my supposition that political parties construct economic ideologies and successfully propagate them. Because of this, citizens in both partisan camps are able to support very different economic policy agendas with deep conviction that the policies they support are both practical and fair.

Contributions to Scholarly Literatures

This book contributes to a number of scholarly literatures and debates. First and foremost, it serves as an update to publications from decades ago, such as Kluegel and Smith's venerable *Beliefs About Inequality*, that provided a broad overview of Americans' explanations for inequality.[2] Much has changed since their book came out in 1986. Americans today are much more likely to reject the idea that the economy rewards merit, including when considering racial minorities. I have also expanded the long-standard focus on why poor people, women, and many racial minority groups earn less than others to consider why rural and White Americans have fallen behind (some) others. Americans' answers to these questions in some instances defy conventional wisdom. Finally, I have situated the study of explanations for inequality within the study of politics, which I argue influences and is influenced by partisan economic narratives.

This book also contributes to the rapidly expanding literature—in the disciplines of economics, political science, psychology, and sociology, among others—on the topic of economic inequality more generally. I have sought to convey the importance of causal attributions for unequal economic outcomes to party politics and political attitudes. Most Americans do not perceive the economy in a political vacuum but instead view it through partisan lenses, as Angus Campbell and colleagues argued in their canonical work *The American Voter*.[3] Only by appreciating these partisan narratives can we understand why so many people support a given party's policy agenda with conviction—often against their personal economic interests. The long-standing belief, especially within the Republican Party, that deeply unequal economic rewards are nonetheless distributed meritocratically helps us to understand better how political leaders could carry on for so long without taking job loss and stagnating wages among working class Americans more seriously. Even after the Great Recession, a surprising number of Americans on the right blamed ordinary working people for their economic woes. More recently, Democrats have emphasized (and in some instances probably exaggerated) structural barriers to success, helping to explain the unexpected progressive zeal of many college-educated, White reformers.

Within the field of political science in particular, I add to the study of political polarization and related debates over the extent to which political ideology among members of the public is real. With respect to the study of polarization, my colleagues have spilled a great deal of proverbial ink over increasing attitudinal polarization (partisans disagreeing over what policies the government ought to pursue or which candidates should serve in office) and affective polarization (partisans disliking those on the other side of the aisle). Factual belief polarization deserves to join the pantheon of polarizations. Other scholars, including myself, have written about disagreements over "the facts." Yet, too often, researchers have framed these disagreements as the result of disinformation mostly propagated by the political right. I argue that both parties engage in a more subtle process of misinforming the public by sharing simple, stylized narratives and cherry-picked facts as opposed to lying. Within the echo chambers of partisan communities, in person and online, these agenda-supporting narratives become partisan common knowledge. Together, policy preferences and supporting arguments (including both value and fact claims) constitute ideology as it is most often understood. These partisan ideologies are very real but socially constructed and flexible. They are also more evident among ordinary citizens today than when Philip Converse wrote his famous piece on belief systems.[4] As other researchers have emphasized, the two parties' reversal over civil rights[5] and intense competition over elections[6] have played a role in this; however, an overlooked contributor to polarization in recent decades has been the Democratic Party's greater responsiveness to economic inequality.

Finally, I challenge the assumption among some scholars that the primary motivation for Republican Party opposition to social welfare, broadly understood, is racism. Two sets of findings undermine this idea. First, Americans' explanations for unequal opportunity in general and for women are more predictive of their redistributive policy preferences than their explanations for unequal opportunity among Black and Latino Americans. Second, these explanations themselves are shaped more by party affiliation and left–right ideology than racism (or sexism). The argument by some academics that racism largely fuels partisan polarization stems in part from a misinterpretation of the strong relationship between racial resentment and conservative policy views. As a concept, racial resentment integrates affective prejudice with factual beliefs about the origins of racial inequality, arguing that the former causes the latter. However, as a measure, racial resentment almost entirely gauges factual beliefs.[7] Scholars increasingly argue that the racial resentment scale ought to be labeled for what it measures most directly: views of racial inequality[8] or structural versus individual attributions for Black Americans' economic and social status.[9] Because of the Republican Party's long-standing commitment to American Dream optimism and resistance to structural explanations for social inequalities, Republicans will likely score high on racial resentment regardless of how they feel about Black Americans specifically.[10] Using the racial resentment measure without controlling for a person's attributional style likely overstates the relationship between racial prejudice and policy conservatism.

Key Limitations and Future Research

The research presented in this book has been significantly aimed at understanding the political world descriptively. In the arena of public opinion, it is important to understand who believes what, and how beliefs and opinions are correlated. More careful attention to causal processes would be a welcome next step for scholars interested in how beliefs about the fairness of the economy fit into Americans' political perspectives and, ultimately, behaviors. Controlled experimentation, in particular, would allow for careful inspection of the assumption that party elites indeed influence Americans' causal narratives about economic inequality and opportunity, and that these narratives influence citizens' political preferences. Experimentation cannot answer all of our causal questions, however. There are many real-world processes—such as socialization within the family or decision-making within parties—for which experimentation is impossible, or, at least, unethical. Other methods are available to better understand these processes. Panel studies of parents and children—such as the famous study launched by Kent Jennings and Richard Niemi—are expensive but extraordinarily informative about political socialization, which begins when children are very young.[11] Political science as a field also has a poor understanding of the micro-processes that underlie parties' constructions of their platforms. Case studies that incorporate process-tracing would likely shed light on the opaque inner workings of political parties and the influence of donors, interest groups, and activists.

This leads me to a second limitation of this study: I have placed ideology and expression ahead of action, such as policymaking by parties and actual voting decisions by citizens. As the expression goes, talk is cheap. Although platforms are relatively good predictors of what a party attempts to do,[12] they of course vary in their predictive power. One suspicion of some social scientists who study economic inequality is that the Democratic Party sometimes exaggerates its commitment to equality to please important pressure groups and prospective voters. When push comes to shove, the party caters more to the influence of affluent donors and business interests than is apparent in its formal communications. We might make a similar conjecture about Democratic identifiers in the public. How many affluent Democrats say that the nation's resource distribution is unfair and support redistribution in theory but would avoid voting for a candidate who promised to substantially raise their taxes? This is likely why, in 2020, candidate Joe Biden promised not to raise taxes on households earning less than $400,000. Those at this threshold were in the top 3 percent of households—not quite the 1 percent, but still highly affluent.[13] On a related note, how many White Democrats say that they support improved educational opportunities for Black children due to historical racism but would oppose real efforts to better integrate public schools across class and racial lines in their own communities? This book has provided evidence that, once parties determine their agendas, ideology takes over. However, more attention to the realm of action would probably reveal a greater role for self-interest.

A third limitation concerns the many types of political communication outside of the party platforms. I am under no illusion that many people read the platforms; rather, I have argued that party platforms reflect the points of view of influential members of a party's coalition and serve as coordinating devices, helping to make sure that those who wish to advance the party's message are on the same page. The extent to which the actors who make up the parties and are allied with them—including interest groups and, importantly, partisan media—reinforce, expand on, and sometimes undermine the official party line deserves attention. In preliminary research, I explored partisan media—especially Fox News and MSNBC—and found mostly overlapping messaging with the parties but also some notable exceptions. For example, Tucker Carlson—former host on the conservative Fox News network—argued frequently in recent years that the American Dream was fading, especially for men. Attention to more discursive sources would likely unearth a wider range of causal narratives regarding inequality, including some that are too politically incorrect or radical for the relatively sanitized party platforms.

Assessing the American Dream

There are many compelling, and competing, narratives about the American Dream. Many political observers seem to accept this as an inevitable reality, even treating disagreements as differences of opinion—to each their own. Yet, resigning ourselves to either agnosticism or partisan narrative would be a mistake. There is utility in trying to separate fact from fiction. Drawing on high-quality social scientific evidence, I reach what I believe to be reasonable, if tentative, conclusions about the narratives surrounding economic opportunity and inequality in political discourse. Speaking generally, each party's explanations for socioeconomic inequality hold a degree of truth. But some truths provide more explanatory value than others. In what follows, I consider the empirical bases for each of the partisan inequality narratives investigated in this book from the perspective of an expansive research literature. This kind of analysis is always timebound. Given the time period addressed in this book, I focus on the American economy leading up to and through the recent Biden administration.

Educational Opportunity

For decades, Democrats have focused on disparities in education, especially those linked to unequal funding. In the past, their arguments have centered on unequal public schools, especially poor schools attended by Black and Hispanic students. More recently, the party has widened its focus to include unequal access to higher education. To a lesser extent, Republicans have also paid some attention to education inequity, especially, as discussed in chapter 2, during George W. Bush's presidency.

How unequal is the American educational landscape? Evidence suggests that American education is probably more equal than many on the left assume, at least with respect to the public school system. While primary and secondary public school financing once varied markedly between locales within states, this is less true today as state and federal funding steadily increased relative to local funding in the latter half of the twentieth century.[14] One careful study found that, within states, per-pupil spending is in fact progressive with respect to class and race on average.[15] In addition, structural sex-based discrimination, such as preventing women from studying certain subjects or obtaining doctorates, has largely subsided. And women now surpass men in earning high school, college, and advanced degrees.[16]

Nevertheless, important educational disparities remain. Nationally, per-pupil education spending appears to be regressive with respect to class and race because Black, Hispanic, and lower-income students disproportionately live in states that spend less on education.[17] Black and Hispanic students are also more likely to attend schools with less experienced instructors.[18] Schools have become more segregated by class in recent years, and Black and Hispanic students are much more likely than Asian American and White students to attend high-poverty schools.[19] The makeup of a student body affects the learning environment. Schools with concentrated disadvantage are associated with fewer advanced courses and more student absenteeism and disciplinary problems. One high-quality experimental study of the effect of schools in the Harlem Children's Zone suggests that higher-quality schools and instructors alone could close Black–White achievement gaps in math and English language ability.[20] The foregoing, in focusing on public schools, does not take into account the obvious advantages of private schools and tutoring, almost exclusively the province of affluent children. In addition to providing a high-quality education, elite schools and tutors provide students with cultural and social capital and considerable assistance obtaining entry to the nation's top colleges and universities.[21]

Higher education in the United States likely plays at least as significant a role in perpetuating socioeconomic inequality as primary and secondary schooling. U.S. colleges are among the most expensive in the world. Unsurprisingly, the most common reason Americans do not attend (or graduate from) college is lack of affordability or, relatedly, the need to work.[22] Rates of college attendance and graduation for young people decrease with declining parental income and wealth. Lack of affordability also contributes to racial and ethnic gaps in earning a college diploma. Survey data from 2021 indicates that, among adults twenty-five and older, 42 percent of White Americans and 61 percent of Asian Americans had a college education; only 28 percent of Black Americans and 21 percent of Hispanic Americans did.[23] Given the very large average earnings gaps between college graduates and people without a college degree, these differential rates of college attendance and graduation perpetuate preexisting economic inequalities across generations.

That said, because college has become so expensive, the wealth premium of attending college—the wealth gap between college graduates and people without a college degree—has likely declined substantially.[24] On the one hand, this suggests that some people who do not attend college are in fact making a wise financial choice given their circumstances. Because of the high cost of attending college, we should not assume that higher education benefits every individual financially. Attending college will be especially counterproductive financially for self-funders who never graduate.[25] On the other hand, the disappearing college wealth premium is in part due to inequities associated with higher education affordability: young people with parents or other relatives who can pay for their higher education reap the financial rewards of attending college without the downside of accumulating, and paying for, debt. A truly meritocratic higher education system would be available to all regardless of their ability to pay.

Where one attends college also matters. The economic outcomes of graduates from different institutions vary substantially.[26] Lower-income college applicants are less likely to attend selective schools (holding test scores constant). This gap is highly consequential, as more selective schools appear to have a causal influence on graduates' incomes (holding constant factors like parental income and racial identity).[27] While in many cases applicants may be selecting into schools for personal reasons, this class gap in college choice also reflects differences in affordability.

If we consider inequities in American education alongside the parties' narratives, the Democratic Party's concerns over educational inequities have been closer to the mark. The Republican Party has certainly not ignored this topic, however. Especially with respect to primary and secondary education, the parties have differed less over diagnosis of the problem and more over how best to improve educational outcomes.

Employment Opportunity

All politicians pay attention to employment during economic downturns, but the Democratic Party stands out for its near-constant concern over a lack of good job opportunities and lack of fairness in the hiring and promotion process. Are Democrats overly pessimistic, or Republicans overly optimistic?

INCOME AND WAGES

Reasons for optimism include, perhaps first and foremost, the fact that U.S. workers tend to earn considerably more than those in most other nations of the world. The United States draws so many immigrants who seek the American Dream for this reason.[28] American household incomes and standard of living have also climbed throughout the decades. Although incomes grew much faster in the mid-twentieth century, typical household incomes continued to grow thereafter. Growth was greatest and occurred across all income brackets when taxes and transfers are included.[29] We should not overstate this optimism, especially as much of this growth is the result of women entering the labor force. Yet, individual wages have also increased over time, with especially strong wage growth across all education levels during the first Trump and Biden administrations.[30]

Wage growth among lower-income earners has been strong enough in recent years that income inequality appears to have stabilized and may be decreasing.[31] Unemployment has been historically low,[32] with more job vacancies than people seeking work.[33] Recent scholarship measuring poverty using anchored measures, as opposed to more typical relative measures, reveals major declines in poverty since the 1960s, especially for Black Americans.[34] This all supports Republican optimism about the widespread availability of economic opportunity.

Yet, on balance, available evidence and analysis suggest that the American economy has not in fact supplied abundant jobs with pay adequate to keep up with rising prices. At $7.25 per hour, the federal minimum wage—which translates into an annual income of $14,500 for a full-time worker—is no longer enough to keep even a person with no dependents out of poverty.[35] Admittedly, very few workers earn a wage so low. Earners at the 10th percentile make approximately $13.50 per hour, or $27,000 per year for full-time work.[36] This is enough to keep an adult with up to two dependents out of poverty. However, the poverty threshold is a low bar. Many economists argue that wages must be much higher to meet what most people would consider to be a minimal threshold for comfortable living. Jeffrey Fuhrer estimates that 43 percent of U.S. families have resources below a reasonable family budget focused on necessities.[37] An important reason why so many Americans are struggling to make ends meet is what Annie Lowrey has called an "affordability crisis."[38] Lowrey, Fuhrer, and others argue that the effective inflation rate for most Americans has been higher than the standard Consumer Price Index for many years because of disproportionate price increases for necessities, especially housing.[39] Amy Glasmeier and her team at the Massachusetts Institute of Technology calculate living wages that take into account realistic expenditures for a modest lifestyle—what we might consider to be the entry point into the middle class.[40] According to this measure, the lowest living wage for a single adult with no dependents anywhere in the country in 2023 was approximately $15 per hour. Single adults with one dependent had to earn at least $30 to $40 per hour, depending on where they lived. This is far above what the median U.S. worker made at the time—$22 per hour.[41] In most states, this median wage was only a living wage for people without dependents or with a working partner and only one child. In other words, most median-wage working parents with more than one child or without a partner will struggle to make ends meet.[42] Finally, it is important to point out that wage rates are not everything—many Americans continue to have difficulty finding stable employment or full-time hours at their place of work. Eugene Ludwig points out in a recent essay that the combined number of American adults who are unemployed, underemployed, or earning a poverty wage is approximately 24 percent.[43]

These realities better reflect Democratic concerns over economic inequality and low wages, although it is important to point out that Democratic messaging also often exaggerates economic problems and fails to recognize economic "good news."

EQUAL ACCESS TO JOB OPPORTUNITIES

The second way in which the American Dream sets a high bar is insisting that economic opportunities be distributed according to merit. The notion that the United States is a meritocracy would suggest that people have similar abilities to apply for a wide variety of employment opportunities and that employers consider only their job-relevant qualifications during the hiring and promotion process. The United States falls far short of this expectation. I discuss consideration of labor market discrimination based on race, sex, and other ascriptive characteristics, which is illegal by law, in a later section. Here I want to consider more subtle—and legal—forms of bias that are nevertheless quite impactful.

The first is the fact that place matters. The average worker lives within thirty miles of their workplace.[44] Unless they can work remotely, American workers simply cannot take jobs that are distant from where they live.[45] In the latter part of the twentieth century, concerns about the links between job opportunity and place of residence focused on a dearth of jobs in inner cities.[46] While depressed central cities remain a concern in many places, a more recent serious problem is disparate job growth between large metropolitan areas, where jobs are plentiful, and more remote rural areas.[47] Transportation is a particular problem for lower-income rural residents, as public transport in most of the United States is poor or nonexistent. Of course, individuals without good employment opportunities can relocate, but relocation has many practical barriers. Lower-income people often do not move because of the difficulty and expense of locating adequate housing in a new area.[48] Perhaps the most famous recent illustration of the importance of place in Americans' economic well-being is the spatially concentrated China shock of the 2000s. As China exported many more inexpensive goods, a trend accelerated by its entry into the World Trade Organization, an estimated two million U.S. jobs linked to manufacturing disappeared. The negative effects were not just short term, as many economists predicted at the time. Many workers who lost their jobs shifted to lower-paid service-sector work and others never returned to work.[49]

Regardless of where one lives, one's social network also affects employment opportunity. Social scientists generally agree that people more readily find jobs via social connections. Historical estimates suggest that approximately half of employees find jobs through family, friends, or acquaintances.[50] Interviews with hiring companies and recruiters suggest similar levels of hiring via referral today. Counterintuitively, the ability to easily apply for jobs online has overwhelmed many employers with applications, often leading to continued reliance on referrals.[51] Job candidates with referrals are advantaged by both learning of job opportunities beforehand and being preferred over the course of the hiring process. One study by a hiring-software company found that job applicants with a referral were six times more likely to be hired.[52] Having connections is an important contributor to upward mobility, meaning that people without such connections are left behind.[53] A study of male workers finds that rates of upward mobility via referrals were much lower among men without a college degree and Black and Hispanic men due to labor market segmentation.[54] Similar patterns likely apply to other people with limited access to potential referrals, including women seeking work in male-dominated or higher-paying roles.[55] Social networks appear to be even more important in rural than urban areas.[56]

In a general sense, these concerns most reflect Democrats' more skeptical perspective of economic fairness in the United States; yet, the party, in recent years, has said little about geographic inequality. This lack of attention created room for Trump, in 2016 in particular, to effectively campaign on a promise to bring jobs back to rural areas and the Rust Belt.

CHILDCARE AND FAMILY LEAVE

Children represent our future and, of course, are deeply loved by their parents. Yet, children inevitably challenge families' finances and parents' access to work. Unfortunately, the United States stands out among developed nations for its lack of support of parents. It is the only developed nation to not guarantee paid parental leave by law.[57] It also subsidizes childcare costs at a much lower rate than similar nations.[58] Together, the lack of guaranteed paid leave and the relative lack of subsidized childcare have substantial negative effects on American families' finances: many parents, most often mothers, must either leave their job or return to work and pay for expensive childcare. Depending on where one lives, childcare costs for one child ranged between approximately $5,000 and $17,000 in 2022.[59] On at least one measure of childcare affordability, in Grover Whitehurst's words, "the U.S. ranks dead last among developed nations."[60]

The lack of paid parental leave and high childcare expenses negatively affect women's earnings in particular. Many expecting mothers quit their jobs given unreasonably short periods of available leave or the lack of affordable childcare options. Economists increasingly believe that American women's roles bearing and caring for children, including school-age children, are the primary reason for what remains of the average gap in earnings between men and women.[61] The lack of government financial support is a significant problem,[62] but so too are the inflexible hours and demands of many contemporary workplaces.[63]

The Democratic Party has consistently criticized this state of affairs, and the Republican Party has tended to oppose reform. That said, this is one area where the Republican Party has begun to acknowledge the need for change by, for example, supporting expanded child tax credits in its 2024 platform.

Discrimination

No topic in the United States is as debated politically as discrimination. Complicating matters is the fact that discrimination means different things to different people. As we saw in chapter 4, some Americans focus on present-day discrimination (or the lack thereof) and some on historical discrimination. Some think about interindividual discrimination and some about discrimination embedded in laws and organizations. The Democratic Party in recent years has emphasized the harmful effects of all types of discrimination on racial and ethnic minorities, especially Black, Hispanic, and Native Americans, and, to a lesser extent, women. The Republican Party tends to argue that discrimination is almost entirely a phenomenon of the past, and, even then, often downplays discrimination.

RACIAL DISCRIMINATION

Given the large literature on this topic, I focus in this section primarily on the experiences of Black Americans.[64] Until the late twentieth century, Black Americans were the largest racial minority group in the country, and they have faced severe discrimination throughout the nation's history. Prior to the Civil War, most Black Americans were enslaved. Even if all unequal treatment had ended with slavery, it still would have had lasting effects. Enslaved people could not accumulate wealth and almost all were prevented from obtaining an education, including learning how to read. Thus, the beginning conditions for Black Americans as they became independent actors in the economy and in society were more deprived than any other large social group—their starting line in the proverbial economic race far behind others.

Of course, discrimination did not stop with the end of slavery. Substantial economic, social, and political discrimination continued for another century and was especially severe in the American South. There, most Black Americans were tenant farmers or sharecroppers, leaving them economically vulnerable. The small minority of Black property owners were constantly at risk of White people taking or destroying their property. While school availability improved for Black Americans during and after Reconstruction, Black schools tended to receive much less funding and to be open fewer days of the year compared to White schools.[65] Black Americans in the North experienced somewhat better conditions but still faced rampant employment and housing discrimination, forcing them into lower-paying jobs and poor (but often overpriced) housing. As we think about the impact of discrimination on racial inequality, we should consider White Americans' favorable treatment, including their disproportionate access to federal government benefits in the first half of the twentieth century, as government programs became more generous. Although Black Americans received some of the benefits provided by programs such as Social Security and the GI Bill, Southern Democrats in Congress made certain that the aid flowing to Black people living in the South would be relatively low. Thus, while these programs did assist Black Americans, they had the counterintuitive effect of widening racial gaps in economic outcomes.[66]

The legal landscape would be transformed in the 1950s, with important Supreme Court decisions (such as *Brown v. Board of Education*), and especially the 1960s (with the enactment of the Civil Rights and Voting Rights Acts). Most racial discrimination became illegal in this era, although this does not mean that people no longer discriminated by race. Yet, even if all forms of discrimination had ended in this era, the effects of historical discrimination would linger to this day. Very few Black Americans could become middle class, let alone affluent, before the 1970s. Many people whose livelihoods were directly affected by this discrimination are still alive, the parents and grandparents of middle-aged Black Americans today. Few of that older generation have much wealth to pass to their children. As a result, White children are much more likely to receive an inheritance than Black children, and their inheritances are much larger in size.[67] Making matters worse, just as racial discrimination began to lessen in the latter half of the twentieth century, the American economy as a whole deteriorated, and economic inequality (regardless of a person's race) began to increase.[68] Beginning in the late 1970s and for at least several decades thereafter, income growth slowed for all Americans except for those in the top 1 percent, whose income dramatically increased. Income growth worsened the further down the economic ladder one went.[69] As Black Americans were more likely to be low income, they were disproportionately negatively affected by these changes.[70]

Racial discrimination has lessened considerably as the decades have progressed. It is the extraordinary racism of the past that explains much of the contemporary Black–White gap in income and wealth. Yet, job market discrimination against Black Americans—as well as other racial minorities—persists, net of any affirmative action policies. One meta-analysis of audit studies conducted in the 1990s, 2000s, and 2010s found that fictitious White job applicants received 38 percent more callbacks than otherwise identical Black applicants, and 23 percent more callbacks than Latino applicants. These differences did not decline during the period under study.[71] A separate meta-analysis of a dozen studies finds that racial discrimination tends to continue at later stages of the interview process, further increasing the chance that a White job candidate will receive a job offer and decreasing the chance that a Black candidate will receive one.[72] A study conducted between 2019 and 2021—the largest to date—suggests that racial discrimination has lessened more recently. However, the Black–White gap in being contacted for a job (in White candidates' favor) still averaged 24 percent for the most biased companies and 3 percent for the least biased companies.[73] Job-market discrimination harms other racial minorities as well. Quan Mai finds that employers preferred White job applicants over Asian American and Hispanic ones at approximately equal rates, with Black job applicants being least preferred.[74]

This brief historical overview makes clear that the Democratic Party is right to continue to be concerned about racial inequality and discrimination. The Republican Party is wrong to deny that discrimination—whether historical or present-day—no longer matters. Yet, members of the Democratic Party have also at times exaggerated and oversimplified discussions of racial discrimination. The focus in recent years on systemic discrimination has sometimes seemed to suggest that racism embedded in laws and behaviors today are more consequential than the lasting imprint of massive discrimination in the nineteenth and twentieth centuries. In addition, the party has sometimes assumed or implied that the history and experiences of Black Americans are emblematic of all racial and ethnic groups. While all racial and ethnic minority groups have faced challenges, Black and Native Americans undeniably have endured uniquely harsh treatment, with especially pronounced negative effects lingering to this day.

SEX AND GENDER DISCRIMINATION

Women have also faced substantial employment discrimination, at least historically. Due to cultural norms as well as formal discrimination, U.S. women's employment levels were far below men's until the latter decades of the twentieth century. Working women tended to cluster in a small number of fields and roles, including domestic service, nursing, secretarial work, and teaching. Due to the Civil Rights Act (and related laws and legal decisions) as well as changing cultural mores, the 1970s and 1980s saw dramatic increases in women's labor force participation and hourly earnings and decreases in sex segregation in employment. That said, this progress appears to have since stalled.[75]

Discrimination likely plays little direct role in women's labor force participation (currently at 78 percent relative to men's 89 percent).[76] However, it may play a role in women's lower earnings. Across all workers, women earn approximately 85 cents for each dollar a man earns.[77] Recent audit studies, similar to those conducted on racial bias, have found little-to-no discrimination on average against women applicants for job openings in the United States.[78] However, bias remains against women in male-dominated fields and against men in female-dominated fields.[79] Because men's fields pay considerably more on average, discrimination against women in these occupations will increase the female–male earnings gap. Although why women's occupations tend to pay less than men's is a complicated question, evidence strongly suggests that the difference is due in part to widespread devaluing of women's work.[80] Thus, bias against women likely occurs at two junctures: lower pay in fields dominated by women, and the difficulties women face joining male-oriented fields. That said, few social scientists would assert that such bias accounts for the entirety of the female–male pay gap. As discussed, many economists view childbearing and child-rearing as more significant contributors to the gap. The Democratic Party in recent years has emphasized the former at the expense of the latter. The Republican Party has said little about either.

Culture of Poverty

Attributing inequality—especially poverty—to community culture or family upbringing is another politically controversial topic. The Democratic Party has avoided any rhetoric that could be interpreted as "blaming the victim." By way of contrast, Republicans have consistently emphasized the importance of marriage and community values to both children's and adults' outcomes. Decades ago, however, assertions of the importance of culture were commonly found on both the right and left.

Discussion of a possible link between culture and poverty increased in the 1960s, with attention focused especially on poverty among Black Americans. Interestingly, it was a Democrat during the Lyndon B. Johnson administration who popularized the idea of a culture of poverty. Daniel Patrick Moynihan's report *The Negro Family: The Case for National Action* argued that two factors held Black Americans back in economic competition.[81] The first was ongoing racism. The second was pathologies in Black families, especially single motherhood, originally shaped by past racism but in the present an exogenous negative influence on Black children's prospects. Matriarchal households were associated with poor outcomes among boys in particular. Many people who were sympathetic to Black Americans criticized the report. Rather than blaming the deprivation of impoverishment itself as leading to further poverty in a cyclical pattern, the cultural argument asserted that characteristics of Black households had an important independent influence on the perpetuation of poverty. Whatever one thinks of the report, it played a significant role in how culture would be discussed in political as well as academic circles in the decades that followed, with racial liberals in particular loathe to entertain the idea that culture matters much to inequality.

Many social scientists have avoided studying the topic of family structure and inequality, but two recent treatments by prominent researchers offer solid evidence that two-parent homes are beneficial to both parents and children. Note that each study avoids Moynihan's pejorative portrayal of Black families. Ron Haskins and Isabel Sawhill argue that young people who complete a "success sequence" of high school, full-time work, and marriage before having children are very unlikely to fall into poverty.[82] Two recent government reports largely confirm their argument, although the order in which the success sequence is completed does not appear to matter.[83] Melissa Kearney argues persuasively that children are much more likely to flourish academically and, later in life, earn more and get married themselves if they are raised in two-parent homes.[84] Children in single-parent homes likely have worse outcomes on average because their families tend to have fewer resources—time, money, and emotional support.[85] Unfortunately, rates of single parenthood continue to be high in the U.S.

What is left uncertain in this literature, however, is the extent to which culture influences young adults' decision to marry. The evidence is mixed. Considerable evidence shows that lower-income women value marriage highly but have been less likely than others to marry due to low wages and high incarceration rates among men with no college education.[86] However, cultural norms likely matter too. Using a careful statistical design, Raj Chetty and Nathaniel Hendren demonstrate that teen pregnancy and marriage rates in an area had a causal impact on those who lived in or moved to a community.[87] Kearney discusses evidence showing that marriage rates tend to fall after men's employment prospects decline but then stabilize at the lower rate even when those prospects subsequently improve.[88]

Culture is, of course, much more multifaceted than simply the causes and effects of family structure. For example, culture provides people with concrete skills or capital. Consider that low-income children may value certain goals—such as obtaining a college education—but not have the knowledge of how to increase their likelihood of attending a good college.[89] Or consider that affluent families and communities socialize young people into high-status attitudes, knowledge, and behaviors that often serve little value beyond marking status. These cultural markers help affluent people attain entry into high-status schools and industries that exclude non-affluent people who are unaware of the appropriate cultural norms.[90] In both instances, lack of sustained exposure to certain cultures deprives one of the ability to navigate contexts in which they are dominant, even if one desires to do so.[91] Evoking culture in this way certainly does not blame the victim. Rather, it incorporates culture into a structural inequality framework.

Sociologists increasingly point out that culture is a mixed bag for lower-income people. It can lock people out of opportunities, through no fault of their own. It can discourage behaviors helpful to socioeconomic advancement, including marriage as well as educational pursuit.[92] Yet, local cultures have important, often critical, functional elements. People learn to navigate unsafe streets, share resources with family and neighbors, adapt their life goals to what seems possible, and ultimately find meaning in their lives as they are, not what they might be. In sum, culture can be beneficial to day-to-day living while simultaneously impeding upward mobility. Nevertheless, few scholars would argue that culture is an indelible force immune to changing external economic realities, whether positive or negative.[93]

How to assess the parties' perspectives in light of this complex picture? Republicans appear to have been correct in their encouragement of two-parent families in particular. That said, they have tended to ignore the difficult socioeconomic realities that both make finding a spouse difficult for many people and challenge family finances regardless of marital status. For their part, Democrats have been right to avoid using cultural narratives to blame victims—even in those instances where cultural influences may be harmful, individuals have little agency in how they are socialized—however, they have wrongly ignored growing evidence that family structure matters.

Hard Work and Personal Responsibility

In discussions related to the economy, Republican politicians have emphasized primarily the importance of hard work to economic success. To a lesser extent, they have highlighted other characteristics associated with personal responsibility, such as the importance of frugality and saving. At points, Democrats have echoed these themes, which are in keeping with the famed Protestant work ethic. Does a decline in the hours Americans devote to work perhaps explain slowed income growth? To what extent do variation in hard work and responsible spending habits contribute to economic inequality?

As a general matter, Americans work long hours—considerably more than European workers, although fewer than workers in many developing countries, especially in Asia.[94] In recent decades, working hours for individual American workers have remained relatively flat, but working hours within households have increased. This increase is due almost entirely to women in dual-earner households entering the labor force, often out of perceived necessity. The decline of the homemaker model has not come without costs, as homemakers perform valuable work.[95] Time-use surveys show that American parents in dual-earner households have compensated for the lack of a devoted homemaker by tasking fathers with more child-rearing and housework than in the past. Parents are not spending less time with children; in fact, child-rearing hours have risen overall. As a result of mothers' increased work hours outside the home and fathers' increased work hours inside the home, parents have less time for leisure and social activities than in the past and often report a great deal of stress as well.[96] In short, Americans are working outside the home more than ever, while also spending a significant amount of time on child-rearing.

What about the relationship between effort and economic inequality? One simple way of determining whether hard work accounts for inequality is to consider how many hours per week people work at the top and the bottom of the income distribution. According to U.S. Census data, among American earners, a positive, linear relationship exists between hours worked each week and income, resulting in a four-hour difference between those in the top 10 percent (46.6 hours) and those in the bottom 10 percent (42.2).[97] Hours worked thus appears to explain a portion of income inequality among workers, although the variance explained is clearly quite small. In addition, many part-time workers, who are disproportionately at the lower end of the economic hierarchy, desire to work more hours.[98] As already discussed, unemployment is also low.

We might also consider the extent to which irresponsible financial decisions explain why some people have less wealth and more debt than others. Social scientists find little evidence that this contributes much to economic inequality or economic distress in the aggregate. A recent study of the quality of individuals' financial choices finds that they do not vary by economic status.[99] Affluent people save more money because they have more discretionary income, not because they make better financial decisions. Elizabeth Warren and Amelia Warren Tyagi provide evidence that middle-class American families are not spending more on luxury goods than in the past and that nearly all bankruptcies are due to medical problems, job loss, or divorce.[100] While there will always be some variation, on average, poor households spend much less than nonpoor households on what researchers refer to as nonessential items—not only in terms of absolute spending but also as a proportion of their budget. One study found that poor households with children spent approximately 11 percent of their income on entertainment, personal care, home furnishings, alcohol and tobacco, and miscellaneous items, whereas nonpoor households with children spent 15.5 percent.[101] A more recent study of Earned Income Tax Credit recipients finds that the vast majority of these lump-sum payments were allocated toward paying down debt (often for taxes owed and utility bills) and important household needs (such as a used car, new appliance, or home repair) and investments (such as education). Approximately 10 percent was spent on enhanced consumption, a category that included modest treats for the family, such as name-brand clothes for children or dinner out at a nice restaurant. Matthew Desmond's *Poverty, by America* and Barbara Ehrenreich's *Nickel and Dimed* provide compelling accounts of how low-income Americans are successful penny pinchers, despite often facing higher costs than others.[102]

The foregoing description of lower-income Americans as largely hard working and financially responsible overlooks one significant social statistic that to some degree throws my characterization into doubt—the fact that many adults have dropped out of the work force altogether. Economists find a steady drop in labor force participation among prime-age men in particular, from a high of 98 percent in the 1950s to 89 percent in early 2024.[103] Researchers disagree over the reasons for this phenomenon. Some emphasize reduced demand for labor due to automation and competition with China.[104] Another cause appears to be ill health, the most common reason cited by nonparticipants themselves in surveys,[105] although note that this category includes many suffering from opioid addiction.[106] A third important cause of low labor force participation among men in particular is the nation's high rate of felony convictions and incarceration,[107] a major social problem in its own right with its own complicated set of causes.[108]

A final point to consider is whether the design of government programs may contribute to some Americans' decision to not work. Some researchers argue that the current design of the Social Security Disability Insurance program reduces labor force participation more than is necessary among people with minor disabilities, leading to ballooning numbers of Americans younger than sixty-five receiving disability benefits.[109] Further, despite major reforms in the 1990s,[110] social welfare programs at all levels of government continue to include benefit cliffs that can disincentivize work as well as marriage by stopping benefits once a household's income passes a specific threshold.[111] To say that the design and even generosity of government programs influence employment levels is not always equivalent to saying that they should be cut. For example, in the case of benefit cliffs, a sensible reform may be increased expenditures as benefits are slowly phased out at higher income levels.

What do we make of the famed, and much debated, American work ethic? On balance, it seems fair to say that the vast majority of Americans—regardless of income level—work hard. For a long time, the Republican Party has sold the misleading idea that the economically successful owed their success to hard work and the poor their poverty to laziness and poor choices. The Democratic Party has been right to dispute these narratives. Yet, the Democratic Party has its own blind spots, not engaging enough with Republican concerns about the effects of the opioid crisis on work or problematic design elements of many government social welfare programs.

Conclusion

I have provided a brief tour of researchers' perspectives on the American Dream. If we were to boil these conclusions down to their core elements, we might say that the American economy, at least today, provides most hard-working people with the basic necessities of life. And it provides many hard-working people with a comfortable life. For those who fall behind, whatever the reason, government programs tend to protect families from abject poverty. These life chances are better in the United States than in most countries in the world.

Yet, this is not exactly what the American Dream promises. Everyone ought to be able to achieve a middle-class lifestyle with hard work. Here, the United States falls short, especially for parents. Often due to starting conditions, and sometimes due to bad luck, a sizable fraction of Americans is unable to achieve financial comfort and stability. The nation falls short of the American Dream even more dramatically in a second way: the correlation between a person's merit and how much they earn may be positive, but—in the language of statistics—a great deal of variance in economic outcomes is explained by other factors. Where we grow up, how we were raised, the schools we attend, who we know, the social biases we face, and the resources we inherit all play a role in predicting where a person lands on the economic ladder.

Overall, the Democratic Party's persistent concern over economic opportunity and fairness tends to be closer to the mark than the Republican Party's frequent insistence that all is well, save overly generous social welfare programs. Yet, both parties are guilty of stylized narratives that cleanly support their policy agendas. Our messy reality supports neither agenda in full.

Will the partisan divide over the American Dream continue? On the one hand, there is little question that it will in some form. Republicans and Democrats have opposed one another on the question of economic opportunity and fairness since the mid-1800s. Yet, on the other hand, two important changes suggest that the United States has reached—and probably passed—its recent peak in polarization over the American Dream.

Decades of minimal real income growth for most Americans—as incomes and wealth soared at the top of the economic ladder—have spurred political change. At first, only the Democratic Party reacted, critiquing the fairness of growing inequality and moving sharply left on economic policy. Trump eventually emerged to thrill dispirited Republicans and many Independents with his critiques of the economy and promise to disrupt his party's long-reigning ideology for their benefit, launching him toward the presidency. Yet, Trump's relative economic populism, so far centered around tariffs and opposition to immigration, has resulted in few economic gains for Americans of low and modest income. Despite this failure, there are signs of an emerging, and possibly more productive, economic egalitarianism among some Republican party leaders and conservative thinkers. More Republican members of Congress have been collaborating with Democrats to craft bipartisan economic policy.[112] New think tanks, such as American Compass, and publications, such as *Compact*, provide intellectual backing for this emergent brand of conservatism. For the moment, these individuals and organizations are far outnumbered (and outspent) by Republican elites with little interest in the economic welfare of working-class and lower-income Americans, but, given the changing Republican coalition, their influence may grow in the future.

A second important change is growing public frustration with partisan conflict and the government in general.[113] A 2023 Pew Research Center report summarized the public mood as overwhelmingly negative, with majorities saying politics is "dominated by special interests, flooded with campaign cash and mired in partisan warfare." When Americans were asked to convey their "feelings about politics in a word or phrase," the words "divisive" and "corrupt" were most common.[114] Political scientists often critique Americans' political knowledge and judgment but, here, the public clearly is not wrong. Although our political system is stacked against ordinary Americans without means, a dissatisfied and roused public can increase the likelihood of real change. That said, whether democratic responsiveness on the whole advances rather than recedes in the coming years is an open question, depending not only on the Trump administration's actions but also on the actions of many powerful interests that do not have Americans' best interests in mind.

Interparty battles over the nature of the nation's problems will always exist to some degree. However, one mark of a healthy democracy is more honest factual debates. Disingenuous arguments confuse voters, undermining democratic decision-making. They also crowd out worthy debates—including whether the celebrated ideal of the American Dream itself could be improved. As discussed in chapter 2, the American Dream includes an insistence that everyone who works hard deserves at least a middle-class lifestyle—the proverbial house with a white picket fence—but also celebrates entrepreneurs and others who manage to strike it rich. Yet, this celebration of wealth is not universal. Relative to people who live in other nations, Americans are unusually supportive of the idea that the difference between economic failure and success should be accompanied by large resource inequalities.[115] In short, the rungs of the ladder of economic success are very far apart in the United States, and many Americans appear to be okay with that. Yet, we should consider whether enormous differences in income and wealth—of the kind we see today—are ethical even if the distribution of economic opportunities were considerably more meritocratic.[116]

Most damning, factual claims that are biased toward a political party's agenda often harm the policymaking process. As Matthew Yglesias warns in an essay from which the opening quote was drawn, one-sided or misleading information intended to "sell" a policy agenda to voters at election time will misinform the party coalition, including vocal activists and even some policy wonks. A tendency to rely primarily on ideologically congenial evidence will lead to poorer quality legislation and greater difficulty enacting that legislation through the bipartisan compromises the U.S. system normally requires.[117] In sum, a lack of candor about the alleged facts underlying socioeconomic inequality and many other problems undermines policymaking. The conclusions presented in this chapter, and indeed this book as a whole, are one attempt to promote such candor.

Figure A.1 Frequency of Specific Types of Explanations for Economic and Related Inequalities in Party Platforms (1980–2020)

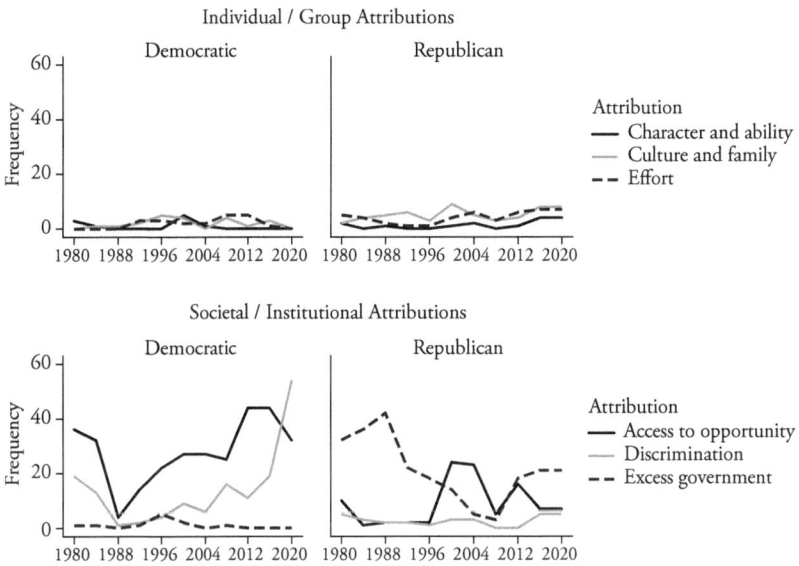

Individual / Group Attributions

Societal / Institutional Attributions

Source: Author's calculations using coded party platform data.

https://doi.org/10.7758/trap6910.5290

Figure A.2 Number of Times Specific Social Groups Mentioned in Conjunction with Concerns over Unequal Opportunity in Republican Party Platforms (1980–2020)

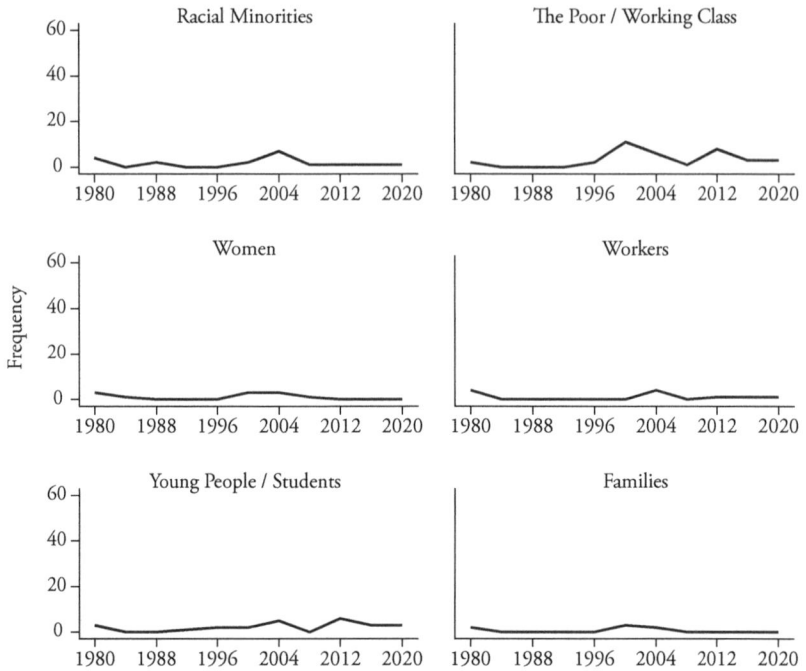

Source: Author's calculations using coded party platform data.

Figure A.3 Predicted Probabilities from Logit Regression with Demographic Controls for "Most Can Make It If They Work Hard" Outcome (Corresponding to Figure 3.1)

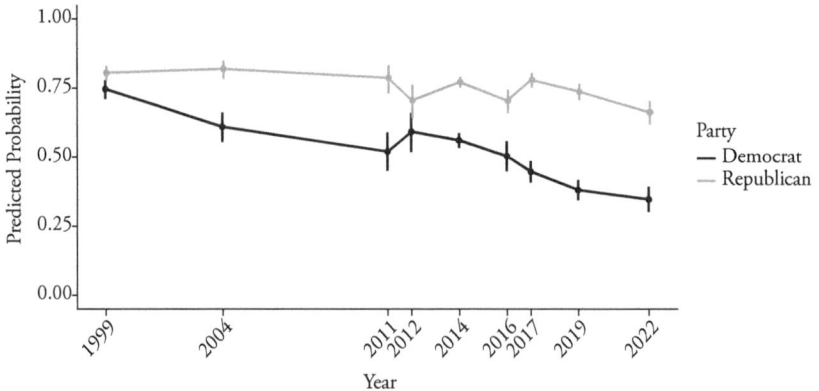

Source: Author's calculations using weighted Pew Research Center data (Pew Research Center 2025).

Figure A.4 Predicted Probabilities from Logit Regression with Demographic Controls for "Poor People Have It Easy" Outcome (Corresponding to Figure 3.2)

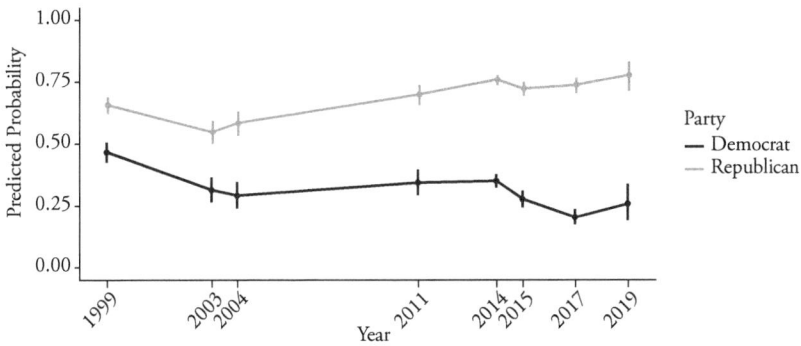

Source: Author's calculations using weighted Pew Research Center data (Pew Research Center 2025).

Figure A.5 Predicted Probabilities from Logit Regression with Demographic Controls for "We Don't Give Everyone an Equal Chance" Outcome (Corresponding to Figure 3.3)

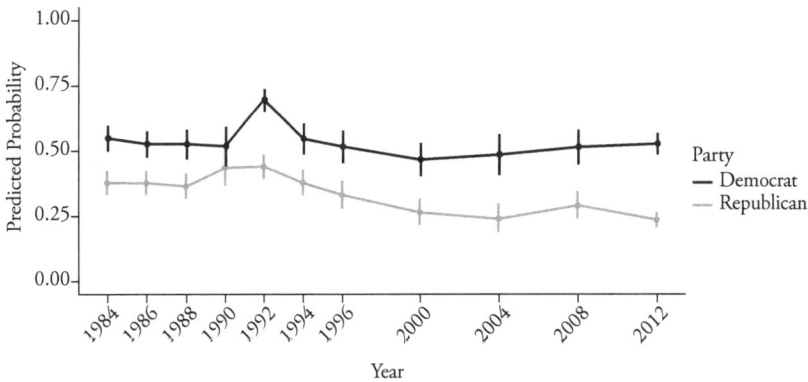

Source: Author's calculations using weighted ANES data (American National Election Studies 2025).

Figure A.6 Predicted Probabilities from Logit Regression with Demographic Controls for Education Explanation for Racial Inequality Outcome (Corresponding to Figure 3.4)

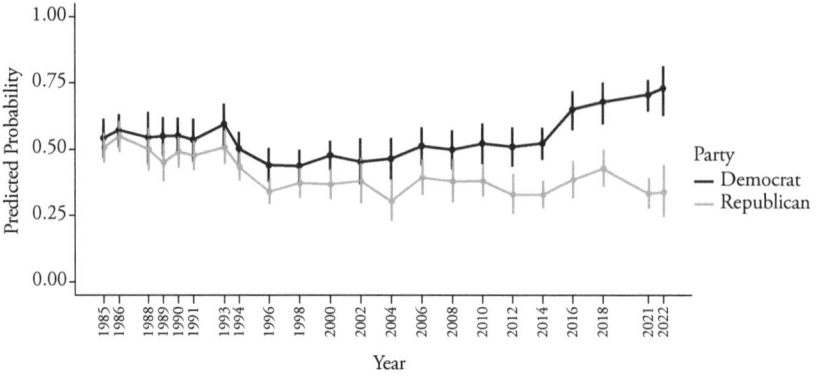

Source: Author's calculations using weighted GSS data (General Social Survey 2025).

Figure A.7 Predicted Probabilities from Logit Regression with Demographic Controls for Discrimination Explanation for Racial Inequality Outcome (Corresponding to Figure 3.5)

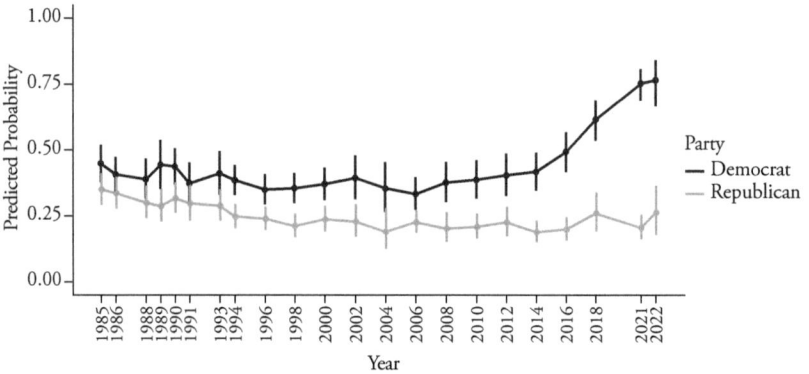

Source: Author's calculations using weighted GSS data (General Social Survey 2025).

Figure A.8 Predicted Probabilities from Logit Regression with Demographic Controls for Lack of Will Explanation for Racial Inequality Outcome (Corresponding to Figure 3.6)

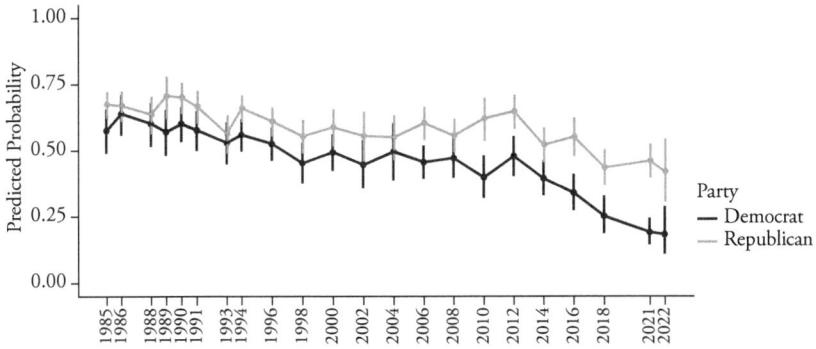

Source: Author's calculations using weighted GSS data (General Social Survey 2025).

Figure A.9 Predicted Probabilities from Logit Regression with Demographic Controls for Inborn Ability Explanation for Racial Inequality Outcome (Corresponding to Figure 3.7)

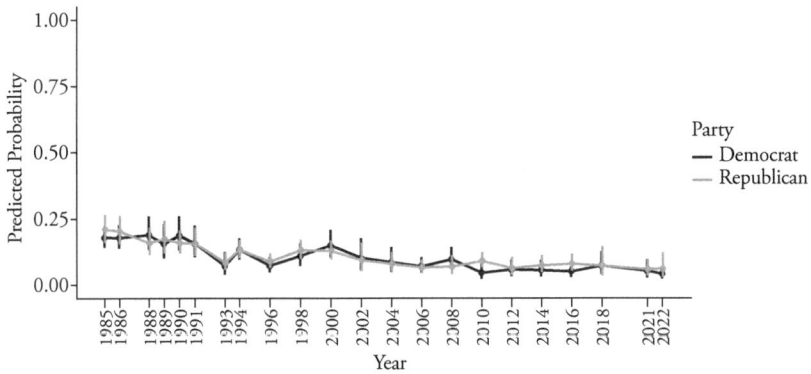

Source: Author's calculations using weighted GSS data (General Social Survey 2025).

Figure A.10 Correlations Among Explanations for Inequality in 2018 Survey

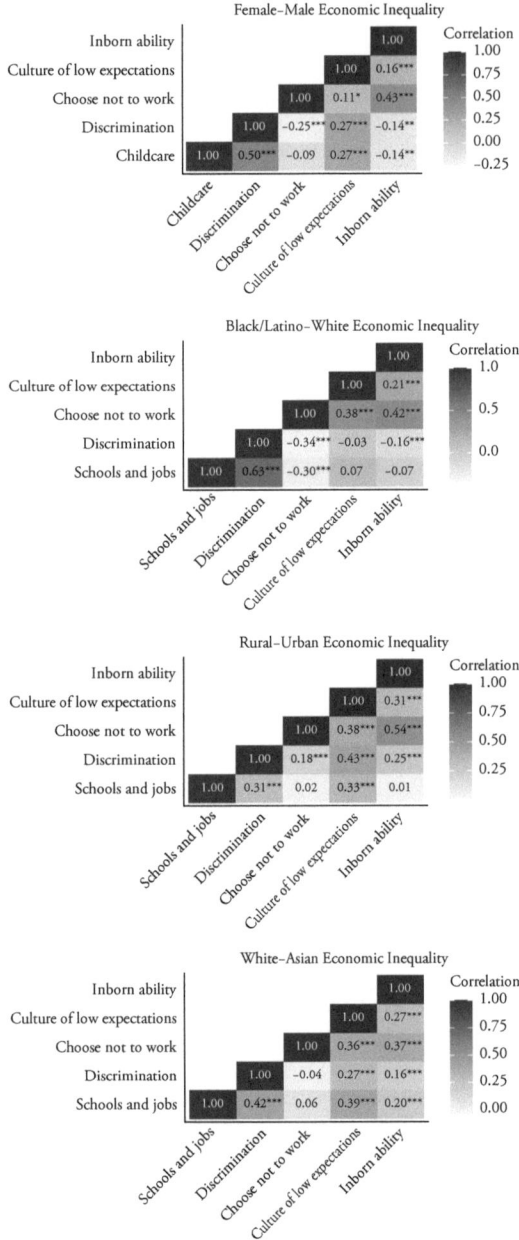

Female–Male Economic Inequality

Black/Latino–White Economic Inequality

Rural–Urban Economic Inequality

White–Asian Economic Inequality

Source: Author's calculations using 2018 EIPS data.

Figure A.11 Coefficient Plot of Unequal Opportunity Difference Measures Regressed onto Demographic Characteristics (2016)

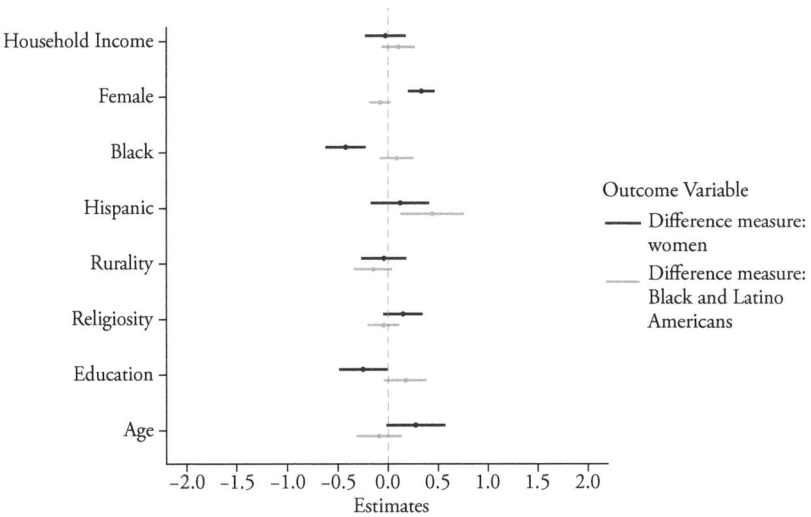

Source: Author's calculations using 2016 EIPS data.

Note: Coefficient plots with estimates from two separate linear regressions. Outcome variables are difference variables: (1) unequal economic opportunity for women – unequal economic opportunity, and (2) unequal economic opportunity for Black and Latino Americans – unequal economic opportunity. Explanatory variables are scored 0 to 1 and outcome variables are scored –5 to 5.

Figure A.12 Associations Between Partisanship and Cultural Explanations for
Socioeconomic Inequality

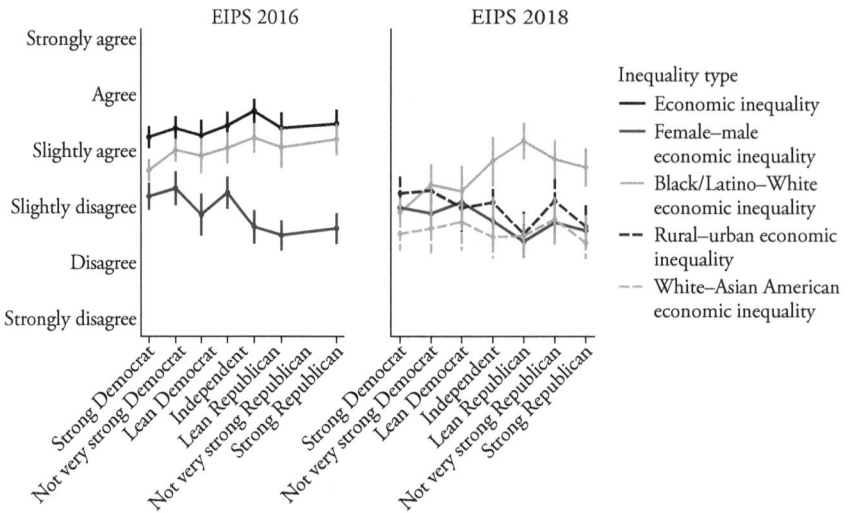

Source: Author's calculations using 2016 and 2018 EIPS data.

Figure A.13 Distributions of Presidential Candidate Feeling Thermometers (2016)

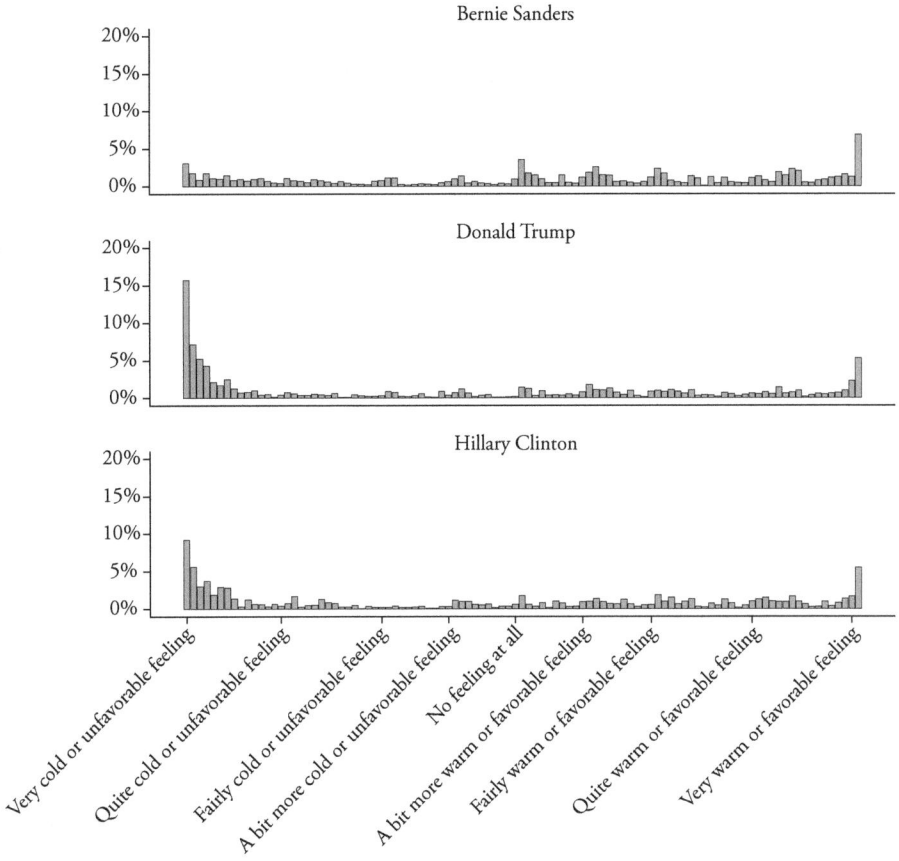

Source: Author's calculations using 2016 EIPS data.

Figure A.14 Coefficient Plots of Political Attitudes Regressed onto Specific Explanations for Economic Inequality (2016)

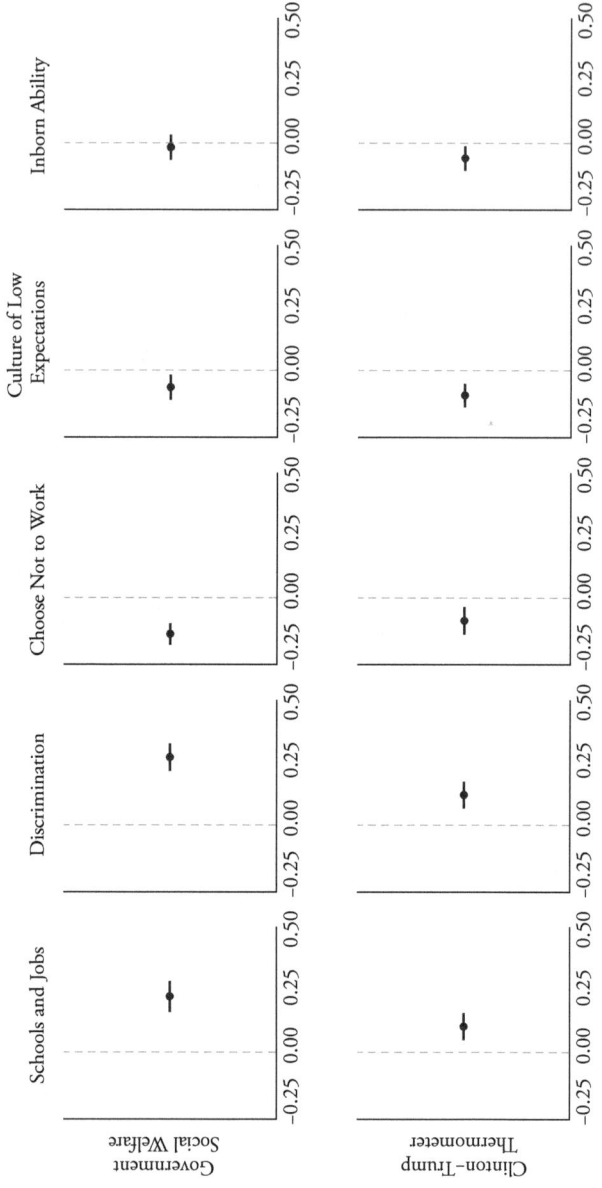

Source: Author's calculations using 2016 EIPS data.
Note: Each coefficient depicted is from an independent linear regression with the indicated explanation for economic inequality as the key predictor of the outcome variable listed on the left-hand side. Control variables include income, sex, race, rurality, religiosity, education, and age. All variables coded 0 to 1.

Figure A.15 Coefficient Plots of Specific Political Attitudes Regressed onto Unequal Opportunity Index (2016)

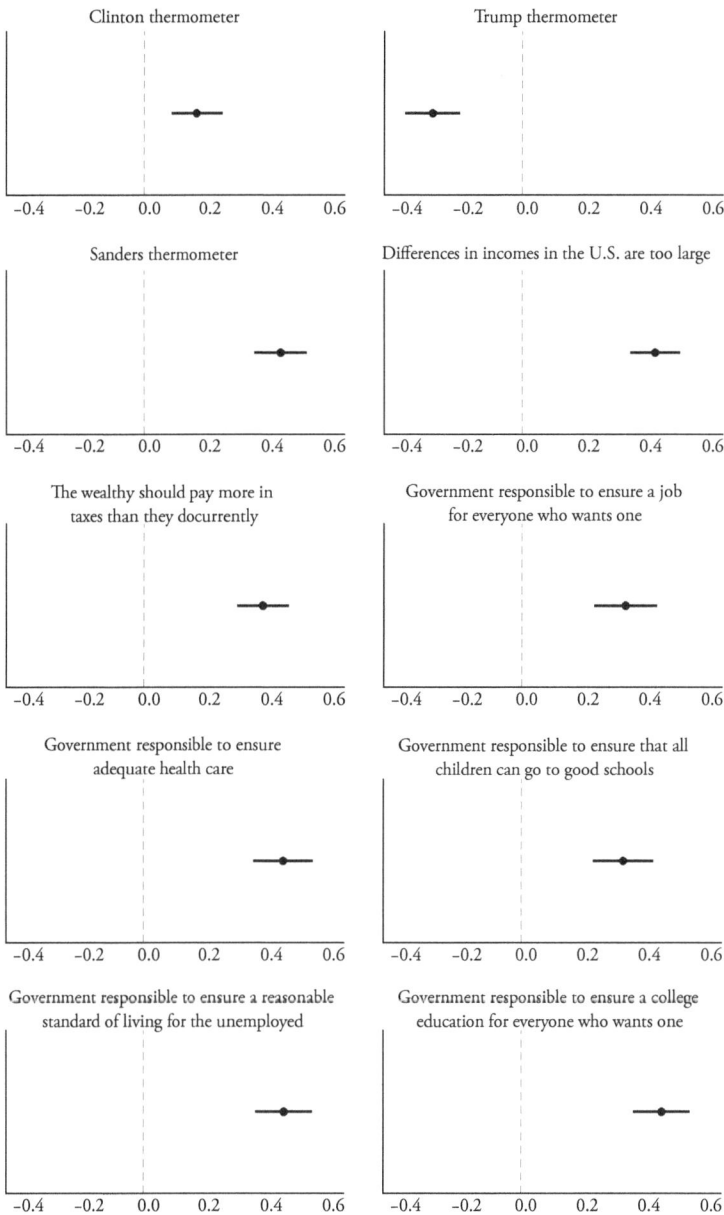

Source: Author's calculations using 2016 EIPS data.
Note: Each coefficient depicted is from an independent linear regression with the unequal economic opportunity index as the key predictor of the outcome variable listed at the top. Control variables include income, sex, race, rurality, religiosity, education, and age. All variables coded 0 to 1.

Figure A.16 Coefficient Plots of Political Attitudes Regressed onto Three Unequal Opportunity Indexes—Racial Subgroups (2016)

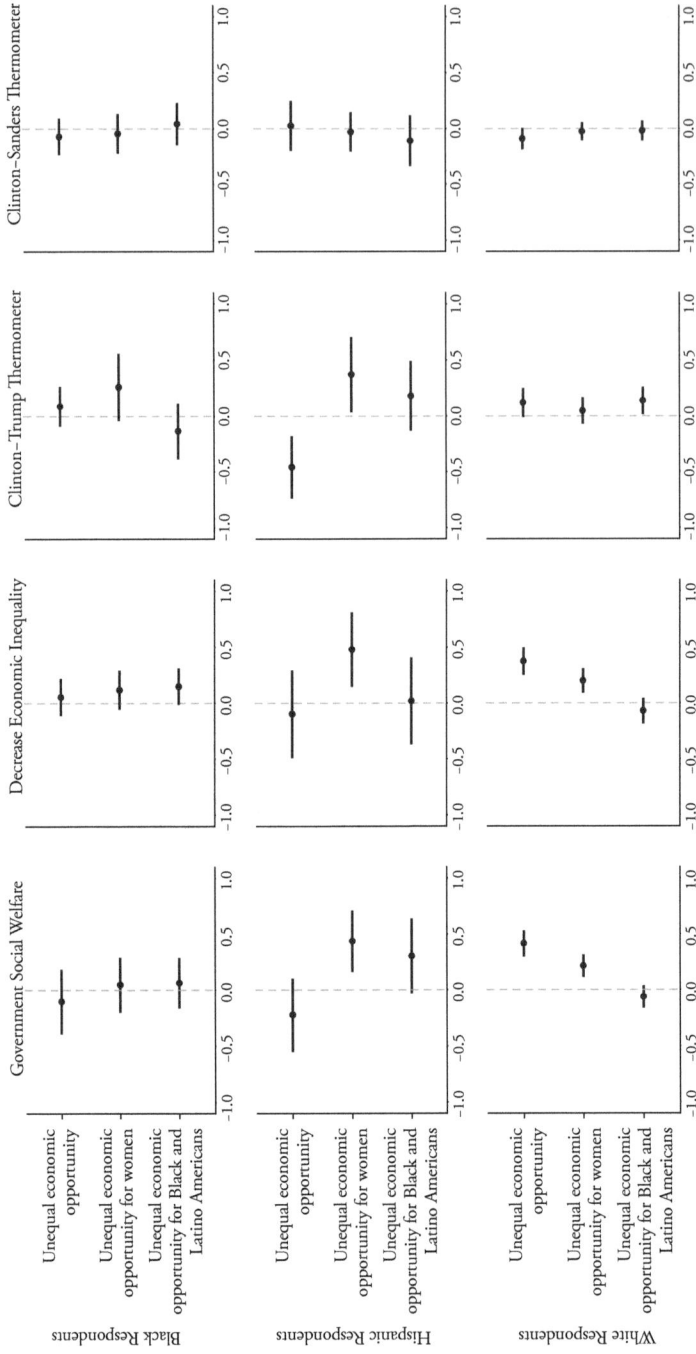

Source: Author's calculations using 2016 EIPS data.
Note: Each panel displays results from one linear regression that includes three indexes as predictors: unequal economic opportunity, unequal economic opportunity for women, and unequal economic opportunity for Black and Latino Americans. Partisanship and demographic variables are included as control variables. Results presented separately for respondents who identify as Black, Hispanic, and White.

Table A.1 Unequal Opportunity Indexes Regressed onto Demographic Characteristics (2016)

	Outcome Variable		
	Unequal economic opportunity (1)	Unequal economic opportunity for women (2)	Unequal economic opportunity for Black and Latino Americans (3)
Household income	−0.172	−0.249**	−0.020
	(0.114)	(0.107)	(0.133)
Female	0.059	0.372***	0.004
	(0.070)	(0.065)	(0.081)
Black	0.671***	0.255***	0.841***
	(0.110)	(0.097)	(0.119)
Hispanic	0.333**	0.461***	0.832***
	(0.147)	(0.157)	(0.202)
Asian American	0.388	0.166	0.179
	(0.244)	(0.199)	(0.248)
Other race	0.020	0.050	0.194
	(0.172)	(0.126)	(0.174)
Rurality	−0.112	−0.141	−0.221
	(0.127)	(0.122)	(0.150)
Religiosity	−0.949***	−0.762***	−1.027***
	(0.104)	(0.105)	(0.128)
Education	0.663***	0.459***	0.862***
	(0.141)	(0.145)	(0.164)
Age	−0.348**	−0.137	−0.441**
	(0.146)	(0.153)	(0.175)
Constant	3.937***	4.340***	4.064***
	(0.128)	(0.126)	(0.157)
R-squared	0.136	0.113	0.163
Observations	1,677	1,674	1,657

Source: Author calculations using 2016 EIPS data.

Note: Coefficients (with standard errors in parentheses) from three linear regressions, with unequal economic opportunity, unequal economic opportunity for women, and unequal economic opportunity for Black and Latino Americans as outcome variables. Explanatory variables are scored 0 to 1 and outcome variables are scored 1 to 6.
* $p < .1$; ** $p < .05$; *** $p < .01$

Table A.2 Unequal Opportunity Indexes Regressed onto Partisanship and Demographic Variables (2016)

	Outcome Variable		
	Unequal economic opportunity (1)	Unequal economic opportunity for women (2)	Unequal economic opportunity for Black and Latino Americans (3)
Party (Republican)	−1.447***	−1.124***	−1.645***
	(0.100)	(0.087)	(0.106)
Household income	−0.102	−0.200**	0.050
	(0.102)	(0.098)	(0.115)
Female	0.014	0.342***	−0.049
	(0.063)	(0.063)	(0.073)
Black	0.189*	−0.144	0.262**
	(0.114)	(0.100)	(0.123)
Hispanic	0.066	0.319**	0.645***
	(0.152)	(0.154)	(0.205)
Asian American	0.257	0.099	0.068
	(0.195)	(0.173)	(0.206)
Other race	−0.019	−0.016	0.134
	(0.173)	(0.126)	(0.150)
Rurality	0.022	−0.020	−0.101
	(0.118)	(0.115)	(0.135)
Religiosity	−0.522***	−0.443***	−0.529***
	(0.095)	(0.101)	(0.109)
Education	0.484***	0.291**	0.662***
	(0.128)	(0.132)	(0.141)
Age	−0.252*	−0.040	−0.286*
	(0.137)	(0.151)	(0.165)
Constant	4.406***	4.711***	4.596***
	(0.114)	(0.123)	(0.139)
R-squared	0.295	0.229	0.324
Observations	1,653	1,648	1,631

Source: Author's calculations using 2016 EIPS data.

Note: Coefficients (with standard errors in parentheses) from three linear regressions, with unequal economic opportunity, unequal economic opportunity for women, and unequal economic opportunity for Black and Latino Americans indexes as outcome variables. Explanatory variables are scored 0 to 1 and outcome variables are scored 1 to 6.

* $p < .1$; ** $p < .05$; *** $p < .01$

Table A.3 Unequal Opportunity Indexes Regressed onto Partisanship, Ideology, and Prejudice Variables (2016)

	Outcome Variable		
	Unequal economic opportunity (1)	Unequal economic opportunity for women (2)	Unequal economic opportunity for Black and Latino Americans (3)
Party (Republican)	−0.934***	−0.662***	−1.070***
	(0.133)	(0.123)	(0.146)
Ideology (conservative)	−1.107***	−0.975***	−1.126***
	(0.190)	(0.183)	(0.202)
Racism	−0.682***	−0.326**	−0.926***
	(0.168)	(0.164)	(0.174)
Sexism	−0.393**	−0.629***	−0.616***
	(0.169)	(0.197)	(0.193)
Household income	−0.088	−0.179*	−0.049
	(0.104)	(0.107)	(0.118)
Female	0.017	0.258***	−0.159**
	(0.071)	(0.068)	(0.078)
Black	0.386***	−0.005	0.455***
	(0.134)	(0.124)	(0.150)
Hispanic	0.0005	0.263*	0.545***
	(0.157)	(0.160)	(0.209)
Asian American	−0.013	−0.114	−0.071
	(0.222)	(0.237)	(0.220)
Other race	−0.128	−0.163	−0.111
	(0.186)	(0.130)	(0.163)
Rurality	−0.023	−0.157	−0.106
	(0.121)	(0.133)	(0.142)
Religiosity	−0.212*	−0.115	−0.201
	(0.112)	(0.124)	(0.127)
Education	0.310**	0.132	0.451***
	(0.140)	(0.152)	(0.158)
Age	0.037	0.043	−0.208
	(0.145)	(0.175)	(0.174)
Constant	4.859***	5.280***	5.392***
	(0.148)	(0.149)	(0.172)
R-squared	0.395	0.306	0.437
Observations	1,290	1,288	1,270

Source: Author's calculations using 2016 EIPS data.

Note: Coefficients (with standard errors in parentheses) from three linear regressions, with unequal economic opportunity, unequal economic opportunity for women, and unequal economic opportunity for Black and Latino Americans indexes as outcome variables. Explanatory variables are scored 0 to 1 and outcome variables are scored 1 to 6.

* $p < .1$; ** $p < .05$; *** $p < .01$

Table A.4 Explanations for Economic Inequality Regressed onto Partisanship and Demographic Variables (2016)

	Outcome Variable				
	Schools and jobs (1)	Discrimination (2)	Choose not to work (3)	Culture of low expectations (4)	Inborn ability (5)
Party (Republican)	−1.227***	−1.841***	1.258***	0.276**	0.228
	(0.124)	(0.143)	(0.152)	(0.139)	(0.148)
Household income	−0.092	0.079	0.285*	0.184	0.119
	(0.133)	(0.145)	(0.154)	(0.142)	(0.169)
Female	0.006	−0.043	−0.050	0.009	−0.080
	(0.082)	(0.093)	(0.095)	(0.088)	(0.102)
Black	0.076	0.576***	0.068	−0.011	−0.234
	(0.152)	(0.150)	(0.163)	(0.155)	(0.170)
Hispanic	0.243	0.253	0.235	0.400**	0.039
	(0.216)	(0.229)	(0.226)	(0.195)	(0.257)
Asian American	0.102	0.593***	−0.088	−0.287	0.097
	(0.207)	(0.183)	(0.314)	(0.219)	(0.278)
Other race	−0.308	−0.004	−0.275	−0.032	−0.474*
	(0.256)	(0.242)	(0.220)	(0.204)	(0.251)
Rurality	0.180	0.034	0.121	0.005	−0.234
	(0.162)	(0.164)	(0.161)	(0.169)	(0.179)
Religiosity	−0.701***	−0.519***	0.352**	0.068	0.126
	(0.124)	(0.141)	(0.142)	(0.147)	(0.165)
Education	0.380**	0.278	−0.826***	−0.133	−0.513**
	(0.172)	(0.198)	(0.179)	(0.171)	(0.213)
Age	−0.320*	−0.268	0.171	−0.063	−0.250
	(0.173)	(0.217)	(0.205)	(0.187)	(0.223)
Constant	5.180***	4.872***	3.887***	4.187***	3.728***
	(0.154)	(0.177)	(0.204)	(0.181)	(0.222)
R-squared	0.163	0.256	0.137	0.015	0.02
Observations	1,708	1,691	1,695	1,660	1,648

Source: Author's calculations using 2016 EIPS data.

Note: Coefficients (with standard errors in parentheses) from five linear regressions with various explanations for generic economic inequality as outcome variables. Explanatory variables are scored 0 to 1 and outcome variables are scored 1 to 6.

* $p < .1$; ** $p < .05$; *** $p < .01$

Table A.5 Economic Policy Attitudes Regressed onto Unequal Opportunity Index and Potential Confounders (2016)

	Outcome Variable					
	Government social welfare			Decrease economic inequality		
	(1)	(2)	(3)	(4)	(5)	(6)
Unequal opportunity index	0.599***	0.361***	0.295***	0.598***	0.326***	0.254***
	(0.033)	(0.041)	(0.043)	(0.034)	(0.035)	(0.036)
Party (Republican)		−0.196***	−0.170***		−0.228***	−0.193***
		(0.030)	(0.027)		(0.026)	(0.026)
Ideology (conservative)		−0.212***	−0.185***		−0.291***	−0.250***
		(0.039)	(0.040)		(0.035)	(0.036)
Social dominance orientation			−0.411***			−0.385***
			(0.046)			(0.052)
Racism			0.093***			0.058
			(0.033)			(0.036)
Sexism			0.037			−0.041
			(0.039)			(0.042)
Household income	−0.062***	−0.051**	−0.046**	−0.077***	−0.065***	−0.057***
	(0.024)	(0.023)	(0.023)	(0.024)	(0.022)	(0.022)
Female	0.030**	0.025*	0.018	0.029*	0.018	0.005
	(0.015)	(0.014)	(0.014)	(0.015)	(0.014)	(0.014)
Black	0.064**	0.006	−0.022	0.129***	0.059***	0.046**
	(0.031)	(0.024)	(0.029)	(0.021)	(0.018)	(0.019)
Hispanic	0.048	0.005	−0.002	0.044	0.005	−0.002
	(0.041)	(0.037)	(0.028)	(0.034)	(0.032)	(0.035)
Asian American	0.123***	0.080	0.084*	0.143***	0.104**	0.114***
	(0.046)	(0.050)	(0.047)	(0.044)	(0.041)	(0.041)
Other race	−0.061*	−0.069**	−0.074***	−0.034	−0.053	−0.060*
	(0.033)	(0.030)	(0.028)	(0.035)	(0.035)	(0.033)
Rurality	−0.049*	−0.047*	−0.038	0.004	0.015	0.020
	(0.027)	(0.026)	(0.025)	(0.029)	(0.027)	(0.027)
Religiosity	−0.031	0.056**	0.057**	−0.142***	−0.022	−0.014
	(0.023)	(0.022)	(0.022)	(0.024)	(0.022)	(0.022)
Education	−0.063*	−0.077**	−0.052*	−0.069**	−0.105***	−0.079***
	(0.033)	(0.032)	(0.030)	(0.032)	(0.028)	(0.028)
Age	−0.120***	−0.088***	−0.093***	−0.038	−0.009	−0.021
	(0.032)	(0.031)	(0.029)	(0.035)	(0.031)	(0.031)
Constant	0.393***	0.666***	0.768***	0.534***	0.876***	0.992***
	(0.039)	(0.047)	(0.053)	(0.039)	(0.040)	(0.042)
R-squared	0.375	0.477	0.53	0.381	0.526	0.566
Observations	1,299	1,239	1,210	1,278	1,220	1,192

Source: Author's calculations using 2016 EIPS data.

Note: Coefficients (with standard errors in parentheses) from six linear regressions, with two policy attitude scales as outcome variables. All variables coded 0 to 1.

* $p < .1$; ** $p < .05$; *** $p < .01$

Table A.6 Presidential Preferences Regressed onto Unequal Opportunity Index and Potential Confounders (2016)

	Outcome Variable					
	Clinton-Trump thermometer			Clinton-Sanders thermometer		
	(1)	(2)	(3)	(4)	(5)	(6)
Unequal opportunity index	0.635***	0.193***	0.172***	−0.027	−0.123***	−0.057*
	(0.044)	(0.041)	(0.045)	(0.025)	(0.029)	(0.031)
Party (Republican)		−0.548***	−0.513***		−0.177***	−0.169***
		(0.030)	(0.034)		(0.021)	(0.023)
Ideology (conservative)		−0.170***	−0.159***		0.040	0.064**
		(0.042)	(0.046)		(0.029)	(0.032)
Social dominance orientation			−0.182***			0.037
			(0.052)			(0.038)
Racism			0.020			0.043*
			(0.035)			(0.026)
Sexism			−0.060			−0.068**
			(0.044)			(0.031)
Household income	0.005	0.031	0.051**	0.017	0.018	0.038**
	(0.033)	(0.023)	(0.024)	(0.021)	(0.020)	(0.019)
Female	0.050**	0.031*	0.014	0.025**	0.018	0.007
	(0.022)	(0.017)	(0.017)	(0.012)	(0.012)	(0.012)
Black	0.227***	0.064**	0.086***	0.067***	0.022	0.038
	(0.036)	(0.026)	(0.029)	(0.023)	(0.022)	(0.024)
Hispanic	0.178***	0.114***	0.129***	0.006	−0.019	0.002
	(0.055)	(0.039)	(0.038)	(0.023)	(0.024)	(0.024)
Asian American	0.061	0.052	0.018	0.002	−0.028	−0.022
	(0.045)	(0.040)	(0.042)	(0.037)	(0.034)	(0.025)
Other race	0.090*	0.051	0.009	0.007	−0.011	0.024
	(0.051)	(0.046)	(0.045)	(0.031)	(0.030)	(0.024)
Rurality	−0.093**	−0.056*	−0.032	−0.084***	−0.073***	−0.045**
	(0.041)	(0.031)	(0.034)	(0.022)	(0.021)	(0.021)
Religiosity	−0.132***	−0.012	−0.013	0.018	0.039*	0.032
	(0.032)	(0.025)	(0.027)	(0.020)	(0.021)	(0.020)
Education	0.091*	0.065*	0.087**	0.010	0.005	−0.004
	(0.047)	(0.035)	(0.036)	(0.024)	(0.023)	(0.021)
Age	−0.067	−0.021	−0.054	0.057**	0.045	0.008
	(0.045)	(0.035)	(0.039)	(0.028)	(0.027)	(0.028)
Constant	0.223***	0.717***	0.770***	0.432***	0.544***	0.494***
	(0.045)	(0.044)	(0.049)	(0.031)	(0.037)	(0.037)
R-squared	0.371	0.663	0.686	0.05	0.133	0.122
Observations	1,207	1,145	932	1,210	1,159	947

Source: Author's calculations using 2016 EIPS data.

Note: Coefficients (with standard errors in parentheses) from six linear regressions, with two presidential candidate feeling thermometer variables—a preference for Clinton over Trump, and a preference for Clinton over Sanders—as outcome variables. All variables coded 0 to 1.

* $p < .1$; ** $p < .05$; *** $p < .01$

Table A.7 Political Attitudes Regressed onto Unequal Opportunity Index, Party Identification, and Their Interaction (2016)

	Outcome Variable			
	Government social welfare (1)	Decrease economic inequality (2)	Clinton-Trump thermometer (3)	Clinton-Sanders thermometer (4)
Unequal opportunity index	0.263***	0.239***	0.195***	−0.090**
	(0.049)	(0.038)	(0.056)	(0.041)
Party (independent)	−0.310***	−0.232***	−0.389***	−0.092
	(0.057)	(0.067)	(0.085)	(0.064)
Party (Republican)	−0.357***	−0.413***	−0.483***	−0.079**
	(0.045)	(0.044)	(0.045)	(0.032)
Household income	−0.046**	−0.062***	0.019	0.011
	(0.021)	(0.022)	(0.023)	(0.019)
Female	0.020	0.016	0.033**	0.024**
	(0.014)	(0.014)	(0.016)	(0.012)
Black	−0.004	0.053***	0.067**	0.033
	(0.027)	(0.018)	(0.027)	(0.022)
Hispanic	0.002	0.003	0.122***	−0.010
	(0.033)	(0.030)	(0.040)	(0.025)
Asian American	0.079*	0.107***	0.048	−0.026
	(0.048)	(0.041)	(0.044)	(0.034)
Other race	−0.056*	−0.059*	0.038	0.011
	(0.030)	(0.034)	(0.036)	(0.030)
Rurality	−0.038	0.030	−0.040	−0.071***
	(0.025)	(0.028)	(0.031)	(0.021)
Religiosity	0.028	−0.081***	−0.050**	0.035*
	(0.021)	(0.022)	(0.023)	(0.019)
Education	−0.075**	−0.088***	0.050	−0.007
	(0.029)	(0.030)	(0.032)	(0.023)
Age	−0.094***	−0.014	−0.038	0.048*
	(0.031)	(0.032)	(0.033)	(0.026)
Unequal opportunity index*party (independent)	0.350***	0.220**	0.171	−0.055
	(0.091)	(0.095)	(0.138)	(0.099)
Unequal opportunity index*party (Republican)	0.251***	0.294***	0.005	−0.056
	(0.089)	(0.084)	(0.081)	(0.063)
Constant	0.651***	0.816***	0.639***	0.525***
	(0.042)	(0.039)	(0.048)	(0.037)
R-squared	0.476	0.508	0.643	0.137
Observations	1,284	1,262	1,235	1,229

Source: Author's calculations using 2016 EIPS data.

Note: Coefficients (with standard errors in parentheses) from four linear regressions, with four political attitude outcome variables. Models allow the coefficient on the Unequal Economic Opportunity Index to vary by partisanship. All variables coded 0 to 1.

* $p < .1$; ** $p < .05$; *** $p < .01$

Table A.8 Political Attitudes Regressed onto Three Unequal Opportunity Indexes (2016)

	Outcome Variable			
	Government social welfare (1)	Decrease economic inequality (2)	Clinton-Trump thermometer (3)	Clinton-Sanders thermometer (4)
Unequal economic opportunity	0.350***	0.309***	0.061	–0.092**
	(0.055)	(0.056)	(0.058)	(0.042)
Unequal economic opportunity	0.174***	0.177***	0.087*	–0.042
for women	(0.046)	(0.048)	(0.052)	(0.036)
Unequal economic opportunity	–0.013	–0.004	0.155***	–0.004
for Blacks and Latinos	(0.047)	(0.052)	(0.055)	(0.039)
Party (Republican)	–0.041***	–0.049***	–0.096***	–0.026***
	(0.005)	(0.004)	(0.004)	(0.003)
Household income	–0.044*	–0.061***	0.031	0.029
	(0.023)	(0.022)	(0.022)	(0.019)
Female	0.016	0.012	0.028*	0.023*
	(0.015)	(0.015)	(0.016)	(0.012)
Black	0.029	0.060***	0.054**	0.006
	(0.027)	(0.018)	(0.027)	(0.020)
Hispanic	0.011	0.008	0.079**	–0.015
	(0.034)	(0.034)	(0.036)	(0.024)
Asian American	0.097*	0.118***	0.049	–0.058**
	(0.053)	(0.045)	(0.039)	(0.025)
Other race	–0.052*	–0.044	0.053	–0.0003
	(0.030)	(0.035)	(0.038)	(0.030)
Rurality	–0.029	0.019	–0.058*	–0.073***
	(0.026)	(0.029)	(0.031)	(0.020)
Religiosity	0.016	–0.070***	–0.041*	0.050***
	(0.022)	(0.023)	(0.023)	(0.019)
Education	–0.072**	–0.094***	0.052	0.012
	(0.031)	(0.031)	(0.033)	(0.022)
Age	–0.112***	–0.026	–0.057	0.051*
	(0.033)	(0.035)	(0.035)	(0.026)
Constant	0.536***	0.725***	0.708***	0.574***
	(0.050)	(0.050)	(0.048)	(0.038)
R-squared	0.477	0.49	0.661	0.121
Observations	1,211	1,191	1,165	1,170

Source: Author's calculations using 2016 EIPS data.

Note: Coefficients (with standard errors in parentheses) from four linear regressions, with four political attitude outcome variables. All variables coded 0 to 1.

* $p < .1$; ** $p < .05$; *** $p < .01$

Table A.9 Affirmative Action Support Regressed onto Two Unequal Opportunity Indexes (2018)

	Outcome Variable	
	Affirmative action: gender (1)	Affirmative action: race (2)
Unequal economic opportunity for women	0.457***	0.362***
	(0.092)	(0.086)
Unequal economic opportunity for Black and Latino Americans	0.192**	0.291***
	(0.092)	(0.081)
Party (Republican)	−0.222***	−0.244***
	(0.048)	(0.051)
Household income	−0.055	−0.039
	(0.047)	(0.049)
Female	0.012	−0.005
	(0.030)	(0.030)
Black	0.161***	0.163***
	(0.061)	(0.055)
Hispanic	0.045	−0.004
	(0.047)	(0.054)
Asian American	0.188**	0.072
	(0.093)	(0.101)
Other race	0.030	−0.011
	(0.070)	(0.082)
Rurality	−0.004	0.010
	(0.053)	(0.056)
Religiosity	−0.044	−0.020
	(0.044)	(0.045)
Education	−0.096*	−0.020
	(0.056)	(0.066)
Age	0.042	−0.114
	(0.065)	(0.070)
Constant	0.106	0.137
	(0.081)	(0.092)
R-squared	0.419	0.445
Observations	367	369

Source: Author's calculations using 2018 EIPS data.

Note: Coefficients (with standard errors in parentheses) from two linear regressions, with two affirmative action preference measures as outcome variables. All variables coded 0 to 1.

* $p < .1$; ** $p < .05$; *** $p < .01$

NOTES

Introduction

1. Huber and Form 1973; Kluegel and Smith 1986.
2. Cheng and Wen 2019; see especially McCall 2016; Piston 2018.
3. Sousa 2024; Wolfe 2024; Zitner 2023.
4. Gordon 2016.
5. Organisation for Economic Co-operation and Development 2023.
6. Aeppli and Wilmers 2022.
7. Chetty et al. 2017.
8. See, for example, Wolak and Peterson 2020a.
9. On the two parties' agendas and supporting coalitions, see Gerring 1998; Grossmann et al. 2021; Hacker and Pierson 2010; Hertel-Fernandez 2019; Piketty 2019; Witko et al. 2021.
10. J. Hochschild 1981; Kluegel and Smith 1986; Petersen 2012; Piketty 2019.
11. Grossman and Hopkins 2023; Piketty 2019; Zacher 2023.
12. Hacker et al. 2023.
13. Burns et al. 2016; Ferguson et al. 2020.
14. Harrs and Sterba 2023; McClosky and Zaller 1984; Wolak and Peterson 2020a.
15. Brewer and Stonecash 2015; Spinner-Halev and Theiss-Morse 2024.

Chapter 1: Debating the American Dream

1. American National Election Studies 2025.
2. Also see Bartels 2016.
3. Feagin 1975, 95.
4. Kluegel and Smith 1986.
5. McCall 2013.
6. McCall 2016.

7. Piston 2018.

8. Cheng and Wen 2019.

9. Lindert and Williamson 2016.

10. On economic inequality, see McCall 2013; on the availability of opportunity, see Wolak and Peterson 2020a.

11. McCall et al. 2017.

12. For example, see Alesina et al. 2001; McClosky and Zaller 1984; Piketty 2019.

13. Bawn et al. 2012; Hacker and Pierson 2014; Karol 2009; Layman et al. 2010; D. Schlozman and Rosenfeld 2019.

14. Gerring 1998; Lowi et al. 2022.

15. Lowi et al. 2022.

16. Brown and Mettler 2024; Maxwell and Shields 2019; Rodden 2019.

17. Gerring 1998; Lowi et al. 2022; Schickler 2016.

18. Rodden 2019.

19. Hacker et al. 2023; Zacher 2023.

20. Izaguirre and Oprysko 2024; Page et al. 2018; Witko et al. 2021.

21. Izaguirre and Oprysko 2024.

22. Bartels 2016; Gilens 2012; Kelly 2019; Witko et al. 2021.

23. Adam Bonica and colleagues (2013) document that the top .01 percent of U.S. households with respect to income contributed more than 40 percent of all campaign contributions in 2012. Benjamin Page and Martin Gilens report that, in the first half of 2015, "nearly half of all the money backing a Republican or Democratic candidate—$179 million of it—came from just 158 families and the companies they owned or controlled. Each of those families contributed $250,000 or more, mainly to super PACs with no limit on the size of contributions" (2017, 104). In 2020, the top twenty donors contributed a combined 2.3 billion dollars in federal elections (Tindera 2021).

24. Barber 2016; Kujala 2019; see also Terris 2023; Zengerle 2015.

25. Bartels 2016; Page et al. 2018.

26. Schattschneider 1960; K. L. Schlozman et al. 2018.

27. Berry and Wilcox 2018; Grumbach 2019; Hertel-Fernandez 2019.

28. K. L. Schlozman et al. 2018.

29. Grossmann et al. 2021.

30. K. L. Schlozman et al. 2018; Grossman et al. 2021.

31. The definition of *neoliberalism* is similar to that of *libertarianism* but has a slightly different emphasis, not only advocating for small government and limited regulation of economic and social actors but also celebrating markets as superior institutions to government (Gerstle 2022; Mudge 2018).

32. Grossmann and Hopkins 2016; Noel 2014; Saldin and Teles 2020.

33. Gerstle 2022; Janda 2022.

34. On farmers, see Jares 2023; on technology companies, see U.S. Chamber of Commerce 2022.

35. Pierson 2017; Stiglitz 2019. The early Republican Party and its predecessor, the Whig

Party, advanced a different economic agenda, eagerly promoting a strong national government, including a national bank, the development of infrastructure, and tariffs (Gerring 1998). Early in the nation's history, these policies worked to the advantage of the affluent and business interests. As the Democratic Party turned to government in the twentieth century as a tool of economic regulation and redistribution, the Republican Party grew more opposed to big government. Trump's growing emphasis on tariffs mirrors this earlier Republican era.

36. Gerring 1998. Early in its history, the Democratic Party famously opposed a powerful central government; its agrarian and southern base viewed the government as being in the pocket of northern industrialists.
37. Fraser and Gerstle 1989; Gerring 1998.
38. Karol 2009; Zaller 2012.
39. Hacker and Pierson 2010; Gerstle 2022; Mudge 2018.
40. Brewer and Stonecash 2015.
41. Hacker et al. 2023; Domestic Policy Council 2023.
42. Lasswell 1936.
43. Skowronek 1984.
44. Rosenblum 2008; Schattschneider 1960.
45. F. Lee 2016.
46. Stokes 1963.
47. Bawn et al. 2012.
48. Gerring 1998; Grossmann and Hopkins 2016.
49. Gerstle 2022.
50. Gerring 1998.
51. See Gerring 1997.
52. Suhay and Druckman 2015; Suhay 2017.
53. Brulle 2014; Dunlap and McCright 2011; Mayer 2016; Oreskes and Conway 2010.
54. Grossmann 2021.
55. For a historical perspective, see Milanovic 2023.
56. King 2016; McCloskey 2014; Piketty 2013.
57. Sargent 2021.
58. Rizzo 2019.
59. Warren 2023.
60. Gramm et al. 2022; Strain 2020b.
61. Grossmann et al. 2021.
62. Ferreira 2023.
63. McCall 2016.
64. See Roemer 2000.
65. J. Hochschild 1995.
66. Brewer and Stonecash 2015; Gerring 1998.
67. D. Trump 2020.
68. Trump 2025.

69. Levin 2023.

70. Brewer and Stonecash 2015.

71. Jost, Blount, et al. 2003.

72. Brewer and Stonecash 2015; Gerring 1998.

73. Clinton 2015.

74. Underwood and Murray 2021.

75. Malpas and Hilton 2021.

76. See Chong and Druckman 2007.

77. Abelson 1981, 717.

78. Roos and Reccius 2024, 314.

79. Brewer and Stonecash 2015; Peck 2019.

80. J. Hochschild 1995; E. Kim 2023.

81. Lyons 2017; Valentino and Sears 1998.

82. Gerring 1998; Lewis 2019.

83. Cameron and Kastellec 2023; D. Schlozman and Rosenfeld 2019.

84. Fagan 2018. See Gerring 1998 on the usual correspondence between party platforms and how presidents govern.

85. Campbell et al. 1960; Jennings and Niemi 1981.

86. Lay et al. 2023.

87. Berelson et al. 1954; Jennings et al. 2009; Lyons 2017; Valentino and Sears 1998.

88. Jennings et al. 2009; also see Anoll et al. 2022.

89. Lyons 2017.

90. Campbell et al. 1960.

91. Layman et al. 2010.

92. Barber and Pope 2019; Lenz 2012; McClosky and Zaller 1984; Sides et al. 2022; Zaller 1992.

93. Bullock 2020; Leeper and Slothuus 2014.

94. Slothuus 2010.

95. Levendusky 2013; Stroud 2011.

96. Katz and Lazarsfeld 1955; Lippmann 1922; Siegel 2013.

97. T. Lee 2002; Zaller 2012.

98. Suhay 2015; Toff and Suhay 2019.

99. Diehl et al. 2016.

100. N. Lee et al. 2021; Suhay et al. 2022; also see Barker et al. 2022.

101. Abramowitz 2011; Levendusky 2009.

102. Iyengar et al. 2012; Iyengar and Westwood 2015; Mason 2018.

103. Bisgaard and Slothuus 2018; Slothuus 2010.

104. Groenendyk 2015.

105. Bafumi and Herron 2010; McCarty 2019.

106. Lauderdale 2013.

107. Klar and Krupnikov 2016; Lowi et al. 2022.

108. Huber and Form 1973; Kluegel and Smith 1986; McClosky and Zaller 1984; Piketty 2019.

109. Cohn 2021; Horowitz et al. 2020.
110. Edsall 2022; Pocasangre and Drutman 2023.
111. Hacker et al. 2023; Zacher 2023.
112. Pierson 2017; Stiglitz 2019.
113. Egan 2013; D. Schlozman and Rosenfeld 2019.
114. Meltzer and Richard 1981.
115. See, for example, Page and Jacobs 2009; Piston 2018.
116. Gilens 2012; Hacker and Pierson 2010.
117. Bartels 2016.
118. Ellis and Stimson 2012; Frank 2004.
119. A. Hochschild 2016, 2024.
120. Curry and Lee 2020; Hacker and Pierson 2010.

Chapter 2: The Politics of the American Dream in Historical Perspective

1. Quoted in Gerring 1998.
2. Transcript provided by the Living Room Candidate (livingroomcandidate.org).
3. Churchwell 2018.
4. Adams (1931) 2001, 404.
5. Adams (1931) 2001, 411.
6. Adams (1931) 2001, 414.
7. Churchwell 2018.
8. Adams (1931) 2001; Lindert and Williamson 2016; Lipset 1977.
9. Adams (1931) 2001.
10. Skowronek 1982.
11. Gerring 1998; Lewis 2019.
12. Gerstle 2022.
13. Young 1958.
14. McCall 2013; Sandel 2020.
15. Some prominent scholars, such as John Roemer (2000), define equal opportunity differently—a society with equal opportunity is sensitive to differences in effort but not innate talent. In other words, in an equal opportunity society, economic inequality is only permissible to the extent that individuals vary in their level of effort or responsibility. Policies should be in place that ameliorate inequalities linked to innate characteristics.
16. Dobbin 2011.
17. My notes indicate that I decided to incorporate into this book the idea of abundance, in addition to meritocracy, at some point in 2022. While I had not read Derek Thompson's influential essay "A Simple Plan to Solve All of America's Problems" (Thompson 2022) at the time, I almost certainly was indirectly influenced by it via the national conversation it inspired. Although the current conversation around abundance focuses primarily on the availability of goods and services, such as housing and health care

(see Klein and Thompson 2025), the idea of abundance is of course also relevant to income and wealth.

18. J. Hochschild 1995.
19. J. Hochschild 1995.
20. For example, see Roemer 1996.
21. R. Smith 1993.
22. McClosky and Zaller 1984. Also see Anderson 2017; Herzog 2020.
23. McClosky and Zaller 1984, 2–3.
24. R. Smith 1993.
25. Lipset 1977.
26. Hartz 1955; Tocqueville (1835) 2004.
27. Blasi et al. 2013; Turner 1893.
28. Lindert and Williamson 2016; Lipset 1977.
29. Lindert and Williamson 2016, 37.
30. Swidler 1986.
31. Blasi et al. 2013; Lindert and Williamson 2016.
32. Piketty and Saez 2014.
33. Lowi et al. 2022.
34. Gerring 1998.
35. G. Feldman 2013.
36. Gerring 1998; Lipset 1977.
37. Gerring 1998; Watson 2006.
38. Golway 2012.
39. Gerring 1998, 226.
40. Reichley 1992; Pestritto 2005.
41. Bonacich 1975.
42. Gerring 1998, 58.
43. It is worth noting that Roosevelt was an "accidental" president, in that he became president after President McKinley was assassinated early in his second term. This might explain his highly unusual status as a somewhat anti-capitalist Republican—the party never intended for him to assume the presidency. I thank Larry Bartels for pointing out this historical detail and hypothesis.
44. Quoted in Gerring 1998, 130–31.
45. Reichley 1992.
46. Hoover 1934, quoted in Brewer and Stonecash 2015, 93.
47. Suhay and Jayaratne 2013.
48. Reichley 1992.
49. Skowronek 1984.
50. Fraser and Gerstle 1989.
51. University of California Santa Barbara, n.d. All party platforms discussed in this chapter were collected by The American Presidency Project, housed at the University of California Santa Barbara. Platforms are available at their website.
52. Katznelson 2005.

53. Weiss 1983.
54. Schickler 2016.
55. University of California Santa Barbara, n.d.
56. Lowi et al. 2022.
57. Zelizer 2015.
58. Gerring 1998.
59. T. Lee 2002; Kinder and Sanders 1996.
60. Gerstle 2022.
61. Gerstle 2022.
62. University of California Santa Barbara, n.d.
63. Quoted in Lipset 1977, 113.
64. Whitaker 1996.
65. Karol 2009; Maxwell and Shields 2019.
66. More radical ideas could be found on both ends of the political spectrum. On the left, economic progressives pressed for a guarantee of equal outcomes, regardless of perceived effort or talent (see Brewer and Stonecash 2015; Lipset 1977). Along these lines, in his 1944 State of the Union address, Franklin Delano Roosevelt proposed a "Second Bill of Rights," which would guarantee for all a living wage, housing, and health care, among other things. This proposal was primarily motivated—at least publicly—not by a commitment to fairness but, rather, by a wartime concern that people with economic difficulties were more likely to support fascism. On the right, libertarians argued for a bare bones government devoted mainly to ensuring national defense and law-abidingness. In this case as well, the reasoning stemmed not from concern over fairness but from concern that it was government involvement in economic affairs that led to fascism (Hayek 1944). However, neither of these more extreme ideas gained widespread acceptance among American political leaders or the public.
67. McCloskey and Zaller 1984, 82.
68. McCloskey and Zaller 1984, 82.
69. Gerstle 2022.
70. An earlier version of this analysis appears in Suhay et al. 2022.
71. A research assistant read each platform carefully, coding every attribution for economic or related inequalities that appeared in a platform. Most of the platforms were long, averaging more than 28,000 words. After the assistant completed his initial coding, I reviewed each platform and the corresponding codes and occasionally recommended coding changes.
72. Attributional statements could be coded into multiple categories. Also note that, in addition to the six categories discussed herein, statements could be coded as blaming some nonhuman phenomenon, such as a natural disaster, or blaming the actions of the other political party but without reference to the design of government programs. The small proportion of attributions that did not fit into any of the predetermined categories were coded as "other."
73. Douthat and Salam 2009; Gerstle 2022; Hacker and Pierson 2010.
74. Maxwell and Shields 2019.

75. Douthat and Salam 2009; Pierson 1994.

76. Bartels 2016.

77. See, for example, Kinder and Sanders 1996.

78. Mendelberg 2001.

79. Mudge 2018. An underappreciated reason for the neoliberal turn in the 1990s is the fall of the Soviet Union in 1989, which suggested that communism and socialism were failed ideologies and removed them as viable political options for a disgruntled working class (Gerstle 2022).

80. Hacker and Pierson 2010.

81. Erikson et al. 2002.

82. Kinder and Sanders 1996; McGhee 2021.

83. Weaver 2000. That said, Clinton did not reduce total spending on aid to low-income Americans, as conventional wisdom suggests. While the new Temporary Aid to Needy Families program (which replaced Aid to Families with Dependent Children) included various limits and provided fewer benefits, Clinton also greatly expanded the Earned Income Tax Credit.

84. Bartels 2016.

85. Gerstle 2022.

86. Douthat and Salam 2009.

87. Bartels 2016; Gerstle 2022.

88. Bartels 2016.

89. Sandel 2020.

90. Brooks and Manza 2013.

91. Bartels 2013.

92. Douthat and Salam 2009.

93. Mayer 2016.

94. Skocpol and Williamson 2016.

95. Douthat and Salam 2009; Saldin and Teles 2020.

96. Glasser 2018.

97. Wolak and Peterson 2020b.

98. See, for example, Ferguson et al. 2020.

99. Saldin and Teles 2020.

100. Ferguson et al. 2020.

101. Greenstein 2024.

102. Pierson 2017.

103. See Zelizer 2022 for an overview of Trump's presidency.

104. J. Green 2024.

105. See Nelson 2021 and Sides et al. 2022 for overviews of the 2020 election.

106. Biden-Sanders Unity Task Force 2020; Detrow 2020.

107. Medina 2021.

108. See Foer 2023 for an overview of Biden's first two years in office.

109. The complete list of groups identified is as follows: people in general; the middle class; the poor/working class; workers; women; racial minorities (Black, Latino, Native, and

Asian Americans); the racial majority; LGBTQ+; rural people; urban people; families; young people and students; the elderly; other. Note that "workers" differ from the "working class" in that the former are employees (and often mentioned in conjunction with their employment) whereas the latter category, less often mentioned, designates Americans who are lower income but not poor.

110. Nehamas and Duehren 2024.
111. Karol 2009.
112. Goldmacher et al. 2024.
113. Hirsh 2025.

Chapter 3: Americans' Beliefs About Inequality and Opportunity over Four Decades

1. Used with permission of Princeton University Press from *Democracy for Realists: Why Elections Do Not Produce Responsive Government*, by Christopher H. Achen and Larry M. Bartels, copyright 2016. Permission conveyed through Copyright Clearance Center, Inc.
2. Gerstle 2022.
3. Lane 1959.
4. For further development of this idea, see Jost 2017.
5. Harrington 1962.
6. Feagin 1975.
7. Feagin 1975, 95–97.
8. Kluegel and Smith 1986.
9. McCall 2013.
10. Condon and Wichowsky 2020; Branch and Hanley 2022.
11. Davidai and Gilovich 2015; Kraus and Tan 2015.
12. Alesina and Angeletos 2005.
13. Almås et al. 2020.
14. Kluegel and Smith 1986, chapter 7.
15. Gilens, 1999, 158.
16. Gilens 1999, 140.
17. Kinder and Sanders 1996, 107.
18. Branch and Hanley 2022.
19. Kinder and Sanders 1996; Kluegel and Smith 1986.
20. Hunt 2007; Branch and Hanley 2022.
21. Huber and Form 1973.
22. J. Hochschild 1981.
23. J. Hochschild 1981, 255.
24. Kluegel and Smith 1986.
25. Kluegel and Smith 1986, 292–93.
26. McClosky and Zaller 1984.
27. Alesina et al. 2001.

28. McCall 2013, 146.
29. Feagin 1975; Kluegel and Smith 1986.
30. McCall 2013, 156.
31. McCall 2016.
32. Cheng and Wen 2019; Piston 2018.
33. Lindert and Williamson 2016. This was true in many countries beyond the United States as well.
34. Lindert and Williamson 2016; Piketty et al. 2018.
35. Binder and Bound 2019.
36. Chetty et al. 2017.
37. Bayer and Charles 2018; Lindert and Williamson 2016.
38. Lindert and Williamson 2016.
39. Wolak and Peterson 2020a. The authors carry out a methodologically sophisticated analysis linking shifting economic indicators to belief in the American Dream (measured differently than I do here, with a wider array of questions that focus more on economic growth). Future research might use this method, which combines hundreds of questions into a summary measure of "public mood" (Stimson 1999), to analyze the relationship between partisan rhetoric and economic narratives about inequality and opportunity.
40. McCall 2013.
41. McCall et al. 2017; see also K. Trump 2020.
42. Steele 2022.
43. McCall 2013.
44. Culpepper et al. 2024.
45. J. Hochschild 1981.
46. Roos and Reccius 2024.
47. Bisgaard and Slothuus 2018; Slothuus 2010.
48. Lodge and Taber 2013; Zaller 1992.
49. Fiorina 1981.
50. Earlier versions of the survey analyses in this section were published in Suhay et al. 2022.
51. These questions are also often phrased in a manner problematic for this book, leaving uncertain who or what the survey respondent believes is ultimately responsible for success—the individual or societal structures. For example, the survey refers to the importance of education without specifying whether people with low education are to blame for not advancing their education or, rather, are the victim of an unequitable educational system. Similarly, the survey asks about the importance of race and sex to getting ahead without clarifying whether that points to the influence of societal discrimination or, to the contrary, the belief that innate differences between racial groups or women and men cause differential economic outcomes.
52. Pew Research Center 2022.
53. U.S. Bureau of Labor Statistics 2021.
54. V. Wilson 2020.

55. Pew Research Center 2016.
56. Schuman et al. 1985,
57. Kinder and Sanders 1996.
58. Levendusky 2009.
59. Conley and Fletcher 2017; Hammonds and Herzig 2008.
60. Kinder and Sanders 1996; Mendelberg 2001.
61. This is not to say that no political actors today espouse explicit racism (and corresponding racially discriminatory policies). Recent years have seen a resurgence of White nationalism mainly associated with political conservatives and Republicans (Fording and Schram 2020). Acolytes in this movement, including the insurgency that sought to keep Trump in the White House in 2021, have engaged in violence (Washington Post Staff 2021). Yet, the survey data here suggests either that such individuals do not embrace biological racism or that their numbers are so small in a proportional sense that they barely register in representative public opinion surveys.
62. Suhay et al. 2022.
63. Note that the appendix figures using GSS data begin in 1985 due to data limitations.
64. See, for example, Berinsky 2009; Zaller 1992.
65. Answers included "not at all interested, "not very interested," "somewhat interested" (in some years), "fairly interested," and "very interested."
66. Hartig 2022; Kennedy and Johnson 2020.
67. See, for example, Barber and Pope 2019; Hare 2022; Layman et al. 2010; Lenz 2012; Levendusky 2009; Zaller 2012.
68. Fiorina et al. 2010.
69. See Levendusky 2009; Maxwell and Shields 2019.

Chapter 4: How Americans Explain Socioeconomic Inequalities

1. This question wording mirrors that found in the GSS Black–White inequality questions. The racial inequality series, in asking survey respondents to contrast a lower earning group with a higher earning one, strikes a balance between questions that focus on success—which may spur especially optimistic, aspirational thinking—and those that focus on poor people—which may prime skepticism about the economy. In comparing those who are more and less successful, such wording also ought to make it easier for respondents to isolate factors that they believe make the difference between economic success and struggle.
2. For example, Iyengar 1991; Kluegel and Smith 1986; Weiner 1995.
3. Kruglanski et al. 1978; Levy et al. 2006.
4. Heider 1958; Weiner 1995.
5. Kluegel and Smith 1986.
6. Iyengar 1991.
7. Morgan et al. 2010; Skitka et al. 2002.
8. Feagin 1975, 95.

9. Van Oorschot and Halman 2000.
10. Weiner 1995; Weiner, Osborne, and Rudolph 2011.
11. Lepianka et al. 2009; K. Smith and Stone 1989.
12. Weiner 1995; Weiner et al. 2011.
13. In other words, each of the cells in table 4.1 also has a stable or unstable dimension. See Weiner 1995. Genetic determinism falls in the individual lack-of-blame cell.
14. Suhay 2017; Weiner 1995.
15. Ickes and Layden 1978; C. Peterson et al. 1982.
16. Hussak and Cimpian 2015, 2016; Keller 2005.
17. Alesina and Angeletos 2005; M. Morris and Peng 1994.
18. Brewer and Stonecash 2015.
19. Morgan et al. 2010.
20. What underlies the ideo-attribution effect? Some scholars argue that attributional styles develop early in life and draw people to their political ideologies (for example, Hussak and Cimpian 2015, 2016). Others argue that attributions operate as post-hoc justifications for ideological commitments that are important to people, such as a desire for social hierarchy (Jost, Glaser, et al. 2003; Sidanius and Pratto 1999). Few political psychologists have considered the possibility of party influence, as I do here. I discuss these ideas further in chapter 6.
21. J. Hochschild 1981; Kluegel and Smith 1986.
22. Kluegel and Smith 1986; see also Hughes and Tuch 2000. This also offers an important lesson for survey methodology: when inquiring about people's inequality beliefs, one should not ask them to choose between presumably opposite explanations; rather, ask them to evaluate each distinct explanation one at a time.
23. Hunt and Bullock 2016; see also Robinson 2009.
24. J. Hochschild 1981.
25. T. Lee 2002.
26. Suhay and Jayaratne 2013; Suhay 2017.
27. Brady 2019.
28. Kluegel and Smith 1986.
29. Hughes and Tuch 2000.
30. Surveys were open to all U.S. adult residents and not restricted to citizens. A small number of respondents were noncitizens; for example, in the initial survey, 40 (2 percent) of 2,000 respondents were not citizens.
31. Stoker and McCall 2017; Twyman 2008.
32. Silver 2023.
33. This survey is now called the Cooperative Election Study. Conducted yearly, it brings together many teams of researchers. A common core of questions is administered to a sample of more than 50,000 Americans, and separate questionnaires designed by the individual teams are administered to subsets of the sample. See Cooperative Election Study 2025.
34. The demographic profiles of the split-samples are nearly identical, meaning the characteristics of the whole sample is mirrored in the set of respondents analyzed here.

35. Unfortunately, surveys were only available in English; the lack of a Spanish-language version may have hindered Hispanic survey participation.

36. Feagin 1975; Kluegel and Smith 1986.

37. See 2002 American National Election Studies data (American National Election Studies 2025); McCall 2013.

38. In 2016, respondents could choose "don't know" as well, an option not provided in 2018 to discourage people from opting out due to social desirability concerns (see Berinsky 2004).

39. I purposely asked about inequality in general first to avoid the possibility that the specific domains of race or sex inequality might bias these results.

40. Hughes and Tuch 2000, 181.

41. Note that the original "worse jobs" wording, borrowed from the ANES, was intended to capture how many academics think about economic class—as a combination of job category (such as, blue-collar versus white-collar) and income. For this reason, the original 2016 wording has some advantages. I revised the wording for two reasons. First, it seems inappropriately disparaging to refer to blue-collar or service-sector jobs as inherently worse than others. Second, especially as we consider comparisons between social groups, it is important to consider wealth disparities.

42. U.S. Department of Commerce 2023.

43. U.S. Department of Commerce 2023.

44. Carr and Kefalas 2010.

45. While economic inequality is especially high among Asian Americans, the proportion of Asian American subgroups and households earning less than the U.S. median is relatively small; in other words, the unusually high inequality found among Asian Americans is primarily driven by a large proportion of affluent households and subgroups (Budiman and Ruiz 2021; Jin 2021).

46. Semega and Kollar 2022, 2.

47. Other patterns emerged in the full set of data. For example, for female–male and Black/Latino–White inequalities, innate explanations were negatively correlated with schools/jobs and discrimination. This is suggestive of a social prejudice dimension to some responses, an idea I return to in chapter 6.

48. Zaller and Feldman 1992.

49. See Couch and Keniston 1960.

50. See Nederhof 1985. While concerns over social desirability have been long-standing, social desirability and related biases appear to be much rarer in self-administered online surveys like the ones I conducted when compared with live interviewer surveys (Tourangeau et al. 2000).

51. Charmaz 2014.

52. An exception is the "other" category. Answers were placed there, and only there, if they could not be placed in a substantive category.

53. About 1 to 2 percent of all answers simply weren't interpretable or didn't answer the question. Often these answers were meaningless phrases; however, some were coher-

ent but irrelevant to the task at hand, such as people who took the opportunity to affirm their normative commitment to equal opportunity.

54. J. Lee 2021.

Chapter 5: Demographic Divides over Explanations for Socioeconomic Inequality

1. Mason and Wronski 2018; Pew Research Center 2018.
2. Swidler 1986.
3. Kluegel and Smith 1986; Lamont 1992.
4. Huckfeldt and Sprague 1995; Katz and Lazarsfeld 1955; Suhay 2015.
5. See Levy et al. 2006.
6. Thal 2017.
7. See Piketty 1995; Suhay et al. 2021.
8. Hewstone 1990; Pettigrew 1979.
9. Sidanius and Pratto 1999.
10. Hewstone 1990.
11. Jost et al. 2004.
12. Jennings et al. 2009.
13. Jennings and Niemi 1981.
14. Braungart and Braungart 1986; Grasso et al. 2019; Sears and Valentino 1997.
15. Braungart and Braungart 1986.
16. Note that the COVID-19 pandemic and associated economic recession occurred after the data discussed in this chapter was collected.
17. Gale et al. 2020.
18. Pew Research Center 2019.
19. Braungart and Braungart 1986; Jennings and Niemi 1981.
20. J. Peterson et al. 2020.
21. Blanchard-Fields 1994.
22. See Grusec and Hastings 2015.
23. Wentzel 2015.
24. Jennings and Niemi 1981; Niemi and Sobieszek 1977.
25. Ehman 1980.
26. Johnston et al. 2017.
27. Alwin et al. 1991; Hunt 2007; Surridge 2016.
28. Kluegel and Smith 1986, 89; Lukianoff and Haidt 2018.
29. Rockenbach et al. 2020; Rothman et al. 2005.
30. Gethin et al. 2021.
31. Khan 2011.
32. Sandel 2020.
33. Surridge 2016, 151.
34. Mendelberg et al. 2017.
35. Jennings and Niemi 1981.

36. Bradley 1978.
37. Weber 1930. The reason for this was deeply religious and, as Weber pointed out, also somewhat illogical. It was thought that God would only allow a group of "elect" people into Heaven. While this designation was predetermined by God, devotion to a calling, sober living, and prosperity were signs of being among the elect. This, then, encouraged Protestants to embody the qualities of the elect. By way of contrast, Catholic teachings tended to emphasize that poverty is a sign of God's grace (Lepianka et al. 2010).
38. Feagin 1975; Hayward and Kemmelmeier 2011; Lepianka et al. 2010.
39. Hunter 1991.
40. Hunt 2007.
41. Putnam and Campbell 2010.
42. Solt et al. 2011.
43. Scheve and Stasavage 2006. In addition, in their study using World Values Survey data, David Hayward and Markus Kemmelmeier (2011) show that non-Protestants become more market oriented with increasing levels of religiosity—a finding that holds across nations and religious traditions.
44. Marx 1970.
45. Scheve and Stasavage 2006; Solt, Habel, and Grant 2011.
46. Gerstle 2022; Maxwell and Shields 2019.
47. Bowler 2013.
48. Rodden 2019; Pew Research Center 2018.
49. Gimpel et al. 2020; Wuthnow 2018.
50. Rodden 2019.
51. Cramer 2016; also see Munis 2022.
52. A. Hochschild 2016.
53. See, for example, Huber and Form 1973.
54. Freeland 2012; Huber and Form 1973; Kraus and Keltner 2013; Suhay et al. 2021.
55. See Cozzarelli et al. 2001; Feagin 1975; Hunt 1996, 2007; Kluegel and Smith 1986; Robinson 2009.
56. Sidanius and Pratto 1999, 45.
57. Sidanius and Pratto 1999, 46.
58. Hierarchy-enhancing myths do not go unchallenged. Sidanius and Pratto also acknowledge the existence of "hierarchy attenuating" myths that challenge the status quo. Here, they emphasize broad ideologies—such as socialism—rather than a set of contrasting causal attributions, such as assertions of discrimination or a lack of opportunity. These ideas are less developed by the authors.
59. Tajfel 1974; Tajfel and Turner 1979.
60. Deaux 1993.
61. Bradley 1978; Hewstone 1990; Pettigrew 1979.
62. Hunt and Bullock 2016.
63. Jost 2020; Jost et al. 2004.

64. Jost 2017; see also Lane 1959. Lerner (1980) originated the concept of "just world beliefs."
65. Jost, Banaji, and Nosek 2004. Sidanius and Pratto's Social Dominance Theory is similar to the idea of "false consciousness" originated by Marx and Engels and developed further by those working in a Marxist tradition. These scholars argue that societal elites propagate ideologies about the economy and society that mask subordinate classes' exploitation (Eyerman 1981). Because elites have more influence over culture than others, such ideas become the "dominant ideology," absorbed even by many in the lower classes who have little to gain from them (Huber and Form 1973).
66. J. Hochschild 1995.
67. Again, when examining beliefs about economic inequality between women and men, the "schools and jobs" wording is replaced by reference to a lack of access to childcare.
68. The Cronbach's alphas are adequate-to-good for unequal economic opportunity (.67) and unequal economic opportunity for Black and Latino Americans (.7). The alpha is lower than ideal for unequal economic opportunity for women (.53); I nevertheless use this index to allow comparison across domains as well as for the sake of parsimony.
69. Wealth was originally captured by asking people to place their household wealth within a given range. However, creating a variable for wealth proved difficult, as approximately 40 percent of respondents reported little-to-no wealth (in line with national averages). Given the minimal variation on this variable, I do not include it in analyses.
70. YouGov used the term "Hispanic" in its question on respondent race and ethnicity; thus, I use this terminology when discussing how respondents self-identify.
71. I divided the number of people living in a postal zip code by the square mileage of the area. The resulting ratio—with large numbers indicating higher-density urban areas and small numbers indicating lower-density rural areas—was then placed on a 0 to 1 interval and reversed so that 1 equals the most rural and 0 equals the most urban place.
72. Rodden 2019.
73. Putnam and Campbell 2010.
74. National Center for Education Statistics 2023.
75. Conley and Fletcher 2017.
76. Garretson and Suhay 2016; Harden 2021.
77. Gethin et al. 2021.

Chapter 6: Partisan Divides over Explanations for Socioeconomic Inequality

1. Campbell et al. 1960; D. Green et al. 2004.
2. See Jost 2021.
3. See Kinder and Sanders 1996.
4. Gill and Andreychik 2014. Empirical results in chapter 4 cast doubt on the likelihood

of finding such a systematic difference in the public. Nevertheless, such consistency could emerge among partisan subgroups.

5. For example, see Alesina et al. 2018; Azevedo et al. 2017; Brewer and Stonecash 2015; Hunt and Bullock 2016; Ternullo 2024.

6. Morgan et al. 2010.

7. Levendusky 2013.

8. Hetherington and Weiler 2009; Johnston et al. 2017; Jost 2021.

9. Although an uncommon view in the literature, I would argue that explanations for inequality that focus on the individual as cause are not always more simple than those that focus on the influence of society. For example, one person could have a complex view of how genetic and other biological phenomena influence human development and another person could have a simple, Pavlovian view of how the environment influences people.

10. Hasson et al. 2018; S. Morris 2020.

11. Lakoff 2016.

12. Alesina and Angeletos 2005; Jost 2021.

13. Gill and Andreychik 2014; McCall 2013.

14. Cooley et al. 2019.

15. Morgan et al. 2010.

16. In the past, affluent Americans disproportionately identified as Republicans, but as discussed in chapter 1, in recent years identification with either party has neared parity (see Zacher 2023).

17. For evidence on this, see Kim and Zilinsky 2022.

18. Kane et al. 2021, 1796. Americans' perceptions of which social groups affiliate with which party are quite accurate (Kane et al. 2021), although people tend to exaggerate how strongly affiliated groups prefer one party over another (Ahler and Sood 2018). This exaggeration should increase the likelihood of the type of bias I describe here.

19. Conover and Feldman 1981.

20. See Iyengar et al. 2012; Iyengar and Westwood 2015; Mason 2018.

21. Hewstone 1990.

22. For example, Alesina and Angeletos 2005; Huber and Form 1973; Piketty 2019.

23. Kluegel and Smith 1986.

24. Kinder and Sanders 1996; Mendelberg 2001.

25. I thank Allison Anoll for suggesting that I differentiate between specific explanation and domain of inequality.

26. Toff 2021.

27. Katz and Lazarsfeld 1955; Settle 2018; Siegel 2020.

28. Strömbäck et al. 2012; Stroud 2011.

29. Bullock 2020; Leeper and Slothuus 2014; Lodge and Taber 2013; Zaller 2012.

30. Berinsky 2009; Lodge and Taber 2013; Zaller 1992.

31. Coppock 2023.

32. See, for example, Ellis and Stimson 2012; S. Feldman and Johnston 2014; Gerring 1997; Kinder and Kalmoe 2017.

33. See Brewer and Stonecash 2015; Ellis and Stimson 2012; S. Feldman and Johnston 2014; Jost 2021; F. Lee 2009.

34. Ellis and Stimson 2012.

35. The correlation between party identification and liberal-conservative ideology in the 2016 EIPS is .64.

36. Jardina and Ollerenshaw 2022; Tesler 2013.

37. Gilens 1999.

38. Condon and Wichowsky 2020. In a study of the American public, Condon and Wichowsky asked participants to imagine a person at the bottom of the income ladder and, later, asked them to describe this person. Approximately 45 percent of study participants reported imagining a poor White person, 30 percent imagined a poor Black person, and 25 percent imagined a poor Latino person.

39. Cooley et al. 2022.

40. Piston 2010.

41. Although cultural explanations for inequality have been a recent mainstay of the Republican Party, answers to this item were not consistently correlated with the other index items. I examine beliefs about culture, as well as innate ability, separately.

42. I leave to the side the small number of people who do not fall into one of these categories.

43. Racism and sexism are notoriously difficult to define and measure. While there are alternate measures of both types of prejudice, these seem best suited to this project. Each measurement index is intended to tap "traditional" forms of prejudice against racial or ethnic out-groups or women that are likely still subscribed to by many people today—a desire for racial/ethnic segregation and separate spheres for men and women. Note that "modern" or "new" forms of sexism and racism (such as modern sexism and racial resentment) overlap conceptually with the unequal opportunity index items and thus are not appropriate controls.

44. The ANES question wording included two variants. In one variant, the survey asked respondents why some individuals and groups earned less than higher-earning groups. In another variant, it asked respondents why some individuals and groups earned more than lower-earning groups. In this chapter, I only examine the first version, because the wording is most similar to my own question.

45. Note that the ANES question in 2002 focused only on educational access, and my questions on inequality by sex asked about childcare instead of education or jobs.

46. Note that left–right ideology is associated with the various explanations across multiple domains of inequality in approximately the same way as partisanship, suggesting again their overlapping nature. The primary exception to this is a positive association between relative conservatism and innate explanations for inequality that is larger than that for Republicanism and innate explanations (analyses not shown). See also Suhay and Jayaratne 2013.

47. Strong Republicans were nearly twice as likely to mention access to opportunity with respect to women's lower incomes and about half as likely as strong Democrats to mention the influence of culture in this domain. (Recall that culture in this instance often involved concerns over a sexist culture.) Republicans were considerably more

likely to mention culture when considering Black/Latino versus White inequality. In the rural–urban domain, strong Republicans were less likely to mention discrimination but more likely to mention intrinsic traits (which were more likely to be positive than negative). Finally, with respect to White–Asian inequality, strong Republicans were more than twice as likely to mention discrimination than strong Democrats.

48. Doell et al. 2021; Jones 2020.

49. This wording is borrowed from the ANES. Scholars have conceptualized and measured what I call political attentiveness in different ways. Zaller (1992) relies primarily on neutral political knowledge to measure political awareness; exploratory investigations using such a measure revealed similar, although weaker, patterns as those discussed here. Education is also sometimes used as a proxy for attentiveness; however, these two variables are only moderately associated (Luskin 1990), and additional years of education do not appear to increase interest (Highton 2009). Furthermore, as the empirical findings in chapter 5 made clear, higher levels of education in the United States are associated with learning fact claims that may not be politically neutral.

50. See Zaller 1992.

51. The fact that lay partisan polarization over the importance of work ethics does not increase with political attention may be because Republican elites have emphasized this narrative for decades, whereas Democratic elites' heavy emphasis on structural barriers to success—and Republicans' sharp pushback—is relatively more recent.

Chapter 7: Political Preferences and Explanations for Inequality

1.. *What's Fair? American Beliefs About Distributive Justice* by Jennifer L. Hochschild, Cambridge, Mass: Harvard University Press, Copyright © 1981 by the President and Fellows of Harvard College. Used by permission. All rights reserved.

2. Schuman et al. 1985.

3. *New York Times* Editorial Board 2020.

4. For example, Achen 2002; Jennings and Niemi 1981; Jennings et al. 2009.

5. For example, Berinsky 2009; Lenz 2012; Zaller 1992.

6. Groenendyk 2015.

7. Bernard Weiner, a foundational figure in the study of causal attributions, argues in favor of this "politics before and after" perspective. He and his colleagues argue that people's initial attributions for a social problem, such as poverty, are heavily shaped by ideology but that the attributions that result also motivate people to assist, or not assist, those experiencing difficulties (Weiner et al. 2011).

8. Kluegel and Smith 1986. See also Hunt (2007), who focuses on explanations for Black–White inequality.

9. Iyengar 1991.

10. Hunt and Bullock 2016.

11. Piff et al. 2020.

12. Alberto and Angeletos 2005.

13. Appelbaum 2001; see also Slothuus 2007.

14. Piff et al. 2020; Gurevich et al. 2012).

15. Petersen et al. 2012.
16. Nearly all the experimental work providing evidence of a deservingness effect on attitudes has focused on low-income people, but presumably a corollary effect would also occur with respect to high-income people. For example, one would expect that high-income people viewed as lazy—for example, those who have inherited wealth—would not be viewed as deserving of their resources, leading to a desire to increase taxes on the wealthy (see Piston 2018).
17. Petersen et al. 2010, 2012.
18. Brewer and Stonecash 2015; Cook and Barrett 1992; Gilens 1999; McCall 2013; Robinson 2009; van Oorschot 2006; Weiner et al. 2011.
19. Deservingness and fairness may be driven by underlying expectations of reciprocity (Petersen et al. 2012)—that the undeserving are takers who refuse to help themselves, let alone others.
20. Weiner et al. 2011, 206.
21. Petersen et al. 2012; Weiner 1995; 2006.
22. Goudarzi et al. 2020.
23. Weiner 1995.
24. Harvey and Reed 1996; Small et al. 2010; W. Wilson 2009.
25. Guetzkow 2010.
26. Nunnally and Carter 2012.
27. For example, C. Jensen and Petersen 2017; Weiner et al. 2011.
28. Harden 2021; Schneider et al. 2018.
29. Dar-Nimrod and Heine 2011; Keller 2005; Suhay and Jayaratne 2013.
30. Gelman 2003; Hussak and Cimpian 2015, 2016; Suhay 2017.
31. Appelbaum 2001.
32. Henry et al. 2004.
33. Gilens 1999, 2003; Kinder and Sanders 1996.
34. Cramer 2016; Munis 2022; A. Hochschild 2016.
35. Gilens 1999.
36. Gilens 1999.
37. Gilens 1999; T. Nelson 1999.
38. Converse (1964) 2006.
39. Respondents were shown a response scale, with 1 marked "Not the government's responsibility at all" and 7 marked "Entirely the government's responsibility." They could also choose "don't know." These items were modelled on similar items in the International Social Survey Programme and developed with Marko Klašnja and Gonzalo Rivero (see Suhay et al. 2021).
40. The Cronbach's alpha is .90 (2016).
41. The two items are correlated at .68.
42. Researchers argue that this subtraction method conveys preferences more precisely than examining each measure alone. Many people have response styles that involve rating all politicians warmly or coolly, meaning that using the measures independently can confuse general attitudes toward politicians for preference as between two candidates.

43. Specifically, the 2016 EIPS asked respondents to estimate how much a typical CEO and a typical unskilled worker earn each year. The final perceived inequality measure was the CEO to unskilled worker income ratio, calculated separately for each respondent.

44. For the sake of brevity, I use the combined sample. The coefficients in the policy models are larger for Hispanic and White Americans, and the coefficients in the Clinton–Trump models are larger for White Americans.

45. Bartels 2018. In a series of regression analyses in the appendix, I demonstrate that the coefficient on the Unequal Opportunity Index is similar in size across the individual components of the policy attitude indexes (Government Social Welfare and Decrease Economic Inequality) and varies as expected across the individual presidential candidate feeling thermometers (negative for Trump, positive for Clinton, and even more positive for Sanders). See figure A.15.

46. As discussed in chapter 6, vanishingly few Republicans appeared in the top 25 percent of the range of the answer scale.

47. Gilens 1999; T. Nelson 1999.

48. Wooldridge 2019.

49. Some people may wonder whether there may be methodological reasons for why the unequal economic opportunity for Black and Latino Americans index was not more predictive of support for government programs to help lower-income people. One possible methodological issue is the fact that my measure mentions Latinos in addition to Black Americans, perhaps changing the nature of survey responses. Yet, in an analysis of the 2018 EIPS—which included a question variant that only included mention of Black Americans—a similar pattern appears. Another possibility is that the government responsibility for social welfare measure is very broad, including more popular programs, such as the provision of education and health care. However, if I narrow the measure to welfare as it is more colloquially understood (that is, a guaranteed income), results are again similar.

50. Of course, not everyone will call to mind the same prototypical person when asked why some people earn less than others—the imagined poor will vary by race, sex, or any number of other traits. The unequal economic opportunity index has the advantage of allowing survey takers to respond with their modal low-income person or people in mind.

51. For example, T. Nelson 1999. On a methodological note, Nelson measures attributions for economic inequality in general and by race with two quite different batteries of questions, which may have introduced bias into the analysis and results. To best compare the effects of causal attributions in different inequality domains, surveyors should use similar question wording.

52. Teixeira and Judis 2023; Michaels and Reed 2023.

53. Note, further, that social desirability bias tends to be low on self-administered online surveys like mine (as opposed to surveys with a live interviewer). See Tourangeau et al. 2000.

54. There are two exceptions. Perceiving discrimination against rural Americans was

associated with support for Clinton, and perceiving discrimination against White Americans was associated with support for Trump.

55. Gilens 1999; T. Nelson 1999.
56. Hacker and Pierson 2010; Lindh and McCall 2023.
57. For a recent treatment, see Mutz 2021.

Chapter 8: The American Dream: Belief, Rhetoric, and Reality

1. See E. Kim 2023.
2. Kluegel and Smith 1986.
3. Campbell et al. 1960.
4. Converse (1964) 2006.
5. Levendusky 2009; Maxwell and Shields 2019.
6. F. Lee 2016.
7. The most common scale items include the following: 1) Generations of slavery and discrimination have created conditions that make it difficult for Black Americans to work their way out of the lower class. 2) Irish, Italian, Jewish and many other American minority groups overcame prejudice and worked their way up. Black Americans should do the same without any special favors. 3) It's really a matter of some people not trying hard enough; if Black Americans would only try harder, they could be just as well off as White Americans. 4) Over the past few years, Black Americans have gotten less than they deserve.
8. Sides et al. 2018.
9. Cramer 2020; Kam and Burge 2018, 2019.
10. See also Feldman and Huddy 2005; Sniderman et al. 2000.
11. Jennings and Niemi 1981; also see Jennings et al. 2009. One can even purchase partisan onesies for infants. Whether socialization is successful at that age is beyond my expertise.
12. Gerring 1998.
13. See Hacker et al. 2023; Slothuus and Bisgaard 2021; and Zacher 2024 for evidence in support of these suppositions.
14. Peterson Foundation 2024.
15. H. Lee et al. 2022.
16. Reeves 2022. Normative perspectives regarding this achievement by women vary. Some people view women surpassing men in educational achievement as a necessary evil because women must become more educated than men to earn the same pay. Others, such as Reeves, are concerned that this educational inequality is a symptom of a cultural crisis among males.
17. H. Lee et al. 2022.
18. Owens 2020.
19. Fahle et al. 2020; Owens 2020.
20. Dobbie and Fryer 2011.
21. Khan 2011.

22. Schaeffer 2022.
23. Schaeffer 2022.
24. Emmons et al. 2019.
25. Cappelli 2020; Lockwood and Webber 2023.
26. Cappelli 2020.
27. Chetty et al. 2020.
28. Schumacher et al. 2023.
29. Blanchet et al. 2023; Horowitz et al. 2020; Siripurapu 2022; Strain 2020b.
30. Fry et al. 2024; U.S. Bureau of Labor Statistics 2023b.
31. Aeppli and Wilmers 2022; Blanchet et al. 2023.
32. U.S. Bureau of Labor Statistics 2024.
33. Gascon and Martorana 2024.
34. Burkhauser et al. 2024; Wimer et al. 2016.
35. U.S. Census Bureau 2023.
36. Gould and deCourcy 2024; U.S. Bureau of Labor Statistics 2023a.
37. Fuhrer 2024a.
38. Lowrey 2020.
39. Fuhrer 2024b.
40. Glasmeier 2025. Costs are included for childcare, health care, housing, transportation, broadband Internet, and limited expenditures for miscellaneous other expenses (personal care products, apparel, and some entertainment).
41. U.S. Bureau of Labor Statistics 2023a.
42. This perspective is echoed in separate analyses by the right-leaning think tank American Compass (2023) as well as the left-leaning Economic Policy Institute (Gould and deCourcy 2024). The Economic Policy Institute hosts a helpful cost-of-living calculator at https://www.epi.org/resources/budget.
43. Ludwig 2025.
44. Akan et al. 2024.
45. Remote work tends to be more available in higher-income professions (Akan et al. 2024), meaning remote work is usually not a viable option for workers in lower-earning professions who would most benefit from it.
46. Massey and Denton 1993; W. Wilson 2009.
47. Carr and Kefalas 2010; Goetz et al. 2018; U.S. Department of Commerce 2023.
48. Bergman et al. 2024.
49. Autor et al. 2016; Autor et al. 2025.
50. Montgomery 1991; Wanberg 2010.
51. Borchers and Ellis 2024.
52. Borchers and Ellis 2024.
53. Borchers and Ellis 2024; Granovetter 1983.
54. Villarreal 2020.
55. Borchers and Ellis 2024; Wanberg 2010.
56. Wanberg 2010.
57. Livingston and Thomas 2019.

58. Miller 2021.
59. Grundy 2024.
60. Whitehurst 2017.
61. Cortés and Pan 2023.
62. Ortiz-Ospina and Roser 2018.
63. Goldin 2014.
64. See Baker and Kelly 2014; Massey and Denton 1993; Myrdal 1944; and Rae 2018 for historical overviews.
65. Collins and Margo 2006.
66. Katznelson 2005.
67. Moss et al. 2020.
68. Gordon 2016.
69. Saez and Zucman 2020.
70. Bayer and Charles 2018.
71. Quillian and Midtbøen 2021. The authors also found substantial discrimination in housing as well, although this has declined over time.
72. Quillian et al. 2020.
73. Kline et al. 2024.
74. Mai 2023.
75. Aragão 2023; England et al. 2020.
76. The Federal Reserve Bank of St. Louis provides monthly updates on labor force participation for men and women.
77. Fry and Aragão 2025.
78. Birkelund et al. 2022; Kline et al. 2024; Lippens et al. 2023.
79. Kline et al. 2024.
80. Levanon et al. 2009.
81. Moynihan 1965.
82. Haskins and Sawhill 2009.
83. Goesling et al. 2020; Inanc et al. 2021.
84. Kearney 2023.
85. Bianchi 2011; Kearney 2023.
86. Autor et al. 2019; Edin and Kefalas 2005; W. Wilson 1996.
87. Chetty and Hendren 2018.
88. Kearney 2023.
89. See Swidler 1986.
90. Lamont and Lareau 1988.
91. Swidler 1986.
92. Sanchez-Jankowski 2008; Vaisey 2010; W. Wilson 2009.
93. Edin and Kefalas 2005; Small et al. 2010; Vaisey 2010; W. Wilson 2009.
94. Giattino and Ortiz-Ospina 2020.
95. Folbre 2009.
96. Bianchi 2011.
97. Ang 2022.

98. L. Jensen and Slack 2003; Reynolds 2004.
99. Ruggeri et al. 2023.
100. Warren and Tyagi 2003.
101. Lino 1996, 9.
102. Desmond 2023; Ehrenreich 2001.
103. Puri and Malde 2024.
104. Abraham and Kearney 2018; Autor et al. 2016.
105. Puri and Malde 2024; Rothstein 2020.
106. Krueger 2017.
107. Eberstadt 2022; Rothstein 2020.
108. Rothstein 2020.
109. Autor et al. 2015; Maestas et al. 2013.
110. Edin and Lein 1997.
111. Ilin and Sanchez 2023; Cohen 2024.
112. Senators Josh Hawley and Elizabeth Warren have been especially involved in bipartisan cooperation on economic legislation. See, for example, Hawley 2024.
113. Krupnikov and Ryan 2022.
114. Pew Research Center 2023.
115. Almås et al. 2020, 2022.
116. Sandel 2020; Young 1958.
117. Yglesias 2025.

REFERENCES

Abelson, Robert P. 1981. "Psychological Status of the Script Concept." *American Psychologist* 36(7): 715–29. https://doi.org/10.1037/0003-066X.36.7.715.

Abraham, Katherine G., and Melissa S. Kearney. 2018. "Explaining the Decline in the U.S. Employment-to-Population Ratio: A Review of the Evidence." NBER Working Paper 24333. National Bureau of Economic Research. https://www.nber.org/system/files/working_papers/w24333/w24333.pdf.

Abramowitz, Alan I. 2011. *The Disappearing Center: Engaged Citizens, Polarization, and American Democracy.* Yale University Press.

Achen, Christopher H. 2002. "Parental Socialization and Rational Party Identification." *Political Behavior* 24(2): 151–70.

Achen, Christopher H., and Larry M. Bartels. 2016. *Democracy for Realists: Why Elections Do Not Produce Responsive Government.* Princeton Studies in Political Behavior. Princeton University Press.

Adams, James Truslow. (1931) 2001. *The Epic of America.* Simon Publications.

Aeppli, Clem, and Nathan Wilmers. 2022. "Rapid Wage Growth at the Bottom Has Offset Rising US Inequality." *Proceedings of the National Academy of Sciences* 119(42): e2204305119. https://doi.org/10.1073/pnas.2204305119.

Ahler, Douglas J., and Gaurav Sood. 2018. "The Parties in Our Heads: Misperceptions About Party Composition and Their Consequences." *Journal of Politics* 80(3): 964–81. https://doi.org/10.1086/697253.

Akan, Kert, Nicholas Bloom, Shelby Buckman, Jose Maria Barrero, Steven J. Davis, Tom Bowen, and Liz Wilke. 2024. "Americans Now Live Farther From Their Employers." Gusto. March 3. https://gusto.com/company-news/americans-now-live-farther-from-their-employers.

Alesina, Alberto, and George-Marios Angeletos. 2005. "Fairness and Redistribution." *American Economic Review* 95(4): 960–80. https://doi.org/10.1257/0002828054825655.

Alesina, Alberto, Edward Glaeser, and Bruce Sacerdote. 2001. "Why Doesn't the United

States Have a European-Style Welfare State?" NBER Working Paper 8524. https://www
.nber.org/system/files/working_papers/w8524/w8524.pdf.

Alesina, Alberto, Stefanie Stantcheva, and Edoardo Teso. 2018. "Intergenerational Mobility
and Preferences for Redistribution." *American Economic Review* 108(2): 521–54. https://
doi.org/10.1257/aer.20162015.

Almås, Ingvild, Alexander W. Cappelen, Erik Sørensen, and Bertil Tungodden. 2020. "Fairness Across the World: Preferences and Beliefs." Presented at the FAIR Workshop,
October 14. https://www.ifs.org.uk/inequality/wp-content/uploads/2020/11/Fairness
-across-the-world-Preferences-and-beliefs.pdf.

Almås, Ingvild, Alexander W. Cappelen, Erik Sørensen, and Bertil Tungodden. 2022. "Attitudes to Inequality: Preferences and Beliefs." Institute for Fiscal Studies.

Alwin, Duane Francis, Ronald Lee Cohen, and Theodore Mead Newcomb. 1991. *Political
Attitudes Over the Life Span: The Bennington Women After Fifty Years.* University of Wisconsin Press.

American Compass. 2023. *Rebuilding American Capitalism: A Handbook for Conservative
Policymakers.* https://americancompass.org/wp-content/uploads/2023/06/AC-Rebuil
ding-American-Capitalism_Digital.pdf.

American National Election Studies. 2025. Data Center. https://electionstudies.org/data
-center.

Anderson, Elizabeth. 2017. *Private Government: How Employers Rule Our Lives (and Why We
Don't Talk About It).* Princeton University Press.

Ang, Carmen. 2022. "Do Top Earners Work More Hours? It Depends Which Country They
Live In." World Economic Forum. September 27. https://www.weforum.org/agenda
/2022/09/working-hours-america-income-economy/.

Anoll, Allison P., Andrew M. Engelhardt, and Mackenzie Israel-Trummel. 2022. "Black
Lives, White Kids: White Parenting Practices Following Black-Led Protests." *Perspectives
on Politics* 20(4): 1328–45. https://doi.org/10.1017/S1537592722001050.

Appelbaum, Lauren. 2001. "The Influence of Perceived Deservingness on Policy Decisions
Regarding Aid to the Poor." *Political Psychology* 22(3): 419–42. https://doi.org/10.1111
/0162-895X.00248.

Aragão, Carolina. 2023. "Gender Pay Gap in U.S. Hasn't Changed Much in Two Decades."
Pew Research Center. March 1. https://www.pewresearch.org/short-reads/2023/03/01
/gender-pay-gap-facts/.

Autor, David H., David Dorn, and Gordon H. Hanson. 2016. "The China Shock: Learning
from Labor-Market Adjustment to Large Changes in Trade." *Annual Review of Economics* 8(1): 205–40. https://doi.org/10.1146/annurev-economics-080315-015041.

Autor, David H., David Dorn, and Gordon H. Hanson. 2019. "When Work Disappears:
Manufacturing Decline and the Falling Marriage Market Value of Young Men." *American Economic Review: Insights* 1(2): 161–78. https://doi.org/10.1257/aeri.20180010.

Autor, David H., David Dorn, Gordon H. Hanson, Maggie R. Jones, and Bradley Setzler.
2025. "Place Versus People: The Ins and Outs of Labor Market Adjustment to Globalization." NBER Working Paper 33424. National Bureau of Economic Research. https://
www.nber.org/system/files/working_papers/w33424/w33424.pdf.

Autor, David H., Mark Duggan, Kyle Greenberg, and David S. Lyle. 2015. "The Impact of Disability Benefits on Labor Supply: Evidence from the VA's Disability Compensation Program." NBER Working Paper 21144. National Bureau of Economic Research. https://www.nber.org/system/files/working_papers/w21144/w21144.pdf.

Azevedo, Flávio, John T. Jost, and Tobias Rothmund. 2017. "'Making America Great Again': System Justification in the U.S. Presidential Election of 2016." *Translational Issues in Psychological Science* 3(3): 231–40. https://doi.org/10.1037/tps0000122.

Bafumi, Joseph, and Michael C. Herron. 2010. "Leapfrog Representation and Extremism: A Study of American Voters and Their Members in Congress." *American Political Science Review* 104(3): 519–42.

Baker, Bruce, and Brian Kelly, eds. 2014. *After Slavery: Race, Labor, and Citizenship in the Reconstruction South*, illustrated edition. University Press of Florida.

Barber, Michael J. 2016. "Representing the Preferences of Donors, Partisans, and Voters in the U.S. Senate." *Public Opinion Quarterly* 80(S1): 225–49. https://doi.org/10.1093/poq/nfw004.

Barber, Michael J., and Jeremy C. Pope. 2019. "Does Party Trump Ideology? Disentangling Party and Ideology in America." *American Political Science Review* 113(1): 38–54. https://doi.org/10.1017/S0003055418000795.

Barker, David C., Ryan Detamble, and Morgan Marietta. 2022. "Intellectualism, Anti-intellectualism, and Epistemic Hubris in Red and Blue America." *American Political Science Review* 116(1): 38–53. https://doi.org/10.1017/S0003055421000988.

Bartels, Larry M. 2013. "Political Effects of the Great Recession." *Annals of the American Academy of Political and Social Science* 650: 47–75.

Bartels, Larry M. 2016. *Unequal Democracy: The Political Economy of the New Gilded Age*, 2nd ed. Russell Sage Foundation and Princeton University Press.

Bartels, Larry M. 2018. "Partisanship in the Trump Era." *Journal of Politics* 80(4): 1483–94. https://doi.org/10.1086/699337.

Bawn, Kathleen, Martin Cohen, David Karol, Seth Masket, Hans Noel, and John Zaller. 2012. "A Theory of Political Parties: Groups, Policy Demands and Nominations in American Politics." *Perspectives on Politics* 10(3): 571–97. https://doi.org/10.1017/S1537592712001624.

Bayer, Patrick, and Kerwin Kofi Charles. 2018. "Divergent Paths: A New Perspective on Earnings Differences Between Black and White Men Since 1940." *Quarterly Journal of Economics* 133(3): 1459–501. https://doi.org/10.1093/qje/qjy003.

Berelson, Bernard R., Paul F. Lazarsfeld, and William N. McPhee. 1954. *Voting: A Study of Opinion Formation in a Presidential Campaign*. University of Chicago Press. https://press.uchicago.edu/ucp/books/book/chicago/V/bo3616092.html.

Bergman, Peter, Raj Chetty, Stefanie DeLuca, Nathaniel Hendren, Lawrence F. Katz, and Christopher Palmer. 2024. "Creating Moves to Opportunity: Experimental Evidence on Barriers to Neighborhood Choice." *American Economic Review* 114(5): 1281–1337.

Berinsky, Adam J. 2004. *Silent Voices: Public Opinion and Political Participation in America*. Princeton University Press.

Berinsky, Adam J. 2009. *In Time of War*. University of Chicago Press.

Berry, Jeffrey M., and Clyde Wilcox. 2018. *The Interest Group Society*, 6th ed. Routledge.

Bianchi, Suzanne M. 2011. "Family Change and Time Allocation in American Families." *Annals of the American Academy of Political and Social Science* 638: 21–44.

Biden-Sanders Unity Task Force. 2020. "Biden-Sanders Unity Task Force Recommendations." Accessed August 1, 2023. https://joebiden.com/wp-content/uploads/2020/08/UNITY-TASK-FORCE-RECOMMENDATIONS.pdf.

Binder, Ariel J., and John Bound. 2019. "The Declining Labor Market Prospects of Less-Educated Men." *Journal of Economic Perspectives* 33(2): 163–90. https://doi.org/10.1257/jep.33.2.163.

Birkelund, Gunn Elisabeth, Bram Lancee, Edvard Nergård Larsen, Javier G Polavieja, Jonas Radl, and Ruta Yemane. 2022. "Gender Discrimination in Hiring: Evidence from a Cross-national Harmonized Field Experiment." *European Sociological Review* 38(3): 337–54. https://doi.org/10.1093/esr/jcab043.

Bisgaard, Martin, and Rune Slothuus. 2018. "Partisan Elites as Culprits? How Party Cues Shape Partisan Perceptual Gaps." *American Journal of Political Science* 62(2): 456–69. https://doi.org/10.1111/ajps.12349.

Blanchard-Fields, Fredda. 1994. "Age Differences in Causal Attributions from an Adult Developmental Perspective." *Journal of Gerontology* 49(2): 43–51. https://doi.org/10.1093/geronj/49.2.P43.

Blanchet, Thomas, Emmanuel Saez, and Gabriel Zucman. 2023. "Who Benefits from Income and Wealth Growth in the United States?" Realtime Inequality. https://realtimeinequality.org/.

Blasi, Joseph R., Richard B. Freeman, and Douglas L. Kruse. 2013. *Citizen's Share: Reducing Inequality in the 21st Century*. Yale University Press.

Bonacich, Edna. 1975. "Abolition, the Extension of Slavery, and the Position of Free Blacks: A Study of Split Labor Markets in the United States, 1830–1863." *American Journal of Sociology* 81(3): 601–28. https://doi.org/10.1086/226110.

Bonica, Adam, Nolan McCarty, Keith T. Poole, and Howard Rosenthal. 2013. "Why Hasn't Democracy Slowed Rising Inequality?" *Journal of Economic Perspectives* 27(3): 103–24. https://doi.org/10.1257/jep.27.3.103.

Borchers, Callum, and Lindsay Ellis. 2024. "Landing a Job Is All About Who You Know (Again)." *Wall Street Journal*, May 30.

Bowler, Kate. 2013. *Blessed: A History of the American Prosperity Gospel*. Oxford University Press.

Bradley, Gifford Weary. 1978. "Self-Serving Biases in the Attribution Process: A Reexamination of the Fact or Fiction Question." *Journal of Personality and Social Psychology* 36(1): 56–71.

Brady, David. 2019. "Theories of the Causes of Poverty." SSRN Scholarly Paper. Social Science Research Network. https://doi.org/10.1146/annurev-soc-073018-022550.

Branch, Enobong Hannah, and Caroline Hanley. 2022. *Work in Black and White: Striving for the American Dream*. Russell Sage Foundation.

Braungart, Richard G., and Margaret M. Braungart. 1986. "Life-Course and Generational Politics." *Annual Review of Sociology* 12 :205–31.

Brewer, Mark D., and Jeffrey M. Stonecash. 2015. *Polarization and the Politics of Personal Responsibility*. Oxford University Press.

Brooks, Clem, and Jeff Manza. 2013. "A Broken Public? Americans' Responses to the Great Recession." *American Sociological Review* 78(5): 727–48. https://doi.org/10.1177/000312 2413498255.

Brown, Trevor E., and Suzanne Mettler. 2024. "Sequential Polarization: The Development of the Rural-Urban Political Divide, 1976–2020." *Perspectives on Politics* 22(3): 630–58. https://doi.org/10.1017/S1537592723002918.

Brulle, Robert J. 2014. "Institutionalizing Delay: Foundation Funding and the Creation of U.S. Climate Change Counter-movement Organizations." *Climate Change* 122(4): 681–94. https://doi.org/10.1007/s10584-013-1018-7.

Budiman, Abby, and Neil G. Ruiz. 2021. "Key Facts About Asian Origin Groups in the U.S." Pew Research Center. April 29. https://www.pewresearch.org/short-reads/2021/04/29 /key-facts-about-asian-origin-groups-in-the-u-s/.

Bullock, John G. 2020. "Party Cues." In *The Oxford Handbook of Electoral Persuasion*, edited by Elizabeth Suhay, Bernard Grofman, and Alexander H. Trechsel. Oxford University Press.

Burkhauser, Richard V., Kevin Corinth, James Elwell, and Jeff Larrimore. 2024. "Evaluating the Success of the War on Poverty Since 1963 Using an Absolute Full-Income Poverty Measure." *Journal of Political Economy* 132(1): 1–47. https://doi.org/10.1086/725705.

Burns, Alexander, Binyamin Appelbaum, and Neil Irwin. 2016. "Donald Trump Vows to Create 25 Million Jobs Over Next Decade." *New York Times*, September 15. https://www .nytimes.com/2016/09/16/us/politics/donald-trump-economy-speech.html.

Cameron, Charles M., and Jonathan P. Kastellec. 2023. *Making the Supreme Court: The Politics of Appointments, 1930–2020*. Oxford University Press.

Campbell, Angus, Phillip Converse, Warren Miller, and Donald Stokes. 1960. *The American Voter*. University of Michigan Press.

Cappelli, Peter. 2020. "The Return on a College Degree: The US Experience." *Oxford Review of Education* 46: 30–43. https://doi.org/10.1080/03054985.2019.1689939.

Carr, Patrick J., and Maria J. Kefalas. 2010. *Hollowing Out the Middle: The Rural Brain Drain and What It Means for America*. Beacon Press.

Charmaz, Kathy. 2014. *Constructing Grounded Theory*, 2nd ed. Sage Publications.

Cheng, Siwei, and Fangqi Wen. 2019. "Americans Overestimate the Intergenerational Persistence in Income Ranks." *Proceedings of the National Academy of Sciences* 116(28): 13909–14. https://doi.org/10.1073/pnas.1814688116.

Chetty, Raj, John N. Friedman, Emmanuel Saez, Nicholas Turner, and Danny Yagan. 2020. "Income Segregation and Intergenerational Mobility Across Colleges in the United States." *Quarterly Journal of Economics* 135(3): 1567–633. https://doi.org/10.1093/qje /qjaa005.

Chetty, Raj, David Grusky, Maximilian Hell, Nathaniel Hendren, Robert Manduca, and Jimmy Narang. 2017. "The Fading American Dream: Trends in Absolute Income Mobility Since 1940." *Science* 356: 398–406. https://doi.org/10.1126/science.aal4617.

Chetty, Raj, and Nathaniel Hendren. 2018. "The Impacts of Neighborhoods on Intergenerational Mobility I: Childhood Exposure Effects." *Quarterly Journal of Economics* 133(3): 1107–62. https://doi.org/10.1093/qje/qjy007.

Chong, Dennis, and James N. Druckman. 2007. "Framing Theory." *Annual Review of Political Science* 10: 103–26. https://doi.org/10.1146/annurev.polisci.10.072805.103054.

Churchwell, Sarah Bartlett. 2018. *Behold, America: The Entangled History of "America First" and "the American Dream."* Basic Books.

Clinton, Hillary. 2015. "Hillary Clinton Transcript: Building the 'Growth and Fairness Economy.'" *Wall Street Journal*, July 13. http://blogs.wsj.com/washwire/2015/07/13/hillary-clinton-transcript-building-the-growth-and-fairness-economy.

Cohen, Rachel. 2024. "Could Tweaks to the Tax Code Lead to More Marriages—And More Kids?" *Vox*, November 26. https://www.vox.com/policy/387818/could-tweaks-to-the-tax-code-lead-to-more-marriages-and-more-kids.

Cohn, Nate. 2021. "How Educational Differences Are Widening America's Political Rift." *New York Times*, September 8. https://www.nytimes.com/2021/09/08/us/politics/how-college-graduates-vote.html.

Collins, William J., and Robert A. Margo. 2006. "Historical Perspectives on Racial Differences in Schooling in the United States." In *Handbook of the Economics of Education*, edited by E. Hanushek and F. Welch. Elsevier. https://doi.org/10.1016/S1574-0692(06) 01003-8.

Condon, Meghan, and Amber Wichowsky. 2020. *The Economic Other: Inequality in the American Political Imagination.* University of Chicago Press.

Conley, Dalton, and Jason Fletcher. 2017. *The Genome Factor: What the Social Genomics Revolution Reveals About Ourselves, Our History, and the Future.* Princeton University Press.

Conover, Pamela Johnston, and Stanley Feldman. 1981. "The Origins and Meaning of Liberal/Conservative Self-Identifications." *American Journal of Political Science* 25 (4): 617–45. https://doi.org/10.2307/2110756.

Converse, Philip (1964) 2006. "The Nature of Belief Systems in Mass Publics." *Critical Review* 18: 1–74. https://doi.org/10.1080/08913810608443650.

Cook, Fay Lomax, and Edith J. Barrett. 1992. "Support for the American Welfare State." Columbia University Press.

Cooley, Erin, Jazmin L. Brown-Iannuzzi, Ryan F. Lei, and William Cipolli. 2019. "Complex Intersections of Race and Class: Among Social Liberals, Learning About White Privilege Reduces Sympathy, Increases Blame, and Decreases External Attributions for White People Struggling with Poverty." *Journal of Experimental Psychology: General* 148(12): 2218–28. https://doi.org/10.1037/xge0000605.

Cooley, Erin, Jazmin L. Brown-Iannuzzi, Ryan F. Lei, William Cipolli, and Lauren E. Philbrook. 2022. "Beliefs That White People Are Poor, Above and Beyond Beliefs That Black People Are Poor, Predict White (But Not Black) Americans' Attitudes Toward Welfare Recipients and Policy." *Personality and Social Psychology Bulletin* 50(3): 450–65. https://doi.org/10.1177/01461672221139071.

Cooperative Election Study 2025. "2020 Cooperative Election Study." Tufts University. https://tischcollege.tufts.edu/research-faculty/research-centers/cooperative-election-study.

Coppock, Alexander. 2023. *Persuasion in Parallel: How Information Changes Minds about Politics*. Chicago Studies in American Politics. University of Chicago Press. https://press.uchicago.edu/ucp/books/book/chicago/P/bo181475008.html.

Cortés, Patricia, and Jessica Pan. 2023. "Children and the Remaining Gender Gaps in the Labor Market." *Journal of Economic Literature* 61(4): 1359–409. https://doi.org/10.1257/jel.20221549.

Couch, Arthur, and Kenneth Keniston. 1960. "Yeasayers and Naysayers: Agreeing Response Set as a Personality Variable." *Journal of Abnormal and Social Psychology* 60(2): 151–74. https://doi.org/10.1037/h0040372.

Cozzarelli, Catherin, Anna V. Wilkinson, and Michael J. Tagler. 2001. "Attitudes Toward the Poor and Attributions for Poverty." *Journal of Social Issues* 57(2): 207–27. https://doi.org/10.1111/0022-4537.00209.

Cramer, Katherine J. 2016. *The Politics of Resentment: Rural Consciousness in Wisconsin and the Rise of Scott Walker*. University of Chicago Press.

Cramer, Katherine J. 2020. "Understanding the Role of Racism in Contemporary US Public Opinion." *Annual Review of Political Science* 23(1): 153–69. https://doi.org/10.1146/annurev-polisci-060418-042842.

Culpepper, Pepper D., Ryan Shandler, Jae-Hee Jung, and Taeku Lee. 2024. "'The Economy Is Rigged': Inequality Narratives, Fairness, and Support for Redistribution in Six Countries." *Comparative Political Studies*, May 13. https://doi.org/10.1177/00104140241252072.

Curry, James M., and Frances E. Lee. 2020. *The Limits of Party: Congress and Lawmaking in a Polarized Era*. Chicago Studies in American Politics. University of Chicago Press. https://press.uchicago.edu/ucp/books/book/chicago/L/bo51795068.html.

Dar-Nimrod, Ilan, and Steven J. Heine. 2011. "Genetic Essentialism: On the Deceptive Determinism of DNA." *Psychological Bulletin* 137(5): 800–18. https://doi.org/10.1037/a0021860.

Davidai, Shai, and Thomas Gilovich. 2015. "Building a More Mobile America—One Income Quintile at a Time." *Perspectives on Psychological Science* 10(1): 60–71. https://doi.org/10.1177/1745691614562005.

Deaux, Kay. 1993. "Reconstructing Social Identity." *Personality and Social Psychology Bulletin* 19(4): 4–12. https://doi.org/10.1177/0146167293191001.

Desmond, Matthew. 2023. *Poverty, by America*. Penguin Random House.

Detrow, Scott. 2020. "Democrats Meet Virtually to Approve Platform That Builds Off Biden-Sanders Effort." NPR, July 27. https://www.npr.org/2020/07/27/895800475/democrats-meet-virtually-to-approve-platform-that-builds-off-of-biden-sanders-ef.

Diehl, Trevor, Brian E Weeks, and Homero Gil de Zúñiga. 2016. "Political Persuasion on Social Media: Tracing Direct and Indirect Effects of News Use and Social Interaction." *New Media & Society* 18(9): 1875–95. https://doi.org/10.1177/1461444815616224.

Dobbie, Will, and Roland G. Fryer. 2011. "Are High-Quality Schools Enough to Increase Achievement Among the Poor? Evidence from the Harlem Children's Zone." *American Economic Journal: Applied Economics* 3(3): 158–87.

Dobbin, Frank. 2011. *Inventing Equal Opportunity*. Princeton University Press.

Doell, Kimberly C., Philip Pärnamets, Elizabeth A. Harris, Leor M. Hackel, and Jay J. Van

Bavel. 2021. "Understanding the Effects of Partisan Identity on Climate Change." *Current Opinion in Behavioral Sciences* 42: 54–59. https://doi.org/10.1016/j.cobeha.2021 .03.013.

Domestic Policy Council. 2023. "Delivering on Equity, Access, and Opportunity for the American People." https://www.whitehouse.gov/wp-content/uploads/2023/02/Equity -EO-Agency-Highlights.pdf.

Douthat, Ross, and Reihan Salam. 2009. *Grand New Party: How Republicans Can Win the Working Class and Save the American Dream*, reprint ed. Knopf Doubleday Publishing Group.

Dunlap, Riley E., and Aaron M. McCright. 2011. "Organized Climate Change Denial." In *The Oxford Handbook of Climate Change and Society*, edited by John S. Dryzek, Richard B. Norgaard, and David Schlosberg. Oxford University Press.

Eberstadt, Nicholas. 2022. *Men Without Work: Post-pandemic Edition*. Templeton Press.

Edin, Kathryn, and Maria J. Kefalas. 2005. *Promises I Can Keep: Why Poor Women Put Motherhood Before Marriage*. University of California Press.

Edin, Kathryn, and Laura Lein. 1997. *Making Ends Meet: How Single Mothers Survive Welfare and Low-Wage Work*. Russell Sage Foundation.

Edsall, Thomas B. 2022. "Red and Blue America Will Never Be the Same." *New York Times*, July 27. https://www.nytimes.com/2022/07/27/opinion/trump-red-blue-america.html.

Egan, Patrick J. 2013. *Partisan Priorities: How Issue Ownership Drives and Distorts American Politics*. Cambridge University Press.

Ehman, Lee H. 1980. "The American School in the Political Socialization Process." *Review of Educational Research* 50(1): 99–119. https://doi.org/10.2307/1170032.

Ehrenreich, Barbara. 2001. *Nickel and Dimed: On (Not) Getting By in America*. Metropolitan Books.

Ellis, Christopher, and James A. Stimson. 2012. *Ideology in America*. Cambridge University Press. https://doi.org/10.1017/CBO9781139094009.

Emmons, William R., Ana H. Kent, and Lowell R. Ricketts. 2019. "Is College Still Worth It? The New Calculus of Falling Returns." *Review* 101(4): 297–329. https://doi.org/10 .20955/r.101.297-329.

England, Paula, Andrew Levine, and Emma Mishel. 2020. "Progress Toward Gender Equality in the United States Has Slowed or Stalled." *Proceedings of the National Academy of Sciences* 117(13): 6990–97. https://doi.org/10.1073/pnas.1918891117.

Erikson, Robert S., Michael B. MacKuen, and James A. Stimson. 2002. *The Macro Polity*. Cambridge University Press. https://doi.org/10.1017/CBO9781139086912.

Eyerman, Ron. 1981. "False Consciousness and Ideology in Marxist Theory." *Acta Sociologica* 24(1–2): 43–56. https://doi.org/10.1177/000169938102400.

Fagan, E. J. 2018. "Marching Orders? U.S. Party Platforms and Legislative Agenda Setting 1948–2014." *Political Research Quarterly* 71(4): 949–59. https://doi.org/10.1177/10659129 18772681.

Fahle, Erin M., Sean F. Reardon, Demetra Kalogrides, Ericka S. Weathers, and Heewon Jang. 2020. "Racial Segregation and School Poverty in the United States, 1999–2016." *Race and Social Problems* 12(1): 42–56. https://doi.org/10.1007/s12552-019-09277-w.

Feagin, Joe R. 1975. *Subordinating the Poor: Welfare and American Beliefs.* Prentice-Hall. https://doi.org/10.1017/S0047279400006528.

Feldman, Glenn. 2013. *The Irony of the Solid South: Democrats, Republicans, and Race, 1865–1944.* University Alabama Press.

Feldman, Stanley, and Leonie Huddy. 2005. "Racial Resentment and White Opposition to Race-Conscious Programs: Principles or Prejudice?" *American Journal of Political Science* 49(1): 168–83. https://doi.org/10.2307/3647720.

Feldman, Stanley, and Christopher Johnston. 2014. "Understanding the Determinants of Political Ideology: Implications of Structural Complexity." *Political Psychology* 35(3): 337–58. https://doi.org/10.1111/pops.12055.

Ferguson, Thomas, Benjamin I. Page, Jacob Rothschild, Arturo Chang, and Jie Chen. 2020. "The Roots of Right-Wing Populism: Donald Trump in 2016." *International Journal of Political Economy* 49(2): 102–23. https://www.tandfonline.com/doi/abs/10.1080/08911916.2020.1778861.

Ferreira, Francisco H. G. 2023. "Is There a 'New Consensus' on Inequality?" IZA Discussion Paper 16422. Institute of Labor Economics. https://ideas.repec.org//p/iza/izadps/dp16422.html.

Fiorina, Morris P. 1981. *Retrospective Voting in American National Elections.* Yale University Press.

Fiorina, Morris P., Samuel J. Abrams, and Jeremy C. Pope. 2010. *Culture War? The Myth of a Polarized America*, 3rd ed. Longman.

Foer, Franklin. 2023. *The Last Politician: Inside Joe Biden's White House and the Struggle for America's Future.* Penguin Press.

Folbre, Nancy. 2009. "Inequality and Time Use in the Household." In *The Oxford Handbook of Economic Inequality*, edited by Wiemer Salverda, Brian Nolan, and Timothy M. Smeeding. Oxford University Press.

Fording, Richard C., and Sanford F. Schram. 2020. *Hard White: The Mainstreaming of Racism in American Politics.* Oxford University Press.

Frank, Thomas. 2004. *What's the Matter with Kansas: How Conservatives Won the Heart of America.* Metropolitan Books.

Fraser, Steve, and Gary Gerstle. 1989. *The Rise and Fall of the New Deal Order, 1930–1980.* Princeton University Press.

Freeland, Chrystia. 2012. *Plutocrats: The Rise of the New Global Super-Rich and the Fall of Everyone Else.* Penguin Press.

Fry, Richard, and Carolina Aragão. 2025. "Gender Pay Gap in the U.S. Has Narrowed Slightly Over 2 Decades." Pew Research Center, March 4. https://www.pewresearch.org/short-reads/2025/03/04/gender-pay-gap-in-us-has-narrowed-slightly-over-2-decades/.

Fry, Richard, Dana Braga, and Kim Parker. 2024. "Is College Worth It?" Pew Research Center. May 23. https://www.pewresearch.org/social-trends/2024/05/23/is-college-worth-it-2/.

Fuhrer, Jeffrey C. 2024a. "How Many Are in Need in the US? The Poverty Rate Is the Tip of the Iceberg." Brookings, June 20. https://www.brookings.edu/articles/how-many-are-in-need-in-the-us-the-poverty-rate-is-the-tip-of-the-iceberg/.

Fuhrer, Jeffrey C. 2024b. "The Cost of Being Poor Is Rising. And It's Worse for Poor Fam-

ilies of Color." Brookings, July 29. https://www.brookings.edu/articles/the-cost-of
-being-poor-is-rising-and-its-worse-for-poor-families-of-color/.

Gale, William G, Hilary Gelfond, Jason J. Fichtner, and Benjamin H. Harris. 2020. "The
Wealth of Generations, with Special Attention to the Millennials." NBER Working
Paper 27123. National Bureau of Economic Research. https://doi.org/10.3386/w27123.

Garretson, Jeremiah, and Elizabeth Suhay. 2016. "Scientific Communication About Biological Influences on Homosexuality and the Politics of Gay Rights." *Political Research
Quarterly* 69(1): 17–29. https://doi.org/10.1177/1065912915620050.

Gascon, Charles S., and Joseph Martorana. 2024. "Labor Market Conditions Have Eased,
but Why? A State-Level View." Federal Reserve Bank of St. Louis. https://www.stlouis
fed.org/publications/regional-economist/2024/feb/labor-market-conditions-eased-state
-level-view.

Gelman, Susan. 2003. *The Essential Child: Origins of Essentialism in Everyday Thought.* Oxford University Press.

General Social Survey. 2025. NORC at the University of Chicago. https://gss.norc.org/us
/en/gss/get-the-data.html.

Gerring, John. 1997. "Ideology: A Definitional Analysis." *Political Research Quarterly* 50(4):
957–94. https://doi.org/10.2307/448995.

Gerring, John. 1998. *Party Ideologies in America 1828–1996.* Cambridge University Press.

Gerstle, Gary. 2022. *The Rise and Fall of the Neoliberal Order: America and the World in the
Free Market Era.* Oxford University Press.

Gethin, Amory, Clara Martínez-Toledano, and Thomas Piketty. 2021. "Brahmin Left Versus
Merchant Right: Changing Political Cleavages in 21 Western Democracies, 1948–2020."
Quarterly Journal of Economics 137(1): 1–48. https://doi.org/10.1093/qje/qjab036.

Giattino, Charlie, and Esteban Ortiz-Ospina. 2020. "Do Workers in Richer Countries Work
Longer Hours?" Our World in Data, December 21. https://ourworldindata.org/rich
-poor-working-hours.

Gilens, Martin. 1999. *Why Americans Hate Welfare: Race, Media, and the Politics of Antipov-
erty Policy.* University of Chicago Press.

Gilens, Martin. 2003. "How the Poor Became Black: The Racialization of American Poverty
in the Mass Media." In *Race and the Politics of Welfare Reform*, edited by Sanford F.
Schram, Joe Soss, and Richard C. Fording. University of Michigan Press.

Gilens, Martin. 2012. *Affluence and Influence: Economic Inequality and Political Power in
America.* Princeton University Press.

Gill, Michael J., and Michael R. Andreychik. 2014. "The Social Explanatory Styles Questionnaire: Assessing Moderators of Basic Social-Cognitive Phenomena Including Spon-
taneous Trait Inference, the Fundamental Attribution Error, and Moral Blame." *PLOS
ONE* 9(7). https://doi.org/10.1371/journal.pone.0100886.

Gimpel, James G., Nathan Lovin, Bryant Moy, and Andrew Reeves. 2020. "The Urban–
Rural Gulf in American Political Behavior." *Political Behavior* 42(4): 1343–68. https://
doi.org/10.1007/s11109-020-09601-w.

Glasmeier, Amy. 2025. "Living Wage Calculator." https://livingwage.mit.edu/.

Glasser, Susan B. 2018. "The Man Who Put Andrew Jackson in Trump's Oval Office." *Po-*

litico, January 22. https://www.politico.com/magazine/story/2018/01/22/andrew-jackson-donald-trump-216493.

Goesling, Brian, Hande Inanc, and Angela Rachidi. 2020. "Success Sequence: A Synthesis of the Literature." OPRE Report 2020–41.

Goetz, Stephan J., Mark D. Partridge, and Heather M. Stephens. 2018. "The Economic Status of Rural America in the President Trump Era and Beyond." *Applied Economic Perspectives and Policy* 40(1): 97–118. https://doi.org/10.1093/aepp/ppx061.

Goldin, Claudia. 2014. "A Grand Gender Convergence: Its Last Chapter." *American Economic Review* 104(4): 1091–119. https://doi.org/10.1257/aer.104.4.1091.

Goldmacher, Shane, Maggie Haberman, and Jonathan Swan. 2024. "How Donald Trump Is Making Big Promises to Big Business." *New York Times*, October 26. https://www.nytimes.com/2024/10/26/us/politics/trump-industry-promises.html.

Golway, Terry, ed. 2012. *American Political Speeches*. Penguin Books.

Gordon, Robert J. 2016. *The Rise and Fall of American Growth: The U.S. Standard of Living Since the Civil War*. Princeton University Press.

Goudarzi, Shahrzad, Ruthie Pliskin, John T. Jost, and Eric D. Knowles. 2020. "Economic System Justification Predicts Muted Emotional Responses to Inequality." *Nature Communications* 11(1): 383. https://doi.org/10.1038/s41467-019-14193-z.

Gould, Elise, and Katherine deCourcy. 2024. "Fastest Wage Growth over the Last Four Years Among Historically Disadvantaged Groups: Low-Wage Workers' Wages Surged After Decades of Slow Growth." Economic Policy Institute. March 21. https://www.epi.org/publication/swa-wages-2023/.

Gramm, Phil, Robert Ekelund, and John Early. 2022. *The Myth of American Inequality: How Government Biases Policy Debate*. Rowman and Littlefield Publishers.

Granovetter, Mark. 1983. "The Strength of Weak Ties: A Network Theory Revisited." *Sociological Theory* 1: 201–33. https://doi.org/10.2307/202051.

Grasso, Maria Teresa, Stephen Farrall, Emily Gray, Colin Hay, and Will Jennings. 2019. "Thatcher's Children, Blair's Babies, Political Socialization and Trickle-Down Value Change: An Age, Period and Cohort Analysis." *British Journal of Political Science* 49(1): 17–36. https://doi.org/10.1017/S0007123416000375.

Green, Donald P., Bradley Palmquist, and Eric Schickler. 2004. *Partisan Hearts and Minds: Political Parties and the Social Identities of Voters*. Yale University Press.

Green, Joshua. 2024. *The Rebels: Elizabeth Warren, Bernie Sanders, Alexandria Ocasio-Cortez, and the Struggle for a New American Politics*. Penguin Press.

Greenstein, Robert. 2024. "Trump Administration Budgets and Social Programs." Hamilton Project. September 3. https://www.hamiltonproject.org/publication/post/trump-administration-budgets-and-programs-for-people-of-limited-means/.

Groenendyk, Eric W. 2015. *Competing Motives in the Partisan Mind: How Loyalty and Responsiveness Shape Party Identification and Democracy*. Series in Political Psychology. Oxford University Press.

Grossmann, Matt. 2021. *How Social Science Got Better: Overcoming Bias with More Evidence, Diversity, and Self-Reflection*. Oxford University Press.

Grossmann, Matt, Kayla Hamann, Jennifer Lee, Gabrielle Levy, Brendan Nyhan, and Victor Wu. 2021. "Republicans Are More Optimistic About Economic Mobility, but No Less Accurate." *Research and Politics* (October–December): 1–8.

Grossman, Matt, and David A. Hopkins. 2023. *Polarized by Degrees: How the Diploma Divide and the Culture War Transformed American Politics.* Cambridge University Press.

Grossmann, Matt, and David A. Hopkins. 2016. *Asymmetric Politics: Ideological Republicans and Group Interest Democrats.* Oxford University Press.

Grossmann, Matt, Zuhaib Mahmood, and William Isaac. 2021. "Political Parties, Interest Groups, and Unequal Class Influence in American Policy." *Journal of Politics* 83(4): 1706–20. https://doi.org/10.1086/711900.

Grumbach, Jacob. 2019. "Interest Group Activists and the Polarization of State Legislatures." *Legislative Studies Quarterly* 45(1): 5–34. https://doi.org/10.1111/lsq.12244.

Grundy, Adam. 2024. "Estimated Revenue for Child Day Care Services Climbed as Child Care Options Declined in 2021." U.S. Census Bureau. January 9. https://www.census.gov/library/stories/2024/01/rising-child-care-cost.html.

Grusec, Joan E., and Paul D. Hastings. 2015. *Handbook of Socialization: Theory and Research*, 2nd ed. Guilford Press.

Guetzkow, Joshua. 2010. "Beyond Deservingness: Congressional Discourse on Poverty, 1964–1996." *The Annals of the American Academy of Political and Social Science* 629(1): 173–97. https://doi.org/10.1177/0002716209357404.

Gurevich, Gregory, Doron Kliger, and Bernard Weiner. 2012. "The Role of Attribution of Causality in Economic Decision Making." *The Journal of Socio-Economics* 41(4): 439–44. https://doi.org/10.1016/j.socec.2011.07.005.

Hacker, Jacob S., Amelia Malpas, Paul Pierson, and Sam Zacher. 2023. "Bridging the Blue Divide: The Democrats' New Metro Coalition and the Unexpected Prominence of Redistribution." *Perspectives on Politics* 22(3): 609–29. https://doi.org/10.1017/S1537592723002931.

Hacker, Jacob S., and Paul Pierson. 2010. *Winner-Take-All Politics: How Washington Made the Rich Richer—and Turned Its Back on the Middle Class.* Simon & Schuster.

Hacker, Jacob S., and Paul Pierson. 2014. "After the 'Master Theory': Downs, Schattscheider, and the Rebirth of Policy-Focused Analysis." *Perspectives on Politics* 12(3): 643–62. https://doi.org/10.1017/S1537592714001637.

Hammonds, Evelynn Maxine, and Rebecca M. Herzig, eds. 2008. *The Nature of Difference: Sciences of Race in the United States from Jefferson to Genomics.* MIT Press.

Harden, Kathryn Paige. 2021. *The Genetic Lottery: Why DNA Matters for Social Equality.* Princeton University Press.

Hare, Christopher. 2022. "Constrained Citizens? Ideological Structure and Conflict Extension in the US Electorate, 1980–2016." *British Journal of Political Science* 52(4): 1602–21. https://doi.org/10.1017/S000712342100051X.

Harrington, Michael. 1962. *The Other America: Poverty in the United States.* Scribner.

Harrs, Sören, and Maj-Britt Sterba. 2023. "Fairness Preferences and Support for Welfare Policies." Working paper. https://behavecon.uni-koeln.de/sites/vhf/user_upload/JMP_Soeren_Harrs.pdf.

Hartig, Hannah. 2022. "Wide Partisan Gaps in Abortion Attitudes, but Opinions in Both Parties Are Complicated." Pew Research Center.

Hartz, Louis. 1955. *The Liberal Tradition in America: An Interpretation of American Political Thought Since the Revolution*. Harcourt. https://doi.org/10.2307/1951399.

Harvey, David L., and Michael H. Reed. 1996. "The Culture of Poverty: An Ideological Analysis." *Sociological Perspectives* 39(4): 465–95. https://doi.org/10.2307/1389418.

Haskins, Ron, and Isabel V. Sawhill. 2009. *Creating an Opportunity Society*. Brookings Institution Press.

Hasson, Yossi, Maya Tamir, Kea S. Brahms, J. Christopher Cohrs, and Eran Halperin. 2018. "Are Liberals and Conservatives Equally Motivated to Feel Empathy Toward Others?" *Personality and Social Psychology Bulletin* 44(10): 1449–59. https://doi.org/10.1177/01461 67218769867.

Hawley, Josh. 2024. "Hawley, Warren Introduce Bipartisan Bill to Control PBMs, Put Patients First." Press release, December 11. https://www.hawley.senate.gov/hawley-warren -introduce-bipartisan-bill-to-control-pbms-put-patients-first/.

Hayek, Friedrich. 1944. *The Road to Serfdom*. University of Chicago Press.

Hayward, R. David, and Markus Kemmelmeier. 2011. "Weber Revisited: A Cross-national Analysis of Religiosity, Religious Culture, and Economic Attitudes." *Journal of Cross-Cultural Psychology* 42(8): 1406–20. https://doi.org/10.1177/0022022111412527.

Heider, Fritz. 1958. *The Psychology of Interpersonal Relations*. John Wiley & Sons. https://doi .org/10.1037/10628-000.

Henry, P. J., Christine Reyna, and Bernard Weiner. 2004. "Hate Welfare But Help the Poor: How the Attributional Content of Stereotypes Explains the Paradox of Reactions to the Destitute in America." *Journal of Applied Social Psychology* 34(1): 34–58.

Hertel-Fernandez, Alexander. 2019. *State Capture: How Conservative Activists, Big Businesses, and Wealthy Donors Reshaped the American States—and the Nation*. Oxford University Press.

Herzog, Don. 2020. *A Little Book of Political Mistakes*. University of Michigan Law School. https://little-book-of-political-mistakes.pubpub.org.

Hetherington, Mark J., and Jonathan D. Weiler. 2009. *Authoritarianism and Polarization in American Politics*. Cambridge University Press. https://doi.org/10.1017/CBO9780511 802331.

Hewstone, Miles. 1990. "The 'Ultimate Attribution Error'? A Review of the Literature on Intergroup Causal Attribution." *European Journal of Social Psychology* 20(4): 311–35. https://doi.org/10.1002/ejsp.2420200404.

Highton, Benjamin. 2009. "Revisiting the Relationship Between Educational Attainment and Political Sophistication." *Journal of Politics* 71(4): 1564–76. https://doi.org/10.1017 /S0022381609990077.

Hirsh, Michael. 2025. "'Beyond My Wildest Dreams': The Architect of Project 2025 Is Ready for His Victory Lap." *Politico*, March 16. https://www.politico.com/news/magazine /2025/03/16/project-2025-paul-dans-qa-00228890/.

Hochschild, Arlie Russell. 2016. *Strangers in Their Own Land: Anger and Mourning on the American Right*. New Press.

Hochschild, Arlie Russell. 2024. *Stolen Pride: Loss, Shame, and the Rise of the Right*. New Press.

Hochschild, Jennifer L. 1981. *What's Fair? American Beliefs About Distributive Justice*. Harvard University Press.

Hochschild, Jennifer L. 1995. *Facing Up to the American Dream: Race, Class, and the Soul of the Nation*. Princeton University Press.

Hoover, Herbert. 1934. *The Challenge to Liberty*. Charles Scribner's Sons.

Horowitz, Juliana, Ruth Igielnik, and Rakesh Kochhar. 2020. "Most Americans Say There Is Too Much Economic Inequality in the U.S., but Fewer Than Half Call It a Top Priority." Pew Research Center, January 9. https://www.pewresearch.org/social-trends /2020/01/09/most-americans-say-there-is-too-much-economic-inequality-in-the-u-s -but-fewer-than-half-call-it-a-top-priority/.

Huber, Joan, and William H. Form. 1973. *Income and Ideology: An Analysis of the American Political Formula*. Free Press.

Huckfeldt, Robert, and John Sprague. 1995. *Citizens, Politics, and Social Communication: Information and Influence in an Election Campaign*. Cambridge University Press. https:// doi.org/10.1017/CBO9780511664113.

Hughes, Michael, and Steven A. Tuch. 2000. "How Beliefs About Poverty Influence Racial Policy Attitudes: A Study of Whites, African Americans, Hispanics, and Asians in the United States." In *Racialized Politics: The Debate About Racism in America*, edited by David O. Sears, Jim Sidanius, and Lawrence Bobo. University of Chicago Press.

Hunt, Matthew O. 1996. "The Individual, Society, or Both? A Comparison of Black, Latino, and White Beliefs about the Causes of Poverty." *Social Forces* 75(1): 293–322. https://doi .org/10.1093/sf/75.1.293.

Hunt, Matthew O. 2007. "African American, Hispanic, and White Beliefs About Black/ White Inequality, 1977–2004." *American Sociological Review* 72(3): 390–415. https://doi .org/10.1177/000312240707200304.

Hunt, Matthew O., and Heather E. Bullock. 2016. "Ideologies and Beliefs About Poverty." In *The Oxford Handbook of the Social Science of Poverty*, edited by David Brady and Linda M. Burton. Oxford University Press.

Hunter, James Davison. 1991. *Culture Wars: The Struggle to Control the Family, Art, Education, Law, and Politics in America*. Basic Books.

Hussak, Larisa J., and Andrei Cimpian. 2015. "An Early-Emerging Explanatory Heuristic Promotes Support for the Status Quo." *Journal of Personality and Social Psychology* 109(5): 739–52. https://doi.org/10.1037/pspa0000033.

Hussak, Larisa J., and Andrei Cimpian. 2016. "Investigating the Origins of Political Views: Biases in Explanation Predict Conservative Attitudes in Children and Adults." *Developmental Science* 21(3). https://doi.org/10.1111/desc.12567.

Ickes, William, and Mary Anne Layden. 1978. "Attributional Styles." In *New Directions in Attribution Research: II*, edited by John H. Harvey, William Ickes, and Robert F. Kidd. Lawrence Erlbaum.

Ilin, Elias, and Alvaro Sanchez. 2023. "Mitigating Benefits Cliffs for Low-Income Families: District of Columbia Career Mobility Action Plan as a Case Study." Federal Reserve Bank of Atlanta. https://www.atlantafed.org/community-development/publications /discussion-papers/2023/09/26/01-a-case-study-mitigating-benefits-cliffs-in-the -district-of-columbia.

Inanc, Hande, Ariella Spitzer, and Brian Goesling. 2021. "Assessing the Benefits of the Success Sequence for Economic Self-Sufficiency and Family Stability." OPRE Report Number 2021–148. https://acf.gov/sites/default/files/documents/opre/opre-assessing-success-sequence-oct-2021.pdf.

Iyengar, Shanto. 1991. *Is Anyone Responsible? How Television Frames Political Issues*. American Politics and Political Economy Series. University of Chicago Press.

Iyengar, Shanto, Gaurav Sood, and Yphtach Lelkes. 2012. "Affect, Not Ideology: A Social Identity Perspective on Polarization." *Public Opinion Quarterly* 76(3): 405–31. https://doi.org/10.1093/poq/nfs038.

Iyengar, Shanto, and Sean J. Westwood. 2015. "Fear and Loathing Across Party Lines: New Evidence on Group Polarization." *American Journal of Political Science* 59(3): 690–707.

Izaguirre, Rosmery, and Caitlin Oprysko. 2024. "Business Donors Overwhelmingly Bet on the GOP. Here's Where It Paid off." *Politico*, November 24. https://www.politico.com/news/2024/11/24/business-election-donations-republicans-00191072.

Janda, Kenneth. 2022. *The Republican Evolution: From Governing Party to Antigovernment Party, 1860–2020*. Columbia University Press.

Jardina, Ashley, and Trent Ollerenshaw. 2022. "The Polls-Trends: The Polarization of White Racial Attitudes and Support for Racial Equality in the US." *Public Opinion Quarterly* 86(S1): 576–87. https://doi.org/10.1093/poq/nfac021.

Jares, Jake Alton. 2023. "Holding on to High Cotton: How Narrow Economic Interests Resist Policy Retrenchment."

Jennings, M. Kent, and Richard G. Niemi. 1981. *Generations and Politics: A Panel Study of Young Adults and Their Parents*. Princeton University Press. https://www.jstor.org/stable/j.ctt7ztk9v.

Jennings, M. Kent, Laura Stoker, and Jake Bowers. 2009. "Politics Across Generations: Family Transmission Reexamined." *Journal of Politics* 71(3): 782–99. https://doi.org/10.1017/s0022381609090719.

Jensen, Carsten, and Michael Bang Petersen. 2017. "The Deservingness Heuristic and the Politics of Health Care." *American Journal of Political Science* 61(1): 68–83. https://doi.org/10.1111/ajps.12251.

Jensen, Leif, and Tim Slack. 2003. "Underemployment in America: Measurement and Evidence." *American Journal of Community Psychology* 32(1–2): 21–31. https://doi.org/10.1023/A:1025686621578.

Jin, Connie Hanzhang. 2021. "6 Charts That Dismantle the Trope of Asian Americans as a Model Minority." NPR. May 25. https://www.npr.org/2021/05/25/999874296/6-charts-that-dismantle-the-trope-of-asian-americans-as-a-model-minority.

Johnston, Christopher D., Howard G. Lavine, and Christopher M. Federico. 2017. *Open Versus Closed: Personality, Identity, and the Politics of Redistribution*. Cambridge University Press. https://doi.org/10.1017/9781316341452.

Jones, Philip Edward. 2020. "Partisanship, Political Awareness, and Retrospective Evaluations, 1956–2016." *Political Behavior* 42: 1295–1317. https://doi.org/10.1007/s11109-019-09543-y.

Jost, John T. 2017. "Working Class Conservatism: A System Justification Perspective." *Current Opinion in Psychology* 18: 73–78. https://doi.org/10.1016/j.copsyc.2017.08.020.

Jost, John T. 2020. *A Theory of System Justification.* Harvard University Press.

Jost, John T. 2021. *Left and Right: The Psychological Significance of a Political Distinction.* Oxford University Press.

Jost, John T., Mahzarin R. Banaji, and Brian A. Nosek. 2004. "A Decade of System Justification Theory: Accumulated Evidence of Conscious and Unconscious Bolstering of the Status Quo." *Political Psychology* 25(6): 881–919. https://doi.org/10.1111/j.1467-9221.2004.00402.x.

Jost, John T., Sally Blount, Jeffrey Pfeffer, and György Hunyady. 2003. "Fair Market Ideology: Its Cognitive-Motivational Underpinnings." *Research in Organizational Behavior* 25: 53–91. https://doi.org/10.1016/S0191-3085(03)25002-4.

Jost, John T., Jack Glaser, Arie W. Kruglanski, and Frank J. Sulloway. 2003. "Political Conservatism as Motivated Social Cognition." *Psychological Bulletin* 129(3): 339–75. https://doi.org/10.1037/0033-2909.129.3.339.

Kam, Cindy D., and Camille D. Burge. 2018. "Uncovering Reactions to the Racial Resentment Scale Across the Racial Divide." *Journal of Politics* 80(1): 314–20. https://doi.org/10.1086/693907.

Kam, Cindy D., and Camille D. Burge. 2019. "Racial Resentment and Public Opinion Across the Racial Divide." *Political Research Quarterly* 72(4): 767–84.

Kane, John V., Lilliana Mason, and Julie Wronski. 2021. "Who's at the Party? Group Sentiments, Knowledge, and Partisan Identity." *Journal of Politics* 83(4): 1783–99. https://doi.org/10.1086/715072.

Karol, David. 2009. *Party Position Change in American Politics.* Cambridge University Press. https://doi.org/10.1017/CBO9780511812620.

Katz, Elihu, and Paul F. Lazarsfeld. 1955. *Personal Influence: The Part Played by People in the Flow of Mass Communications.* Free Press.

Katznelson, Ira. 2005. *When Affirmative Action Was White: An Untold History of Racial Inequality in Twentieth-Century America.* W. W. Norton & Company.

Kearney, Melissa S. 2023. *The Two-Parent Privilege: How Americans Stopped Getting Married and Started Falling Behind.* University of Chicago Press.

Keller, Johannes. 2005. "In Genes We Trust: The Biological Component of Psychological Essentialism and Its Relationship to Mechanisms of Motivated Social Cognition." *Journal of Personality and Social Psychology* 88(4): 686–702. https://doi.org/10.1037/0022-3514.88.4.686.

Kelly, Nathan J. 2019. *America's Inequality Trap.* Chicago Studies in American Politics. University of Chicago Press.

Kennedy, Brian, and Courtney Johnson. 2020. "More Americans See Climate Change as a Priority, but Democrats Are Much More Concerned than Republicans." Pew Research Center, February 28. https://www.pewresearch.org/short-reads/2020/02/28/more-americans-see-climate-change-as-a-priority-but-democrats-are-much-more-concerned-than-republicans/.

Khan, Shamus Rahman. 2011. *Privilege: The Making of an Adolescent Elite at St. Paul's School.* Princeton University Press.

Kim, Eunji. 2023. "Entertaining Beliefs in Economic Mobility." *American Journal of Political Science* 67(1): 39–54. https://doi.org/10.1111/ajps.12702.

Kim, Seo-young Silvia, and Jan Zilinsky. 2022. "Division Does Not Imply Predictability: Demographics Continue to Reveal Little About Voting and Partisanship." *Political Behavior* 46: 67–87. https://doi.org/10.1007/s11109-022-09816-z.

Kinder, Donald R., and Nathan P. Kalmoe. 2017. *Neither Liberal nor Conservative: Ideological Innocence in the American Public.* University of Chicago Press.

Kinder, Donald R., and Lynn M. Sanders. 1996. *Divided by Color: Racial Politics and Democratic Ideals.* University of Chicago Press.

King, J. E. 2016. "The Literature on Piketty." *Review of Political Economy* 29: 1–17. https://doi.org/10.1080/09538259.2016.1173425.

Klar, Samara, and Yanna Krupnikov. 2016. *Independent Politics: How American Disdain for Parties Leads to Inaction.* Cambridge University Press.

Klein, Ezra, and Derek Thompson. 2025. *Abundance.* Simon & Schuster.

Kline, Patrick M., Evan K. Rose, and Christopher R. Walters. 2024. "A Discrimination Report Card." NBER Working Paper 32313. National Bureau of Economic Research. https://www.nber.org/system/files/working_papers/w32313/w32313.pdf.

Kluegel, James R., and Eliot R. Smith. 1986. *Beliefs About Inequality: Americans' Views of What Is and What Ought to Be.* Aldine de Gruyter.

Kraus, Michael W., and Dacher Keltner. 2013. "Social Class Rank, Essentialism, and Punitive Judgment." *Journal of Personality and Social Psychology* 105(2): 247–61. https://doi.org/10.1037/a0032895.

Kraus, Michael W., and Jacinth J. X. Tan. 2015. "Americans Overestimate Social Class Mobility." *Journal of Experimental Social Psychology* 58: 101–11. https://doi.org/10.1016/j.jesp.2015.01.005.

Krueger, Alan B. 2017. "Where Have All the Workers Gone? An Inquiry into the Decline of the U.S. Labor Force Participation Rate." *Brookings Paper on Economic Activity* (2; fall): 1–87. https://doi:10.1353/eca.2017.0012.

Kruglanski, Arie W., Irit Z. Hamel, Shirley A. Maides, and Joseph M. Schwartz. 1978. "Attribution Theory as a Special Case of Lay Epistemology." In *New Directions in Attribution Research*, vol. 2., edited by John H. Harvey, William Ickes, and Robert F. Kidd. Lawrence Erlbaum Associates.

Krupnikov, Yanna, and John Barry Ryan. 2022. *The Other Divide: Polarization and Disengagement in American Politics.* Cambridge University Press.

Kujala, Jordan. 2019. "Donors, Primary Elections, and Polarization in the United States." *American Journal of Political Science* 64(3): 587–602. https://doi.org/10.1111/ajps.12477.

Lakoff, George. 2016. *Moral Politics: How Liberals and Conservatives Think*, 3rd ed. University of Chicago Press.

Lamont, Michèle. 1992. *Money, Morals, and Manners: The Culture of the French and the American Upper-Middle Class.* University of Chicago Press.

Lamont, Michèle, and Annette Lareau. 1988. "Cultural Capital: Allusions, Gaps and Glissandos in Recent Theoretical Developments." *Sociological Theory* 6(2): 153–68. https://doi.org/10.2307/202113.

Lane, Robert E. 1959. "The Fear of Equality." *American Political Science Review* 53(1): 35–51. https://doi.org/10.2307/1951729.

Lasswell, Harold D. 1936. *Politics: Who Gets What, When How.* McGraw-Hill.

Lauderdale, Benjamin E. 2013. "Does Inattention to Political Debate Explain the Polarization Gap Between the U.S. Congress and Public?" *Public Opinion Quarterly* 77: 2–23.

Lay, J. Celeste, Mirya R. Holman, Jill S. Greenlee, Zoe M. Oxley, and Angela L. Bos. 2023. "Partisanship on the Playground: Expressive Party Politics Among Children." *Political Research Quarterly* 76(3): 1249–64. https://doi.org/10.1177/10659129221132223.

Layman, Geoffrey C., Thomas M. Carsey, John C. Green, Richard Herrera, and Rosalyn Cooperman. 2010. "Activists and Conflict Extension in American Party Politics." *American Political Science Review* 104(2): 324–46. https://doi.org/10.1017/S000305541000016X.

Lee, Frances E. 2009. *Beyond Ideology: Politics, Principles, and Partisanship in the U. S. Senate.* University of Chicago Press.

Lee, Frances E. 2016. *Insecure Majorities: Congress and the Perpetual Campaign.* University of Chicago Press.

Lee, Hojung, Kenneth Shores, and Elinor Williams. 2022. "The Distribution of School Resources in the United States: A Comparative Analysis Across Levels of Governance, Student Subgroups, and Educational Resources." *Peabody Journal of Education* 97(4): 395–411. https://doi.org/10.1080/0161956X.2022.2107369.

Lee, Jennifer. 2021. "Reckoning with Asian America and the New Culture War on Affirmative Action." *Sociological Forum* 36(4): 863–88. https://doi.org/10.1111/socf.12751.

Lee, Nathan, Brendan Nyhan, Jason Reifler, and D. J. Flynn. 2021. "More Accurate, But No Less Polarized: Comparing the Factual Beliefs of Government Officials and the Public." *British Journal of Political Science* 51(3): 1315–22. https://doi.org/10.1017/S000712342000037X.

Lee, Taeku. 2002. *Mobilizing Public Opinion: Black Insurgency and Racial Attitudes in the Civil Rights Era.* University of Chicago Press.

Leeper, Thomas J., and Rune Slothuus. 2014. "Political Parties, Motivated Reasoning, and Public Opinion Formation." *Political Psychology* 35(S1): 129–56. https://doi.org/10.1111/pops.12164.

Lenz, Gabriel S. 2012. *Follow the Leader? How Voters Respond to Politicians' Policies and Performance.* Chicago Studies in American Politics. University of Chicago Press.

Lepianka, Dorota, John Gelissen, and Wim van Oorschot. 2010. "Popular Explanations of Poverty in Europe: Effects of Contextual and Individual Characteristics Across 28 European Countries." *Acta Sociologica* 53(1): 53–72. https://doi.org/10.1177/0001699309357842.

Lepianka, Dorota, Wim van Oorschot, and John Gelissen. 2009. "Popular Explanations of Poverty: A Critical Discussion of Empirical Research." *Journal of Social Policy* 38(3): 421–38. https://doi.org/10.1017/S0047279409003092.

Lerner, Melvin. 1980. *The Belief in a Just World: Perspectives in Social Psychology.* Springer.

Levanon, Asaf, Paula England, and Paul Allison. 2009. "Occupational Feminization and Pay: Assessing Causal Dynamics Using 1950–2000 U.S. Census Data." *Social Forces* 88(2): 865–91. https://doi.org/10.1353/sof.0.0264.

Levendusky, Matthew. 2009. *The Partisan Sort: How Liberals Became Democrats and Conservatives Became Republicans.* Chicago Studies in American Politics. University of Chicago Press.

Levendusky, Matthew. 2013. *How Partisan Media Polarize America.* Chicago Studies in American Politics. University of Chicago Press.

Levin, Bess. 2023. "Republicans Think Low-Income Americans Aren't Working Hard Enough to Deserve Food." *Vanity Fair*, March 15. https://www.vanityfair.com/news/2023/03/republicans-food-stamps-work-requirements.

Levy, Sheri R., Chi-yue Chiu, and Ying-yi Hong. 2006. "Lay Theories and Intergroup Relations." *Group Processes & Intergroup Relations* 9(1): 5–24. https://doi.org/10.1177/13684 302060598.

Lewis, Verlan. 2019. *Ideas of Power: The Politics of American Party Ideology Development.* Cambridge University Press.

Lindert, Peter H., and Jeffrey G. Williamson. 2016. *Unequal Gains: American Growth and Inequality Since 1700.* Princeton University Press.

Lindh, Arvid, and Leslie McCall. 2023. "Bringing the Market In: An Expanded Framework for Understanding Popular Responses to Economic Inequality." *Socio-Economic Review* 21(2): 1035–55. https://doi.org/10.1093/ser/mwac018.

Lino, Mark. 1996. "Income and Spending of Poor Households With Children." *Family Economics and Nutrition Review* 9(1): 2–13.

Lippens, Louis, Siel Vermeiren, and Stijn Baert. 2023. "The State of Hiring Discrimination: A Meta-Analysis of (Almost) All Recent Correspondence Experiments." *European Economic Review* 151: 104315. https://doi.org/10.1016/j.euroecorev.2022.104315.

Lippmann, Walter. 1922. *Public Opinion.* Harcourt, Brace and Company.

Lipset, Seymour Martin. 1977. "Why No Socialism in the United States?" In *Radicalism in the Contemporary Age*, vol. 1, edited by Seweryn Bialer. Westview Press.

Livingston, Gretchen, and Deja Thomas. 2019. "Among 41 Countries, Only U.S. Lacks Paid Parental Leave." Pew Research Center. December 16. https://www.pewresearch.org/short-reads/2019/12/16/u-s-lacks-mandated-paid-parental-leave.

Lockwood, Jacob, and Douglas Webber. 2023. "Non-Completion, Student Debt, and Financial Well-Being: Evidence from the Survey of Household Economics and Decisionmaking." Board of Governors of the Federal Reserve System. https://www.federalreserve.gov/econres/notes/feds-notes/non-completion-student-debt-and-financial-well-being-20230821.html.

Lodge, Milton, and Charles S. Taber. 2013. *The Rationalizing Voter.* Cambridge University Press.

Lowi, Theodore J., Benjamin Ginsberg, Kenneth A. Shepsle, Stephen Ansolabehere, and Hahrie Han. 2022. *American Government: Power and Purpose*, 17th ed. W. W. Norton & Company.

Lowrey, Annie. 2020. "The Great Affordability Crisis Breaking America." *Atlantic*, February 7. https://www.theatlantic.com/ideas/archive/2020/02/great-affordability-crisis -breaking-america/606046/.

Ludwig, Eugene. 2025. "Voters Were Right About the Economy. The Data Was Wrong." *Politico*, February 11. https://www.politico.com/news/magazine/2025/02/11/democrats -tricked-strong-economy-00203464.

Lukianoff, Greg, and Jonathan Haidt. 2018. *The Coddling of the American Mind: How Good Intentions and Bad Ideas Are Setting Up a Generation for Failure.* Penguin Press.

Luskin, Robert C. 1990. "Explaining Political Sophistication." *Political Behavior* 12(4): 331– 61. https://doi.org/10.1007/BF00992793.

Lyons, Jeffrey. 2017. "The Family and Partisan Socialization in Red and Blue America." *Political Psychology* 38(2): 297–312. https://doi.org/10.1111/pops.12336.

Maestas, Nicole, Kathleen J. Mullen, and Alexander Strand. 2013. "Does Disability Insurance Receipt Discourage Work? Using Examiner Assignment to Estimate Causal Effects of SSDI Receipt." *American Economic Review* 103(5): 1797–829. https://doi.org/10.1257 /aer.103.5.1797.

Mai, Quan D. 2023. "The Demographic Context of Hiring Discrimination: Evidence from a Field Experiment in 50 Metropolitan Statistical Areas." *Work and Occupations* 50(4): 463–98. https://doi.org/10.1177/07308884221134470.

Malpas, Amelia, and Adam Hilton. 2021. "Retreating from Redistribution? Trends in Democratic Party Fidelity to Economic Equality, 1984–2020." *Forum* 19(2): 283–316. https:// doi.org/10.1515/for-2021-0012.

Marx, Karl. 1970. "Critique of Hegel's Philosophy of Right." Cambridge University Press.

Mason, Lilliana. 2018. *Uncivil Agreement: How Politics Became Our Identity.* University of Chicago Press.

Mason, Lilliana, and Julie Wronski. 2018. "One Tribe to Bind Them All: How Our Social Group Attachments Strengthen Partisanship." *Political Psychology* 39: 257–77. https:// doi.org/10.1111/pops.12485.

Massey, Douglas S., and Nancy A. Denton. 1993. *American Apartheid: Segregation and the Making of the Underclass.* Harvard University Press.

Maxwell, Angie, and Todd Shields. 2019. *The Long Southern Strategy: How Chasing White Voters in the South Changed American Politics.* Oxford University Press.

Mayer, Jane. 2016. *Dark Money: The Hidden History of the Billionaires Behind the Rise of the Radical Right.* Doubleday.

McCall, Leslie. 2013. *The Undeserving Rich: American Beliefs About Inequality, Opportunity, and Redistribution.* Cambridge University Press.

McCall, Leslie. 2016. "Political and Policy Responses to Problems of Inequality and Opportunity: Past, Present, and Future." In *The Dynamics of Opportunity in America: Evidence and Perspectives,* edited by Irwin Kirsch and Henry Braun. Springer International Publishing.

McCall, Leslie, Derek Burk, Marie Laperriere, and Jennifer A. Richeson. 2017. "Exposure to Rising Inequality Shapes Americans' Opportunity Beliefs and Policy Support." *Pro-*

ceedings of the National Academy of Sciences 114(36). https://www.pnas.org/doi/10.1073
/pnas.1706253114.

McCarty, Nolan. 2019. *Polarization: What Everyone Needs to Know.* Oxford University Press.

McCloskey, Deirdre Nansen. 2014. "Measured, Unmeasured, Mismeasured, and Unjustified
Pessimism: A Review Essay of Thomas Piketty's *Capital in the Twenty-First Century.*"
Erasmus Journal for Philosophy and Economics 7(2): 73–115. https://doi.org/10.23941/ejpe
.v7i2.170.

McClosky, Herbert, and John Zaller. 1984. *The American Ethos: Public Attitudes Toward Capitalism and Democracy.* Harvard University Press.

McGhee, Heather. 2021. *The Sum of Us: What Racism Costs Everyone and How We Can Prosper Together.* One World.

Medina, Jennifer. 2021. "Biden Wanted an F.D.R. Presidency. How's He Doing So Far?"
New York Times, October 26. https://www.nytimes.com/2021/10/26/us/politics/biden
-wanted-an-fdr-presidency-hows-he-doing-so-far.html.

Meltzer, Allan H., and Scott F. Richard. 1981. "A Rational Theory of the Size of Government." *Journal of Political Economy* 89(5): 914–27. https://doi.org/10.1086/261013.

Mendelberg, Tali. 2001. *The Race Card: Campaign Strategy, Implicit Messages, and the Norm
of Equality.* Princeton University Press.

Mendelberg, Tali, Katherine T. McCabe, and Adam Thal. 2017. "College Socialization and
the Economic Views of Affluent Americans." *American Journal of Political Science* 61(3):
606–23.

Michaels, Walter Benn, and Adolph Reed Jr. 2023. *No Politics but Class Politics.* Eris.

Milanovic, Branko. 2023. *Visions of Inequality: From the French Revolution to the End of the
Cold War.* Belknap Press.

Miller, Claire Cain. 2021. "How Other Nations Pay for Child Care. The U.S. Is an Outlier."
New York Times, October 6. https://www.nytimes.com/2021/10/06/upshot/child-care
-biden.html.

Montgomery, James D. 1991. "Social Networks and Labor-Market Outcomes: Toward an
Economic Analysis." *American Economic Review* 81(5): 1408–18.

Morgan, G. Scott, Elizabeth Mullen, and Linda J. Skitka. 2010. "When Values and Attributions Collide: Liberals' and Conservatives' Values Motivate Attributions for Alleged
Misdeeds." *Personality and Social Psychology Bulletin* 36(9): 1241–54. https://doi.org
/10.1177/0146167210703806.

Morris, Michael W., and Kaiping Peng. 1994. "Culture and Cause: American and Chinese
Attributions for Social and Physical Events." *Journal of Personality and Social Psychology*
67(6): 949–71. https://doi.org/10.1037/0022-3514.67.6.949.

Morris, Stephen G. 2020. "Empathy and the Liberal-Conservative Political Divide in the
U.S." *Journal of Social and Political Psychology* 8(1): 8–24. https://doi.org/10.5964/jspp
.v8i1.1102.

Moss, Emily, Kriston McIntosh, Wendy Edelberg, and Kristen Broady. 2020. "The Black-
White Wealth Gap Left Black Households More Vulnerable." Brookings Institute. December 8. https://www.brookings.edu/articles/the-black-white-wealth-gap-left-black
-households-more-vulnerable/.

Moynihan, Daniel P. 1965. "The Negro Family: The Case for National Action." U.S. Department of Labor. https://www.dol.gov/general/aboutdol/history/webid-moynihan.

Mudge, Stephanie L. 2018. *Leftism Reinvented: Western Parties from Socialism to Neoliberalism.* Harvard University Press.

Munis, B. Kal. 2022. "Us Over Here Versus Them Over There … Literally: Measuring Place Resentment in American Politics." *Political Behavior* 44(3): 1057–78. https://doi.org/10.1007/s11109-020-09641-2.

Mutz, Diana Carole. 2021. *Winners and Losers: The Psychology of Foreign Trade.* Princeton Studies in Political Behavior. Princeton University Press.

Myrdal, Gunnar. 1944. *An American Dilemma: The Negro Problem and Modern Democracy.* Harper & Brothers.

National Center for Education Statistics. 2023. "Annual Earnings by Educational Attainment." National Center for Education Statistics. https://nces.ed.gov/programs/coe/indicator/cba.

Nederhof, Anton J. 1985. "Methods of Coping with Social Desirability Bias: A Review." *European Journal of Social Psychology* 15(3): 263–80. https://doi.org/10.1002/ejsp.2420150303.

Nehamas, Nicholas, and Andrew Duehren. 2024. "Harris Had a Wall Street-Approved Economic Pitch. It Fell Flat." *New York Times,* November 9. https://www.nytimes.com/2024/11/09/us/politics/harris-trump-economy.html.

Nelson, Michael, ed. 2021. *The Elections of 2020.* University of Virginia Press.

Nelson, Thomas E. 1999. "Group Affect and Attribution in Social Policy Opinion." *Journal of Politics* 61(2): 331–62. https://doi.org/10.2307/2647507.

New York Times Editorial Board. 2020. "Let's Talk About Higher Wages." *New York Times,* November 28. https://www.nytimes.com/2020/11/28/opinion/wages-economic-growth.html.

Niemi, Richard G., and Barbara I. Sobieszek. 1977. "Political Socialization." *Annual Review of Sociology* 3: 209–33. https://doi.org/10.1146/annurev.so.03.080177.001233.

Noel, Hans. 2014. *Political Ideologies and Political Parties in America.* Cambridge University Press. https://doi.org/10.1017/CBO9781139814775.

Nunnally, Shayla C., and Niambi M. Carter. 2012. "Moving from Victims to Victors: African American Attitudes on the 'Culture of Poverty' and Black Blame." *Journal of African American Studies* 16(3): 423–55. https://doi.org/10.1007/S121.

Oreskes, Naomi, and Eric M. Conway. 2010. *Merchants of Doubt: How a Handful of Scientists Obscured the Truth on Issues from Tobacco Smoke to Global Warming.* Bloomsbury Press.

Organisation for Economic Co-operation and Development. 2023. "Income Inequality." OECD Data. http://data.oecd.org/inequality/income-inequality.htm.

Ortiz-Ospina, Esteban, and Max Roser. 2018. "Economic Inequality by Gender." Our World in Data. https://ourworldindata.org/economic-inequality-by-gender.

Owens, Ann. 2020. "Unequal Opportunity: School and Neighborhood Segregation in the USA." *Race and Social Problems* 12(1): 29–41. https://doi.org/10.1007/s12552-019-09274-z.

Page, Benjamin I., and Martin Gilens. 2017. *Democracy in America? What Has Gone Wrong and What We Can Do About It*. University of Chicago Press.

Page, Benjamin I., and Lawrence R. Jacobs. 2009. *Class War? What Americans Really Think About Economic Inequality*. University of Chicago Press.

Page, Benjamin I., Jason Seawright, and Matthew J. Lacombe. 2018. *Billionaires and Stealth Politics*. University of Chicago Press.

Peck, Reece. 2019. *Fox Populism: Branding Conservatism as Working Class*. Cambridge University Press.

Pestritto, Ronald J. 2005. *Woodrow Wilson and the Roots of Modern Liberalism*. Rowman & Littlefield Publishers.

Petersen, Michael Bang. 2012. "Social Welfare as Small-Scale Help: Evolutionary Psychology and the Deservingness Heuristic." *American Journal of Political Science* 56(1): 1–16. https://doi.org/10.1111/j.1540-5907.2011.00545.x.

Petersen, Michael Bang, Rune Slothuus, Rune Stubager, and Lise Togeby. 2010. "Deservingness Versus Values in Public Opinion on Welfare: The Automaticity of the Deservingness Heuristic." *European Journal of Political Research* 50: 24–52. https://doi.org/10.1111/j.1475-6765.2010.01923.x.

Petersen, Michael Bang, Daniel Sznycer, Leda Cosmides, and John Tooby. 2012. "Who Deserves Help? Evolutionary Psychology, Social Emotions, and Public Opinion About Welfare." *Political Psychology* 33(3): 395–418. https://doi.org/10.1111/j.1467-9221.2012.00883.x.

Peterson, Christopher, Amy Semmel, Carl von Baeyer, Lyn Y. Abramson, Gerald I. Metalsky, and Martin E. P. Seligman. 1982. "The Attributional Style Questionnaire." *Cognitive Therapy and Research* 6(3): 287–99. https://doi.org/10.1007/BF01173577.

Peterson Foundation. 2024. "How Is K-12 Education Funded?" Peter G. Peterson Foundation. https://www.pgpf.org/article/how-is-k-12-education-funded/.

Peterson, Johnathan C., Kevin B. Smith, and John R. Hibbing. 2020. "Do People Really Become More Conservative as They Age?" *Journal of Politics* 82(2): 600–611. https://doi.org/10.1086/706889.

Pettigrew, Thomas F. 1979. "The Ultimate Attribution Error: Extending Allport's Cognitive Analysis of Prejudice." *Personality and Social Psychology Bulletin* 5(4): 461–76. https://doi.org/10.1177/014616727900500.

Pew Research Center. 2016. "On Views of Race and Inequality, Blacks and Whites Are Worlds Apart." June 27. https://www.pewresearch.org/social-trends/2016/06/27/on-views-of-race-and-inequality-blacks-and-whites-are-worlds-apart/.

Pew Research Center. 2018. "What Unites and Divides Urban, Suburban and Rural Communities." May 22. https://www.pewresearch.org/social-trends/2018/05/22/what-unites-and-divides-urban-suburban-and-rural-communities/.

Pew Research Center. 2019. "In a Politically Polarized Era, Sharp Divides in Both Partisan Coalitions." December 17. https://www.pewresearch.org/politics/2019/12/17/in-a-politically-polarized-era-sharp-divides-in-both-partisan-coalitions/.

Pew Research Center. 2022. "Biden's Job Rating Slumps as Public's View of Economy Turns

More Negative." July 13. https://www.pewresearch.org/politics/2022/07/13/bidens-job
-rating-slumps-as-publics-view-of-economy-turns-more-negative/.

Pew Research Center. 2023. "Americans' Dismal Views of the Nation's Politics." September
19. https://www.pewresearch.org/politics/2023/09/19/americans-dismal-views-of-the
-nations-politics/.

Pew Research Center. 2025. Datasets. https://www.pewresearch.org/datasets.

Pierson, Paul. 1994. *Dismantling the Welfare State? Reagan, Thatcher and the Politics of Retrenchment.* Cambridge Studies in Comparative Politics. Cambridge University Press.
https://doi.org/10.1017/CBO9780511805288.

Pierson, Paul. 2017. "American Hybrid: Donald Trump and the Strange Merger of Populism
and Plutocracy." *British Journal of Sociology* 68: S105–19. https://doi.org/10.1111/1468-
4446.12323.

Piff, Paul K., Dylan Wiwad, Angela R. Robinson, Lara B. Aknin, Brett Mercier, and Azim
Shariff. 2020. "Shifting Attributions for Poverty Motivates Opposition to Inequality
and Enhances Egalitarianism." *Nature Human Behaviour* 4: 496–505. https://doi.org/10
.1038/s41562-020-0835-8.

Piketty, Thomas. 1995. "Social Mobility and Redistributive Politics." *Quarterly Journal of
Economics* 110(3): 551–84. https://doi.org/10.2307/2946692.

Piketty, Thomas. 2013. *Capital in the Twenty-First Century.* Harvard University Press.

Piketty, Thomas. 2019. *Capital and Ideology.* Harvard University Press.

Piketty, Thomas, and Emmanuel Saez. 2014. "Income Inequality in the United States, 1913–
1998." *Quarterly Journal of Economics* 118(1): 1–39. https://doi.org/10.1162/003355303605
35135.

Piketty, Thomas, Emmanuel Saez, and Gabriel Zucman. 2018. "Distributional National Accounts: Methods and Estimates for the United States." *Quarterly Journal of Economics*
133(2): 553–609. https://doi.org/10.1093/qje/qjx043.

Piston, Spencer. 2010. "How Explicit Racial Prejudice Hurt Obama in the 2008 Election."
Political Behavior 32: 431–51.

Piston, Spencer. 2018. *Class Attitudes in America: Sympathy for the Poor, Resentment of the
Rich, and Political Implications.* Cambridge University Press.

Pocasangre, Oscar, and Lee Drutman. 2023. "Understanding the Partisan Divide: How Demographics and Policy Views Shape Party Coalitions." New America.

Puri, Sneha, and Jack Malde. 2024. "Delving into the Reasons Why Some Prime-Age Men
Are Out of Work." Bipartisan Policy Center. February 29. https://bipartisanpolicy.org
/blog/why-some-prime-age-men-are-out-of-work/.

Putnam, Robert D., and David E. Campbell. 2010. *American Grace: How Religion Divides
and Unites Us.* Simon & Schuster.

Quillian, Lincoln, John J. Lee, and Mariana Oliver. 2020. "Evidence from Field Experiments
in Hiring Shows Substantial Additional Racial Discrimination After the Callback." *Social Forces* 99(2): 732–59. https://doi.org/10.1093/sf/soaa026.

Quillian, Lincoln, and Arnfinn H. Midtbøen. 2021. "Comparative Perspectives on Racial

Discrimination in Hiring: The Rise of Field Experiments." *Annual Review of Sociology* 47(1): 391–415. https://doi.org/10.1146/annurev-soc-090420-035144.

Rae, Noel. 2018. *The Great Stain: Witnessing American Slavery*. Harry N. Abrams.

Reeves, Richard V. 2022. *Of Boys and Men: Why the Modern Male Is Struggling, Why It Matters, and What to Do About It*. Brookings Institution Press.

Reichley, A. James. 1992. *Life of the Parties*. Free Press.

Reynolds, Jeremy. 2004. "When Too Much Is Not Enough: Actual and Preferred Work Hours in the United States and Abroad." *Sociological Forum* 19(1): 89–120. https://doi.org/10.1023/B:SOFO.0000019649.59873.08.

Rizzo, Salvador. 2019. "Joe Biden's Claim That 'Almost Half' of Americans Live in Poverty." *Washington Post*, June 23. https://www.washingtonpost.com/politics/2019/06/20/joe-bidens-claim-that-almost-half-americans-live-poverty.

Robinson, James W. 2009. "American Poverty Cause Beliefs and Structured Inequality Legitimation." *Sociological Spectrum* 29(4): 489–518. https://doi.org/10.1080/02732170902904681.

Rockenbach, Alyssa N., Matthew J. Mayhew, Kevin Singer, and Laura S. Dahl. 2020. "Professors Change Few Minds on Politics—but Conservative Ones May Have More Influence."

Rodden, Jonathan A. 2019. *Why Cities Lose: The Deep Roots of the Urban-Rural Political Divide*. Basic Books.

Roemer, John E. 1996. *Theories of Distributive Justice:* Harvard University Press.

Roemer, John E. 2000. "Equality of Opportunity." In *Meritocracy and Economic Inequality*, edited by Kenneth Arrow, Samuel Bowles, and Steven N. Durlauf. Princeton University Press.

Roos, Michael, and Matthias Reccius. 2024. "Narratives in Economics." *Journal of Economic Surveys* 38(2): 303–41. https://doi.org/10.1111/joes.12576.

Rosenblum, Nancy L. 2008. *On the Side of the Angels: An Appreciation of Parties and Partisanship*. Princeton University Press.

Rothman, Stanley, S. Robert Lichter, and Neil Nevitte. 2005. "Politics and Professional Advancement Among College Faculty." *Forum* 3(1). https://doi.org/10.2202/1540-8884.1067.

Rothstein, Donna S. 2020. "Male Prime-Age Nonworkers: Evidence from the NLSY97." *Monthly Labor Review*, December. Bureau of Labor Statistics. https://doi.org/10.21916/mlr.2020.25.

Ruggeri, Kai, Sarah Ashcroft-Jones, Giampaolo Abate Romero Landini, et al. 2023. "The Persistence of Cognitive Biases in Financial Decisions Across Economic Groups." *Scientific Reports* 13(1): 10329. https://doi.org/10.1038/s41598-023-36339-2.

Saez, Emmanuel, and Gabriel Zucman. 2020. "The Rise of Income and Wealth Inequality in America: Evidence from Distributional Macroeconomic Accounts." *Journal of Economic Perspectives* 34(4): 3–26. https://doi.org/10.1257/jep.34.4.3.

Saldin, Robert P., and Steven M. Teles. 2020. *Never Trump: The Revolt of the Conservative Elites*. Oxford University Press.

Sanchez-Jankowski, Martin. 2008. *Cracks in the Pavement: Social Change and Resilience in Poor Neighborhoods*. University of California Press.

Sandel, Michael. 2020. *The Tyranny of Merit: What's Become of the Common Good?* Farrar, Strauss, & Giroux.

Sargent, Greg. 2021. "Bernie Sanders Calls for Downward 'Transfer' of Wealth of Top One Percent." *Washington Post*, December 2. https://www.washingtonpost.com/blogs/plum -line/wp/2015/05/26/bernie-sanders-calls-for-downward-transfer-of-wealth-of-top-one -percent.

Schaeffer, Katherine. 2022. "10 Facts About Today's College Graduates." Pew Research Center. April 12. https://www.pewresearch.org/short-reads/2022/04/12/10-facts-about -todays-college-graduates.

Schattschneider, Elmer Eric. 1960. *The Semisovereign People: A Realist's View of Democracy in America*. Dryden Press.

Scheve, Kenneth, and David Stasavage. 2006. "Religion and Preferences for Social Insurance." *Quarterly Journal of Political Science* 1(3): 255–86. https://doi.org/10.1561/100.00 005052.

Schickler, Eric. 2016. *Racial Realignment: The Transformation of American Liberalism, 1932– 1965*. Princeton University Press.

Schlozman, Daniel, and Sam Rosenfeld. 2019. "The Hollow Parties." In *Can America Govern Itself?*, edited by Frances E. Lee and Nolan McCarty. Cambridge University Press.

Schlozman, Kay Lehman, Sidney Verba, and Henry E. Brady. 2018. *Unequal and Unrepresented: Political Inequality and the People's Voice in the New Gilded Age*. Princeton University Press.

Schneider, Stephen P., Kevin B. Smith, and John R. Hibbing. 2018. "Genetic Attributions: Sign of Intolerance or Acceptance?" *Journal of Politics* 80(3). https://doi.org/10.1086 /696860.

Schumacher, Shannon, Liz Hamel, Samantha Artiga, Drishti Pillai, Ashley Kirzinger, Audrey Kearney, Marley Presiado, Ana Gonzalez-Barrera, and Mollyann Brodie. 2023. "Understanding the U.S. Immigrant Experience: The 2023 KFF/LA Times Survey of Immigrants." KFF. September 17. https://www.kff.org/report-section/understanding-the -u-s-immigrant-experience-the-2023-kff-la-times-survey-of-immigrants-findings.

Schuman, Howard, Charlotte Steeh, and Lawrence Bobo. 1985. *Racial Attitudes in America: Trends and Interpretations*. Harvard University Press.

Sears, David O., and Nicholas A. Valentino. 1997. "Politics Matters: Political Events as Catalysts for Preadult Socialization." *American Political Science Review* 91(1): 45–65. https:// doi.org/10.2307/2952258.

Semega, Jessica, and Melissa Kollar. 2022. *Income in the United States: 2021*. U.S. Census Bureau. https://www.census.gov/content/dam/Census/library/publications/2022/demo /p60-276.pdf.

Settle, Jaime E. 2018. *Frenemies: How Social Media Polarizes America*. Cambridge University Press. https://doi.org/10.1017/9781108560573.

Sidanius, Jim, and Felicia Pratto. 1999. *Social Dominance: An Intergroup Theory of Social Hierarchy and Oppression*. Cambridge University Press.

Sides, John, Chris Tausanovitch, and Lynn Vavreck. 2022. *The Bitter End: The 2020 Presidential Campaign and the Challenge to American Democracy*. Princeton University Press.

Sides, John, Michael Tesler, and Lynn Vavreck. 2018. *Identity Crisis: The 2016 Presidential Campaign and the Battle for the Meaning of America*. Princeton University Press.

Siegel, David A. 2013. "Social Networks and the Mass Media." *American Political Science Review* 107(4): 786–805.

Siegel, David A. 2020. "Networks and Media Influence." In *The Oxford Handbook of Electoral Persuasion*, edited by Elizabeth Suhay, Bernard Grofman, and Alexander H. Trechsel. Oxford University Press.

Silver, Nate. 2023. "538's Pollster Ratings." FiveThirtyEight. March 9. https://projects.five thirtyeight.com/pollster-ratings.

Siripurapu, Anshu. 2022. "The U.S. Inequality Debate." Council on Foreign Relations. Last updated April 20. https://www.cfr.org/backgrounder/us-inequality-debate.

Skitka, Linda J., Elizabeth Mullen, Thomas Griffin, Susan Hutchinson, and Brian Chamberlin. 2002. "Dispositions, Scripts, or Motivated Correction? Understanding Ideological Differences in Explanations for Social Problems." *Journal of Personality and Social Psychology* 83(2): 470–87. https://doi.org/10.1037/0022-3514.83.2.470.

Skocpol, Theda, and Vanessa Williamson. 2016. *The Tea Party and the Remaking of Republican Conservatism*, updated ed. Oxford University Press.

Skowronek, Stephen. 1982. *Building a New American State: The Expansion of National Administrative Capacities, 1877–1920*. Cambridge University Press.

Skowronek, Stephen. 1984. "Presidential Leadership in Political Time." In *The Presidency and the Political System*, edited by Michael Nelson. CQ Press.

Slothuus, Rune. 2007. "Framing Deservingness to Win Support for Welfare State Retrenchment." *Scandinavian Political Studies* 30(3): 323–44. https://doi.org/10.1111/j.1467-9477 .2007.00183.x.

Slothuus, Rune. 2010. "When Can Political Parties Lead Public Opinion? Evidence from a Natural Experiment." *Political Communication* 27(2): 158–77. https://doi.org/10.1080 /10584601003709381.

Slothuus, Rune, and Martin Bisgaard. 2021. "Party over Pocketbook? How Party Cues Influence Opinion When Citizens Have a Stake in Policy." *American Political Science Review* 115(3): 1090–96. https://doi.org/10.1017/S0003055421000332.

Small, Mario Luis, David J. Harding, and Michèle Lamont. 2010. "Reconsidering Culture and Poverty." *The Annals of the American Academy of Political and Social Science* 629(1): 6–27. https://doi.org/10.1177/0002716210363620.

Smith, Kevin B., and Lorene H. Stone. 1989. "Rags, Riches, and Bootstraps: Beliefs about the Causes of Wealth and Poverty." *Sociological Quarterly* 30(1): 93–107. https://doi.org /10.1111/j.1533-8525.1989.tb01513.x.

Smith, Rogers M. 1993. "Beyond Tocqueville, Myrdal, and Hartz: The Multiple Traditions in America." *American Political Science Review* 87(3): 549–66. https://doi.org/10.2307 /2938735.

Sniderman, Paul M., Gretchen C. Crosby, and Howell, William G. 2000. "The Politics of

Race." In *Racialized Politics: The Debate about Racism in America*, edited by David O. Sears, James Sidanius, and Lawrence Bobo. University of Chicago Press.

Solt, Frederick, Philip Habel, and J.Tobin Grant. 2011. "Economic Inequality, Relative Power, and Religiosity." *Social Science Quarterly* 92(2): 447–65. https://doi.org/10.1111/j.1540-6237.2011.00777.x.

Sousa, Jared. 2024. "American Dream Far from Reality for Most People." ABC News. January 15. https://abcnews.go.com/Politics/american-dream-reality-people-poll/story?id=106339566.

Spinner-Halev, Jeff, and Elizabeth Theiss-Morse. 2024. *Respect and Loathing in American Democracy: Polarization, Moralization, and the Undermining of Equality.* University of Chicago Press.

Steele, Ellen. 2022. "The Distribution of Household Income, 2019." Congressional Budget Office. https://www.cbo.gov/publication/58781.

Stiglitz, Joseph E. 2019. *People, Power, and Profits: Progressive Capitalism for an Age of Discontent.* W. W. Norton & Company.

Stimson, James A. 1999. *Public Opinion in America: Moods, Cycles, and Swings,* 2nd ed. Westview Press.

Stoker, Laura, and Andrew McCall. 2017. "The Quest for Representative Survey Samples." In *The Routledge Handbook of Elections, Voting Behavior and Public Opinion*, edited by Justin Fisher, Edward Fieldhouse, Mark N. Franklin, Rachel Gibson, Marta Cantijoch, and Christopher Wlezien. Routledge.

Stokes, Donald E. 1963. "Spatial Models of Party Competition." *American Political Science Review* 57(2): 368–77. https://doi.org/10.2307/1952828.

Strain, Michael R. 2020a. "The American Dream Is Alive and Well." *Wall Street Journal,* January 31. https://www.wsj.com/articles/the-american-dream-is-alive-and-well-11580486386.

Strain, Michael R. 2020b. *The American Dream Is Not Dead: But Populism Could Kill It.* Templeton Press.

Strömbäck, Jesper, Monika Djerf-Pierre, and Adam Shehata. 2012. "The Dynamics of Political Interest and News Media Consumption: A Longitudinal Perspective." *International Journal of Public Opinion Research* 25(4): 414–35. https://doi.org/10.1093/ijpor/eds018.

Stroud, Natalie Jomini. 2011. *Niche News: The Politics of News Choice.* Oxford University Press.

Suhay, Elizabeth. 2015. "Explaining Group Influence: The Role of Identity and Emotion in Political Conformity and Polarization." *Political Behavior* 37(1): 221–51. https://doi.org/10.1007/s11109-014-9269-1.

Suhay, Elizabeth. 2017. "The Politics of Scientific Knowledge." In *Oxford Research Encyclopedia of Communication*, edited by Jon Nussbaum. Oxford University Press. https://doi.org/10.1093/acrefore/9780190228613.013.107.

Suhay, Elizabeth, and James N. Druckman. 2015. "The Politics of Science: Political Values and the Production, Communication, and Reception of Scientific Knowledge." *Annals of the American Academy of Political and Social Science* 658. https://journals.sagepub.com/toc/anna/658/1.

Suhay, Elizabeth, and Toby Jayaratne. 2013. "Does Biology Justify Ideology? The Politics of Genetic Attribution." *Public Opinion Quarterly* 77(2): 497–521. https://doi.org/10.1093/poq/nfs049.

Suhay, Elizabeth, Marko Klašnja, and Gonzalo Rivero. 2021. "Ideology of Affluence: Explanations for Inequality and Economic Policy Preferences Among Rich Americans." *The Journal of Politics* 83(1): 367–80. https://doi.org/10.1086/709672.

Suhay, Elizabeth, Mark Tenenbaum, and Austin Bartola. 2022. "Explanations for Inequality and Partisan Polarization in the U.S., 1980–2020." *Forum* 20(1): 5–36. https://doi.org/10.1515/for-2022-2052.

Surridge, Paula. 2016. "Education and Liberalism: Pursuing the Link." *Oxford Review of Education* 42(2): 146–64. https://doi.org/10.1080/03054985.2016.1151408.

Swidler, Ann. 1986. "Culture in Action: Symbols and Strategies." *American Sociological Review* 51(2): 283–86. https://doi.org/10.2307/2095521.

Tajfel, Henri. 1974. "Social Identity and Intergroup Behaviour." *Social Science Information* 13(2): 65–93. https://doi.org/10.1177/053901847401300204.

Tajfel, Henri, and John C. Turner. 1979. "An Integrative Theory of Intergroup Conflict." In *The Social Psychology of Intergroup Relations*, edited by W. G. Austin and S. Worchel. Brooks/Cole.

Teixeira, Ruy, and John B. Judis. 2023. *Where Have All the Democrats Gone? The Soul of the Party in the Age of Extremes*. Henry Holt and Co.

Terkel, Studs. 1980. *American Dreams: Lost & Found*. Pantheon Books.

Ternullo, Stephanie. 2024. *How the Heartland Went Red: Why Local Forces Matter in an Age of Nationalized Politics*. Princeton University Press.

Terris, Ben. 2023. *The Big Break: The Weirdos, Wonks, and Wannabes Trying to Win in Washington While America Loses Its Mind*. Twelve.

Tesler, Michael. 2013. "The Return of Old-Fashioned Racism to White Americans' Partisan Preferences in the Early Obama Era." *Journal of Politics* 75(1): 110–23. https://doi.org/10.1017/S0022381612000904.

Thal, Adam. 2017. "Class Isolation and Affluent Americans' Perception of Social Conditions." *Political Behavior* 39(2): 401–24.

Thompson, Derek. 2022. "A Simple Plan to Solve All of America's Problems." *Atlantic*, January 12. https://www.theatlantic.com/ideas/archive/2022/01/scarcity-crisis-college-housing-health-care/621221/.

Tindera, Michela. 2021. "These Billionaire Donors Spent the Most Money on the 2020 Election." *Forbes*, February 25. https://www.forbes.com/sites/michelatindera/2021/02/25/these-billionaire-donors-spent-the-most-money-on-the-2020-election.

Tocqueville, Alexis de. (1835) 2004. *Democracy in America*. Translated by Arthur Goldhammer. Library of America.

Toff, Benjamin. 2021. "The Social Function of News and (Mis)Information Use." In *The Politics of Truth in Polarized America*, edited by David C. Barker and Elizabeth Suhay. Oxford University Press.

Toff, Benjamin, and Elizabeth Suhay. 2019. "Partisan Conformity, Social Identity, and the Formation of Policy Preferences." *International Journal of Public Opinion Research* 31(2): 349–67. https://doi.org/10.1093/ijpor/edy014.

Tourangeau, Roger, Lance J. Rips, and Kenneth Rasinski. 2000. *The Psychology of Survey Response*. Cambridge University Press.

Trump, Donald J. 2020. "Executive Order on Combating Race and Sex Stereotyping – The White House." https://trumpwhitehouse.archives.gov/presidential-actions/executive-or der-combating-race-sex-stereotyping/.

Trump, Donald J. 2025. "Ending Radical and Wasteful Government DEI Programs and Preferencing." The White House, January 20. https://www.whitehouse.gov/presidential -actions/2025/01/ending-radical-and-wasteful-government-dei-programs-and-preferenc ing.

Trump, Kris-Stella. 2020. "When and Why Is Economic Inequality Seen as Fair." *Current Opinion in Behavioral Sciences* 34: 46–51. https://doi.org/10.1016/j.cobeha.2019.12.001.

Turner, Frederick Jackson. 1893. "The Significance of the Frontier in American History." American Historical Association. https://www.historians.org/resource/the-significance -of-the-frontier-in-american-history.

Twyman, Joe. 2008. "Getting It Right: YouGov and Online Survey Research in Britain." *Journal of Elections, Public Opinion and Parties* 18(4): 343–54. https://doi.org/10.1080/17 457280802305169.

Uberti, David. 2025. "Trump Tries to Forge 'Golden Age' Economy of Self-Reliance and Defiance." *Wall Street Journal*, January 25. https://www.wsj.com/politics/policy/trump -economic-vision-policy-plan-e570b32b?st=DdxSkL.

Underwood, Lauren, and Patty Murray. 2021. "Underwood, Murray Introduce Legislation to Protect Women's Retirement Security." Press Release. July 22. https://underwood .house.gov/media/press-releases/underwood-murray-introduce-legislation-protect -womens-retirement-security.

University of California Santa Barbara. n.d. "The American Presidency Project." https:// www.presidency.ucsb.edu/documents/app-categories/elections-and-transitions/party -platforms.

U.S. Bureau of Labor Statistics. 2021. "Labor Force Characteristics by Race and Ethnicity, 2020." BLS Reports. https://www.bls.gov/opub/reports/race-and-ethnicity/2020/home .htm.

U.S. Bureau of Labor Statistics. 2023a. "Compensation Percentile Estimates." June 16, 2023. https://www.bls.gov/ecec/factsheets/compensation-percentile-estimates.htm.

U.S. Bureau of Labor Statistics. 2023b. "Median Weekly Earnings $721 for Workers With- out High School Diploma, $1,864 for Advanced Degree." *TED: The Economics Daily* (blog). November 17. https://www.bls.gov/opub/ted/2023/median-weekly-earnings-721 -for-workers-without-high-school-diploma-1864-for-advanced-degree.htm.

U.S. Bureau of Labor Statistics. 2024. "The Employment Situation - June 2024." https:// www.bls.gov/news.release/pdf/empsit.pdf.

U.S. Census Bureau. 2023. "Poverty Thresholds by Size of Family and Number of Children." https://www.census.gov/data/tables/time-series/demo/income-poverty/historical -poverty-thresholds.html.

U.S. Chamber of Commerce. 2022. "U.S. Chamber Applauds the CHIPS and Science Act as 'Historic Investment in America's Future." August 9. www.uschamber.com/technolo

gy/u-s-chamber-applauds-the-chips-and-science-act-as-historic-investment-in-americas
-future.

U.S. Department of Commerce. 2023. "Geographic Inequality on the Rise in the U.S." June
15. https://www.commerce.gov/news/blog/2023/06/geographic-inequality-rise-us.

Vaisey, Stephen. 2010. "What People Want: Rethinking Poverty, Culture, and Educational
Attainment." *The Annals of the American Academy of Political and Social Science* 629:
75–101.

Valentino, Nicholas A., and David O. Sears. 1998. "Event-Driven Political Communication
and the Preadult Socialization of Partisanship." *Political Behavior* 20(2): 127–54. https://
doi.org/10.1023/A:1024880713245.

Van Oorschot, Wim. 2006. "Making the Difference in Social Europe: Deservingness Perceptions Among Citizens of European Welfare States." *Journal of European Social Policy*
16(1): 23–42. https://doi.org/10.1177/0958928706059.

Van Oorschot, Wim, and Loek Halman. 2000. "Blame or Fate, Individual or Social? An
International Comparison of Popular Explanations of Poverty." *European Societies* 2(1):
1–28. https://doi.org/10.1080/146166900360701.

Villarreal, Andrés. 2020. "The U.S. Occupational Structure: A Social Network Approach."
Sociological Science 7: 187–221. https://doi.org/10.15195/v7.a8.

Wanberg, Connie. 2010. "The Individual Experience of Unemployment." *Annual Review of
Psychology* 63: 369–96. https://doi.org/10.1146/annurev-psych-120710-100500.

Warren, Elizabeth. 2019. "Full Transcript: 2019 Democratic Debate Night One, Sortable by
Topic." NBC News, June 27. https://www.nbcnews.com/politics/2020-election/full
-transcript-first-democratic-primary-debate-2019-n1022816.

Warren, Elizabeth. 2023. "Tax the Ultra-Rich." https://elizabethwarren.com/wealth-gap.

Warren, Elizabeth, and Amelia Warren Tyagi. 2003. *The Two-Income Trap: Why Middle-Class
Mothers and Fathers Are Going Broke*. Basic Books.

Washington Post Staff. 2021. "Identifying Far-Right Symbols That Appeared at the U.S.
Capitol Riot." January 15. https://www.washingtonpost.com/nation/interactive/2021
/far-right-symbols-capitol-riot.

Watson, Harry L. 2006. *Liberty and Power: The Politics of Jacksonian America*. Hill and Wang.

Weaver, R. Kent. 2000. *Ending Welfare as We Know It*. Brookings Institution.

Weber, Max. 1930. *The Protestant Ethic and the Spirit of Capitalism*. HarperCollins.

Weiner, Bernard. 1995. *Judgments of Responsibility: A Foundation for a Theory of Social Conduct*. Guilford Press.

Weiner, Bernard. 2006. *Social Motivation, Justice, and the Moral Emotions: An Attributional
Approach*. Lawrence Erlbaum.

Weiner, Bernard, Danny Osborne, and Udo Rudolph. 2011. "An Attributional Analysis of
Reactions to Poverty: The Political Ideology of the Giver and the Perceived Morality of
the Receiver." *Personality and Social Psychology Review* 15(2): 199–213. https://doi.org/10
.1177/1088868310387615.

Weiss, Nancy Joan. 1983. *Farewell to the Party of Lincoln*. Princeton University Press.

Wentzel, Kathryn R. 2015. "Socialization in School Settings." In *Handbook of Socialization:
Theory and Research*, edited by Joan E. Grusec and Paul D. Hastings. Guilford Press.

Whitaker, John C. 1996. "Nixon's Domestic Policy: Both Liberal and Bold in Retrospect."
  Presidential Studies Quarterly 26(1): 131–53.

White House. 2017. "Off-Camera Briefing of the FY18 Budget by Office of Management
  and Budget Director Mick Mulvaney." Transcript, May 22. https://trumpwhitehouse
  .archives.gov/briefings-statements/off-camera-briefing-fy18-budget-office-management
  -budget-director-mick-mulvaney-052217/.

Whitehurst, Grover J. 2017. "Why the Federal Government Should Subsidize Childcare and
  How to Pay for It." Brookings Institute. March 9. https://www.brookings.edu/articles
  /why-the-federal-government-should-subsidize-childcare-and-how-to-pay-for-it.

Wilson, Valerie. 2020. "Racial Disparities in Income and Poverty Remain Largely Un-
  changed amid Strong Income Growth in 2019." Economic Policy Institute, September
  16. https://www.epi.org/blog/racial-disparities-in-income-and-poverty-remain-largely
  -unchanged-amid-strong-income-growth-in-2019/.

Wilson, William Julius. 1996. *When Work Disappears: The World of the New Urban Poor.*
  Knopf.

Wilson, William Julius. 2009. *More than Just Race: Being Black and Poor in the Inner City.*
  W. W. Norton & Company.

Wimer, Christopher, Liana Fox, Irwin Garfinkel, Neeraj Kaushal, and Jane Waldfogel. 2016.
  "Progress on Poverty? New Estimates of Historical Trends Using an Anchored Supple-
  mental Poverty Measure." *Demography* 53(4): 1207–18. https://doi.org/10.1007/s13524
  -016-0485-7.

Witko, Christopher, Jana Morgan, Nathan J. Kelly, and Peter K. Enns. 2021. *Hijacking the
  Agenda: Economic Power and Political Influence.* Russell Sage Foundation.

Wolak, Jennifer, and David A. M. Peterson. 2020a. "The Dynamic American Dream." *American Journal of Political Science* 64(4): 968–81. https://doi.org/10.1111/ajps.12522.

Wolak, Jennifer, and David A. M. Peterson. 2020b. "Trump Keeps Invoking the 'American
  Dream.' Americans Are Pessimistic That They Can Achieve It." *Washington Post*, September 21. https://www.washingtonpost.com/politics/2020/09/21/trump-keeps-invok
  ing-american-dream-americans-are-pessimistic-that-they-can-achieve-it.

Wolfe, Rachel. 2024. "The American Dream Feels Out of Reach for Most." *Wall Street Journal*, August 28. https://www.wsj.com/economy/consumers/american-dream-poll-us
  -economy-e5ddf640.

Wooldridge, Jeffrey M. 2019. *Introductory Econometrics: A Modern Approach*, 7th ed. Cen-
  gage Learning.

Wuthnow, Robert. 2018. *The Left Behind: Decline and Rage in Small-Town America.* Princeton
  University Press.

Yglesias, Matthew. 2025. "Misinformation Mostly Confuses Your Own Side." *Slow Boring*,
  February 26. https://www.slowboring.com/p/misinformation-mostly-confuses-your.

Young, Michael Dunlop. 1958. *The Rise of the Meritocracy.* Transaction Publishers.

Zacher, Sam. 2023. "Polarization of the Rich: The New Democratic Allegiance of Affluent
  Americans and the Politics of Redistribution." *Perspectives on Politics* 22(2): 338–56.
  https://doi.org/10.1017/S1537592722003310.

Zacher, Sam. 2024. "What Forms of Redistribution Do Americans Want? Understanding

Preferences for Policy Benefit-Cost Tradeoffs." *Policy Research Quarterly* 77(4). https://doi.org/10.1177/10659129241260413.

Zaller, John. 1992. *The Nature and Origins of Mass Opinion*. Cambridge University Press.

Zaller, John. 2012. "What *Nature and Origins* Leaves Out." *Critical Review* 24(4): 569–642. https://doi.org/10.1080/08913811.2012.807648.

Zaller, John, and Stanley Feldman. 1992. "A Simple Theory of Survey Response: Answering Questions Versus Revealing Preferences." *American Journal of Political Science* 36(3): 579–616. https://doi.org/10.2307/2111583.

Zelizer, Julian E. 2015. *The Fierce Urgency of Now: Lyndon Johnson, Congress, and the Battle for the Great Society*. Penguin Press.

Zelizer, Julian E., ed. 2022. *The Presidency of Donald J. Trump: A First Historical Assessment*. Princeton University Press.

Zengerle, Jason. 2015. "Sheldon Adelson Is Ready to Buy the Presidency." *New York Magazine*, September 9. https://nymag.com/intelligencer/2015/09/sheldon-adelson-is-ready-to-buy-the-presidency.html.

Zitner, Aaron. 2023. "Voters See American Dream Slipping Out of Reach, WSJ/NORC Poll Shows." *Wall Street Journal*, November 24. https://www.wsj.com/us-news/american-dream-out-of-reach-poll-3b774892.

INDEX

Tables and figures are listed in **boldface**.

Abelson, Robert, 24
Achen, Chrisopher, 68
Adams, James Truslow, 33
affirmative action, 66, 72, 193, 196, **197**, 209–10, **210**, **263**
age: demographic divides and inequality explanations, 139–40, 149–55, **150**, **152**, **154**, **249**, **255**; partisan divides and inequality explanations, 169–73, **171–72**
Alesina, Alberto, 71, 74, 190
Almås, Ingvild, 71–72
American Community Survey, 107
American Compass, 240, 287*n*42
American Dream, 215–42; American public's belief in, 11–12, 70–78, 102, 104; and culture of poverty, 234–36; defined, 1, 33; and discrimination, 230–34; and economic conditions, 12–13; and education, 223–25; and employment, 226–30; historical perspectives on, 32–67 (*see also* historical perspectives on American Dream); and partisan economic ideologies, 20–22, 29; and political polarization, 2–5, 11–13; research limitations and future research on, 221–23; scholarly literature, contributions to, 219–21; work ethic and, 2–4, 33–34, 236–39 (*see also* meritocracy)
"The American Dream Is Alive and Well" (*Wall Street Journal*), **21**

The American Dream Is Not Dead (Strain), 20
American Dreams (Terkel), 136, 137
The American Ethos (McClosky & Zaller), 37–38
American National Election Study (ANES): data from, 79; on discrimination, 72; on equal opportunity, 11–12, 83, **84**, 91–92, **92**; inequality explanations from, 111, **112**; on partisan divides and inequality explanations, 173–78, **174–77**, 282*nn*44–45
The American Voter (Campbell), 26, 219
Angeletos, George-Marios, 71, 190
Appelbaum, Lauren, 190, 192

Bartels, Larry, 68, 203
Bartola, Austin, 90
Bawn, Kathleen, 18
Beliefs About Inequality (Kluegel & Smith), 12, 71, 219
bias: and demographic divides over inequality, 138; intergroup attributional bias, 162–63; and partisan socialization, 26, 164–65; and policy outcomes, 15, 26, 30; and social desirability, 124, 277*n*50, 285*n*51; and social identity theory, 144–45; in survey results, 74, 108, 277*n*38
Biden, Joe, 18, 20, 62–64, 222
Black Lives Matter, 89

Blanchard-Fields, Freda, 140
Bonica, Adam, 266n23
Branch, Enobong Hannah, 71, 72
Bryan, William Jennings, 40
Bullock, Heather, 106, 190
Bush, George W., 54–55, 223

Campbell, Angus, 26, 219
Campbell, David, 148
Capital in the Twenty-First Century
   (Piketty), 20
capitalism, 19, 23, 37–38, 40, 142
Carlson, Tucker, 223
Cheng, Siwei, 12, 74
Chetty, Raj, 235
childcare and family leave, 116, 130, 229–
   30, **248**
Civil Rights Movement, 18, 44–46
Clinton, Bill, 23, 53–54, 272n83
Clinton, Hillary, 23, 61; political prefer-
   ences and inequality explanations, 197–
   98, **200**, 201–9, **202**, **205–6**, **208**, **251–
   54**, **260–62**
Condon, Meghan, 71, 282n38
Converse, Philip, 220
Cooley, Erin, 162
Coolidge, Calvin, 42
Cooperative Congressional Election Study,
   107–8, 276n33
COVID-19 pandemic, 2, 60, 62, 76
culture: and American Dream, 33; correlations among inequality explanations,
   120–21, **120**, **248**; demographic divides
   and inequality explanations, 153–54, **154**;
   and EIPS responses on inequality, 112,
   115–16, **115**, 125, 131; elite influence in,
   280n65; and gender roles, 130–31; and
   inequality explanations, 104, 106; moral
   traditionalism, 17, 53, 59; partisan divides and inequality explanations, 178,
   250, 282n41; political preferences and
   inequality explanations, 203; of poverty,
   111, 192, 234–36; in rural vs. urban areas,
   143. *See also* socialization

Democratic Party: activists and interest
   groups for, 15, 17, 266n23; on discrimi-

nation, 232; economic ideology of, 2–4,
   6, 17–18, 22–24, 68–69, 76–78, 122, 163–
   64, 267n36; historical perspectives on,
   34, 39–44, 46–50, **48–51**, 271nn71–72;
   on inequality, 20–23, 52, 54, 63, 193,
   217–18, 240, **243**; and partisan socialization, 25–28; policy justification of, 18–
   25, **21**; progressive shift of, 54–56, 61–64,
   66; race and ethnicity, 44, 65. *See also
   specific politicians*
Democrats: American Dream, belief in, 2,
   215–17; characteristics of EIPS respondents, 108, **109–10**; demographics of, 5,
   14–15, **16**, 29, 63, 139–41, 162, 216,
   281n18; on economic mobility, 20–22;
   and EIPS responses on inequality, 118;
   on equal opportunity and racial inequality, 82–90, **86–89**; inequality explanations (*see* partisan divides and inequality
   explanations; political preferences and
   inequality explanations); meritocracy
   and opportunity, 4–5; partisan differences by level of political interest, 91–95,
   92–94; on social welfare programs, 44,
   53–54, 81–82, **82**, 193, 272n83; on work
   ethic, 80–81, **80**
demographic divides and inequality explanations, 8, 136–56; and age, 139–40;
   causes of, 137–38; and dominant vs.
   marginalized groups, 143–45; and education, 140–41; investigations of, 145–54,
   147, **150**, **152**, **154**, **249**, **255**; and religion, 142; and rurality, 143
Desmond, Matthew, 238
discrimination: and American Dream,
   230–34; correlations among inequality
   explanations, 120–21, **120**, **248**; demographic divides and inequality explanations, 146, **147**, 152–53, **152**, **249**; and
   economic outcomes, 2; in education,
   224; and EIPS responses on inequality,
   111, **112**, 115–18, **115**, **117**, 125, 127–30; in
   employment, 22–23, 38–39, 232; and
   equal opportunity, 85–87, **87**, 92–94,
   93, 96; laws against, 22–23, 231; partisan
   divides and inequality explanations,
   166, 173, **175**, 178–80, **179**, 282n43; re-

verse, 59; and sexism, 116, 159, 168–69, 172, **172**, 233–34; social hierarchies enforced through, 144; and White nationalism, 275*n*61. *See also* structural inequalities

economic inequality: blame for, 20, 75–76, 87–90, **88–89**, 94–95, **94**; Democratic vs. Republican views on, 3, 20–23, **49–51**, 52–54, 68–69, 193, 217–18, **243–47**; demographic divides and explanations for, 136–56 (*see also* demographic divides and inequality explanations); and Great Leveling, 12–13; growth of, 1–2; and historical perspective, 36, 38–40; partisan divides and explanations for, 157–85 (*see also* partisan divides and inequality explanations); political preferences and explanations for, 186–214 (*see also* political preferences and inequality explanations); race and ethnicity, 20, 70, 72, 82–90, **86–89**, 193–94; socialization and views on, 13; survey responses on, 70–74, 82–90, **84**, **86–89**. *See also* poverty
Economic Policy Institute, 287*n*42
education: ANES survey question on, 111, **112**; correlations among inequality explanations, 120–21, **120**, **248**; demographic divides and inequality explanations, 140–41, 146–54, **150**, **152**, **154**, 155, **249**, **255**; of EIPS respondents, **109–10**; and EIPS responses on inequality, 115–18, **115**, **117**, 125; and equal opportunity, 32, 85–86, **86**, 92–94, **93**, 223–25, 286*n*16; partisan divides and inequality explanations, 169–73, **171–72**, **174**
Ehrenreich, Barbara, 238
Eisenhower, Dwight, 45
employment: and American Dream, 226–30; correlations among inequality explanations, 120–21, **120**, **248**; declines in, 238; demographic divides and inequality explanations, 146, 152–53, **152**; discrimination in, 22–23, 38–39, 232; EIPS questions on, 112, 113, 277*n*41; and EIPS responses on inequality, 115–18, **115**, **117**,

125; equal opportunity and meritocracy, 37; and marriage rates, 234–35; partisan divides and inequality explanations, 173, **174**; social welfare programs as disincentive for, 51–53
The Epic of America (Adams), 33
equal opportunity: and American Dream, debates over, 22–23; American National Election Study survey question on, 11–12; defined, 35–36, 236*n*15; discrimination inhibiting, 85–87, **87**, 92–94, **93**, 96; historical perspectives on, 32, 35–37, 46, 271*n*66; and New Deal era, 46–47; partisan differences by political interest, 91–95, **92–94**; and Republican Party, 41–43; survey data on, 82–90, **84**, **86–89**. *See also* education; employment
Explanations for Inequality & Politics surveys (EIPS), 7–8, 99–135; administration of, 107–8, 276–77*nn*34–35; causal attribution questions, 109–14, **112**, 134; characteristics of sample, 108, **109–10**; conceptual overview, 102–5, **103**; consistency and inconsistency of responses, 105–7; demographic divides and explanations for inequality, 136–56 (*see also* demographic divides and inequality explanations); explanations for unequal economic outcomes from, 115–18, **115**, **117**; on gender income gap, 99; open-ended question responses, 123–33, **127**, 134–35; overview, 100–102, 275*n*1; partisan divides and explanations for inequality, 157–85 (*see also* partisan divides and inequality explanations); political preferences and explanations for inequality, 186–214 (*see also* political preferences and inequality explanations); response patterns, 118–23, **120**; on rural-urban economic inequality, 99, 113, 116–17, **117**, 129, 131–32

family structure, 53, 59, 234–36
Feagin, Joe, 12, 70–71, 74, 103
Form, William, 72–73
Fuhrer, Jeffrey, 227

gender: ANES survey question on, 111, **112**; childcare and family leave, 116, 130, 229–30, **248**; correlations among inequality explanations, 121, **248**; and Democratic Party platform, **51**, 65; demographic divides and inequality explanations, 143–45, 146–55, **147**, **150**, **152**, **154**, **249**, **255**, 280*n*65; and education, 224, 286*n*16; of EIPS respondents, **109–10**; and EIPS responses on inequality, 101, 112–13, 115–17, **115**, **117**, 129–30; and gender roles, 130–31, 237; and income gap, 23, 75, 99, 230, 233; partisan divides and inequality explanations, 169–81, **171–72**, **174–77**, **179**, **182–83**, **250**; political preferences and inequality explanations, **208**, 209–12, **210–11**; and sexism, 116, 159, 168–69, 172, **172**, 233–34

General Social Survey (GSS), 2, 79, 84–90, 92–95, **93–94**

geographic inequality. *See* rural-urban inequality

Gerring, John, 40

Gilens, Martin, 72, 193, 207, 266*n*23

Glasmeier, Amy, 227

Goldwater, Barry, 50

Gore, Al, 54

Goudarzi, Shahrzad, 191

Gramm, Phil, 20

Great Depression, 17–18, 42–43

Great Leveling (1910–1970), 12–13

Great Recession, 2, 18, 24, 55–56, 76, 80

Greely, Horace, 39–40

Grossman, Matt, 20–21

Halman, Loek, 103, **103**

Hanley, Caroline, 71, 72

Harrington, Michael, 70

Harris, Kamala, 15, 66

Haskins, Ron, 234–35

Hayward, David, 279*n*43

Hendren, Nathaniel, 235

Hewstone, Miles, 281*n*18

historical perspectives on American Dream: 6, 32–67; conservative shift, 50–57; early American political history, 37–43; equal opportunity, meritocracy, and American Dream, 35–37; New Deal era, 43–47; party platforms in Neoliberal era, 47–50, **48–51**; populist shift, 57–64; social groups in platform agendas, **51**, 64–65

Hochschild, Jennifer, 73, 106, 118, 145, 186

Hoover, Herbert, 32, 35, 37, 42–43

household income: demographic divides and inequality explanations, 147–54, **150**, **152**, **154**, **249**, **255**; growth in, 226; partisan divides and inequality explanations, 169–73, **171**; and partisanship, 14–15, **16**; race and ethnicity, 113–14, 277*n*45; and social welfare program eligibility, 239. *See also* poverty

Huber, Joan, 72–73

Hughes, Michael, 107, 113

Hunt, Matthew, 106, 142, 190

ideo-attribution effect, 106, 160, 162, 276*n*20

Independents, 28, 79, 189

individualism: and personal responsibility for poverty, 12–13, 22–23, 32, 36–37, 71–72, 103, 191–92; Republican emphasis on, 56, 58, 123

intelligence: correlations among inequality explanations, 120–21, **120**, **248**; demographic divides and inequality explanations, 153–54, **154**; and EIPS responses on inequality explanations, 115–17, **115**, **117**, 125; partisan divides and inequality explanations, **177**, 178; political preferences and inequality explanations, 203; poverty based on, 192

International Social Survey Programme, 12, 79, 274*n*51

Iyengar, Shanto, 190

Jackson, Andrew, 39–40, 57

Jarrett, Vernon, 136

Jennings, Kent, 221

Johnson, Dusty, 22–23

Johnson, Lyndon B., 18, 32, 37, 44

Jost, John, 145

Kane, John, 162

Kearney, Melissa, 235

Kemmelmeier, Markus, 279n43
Kerry, John, 55
Kinder, Donald, 72
King, Rodney, 84
Kluegel, James, 12, 71–73, 106, 163, 190, 219, 276n22

Lane, Robert, 70
Lasswell, Harold, 18
libertarianism, 17, 67, 266n31, 271n66
Lindert, Peter, 38
Lippmann, Walter, 11
Lowrey, Annie, 227
luck, 74, 79, 103, 190

Mai, Quan, 232
market economy, 13, 23, 29, 58
Marx, Karl, 142, 280n65
McCall, Leslie, 12–13, 71, 74–76
McClosky, Herbert, 37–38, 46, 73
McCracken, Paul, 45
Mendelberg, Tali, 141
meritocracy: American public's belief in, 1, 102; defined, 35; dominant groups favoring, 143–44; and employment access, 227–28; historical perspectives on, 35–37, 42; meritocratic abundance, 5, 36, 68, 99–100; partisan divides and inequality explanations, 160–61; party agendas and views on, 3–5, 14, 22–24; poverty, personal responsibility for, 12–13, 22–23, 32, 36–37, 71–72, 103, 191–92; quantity of opportunity for, 22; survey responses on, 71–72, 79–81, **80**
Morgan, G. Scott, 106, 160, 162
Moynihan, Daniel Patrick, 234
Mulvaney, Mick, 157
Murray, Patty, 23
Musk, Elon, 17, 241
The Myth of American Inequality (Gramm), 20

The Negro Family: The Case for National Action (Moynihan), 234
Nelson, Thomas, 193, 207, 285n51
neoliberalism: and conservative shift, 50–57; defined, 266n31; and party platforms, 47–50, **48–51**, 271nn71–72; and political agendas, 17; and populist shift, 57–64; social groups in platform agendas, **51**, 64–65
Nickel and Dimed (Ehrenreich), 238
Niemi, Richard, 221
Nixon, Richard, 45–46

Obama, Barack, 23, 55–56

Page, Benjamin, 266n23
partisan divides and inequality explanations, 8–9, 157–85; EIPS open-ended responses on, 178–80, **179**; investigations of, 167–80, **170–72, 174–77, 179, 256–58**; literature review, 160–65; by political interest level, 180–81, **182–83**, 282–83n47; survey data on, 86–87, 91–95, **92–94**; symbolic ideology and social prejudice, 165–67
partisan socialization, 25–28, 164–65, 189
Petersen, Michael Bang, 190
Peterson, David, 75, 274n39
Pew Research Center, 2, 79–81, 241
Piff, Paul, 190
Piketty, Thomas, 20
Piston, Spencer, 12, 74, 167
political parties, 14. *See also* Democratic Party; Republican Party
political polarization, 5–6, 11–31; American Dream, belief in, 2–5, 11–13, 29; in Congress, 27; partisan socialization, 25–28; party agenda justifications, 18–25, **21**; party agendas and coalitions, 14–18, **16**, 220, 241–42; public frustration with, 241
political preferences and inequality explanations, 9–10, 186–214; additional variables for, 198–99, 285n43; literature review, 189–94; political attitudes assessed with EIPS, 194–98, **195–97, 251**; unequal economic opportunity index on, 199–204, **200, 202, 205–6, 252–53, 259–61**, 285n45; unequal economic opportunity indices compared, 205–10, **208, 210–11, 254, 262–63**
populism, 2, 56–63, 66–67, 240

poverty: culture of, 111, 192, 234–36; personal responsibility for, 12–13, 22–23, 32, 36–37, 71–72, 103, 191–92; public opinion on, 70–71; rates of, 20, 226–27; Republican views on causes of, 53; socialization to, 32, 45, 191–92. *See also* economic inequality; social welfare programs

Poverty, by America (Desmond), 238

Pratto, Felicia, 144, 279n58, 280n65

protectionism, 57, 67, 240

The Protestant Ethic and the Spirit of Capitalism (Weber), 142

public opinion. *See* Explanations for Inequality & Politics surveys; survey and research data

Putnam, Robert, 148

race and ethnicity: ANES survey question on, 111, **112**; and Civil Rights Movement, 18, 44–46; correlations among inequality explanations, 121, **248**; demographic divides and inequality explanations, 143–55, **147**, **150**, **152**, **154**, **249**, **255**, 280n65; and deservingness, 192–93; and education, 224; of EIPS respondents, 108, **109–10**, 277n35; and EIPS responses on inequality, 100–101, 113, **115**, 116–17, **117**, 127–30, 132–33; and historical perspective on American Dream, 38–39; and household income, 113–14, 277n45; and inequality, 20, 70, 72, 82–90, **86–89**, 193–94; partisan divides and inequality explanations, 169–81, **171–72**, **174–77**, **182–83**, **250**; and party affiliation, 14–15, **51**, 63, 65; political preferences and inequality explanations, 199–200, **200**, 207–12, **208**, **210–11**, 285n49; and populist movements, 66; racial resentment scale, 221, 286n7; racism (*see* discrimination); and Republican views on causes of poverty, 53; and social welfare programs, 43–44, 53, 220–21; stereotypes of, 107, 167, 192–94; and systemic inequality, 4. *See also* structural inequalities

Reagan, Ronald, 4, 50–53, 190

Reccius, Matthias, 24

religion: demographic divides and inequality explanations, 142, 149–55, **150**, **152**, **154**, **249**, **255**; partisan divides and inequality explanations, 169–73, **171–72**

Republican Party: activists and interest groups for, 15; and campaign donations, 266n23; conservative shift of, 50–57, 66–67; on discrimination, 232; economic ideology of, 2–4, 6, 17–18, 22–24, 69, 76–78, 122–23, 164, 266–67n35; historical perspectives on, 34, 41–43, 45–50, **48–51**, 271nn71–72; on inequality, 20–23, 52–54, 193, 217–18, **243–47**; on meritocracy, 22–23; and partisan socialization, 25–28; policy justification of, 18–25, **21**; populist shift of, 59–61; and religion, 142. *See also specific politicians*

Republicans: American Dream, belief in, 2, 215–17; characteristics of EIPS respondents, 108, **109–10**; demographics of, 14–15, **16**, 29, 139–40, 162, 216, 281n18; on economic mobility, 20–22; and EIPS responses on inequality, 118; on equal opportunity and racial inequality, 82–90, **86–89**; inequality explanations (*see* partisan divides and inequality explanations; political preferences and inequality explanations); meritocracy and opportunity, 4–5; partisan differences by level of political interest, 91–95, **92–94**; racism among, 166–67, 275n61; on social welfare programs, 51–53, 81–82, **82**, 193, 220–21; on work ethic, 13, 22, 80–81, **80**

Rodden, Jonathan, 148

Roemer, John, 236n15

Roos, Michael, 24

Roosevelt, Franklin D., 17–18, 43–44, 271n66

Roosevelt, Theodore, 41–42, 270n43

rural-urban inequality: correlations among inequality explanations, 121, **248**; demographic divides and inequality explanations, 143, **147–55**, **150**, **152**, **154**, **249**, **255**; and EIPS responses on inequality, 99, 113, 116–17, **117**, 129, 131–32; and employment access, 228; partisan divides and inequality explanations, 169–73, **171–72, 174–77,** 178–80, **179, 250;** political preferences and inequality explanations, 210–12, **211,** 285–86*n*54; U.S. Department of Commerce report on, 113

Sanders, Bernie, 20, 61–62; political preferences and inequality explanations, 197–98, **202,** 203, **205–6, 208, 251, 253–54, 260–62**
Sanders, Lynn, 72
Sawhill, Isabel, 234–35
Scheve, Kenneth, 142
Sidanius, Jim, 144, 279*n*58, 280*n*65
Skitka, Linda, 106
Smith, Eliot, 12, 71–73, 106, 163, 190, 219, 276*n*22
Smith, Rogers, 38
social identity theory, 144–45
socialization: and conformity, 26; and demographic divides over inequality, 137; and economic knowledge, 13; and education, 140–41; partisan, 25–28, 164–65, 189; to poverty, 32, 45, 111, 191–92, 192, 234–36
social networks, 138, 165, 228–29
social welfare programs: Democrats vs. Republicans on, 17–18, 44, 51–54, 58, 193, 220–21, 272*n*83; disability benefits, 238; employment levels, effect on, 238–39; and political preferences, 190–94, 284*n*16 (*see also* political preferences and inequality explanations); and race and ethnicity, 43–44, 53, 220–21; survey responses on, 72, 81–82, **82;** work requirements for, 22–23, 54
Solt, Frederick, 142
Stasavage, David, 142
stereotypes, 107, 130, 167, 192–94
Strain, Michael, 20
structural inequalities, 4, 18, 23, 103, **103,** 190–91, 217, 284*n*16. *See also* discrimination
Surridge, Paula, 141
survey and research data, 6–7, 68–98; on American Dream, 70–78; deficiencies

in, 100, 158–59; on equal opportunity and racial inequality, 82–90, **84, 86–89;** on hard work and opportunity, 79–82, **80;** partisan differences by level of political interest, 91–95, **92–94;** on social welfare programs, **82;** surveys used, 78–79. *See also* Explanations for Inequality & Politics surveys

Tajfel, Henri, 144
tariffs, 59–60, 240, 267*n*35
Tenenbaum, Mark, 68, 90
Terkel, Studs, 136, 137
Thompson, Derek, 236*n*17
Truman, Harry, 44
Trump, Donald: on American Dream, 216; discrimination, banning discussions on, 22; and economic ideology, 17, 29; political preferences and inequality explanations, 197–98, **200,** 201–9, **202, 205–6, 208,** 251–54, **260–62;** and populism, 57–61, 67, 240; presidential election of 2016, 2, 4, 57–58, 61, 229; presidential election of 2024, 2, 15; racism of, 90; and tariffs, 59–60, 240, 267*n*35
Tuch, Steven, 107, 113
Turner, John, 144
Tyagi, Amelia Warren, 237

Underwood, Lauren, 23
upward mobility. *See* American Dream
U.S. Census Bureau, 107, 113–14, 237
U.S. Department of Commerce, 113

van Oorschot, Wim, 103–4

Warren, Elizabeth, 20, 61–62, 157, 237
wealth gap, 82–83, 111, 139, 224–25, 231–32
Weber, Max, 142, 279*n*37
Weiner, Bernard, 103, **103,** 191, 283*n*7
welfare. *See* social welfare programs
Wen, Fangqui, 12, 74
White nationalism, 275*n*61
Wichowsky, Amber, 71, 282*n*38
Williamson, Jeffrey, 38
Wilson, Woodrow, 40–41
Wolak, Jennifer, 75, 274*n*39

work ethic: and American Dream, 2–4, 33–34, 236–39; correlations among inequality explanations, 120–21, **120**, **248**; demographic divides and inequality explanations, 146, 152–53, **152**; and EIPS responses on inequality, 115–16, **115**, 119, 125, 132; partisan divides and inequality explanations, **176**, 178; and religion, 142; Republicans on, 13, 22, 80–81, **80**; survey responses on, 79–82, **80**

World Values Survey, 71, 74
World War II, 44, 271*n*66

xenophobia, 57
Xu, Qingya, 68

Yglesias, Matthew, 215, 242
YouGov, 107–8, 147–48

Zaller, John, 37–38, 46, 73, 283*n*49